MARY HAYS
(1759–1843)

For Chauncey, with whom it is my joy to share
"the feast of reason and the flow of soul."

Mary Hays
(1759–1843)
The Growth of a Woman's Mind

GINA LURIA WALKER
The New School University, New York City, USA

ASHGATE

Published by
Ashgate Publishing Limited
Gower House
Croft Road
Aldershot
Hampshire GU11 3HR
England

Ashgate Publishing Company
Suite 420
101 Cherry Street
Burlington, VT 05401-4405
USA

Ashgate website: http://www.ashgate.com

British Library Cataloguing in Publication Data
Walker, Gina Luria, 1942–
Mary Hays, (1759–1843) : the growth of a woman's mind
  1.Hays, Mary, 1759 or 60–1843 – Knowledge and learning 2.Hays, Mary, 1759 or 60–1843 – Criticism and interpretation
  I.Title
  823.7

Library of Congress Cataloging-in-Publication Data
Walker, Gina Luria.
  Mary Hays, (1759-1843) : the growth of a woman's mind / by Gina Luria Walker.
     p. cm.
  Includes bibliographical references.
  1. Hays, Mary, 1759 or 60-1843—Political and social views. 2. Politics and literature—Great Britain—History—18th century. 3. Politics and literature—Great Britain—History—19th century. 4. Women's rights—England—History—18th century. 5. Women's rights—England—History—19th century. 6. Radicals—Great Britain—History—18th century. 7. Radicals—Great Britain—History—19th century. I. Title.

PR4769.H6Z93 2006
823'.7—dc22

2006013676

ISBN-13: 978-0-7546-4061-5
ISBN-10: 0-7546-4061-2

Printed and bound in Great Britain by MPG Books Ltd, Bodmin, Cornwall.

Contents

Acknowledgments

The first acknowledgment is for Laura J. Corwin who has supported my work on Mary Hays as intrepid researcher and "perfect reader"—Fanny Burney's term for her sister Susan, and, in the process, has become a trusted critic and dear friend. I also appreciate the many ways in which Portis Hicks, Laura's husband, has supported the work on Hays with wit, cheerful readiness to accompany Laura to the many sites where evidence about Hays might be found, and terrific travel directions.

The next acknowledgment is to Kenneth Neill Cameron (1908–94), who suggested I consider Mary Hays as a dissertation subject in 1969, and directed me to the Carl H. Pforzheimer Library where I have enjoyed encouragement over the years, especially from Doucet Devin Fischer. Among others in the Pforzheimer constellation, Donald R. Reiman, Elizabeth C. Denlinger, Daniel Dibbern, Mihai H. Handrea, Ricki B. Herzfeld, and Robert Yampolsky have provided important support. I am grateful to Stephen Wagner, Curator, the Carl H. Pforzheimer Collection of Shelley and His Circle, New York Public Library, Astor, Lenox, and Tilden Foundations, for his interest in Hays. Frida Knight (1910–96), biographer of William Frend, took me to tea with Raymond Williams (1921–88) at Jesus College, Cambridge University, in 1971, where Williams expressed his interest in knowing more about Hays.

On the advice of Donald Reiman, I tracked down Jill Organ (later Hansen) who had inherited the Mary Hays archive from Hays's first twentieth century editor and collateral descendant, Anne F. Wedd. The Pforzheimer Library provided a travel and research grant so that I could meet Miss Organ in London and review the documents in her possession. I visited her flat in Islington twice during my visit. Miss Organ described her close friendship with Miss Wedd, whom she had called "Tante," and with whom she had attended lectures at Dr. Williams's Library, the Unitarian repository in Gordon Square. She refused to let me see any of the papers until the last night I was in London. Then, after dinner at a nearby restaurant, we went back to her flat. She took me into her bedroom where she pulled out a small weathered chest from under her bed. When she opened it, I saw the letters, as well as a copy of Mary Wollstonecraft's *A Vindication of the Rights of Woman* with Hays's name on the inside cover and her markings on the pages. The Pforzheimer Library purchased the Hays archive from Miss Organ in 1971. Early the next year she wrote to me to say that she had used the money from the sale of the papers as her dowry and had just married her longtime friend, Christian Hansen, who had been pensioned after he was wounded in World War II and had been living in Malta.

Mrs. Hansen continued to be helpful when Laura Corwin traced her to Tunbridge Wells, Kent, in summer 2001 and went to see her. I spoke with Mrs. Hansen by telephone while Laura was there. She referred to her "great age" of 88, but remembered our meeting and repeated what she had said to me 30 years before—that the book about Hays must be published because "Tante" wanted people to know about her. Mrs. Hansen seemed pleased that Wedd had left some of the Hays materials to Dr. Williams's Library. She gave Laura pictures of Anne Wedd, and of herself and her husband. Mrs. Hansen is now deceased. Additional information about Hays and Wedd has subsequently been provided by Philippa Gregory, Hays's great-great-great-great-great-grandniece, who is well known as a historical novelist, but important also for her insights into the writing life and her sense of history in women's lives. Philippa's aunt, Mrs. Mary Wedd, and her cousin, Imogen Wedd, have shared familial perspectives that give Hays and A.F. Wedd new vitality.

I appreciate the generosity of many scholars, especially those to whom I sent electronic queries and who responded helpfully, whether we had previously been in contact or not. Pamela Clemit is first among these for her wise and detailed knowledge of William Godwin and for her continuing friendship. G.M. Ditchfield has been marvelously liberal with his time and erudition about Hannah and Theophilus Lindsey, Jane and John Disney, and early Unitarianism. Helen Braithwaite, Penelope J. Corfield, Elizabeth Dolan, Patricia Fara, John Christian Laursen, Jeanne Moskal, Anthony Page, Pam Perkins, William St. Clair, Tania Smith, and Mary A. Waters have been collegial correspondents indeed. Marilyn L. Brooks made the helpful gift of the portable document format (PDF) of her edition of Hays's correspondence before it was published, and has freely shared information about the circumstances of Hays's early life. James E. Bradley, Nora Crook, Alice Green Fredman (1924–93), Felicia Gordon, Gary Kelly, John Christian Laursen, Clarissa Campbell Orr, Helena Rosenblatt, and Janet Todd have supported my work on Hays in generally inspiring and specific ways. The Gender and Enlightenment Collaborative Research Project (formerly, Feminism and Enlightenment), directed by Barbara Taylor and Sarah Knott, provided a marvelous forum for airing new ideas about Hays in the context of other Enlightenment *femmes philosophes*. I am honored to represent Hays in *Women, Gender and Enlightenment* (Palgrave, 2005), where as editor Barbara Taylor gave me scope to rehearse some of my ideas and offered astute editorial guidance.

Libraries and librarians have been crucial to reconstructing Hays's texts. I am extremely grateful to the Bodleian Library, University of Oxford, for non-exclusive permission to publish material from the the Abinger Collection, to the Keeper of Special Collections and Western Manuscripts (Mr. Richard Ovenden, and especially to Bruce C. Barker-Benfield for his assistance); to Stephen Wagner at the Carl H. Pforzheimer Collection of Shelley and His Circle at NYPL, Astor, Tilden, and Lenox Foundations; Dr. David L. Wykes, Director, and the Trustees of Dr. Williams's Library for advice, assistance, and permission to quote from unpublished manuscripts in their collection; Eric Rupp and the other patient librarians at The Elmer Holmes Bobst Library, New York University; the staff at the Raymond Fogelman Library, New School University; Helen Scott, Librarian, Chawton House Library, Chawton; Margaret Sherry Rich, Reference Librarian/Archivist, Rare Books & Special Collections, Princeton University Library, and her colleagues Tad Bennicoff and Susan Harmon at the Seeley G. Mudd Manuscript Library, Princeton University.

Erika Gaffney was the first editor to welcome me to Ashgate, at the suggestion of Felicia Gordon. Ann Donahue quickly proved to be one of Hays's champions, and she continues to be a wise and abiding presence as the book takes on life. Meredith Coeyman has been responsive and adroit as the Desk Editor. The anonymous Readers for Ashgate have been enthusiastic, encouraging, and instructive. I thank them for urging me on and making such helpful suggestions.

I have benefited from the strenuous efforts and cheerful support of younger scholars and students in completing this project, particularly Arianne J. Chernock, Fiore Sireci, Kate Godin, Danielle La Senna, Shawn Mason, Meghan Roe, and Marta Stemberger. The students in my classes on the history of learned women at The New School, New School University, have been insistent in their attentions to Hays; I am grateful to them for teaching me about her importance to women today. I thank Dean Linda Dunne and my other New School colleagues for their understanding of how much time and attention this book has taken. Stefanie Bendik has transformed the demanding process of completing the manuscript into a collaborative feminist endeavor, and I appreciate her boundless patience and occasional firmness in not letting me make yet another change to the text.

Philippa Gregory continues to provide inspiration for and insights into writing about a woman writer's intellectual life. Finding her has proved to be an unexpected pleasure of the work on Hays. I appreciate Marilyn Brooks's suggestion that I contact Philippa after the broadcast on the BBC-Radio 4's "Woman's Hour" of "Mary Hays in Love," her adaptation of Hays's "Love Letters," in December 2002.

I acknowledge the professionals who make it possible for me to live the life of the mind healthfully and happily: Keith Sedlacek, M.D.; Catherine C. Hart, M.D.; Michele Green; M.D.; Jennie Ann Freiman, M.D.; Dorothy Anderson, Deni Bank, Lynn Foreman, Anni Kuan, and Lorraine Massey.

List of Abbreviations

The following abbreviations are used throughout this edition:

Abinge Bodleian Library, University of Oxford, Abinger Collection.

CMH Brooks, M.L., *The Correspondence (1779–1843) of Mary Hays, British Novelist* (Lewiston: Edwin Mellen Press, 2004).

DWL Dr. Williams's Library.

L&E Hays, M., *Letters and Essays, Moral, and Miscellaneous*, 1793, ed. G. Luria (New York: Garland, 1974).

MAV Godwin, W., *Memoirs of the Author of A Vindication of the Rights of Woman*, ed. P. Clemit and G.L. Walker (Peterborough: Broadview Press, 2001).

MEC Hays, M., *Memoirs of Emma Courtney*, ed. M.L. Brooks (Peterborough: Broadview Literary Texts, 2000).

MW Todd, Janet, *Mary Wollstonecraft: A Revolutionary Life* (London: Weidenfeld & Nicolson, 2000).

Pforz. The Carl H. and Lily Pforzheimer Collection of Shelley and His Circle, New York Public Library, Astor, Lenox, and Tilden Foundations.

VRW Wollstonecraft, M., *A Vindication of the Rights of Woman, The Vindications*, ed. E.L. Macdonald and K. Scherf (Peterborough: Broadview Press, 1997).

Introduction

"In the intellectual advancement of women, and their consequent privileges in society, is to be traced the progress of civilization, or knowledge gradually superseding the dominion of *brute-force*."

Mary Hays, *Memoirs of Mary Wollstonecraft*, 1800

"The denial of women's contributions to intellectual history erases their intellectual heritage."

Wendy Gunther-Canada, *Rebel Writer: Mary Wollstonecraft and Enlightenment Politics*, 2001

The Idea of Being Free

This is the story of Mary Hays's intellectual quest. Hays self-consciously dedicated herself to "the idea of being free,"[1] by which she meant self-determination and understanding (in the sense of both knowledge and enlightenment). During her long life she judged people, politics, morality, and aesthetics by the degree to which they fostered or obstructed her life's work. Hays shared with her Rational Dissenting contemporaries an almost existential sense of urgency that the search for truth was the most direct way to give her existence meaning. Yet Hays's experience was one of constant struggle against traditional social, political, religious, and private assumptions about what women should and should not be or do. Many of Hays's texts express her continuing frustration that despite their progressive views on other subjects, the majority of enlightened men with whom she associated failed to appreciate the depth of her desire to learn or her expectation that she could enjoy equal freedom with them in expressing her views. She responded by insisting that gender must be part of the reformist agenda of Rational Dissent. In this way Hays contributed importantly to the early feminist conversation that helped shape the intellectual project we know as the Enlightenment.[2]

Hays quickly learned that because of her sex she could only participate in the republic of letters as an outsider. Thus the story of her intellectual life is inextricably linked to Enlightenment tensions that roiled gender issues. The necessity of reacting to these issues led, and in some cases forced, Hays to explore modes of feeling, forms of thought, and hybrid genres that her male contemporaries could ignore or at least felt no comparable urgency to consider.

But, while Hays wrestled with the entrenched gender expectations of her time, she reflexively adhered to them herself, even as she tried to reason her way beyond them. Hays's strenuous efforts to find release for her frustrated energies, in her case sexual as well as cognitive, dominate the story of her intellectual life.[3] As a result, female sexual fulfillment, the necessary connection between gender and genre (specifically life-writing and the novel), and the public perils of expressing her convictions in these new forms were some of the areas she experimented with.

Paradoxes of Gender

Hays lived the paradoxes of being a woman who sought enlightenment. She was keenly aware that she had been acculturated like other women to believe herself intellectually inferior to men. At the same time, she consciously resisted such imposed constraints of gender. Her accounts of her experience of these tensions, as well as her own behavior, offer evidence about how women subvert themselves, and the social anxiety this phenomenon arouses in others. Hays aspired to a realm where the mind had no sex, but to her sorrow and anger she learned that the knowledge she sought was controlled and produced by and for men and that women were habitually excluded from the life of the mind. Reluctantly, she also acknowledged that women could not realize the idea or practice of autonomy with the same freedoms as men.

Hays's story is one of neither success nor personal resolution.[4] In her time and for 150 years after, Hays was judged a failure. For many of her contemporaries Hays was at best a pedant, at worst an embarrassment, and, somewhere in between, a clown. Yet it is Hays's very accounts of her resistance to gender prejudice that inform her tale so uniquely. She presaged later public women intellectuals in her stubborn insistence that she would pursue the life of the mind despite the conventional assumption that women were by nature slaves to their feelings and, therefore, generally incapable of reason or the pursuit of knowledge.

Hays was a protean figure who emerged out of a complex set of cultural concerns in the late eighteenth century and who presaged profound social changes in the nineteenth century and beyond. She compiled her first "book" of love letters as an adolescent devotee of the Cult of Sensibility. She willingly involved herself in the controversies of Enlightened Dissent and embraced Unitarianism out of deep theological conviction. She wrestled with the apparent tension and connection between reason and faith, free will and divine decree. She was enthralled by the emerging science of the mind and attempted to replicate scientific methods as a lone empiricist whose subject was herself. She applied the nascent concept of "unlimited toleration" to female experience. Hays is especially intriguing for her experiments with life-writing about women, part of her attempt to speak directly to a burgeoning female audience in a genre that appeared to be more conventional than the subversive uses she made of it. Hays's texts are inextricably linked to the events of her life and to her compelling desire to elevate her existence to that of a seeker after truth no matter where the search might take her.

In her attempts to be recognized as a public woman intellectual, Hays's story raises important questions about how literary reputations are made; her troubled relations with male contemporaries—among them Godwin, Southey, and Coleridge—implicitly question the creation of the received textual canon of the Revolutionary, Romantic, and Victorian periods.[5] The events and works of Hays's life are filtered through political and cultural prejudices that ensnared her. These unhappy episodes show us what it took to be a writer at the end of the eighteenth century, and the particular psychological toll when the writer was female.

Preludes

The subtitle of this book makes deliberate reference to William Wordsworth, Hays's younger contemporary, particularly his epic, *The Prelude,* that he described as "the poem on the growth of my own mind." Wordsworth began writing *The Prelude* in 1798. It was finally published in 1850 after his death the same year. *The Prelude* draws on some of the same ideas, influences, and personal relationships of the vibrant period of British radicalism of the 1790s[6] in which both Hays and Wordsworth were active. These themes are also reflected in Hays's letters, novels, and periodical pieces.[7] Hays also shares with Wordsworth and Coleridge excitement at the new hypotheses about the science of the mind that she, like the men, found useful as metaphors for human experience. Hays portrayed the growth of her own mind and that of other women in her fiction, memoirs, and quasi-journalistic reportage.

But Hays's idiosyncratic intellectual genealogy emerged from a different set of traditions than Wordsworth's. Most crucial was her exclusion because of her sex from the enlightened classical education reserved for men that Wordsworth benefited from.[8] Without participating in the established institutions of teaching and learning, Hays's surviving texts, unlike Wordsworth's, form a series of preludes—beginnings and anticipations—that never achieve substantive, social, artistic, psychological, or formal consistency or resolution.[9] And, unlike Wordsworth, Hays could not resolve the gendered contradictions in her own life, although she was aware that her failure to do so weakened her ability to address the realities of gender that thwarted her and other women intellectuals.[10]

Freedom and Isolation

As an outsider in the republic of letters, Hays made use of whatever cultural forces would enable her to learn and teach through her writings. Her interloper status allowed her unprecedented imaginative freedom that was accompanied by extreme isolation. Her frustration expressed itself as cognitive restlessness. She moved from heterodox sexual interpretations of Sensibility to the discourse of Revolution and from there to a female version of Romanticism[11] that finally led her to withdraw from the social intercourse of public life, although she kept on writing and publishing. In retrospect, Hays can best be understood as one of a new generation of modern intellectuals, bound by a common heritage of ideas that left them socially isolated, rather than by birth, status, religious persuasion, profession, or wealth. Roy Porter cites Hays and Godwin as late eighteenth-century representatives of that self-selecting cohort of individuals who embraced dissent as a new and fluid identity in opposition to the prevailing culture.[12] This offers a coherent way of understanding Hays's self-representations as a "Solitary Wanderer," Rousseau's image of social isolation that Wollstonecraft also adopted.

The awakening, sentient female self was Hays's continuous subject. Like others of her female contemporaries, she labored to craft a lexicon that could convey female understanding in the language of real women.[13] Unlike Wordsworth, the "I" in Hays's texts rarely achieves that oracular transcendence for which she, like the Poet, Wordsworth's persona, longs. The self is always female in Hays's representations, bound to the realities of what she and Wollstonecraft described as "the magic circle" of gender in which a woman's worth is necessarily yoked with the presence or—in Hays's experience—the absence of a man. Yet the narrative persona Hays constructs over time does achieve authority because of her imagined reconstructions of women of the past. Hays ultimately recognized the importance of documenting women's lives for future generations. In *Female Biography* (1802), and *Memoirs of Queens* (1821), she revised history to evoke a continuum of competent women who give hope that in more advanced stages of society women's cognitive freedom would calibrate cultural progress. In these works, Hays anticipated contemporary feminist interest in constructing an intellectual history of women.

As she learned, Hays identified new models of female erudition. She incorporated and rejected the figures that were available to her. Hays's increasingly sophisticated autodidactism modified her sense of self and her expectations of others' responses to her texts and her persona. Her ideas and reactions differed from Wollstonecraft's and others of their female contemporaries. Hays's published and unpublished works demonstrate the dissonance between gendered norms for uncredentialed women and the aspirations and achievements for which Hays first sought, then defied, social approbation. Hays's strategies in negotiating between the private and public spheres allowed her to encroach on the recesses of higher learning to understand, modify, and reinterpret this knowledge for women.

The Hays Persona

Hays provoked strong reactions in her time to her work, to herself personally, and to the persona she created. Early in their relationship, Wollstonecraft criticized Hays's dependence in her texts on the *"shouldering up* of Dr this or that."[14] From her own accounts, Hays was determined to be enlightened no matter what it took in a time when advanced learning for women was difficult to obtain and hazardous to reveal. Unlike Wollstonecraft, she desired to know what men knew not to "interrupt" their conversations,[15] but to learn how to construct an alternative, women-centered discourse that would enlighten other intellectually curious women who were perhaps less ambitious and aggressive than Hays herself. Responses to her by her contemporaries, mainly negative, and her frequently ill-advised reactions to these, are also part of her story. Thus Hays is both the subject of this book and an illuminating figure in the larger questions her story raises of how a woman intellectual was perceived in her time, and how that perception affected the course of her own life.

Hays's story continues to resonate. In discussions with other women, I have been struck by how contemporary is her problem of overcoming her own and others' gender prejudices. Hays's texts arouse and anger readers because she addresses the still unresolved complexities of women's efforts to achieve intellectual independence and craft a new lexicon for and about women. Hays's own equivocations provoke modern readers as they once did her contemporaries.[16] Some readers take exception to Hays's reliance on "generous men," particularly William Godwin, and see this as a denial of her own agency. Others are inspired by Hays's courage in depicting her needs, desires, and ambivalence so honestly. Twenty-first-century reactions to Hays are part of her story, too, because ignorance of and prejudices about learned women endure. Four decades after the beginning of what was then called "the new scholarship on women," we are still uncertain about the validity and nature of or criteria for an intellectual history of women or whether and how to "add in" the contributions of women to the received history of ideas.[17]

Indeed, the growth of Hays's understanding, her interactions with other historical actors, and the texts that emerged from these force us to confront fundamental questions about the enterprise of constructing women's intellectual history because they are the very issues that Hays investigated, represented, and wanted to develop and resolve. These questions include: How can we accurately understand "female education" in the context of women's accounts of their necessary autodidactism?[18] How do we assess women's production of texts and the texts themselves in spite of the persistence of what Michèle Le Doeuff describes as women's "conditional access to knowledge"?[19] Did Kant's definition of "enlightenment"—*"Sapere aude!"* ["Have courage to use your own reason!"] apply to women? During the Enlightenment, did women ever achieve enduring intellectual autonomy? If so, was this recognized by their male contemporaries? By the larger culture? Can we discern reiterative patterns in women's texts that enabled readers and commentators to dismiss them, for example, authorial apology, self-deprecation, and anger? Can we usefully generalize about the history of the reception of women writers and their works? Mary Hays's intellectual journey offers evidence that may help us continue her quest for enlightenment on these and other important questions to understand more fully the women of the past, present, and future, who seek the life of the mind.

Sources

Mary Hays preserved the materials that documented what she described as her "extraordinary destiny." She left the papers she collected to a favorite niece, Sarah Dunkin Wedd. The manuscripts were carefully handed down through subsequent generations of the family. Anne F. Wedd (1875?–1956), Hays's great-grandniece, published a selected edition of the materials as *The Love-Letters of Mary Hays 1779–1781* (1925), and *The Fate of the Fenwicks* (1927).[20] In 1970, the surviving Hays archive consisted of 117 letters to and from Hays, including letters from Wollstonecraft, Godwin, Charlotte Smith, Mary Shelley, and Southey, as well as other manuscript materials. A few documents that Wedd indicated she once held are now missing. Of particular importance, Volume II of the early love letters has disappeared. Wedd claimed that it contained autobiographical fragments that she cited in "The Story of Mary Hays," her introduction to the 1925 edition of *The Love-Letters*. Additional manuscripts have been added to the original collection since the Carl H. and Lily Pforzheimer Library purchased it in 1971 from Jill Organ (later Hansen), who inherited the materials from Anne F. Wedd. Primary materials from the Abinger Collection of the Bodleian Library, the British Library, Dr. Williams's Library, and other archives, including a brief 1843–44 Unitarian memoir of Hays, augment the Hays archive now at the Carl H. Pforzheimer Collection of Shelley and His Circle, the New York Public Library, Astor, Lenox, and Tilden Foundations.

Gina Luria Walker
Rhinebeck, NY

Notes

1   Mary Hays to William Godwin, 13 October 1795, *Pforz.*, MH 8. See Chapter Five.
2   Siep Stuurman argues that "early-modern feminism" is "one of the critical discourses that went into the *making* of the Enlightenment," "The Deconstruction of Gender: Seventeenth–Century Feminism and Modern Equality," in Barbara Taylor and Sarah Knott (eds), *Women, Gender and Enlightenment* (Houndmills, 2005), p. 371.
3   Kate Sopher has recently described the gendered nature of these dilemmas during the Enlightenment in terms that closely echo Hays's representations of her own and other

women's experience. Sopher writes, "For educated women of the [Enlightenment], it seems clear that the main problem was not so much the lack of things to say, or fear of saying, but the resistance of their culture to allowing them access to the means of expression available to their male counterparts. Their particular message is of the frustration of their mental autonomy rather than its underdevelopment ... It is a persistent theme of the prolific writings by women in this period on education that at least in the 'life of the mind', if nowhere else, women could find some relief for their pent up cognitive energy," Kate Sopher, "Feminism and Enlightenment Legacies," *Women, Gender and Enlightenment*, p. 712.

4   Hays's story refutes what E.J. Clery calls the "unreflecting triumphalism at women's achievements, which has been characteristic of feminist literary history," "Bluestocking 'Feminism' and the Fame Game," *British Journal for Eighteenth-Century Studies*, 28/2 (Autumn 2005): 277–8.

5   In *The Madwoman in the Attic: The Woman Writer and the Nineteenth-Century Literary Imagination*, Sandra M. Gilbert and Susan Gubar acknowledged that they were "trying to recover not only a major (and neglected) female literature but a whole (neglected) female history," "Preface," (Yale, 1979), p. xii. Mary Hays's story is part of that ongoing process of recovery. Like other women who have been rediscovered by modern scholars, Hays's story adds to and modifies female intellectual history. Gilbert and Gubar also spoke of the need to understand the "lesser peaks" of minor figures that came between the "mountain peaks" of major women writers. My study of Hays does not argue for her place in a proposed hierarchy of a female canon intended to parallel the male canon. I am interested in examining the story of Hays's intellectual struggle rather than constructing a polemic to argue that Hays's texts should be read more than they are because, as Gilbert and Gubar suggest, these can shed light on Wollstonecraft as the "major peak" in the 1790s.

6   Albert Goodwin, *The Friends of Liberty: The English Democratic Movement in the Age of the French Revolution* (Cambridge, MA, 1979), pp. 74–5.

7   See Nicholas Roe, *Wordsworth and Coleridge: the radical years* (Oxford, 1988).

8   Richard W. Clancy, *Wordsworth's classical undersong: education, rhetoric and poetic truth* (New York, 2000); Ben Ross Schneider, *Wordsworth's Cambridge Education* (Cambridge, 1957).

9   Marilyn Butler, *Romantics, Rebels and Reactionaries: English Literature and its Background 1760–1830* (Oxford, 1982), p. 94.

10   Angela Keane comments that "wandering women" like Hays, Smith, and Wollstonecraft "belong yet are detached and detachable from national tradition, a condition that makes them intellectually free but culturally homeless," *Women Writers and the English Nation in the 1790s: Romantic Belongings* (Cambridge, 2000), p. 160.

11   Anne K. Mellor defines as "'feminine Romanticism' female representations of the period that are simultaneously autobiographical, subversive, and visionary," *Romanticism & Gender* (New York, 1993), pp. 309–12.

12   Roy Porter describes the emergence of a modern "free intelligentsia." Like Hays or Godwin, Porter advises, "Intellectuals came to exude the air of a narcissistic *bien-pensant* coterie writing about each other, surreptitiously propagating the idea that writers and artists were the people who really counted, the true legislators of the world." Roy Porter, "Lasting Light?," *Enlightenment: Britain and the Creation of the Modern World* (London, 2000), pp. 478–9.

13   See Hannah Barker and Elaine Chalus, "Introduction," *Gender in Eighteenth-Century England: Roles, Representations and Responsibilities* (Longman, 1997), pp. 1–28.

14   Wollstonecraft to Hays, 25 November 1792, *Pforz.*, MW 35.

15   Wendy Gunther-Canada, *Rebel Writer: Mary Wollstonecraft and Enlightenment Politics* (DeKalb, 2001), p. 4.

16   These discomforts continue to our day. See Lionel Shriver, on the occasion of her learning of her shortlisting for the Orange Prize (which she subsequently won): "I acted like a man – and prepared for victory." *The Guardian* (13 June 2005).

17   Gina Luria Walker, "'Can Man Be Free/And Woman Be a Slave?' Teaching Eighteenth- and Nineteenth-Century Women Writers in Intersecting Communities," pp. 190–204, as well as the other chapters in *Teaching British Women Writers 1750–1900*, ed. Jeanne Moskal and Shannon R. Wooden (New York, 2005).

18   Barbara J. Whitehead argues that "the principle to be questioned is whether formal training in the humanities was required in order for a woman to be 'educated,'" "Introduction," *Women's Education in Early Modern Europe: A History 1500–1800* (Garland, 1999), p. xi.

19   George Eliot addressed these issues in her portrayal of Dorothea Brooke's aspirations in *Middlemarch:* "[Dorothea] would not have asked Mr. Casaubon at once to teach her the [classical] languages, dreading of all things to be tiresome instead of helpful; but it was not entirely out of devotion to her future husband that she wished to know Latin and Greek. Those provinces of masculine knowledge seemed to her a standing-ground from which all truth could be seen more truly. As it was, she constantly doubted her own conclusions, because she felt her own ignorance." For a more contemporary view, see Michèle Le Doueff, *The Sex of Knowing*, trans. Kathryn Hamer and Lorraine Code (New York, 2003), p. 24.

20   See "Annie Frances Wedd," by Imogen Wedd (unpublished MS, 2004). I appreciate Imogen Wedd's contribution of her accounts of her family.

PART ONE
Preludes

Chapter One

Love Letters

"I fear I have too often swerved from the rules which [prudence] dictates ... Why should we sacrifice sincerity to politeness?"

Mary Hays to John Eccles, *Love Letters*, 1779

Mary Hays was the most purposefully intellectual woman within the tiny community of English Jacobins in the 1790s. From her girlhood, texts for enlightenment and self-expression were integral to the major interests and events of her long life. The evidence reveals her vigorous participation in the creation, response to, acquisition, archiving, and publication of the written word. She lived much of her life through letters and books. She was happiest learning, more comfortable with other people as correspondents than in person, and responded to others' texts as if these embodied the writer. The erotic corollary of this was that she spoke more frankly of love and sex in her letters than face-to-face with the objects of her desire. The passions of her life were self-exploration, the pursuit of knowledge, and recognition for her intellectual talents. Hays's aspirations to learn formed the basis of the creed she constructed for herself out of the various cultural influences to which she had access. Hays valued Rational Dissent's insistence on the "right to private judgment."[1] She embraced optimistic Enlightenment claims about the sensory basis of human thought that argued for the greater importance of environmental influences over inborn qualities.

The love letters Hays exchanged between 1779–80 with John Eccles, a young Baptist, express her early and abiding frustration at the gulf between male and female education, among even so enlightened a group as the Rational Dissenters. Hays's ruminations in the love letters on the propriety of her amorous experiments with Eccles reveal her interest in the possibilities of female freedom, both its perils and its fulfillment. She embraced the cult of Sincerity as a cornerstone of her emotional and intellectual life.[2] In her love letters Hays was eager to chart a fluid, idiosyncratic, and independent self that presages "feminine Romanticism," Anne Mellor's term for female self-writing of the period that is startling and predictive.[3]

At the time of her exchanges with Eccles, Hays lived at Gainsford Street in Southwark, close by the London wharves, with her widowed mother, younger sister Elizabeth, and several other married and unmarried siblings.[4] Steeped in the rich aural and print culture of English Dissent, Hays's girlhood education consisted of informal but avid reading, particularly of poetry and novels; weekly attendance at nonconformist chapels; and familiarity with the musical propaganda and confessions of the spiritual descendants of Bunyan and Milton.[5] During her adolescence, Hays was eager to devise an analogue for herself to the classical paradigm of education reserved for men. She would, in time, look to a succession of "generous men"—John Eccles, Robert Robinson, Joseph Priestley, John Disney, Hugh Worthington, George Dyer, William Frend, and William Godwin—who nourished her intellectual hunger and provided access to the public life of the mind. Her first epistolary relationship was with Eccles. Their extant correspondence reveals the tentative expression of many of her persistent concerns, as well as her discovery of textual interplay as a vehicle for instruction, intimacy, and inquiry.

These earliest surviving manuscripts reveal that Hays was ambitious to learn and curious about the mental processes of learning. From the correspondence, we know that what Eccles admired as Hays's "polished education" consisted of extensive reading of poetry and novels. She had the key to her friend Mrs. Collier's library, where she explored works by the same authors her later fictional heroines read. Even in the midst of her ardent—and illicit—romance with Eccles, she criticized the chasm between men's freedom to learn and the constraints on women's education, noting the "stillness and privacy" of female life.[6] She envied Eccles's classical training, and proposed that he be her tutor instead of her lover. With the precedent of Rousseau's Heloise before her, she sensed the combustible sexual potential when woman and man came together in pursuit of knowledge. She urged him to teach her what he knew as a man without hurting her as a woman.[7]

Hays first looked to literature for instruction. We can conjecture that she organized "Love Letters," the collection of her correspondence with Eccles, as a novel modeled after Richardson, a writer who influenced her strongly.[8] As narrator, Hays strives to take some distance from her youthful literary *persona* Mary Hays—or "Maria" or "Polly" as Eccles variously dubs her—to recreate the story of their "grand affair." This self-consciousness is a continuation of the awareness she and Eccles expressed that they were creating a record of their own (sometimes) "innocent intercourse" while they passed back and forth the volumes of a popular epistolary romance, *Fatal Friendship*, By a Lady (1770). Perhaps the most important model for crafting a collection of love letters in which the lovers were rational, high-minded, virtuous, and ardent is the correspondence of Heloise and Abelard, familiar to Hays at least through Alexander Pope's poem "Eloisa to Abelard" (1717). "M. H.," as she signs herself, writes in the cover of a letter of Friday, 31 July 1779, to Eccles, "Let me hear from you soon, though I must not see you," and adds, "Heaven first taught letters to some wretched maid,/Some banished lover, or some captive's aid," lines 51 and 52 of "Eloisa to Abelard."[9] Hays quotes from memory; the original verse reads, "Heaven first taught letters for some wretch's aid,/ Some banished lover, or some captive maid." Her transposition of the order of marginal subjects to whom "Heaven" *first* provides written language reveals the intensity of her understanding, as well her feelings, about the power of writing and the limitations of female autonomy. Hays's intimate knowledge of the poem, and, therefore, of at least the rudiments of the personal and textual history of the real Heloise and Abelard, suggests an independent source for her observations on the differences between women and men that follow. It also explains in part the zeal with which she took to the clandestine zone that she and Eccles inhabit in their correspondence.

In the love letters Hays meditates on Eloisa's celebration of women's right to love passionately outside the bounds of marriage. Eloisa also serves as an emollient, softening Hays's guilt over her own sexual curiosity and trespasses. If Eloisa's sins could be forgiven because she loved much, surely a (still) virgin daughter could be excused for disobeying her mother. But even as Hays vacillates about the propriety of her erotic explorations with Eccles, in the imaginary sphere of her correspondence she sounds the female voice clear, distinct, and subversive, much as Pope's Eloisa and the historical Heloise do in their epistolary interchanges with men. In her letters Hays also seeks constant reassurance from Eccles that he will be faithful to her because her sensual response to him is complicated by her own vulnerability and subverted by what she has been taught to fear about men's mistreatment of women. The evidence suggests that Eccles himself is reliable. But to Hays, they are gendered figures in a static *tableau* in which men press for illicit sex, and women must hold out for marriage. She voices her emerging consciousness of the different realms in which the two sexes exist, a complex response composed of envy, resentment, admiration, longing, and skepticism. Again and again in the letters, she questions Eccles's ability to be faithful, to withstand the blandishments of the "world and its amusements" because he is a man.

The Setting

The earliest surviving self-conscious text by Hays is a volume in her handwriting of the letters Hays at 19, exchanged with Eccles, then 23. It tells the story of their covert relationship, begun when their respective parents rejected their proposal to marry. It continued with frequent and ardent exchanges until Eccles's sudden death from a fever 18 months later, just as the parents relented and marriage seemed a probability. With her love life abruptly halted, Hays turned to imaginative experiments in the layering of texts and the positioning of real voices in the manuscript "Love Letters," extracting text from life and inserting it back again. Hays's text begins on 12 February 1779, and ends on 23 August 1781, with her "Concluding Note" in observance of "that fatal day, which blasted all the fond hopes of my youth." Hays copied the letters in the year following Eccles' death to form what she called her "book," the first documented instance in which grief galvanized her to create an artifact of her experience.[10]

As Hays transformed them, the letters demonstrate that in the midst of a passionate relationship, Hays used the correspondence to reflect on the differences between women and men. Within the insular nest of family and local Rational Dissenters, she discovered that writing offered freedoms that even romantic love could not provide. Through her girlhood, listening to sermons that extolled God's command "*to add knowledge* to all other Christian virtues,"[11] Hays came to see the search for enlightenment as a legitimate exercise in the ongoing progress of the Christian pilgrim. As she heard learned men analyze controversial political and ethical issues, she observed the forms of discourse. From within the quotidian female culture in which she was inculcated, Hays gestated a stubborn independence, applying Rational Dissenting pragmatism to the seemingly intractable, though usually ignored, problems of woman's competence and women's place. On her own, Hays discerned that female sexuality was an authentic, if dangerous, form of knowledge. Her protestations to Eccles about the "propriety" of their erotic experiments were not just maidenly coyness, as Hays explains in her introduction to the love letters. Rather, she expressed genuine ambivalence about the historical imperative that women preserve their chastity whatever the cost, while men were free to adventure sexually, as well as intellectually. Hays intimates that sexuality may be a vehicle for autonomy, either as personal fulfillment or submission.

The Story

Hays's "Love Letters" book begins with her entrance into the world of romantic travail. Mrs. Hays has asked to meet with Eccles to tell him that he may no longer see Hays. In her preface, Hays writes that "some malevolent and ill grounded aspersion being related to my family, they determined (if possible) to put an end to our connection ... before I acquiesced in their commands, I insisted on having one more interview with the object of my tenderness." Even before the final meeting, in a spirit of subversion, Eccles and Hays conspire about the future. "I am now going to commit a trespass on the respect I owe Mrs. Hays, and on your delicacy," Eccles writes,

> but I cannot help it. I expect to be forbid ever to speak to you again; if so I hope you will not refuse to see me *once* afterwards in private; this favor I think I may claim, for oh! Miss Hays, I have loved you; I adore you; and the greater discouragements I have met with, the more firmly has my heart been attached to you; — this deserves some regard.[12]

Perhaps to test the depths of the young people's affections, perhaps concerned that a youthful flirtation was veering into a serious sexual affair, Hays's mother had acceded to Eccles's father's demand that the couple separate. Since Eccles had rooms in a house just across the street—Hays and Eccles had plain view of each other's bedroom windows—the young people found it possible to stay in contact by a set of ingenious signals, and even in Mrs. Hays's occasional absences, to visit privately behind closed doors. Eccles and Hays wrote to each other at least three times a week while his energies were presumably focused on acquiring the means to support a wife. Hays is the heroine of the "Love Letters" as she configures them, torn between forbidden love and filial duty. In the Hays family's insular world, Hays seemed a relatively good catch on the marriage market: her father had left her an annuity of £70 per annum, dependent on her mother's approval of her choice of a husband. By contrast, Eccles was no bargain: he seems to have had neither occupation, nor savings, nor any annuity; and his father had refused to help him gain independence after an unsuccessful foray into the family business. At first Mrs. Hays and others in their circle suspected that Eccles was after Hays's money. Some went so far as to say that, since Hays was not pretty, an assured income was her only asset. In the course of the lovers' correspondence, Hays acknowledged the truth of this assessment of her looks. Her memory of their "earliest acquaintance was a consciousness that I possessed but few personal charms ... opposition I believe increased my affection, and I determined to persevere."[13] Eccles's father, however, was not impressed with Hays or her bequest. He opined to Eccles that he "was sorry he should trouble so much about one woman, as there were so many in the world."[14]

But Eccles was resolute. He had moved to Southwark from his family's home in Fordingbridge sometime during 1777 and joined the meeting house community that the Hays family participated in. Eccles reminisced, "I shall begin with the first time I saw a little girl with dark hair and features soft as those of the peaceful messengers of heaven. — I cannot express what I then thought (and, shall I say, still think), but I saw everything that was engaging and amiable in her face; she fascinated me, I believe; I could think of no one nor anything but her."[15] Eccles's description of Hays's appearance is the only favorable one that survives.

In her "Love Letters," Hays transforms Eccles into the exemplary "generous man"—his term—against whom she will measure all others. In retrospect, she believes that she has experienced a grand passion that, she insists, allowed her to move beyond the accepted boundaries of female behavior, even implicitly to question traditional assumptions about the genders and the sanctity of marriage. Hays recognizes the power of writing to attest to her dissident experience. Her understanding, like Eccles's, derives in part from the sense and sound of the poetry they endlessly spout, much of it (as their mistakes reveal) from memory. In the dialogue about their relationship, and the nature of male/female connections more generally, this poetic reserve allowed them to mimic the clerical disputation of the nonconformist meeting house in which assertion and response were supported by scriptural precedent and exegesis.

Hays seizes the opportunity for the free exchange that their enforced correspondence allows. "Write your thoughts with freedom, just as they flow," she urges Eccles. Perhaps these appeals between women and men express the curiosity they feel about the mind of the opposite sex. Epistolary exchanges like Hays's and Eccles's extend the discursive boundaries in what women and men say to each

other. And such confidential correspondence offers the possibility of mutual
alliance, not avoidance or antagonism. Hays conserves the writings that chronicle
her existence. Her reasons "for creating a memorial (more lasting than the original
loose papers)," she writes in the introduction to "Love Letters," are several.[16] They
include documenting the "great tenderness" of her friends in her grief, and the
"favorable opinion" they hold of Eccles, whom she describes as "the Friend of my
heart." Hays also represents the letters as instructive, indicating her keen interest in
her own mental development. She recognizes that her reactions may be seen as
excessive and attempts a pre-emptive explanation. Hays predicts that

> should this book ever fall into the hands of those who make the human heart their study,
> they may, it is possible, find some entertainment, should the papers continue legible, in
> tracing the train of circumstances which have contributed to form a character, in some
> respects it may be singular and whimsical, yet affording I trust something to imitate,
> though more to warn and pity.

She confesses "a secret pride which I feel from the consciousness of having
possessed the entire affections of a man, who did honor to humanity,"
foreshadowing the complex textual *persona* she will construct later in life.[17] To
memorialize their love, she has created an object that has the potential to endure.
But, she recognizes, as an independent artifact, her text may be judged harshly for
the kinds of rebellion it reveals. She rationalizes this, like Heloise, as an
appropriate risk because of the loved one's merits:

> If I erred in thus indulging an affection (in opposition to duty) which is implanted in our
> souls by the God of nature, and of love; I have sufficiently expiated it, if floods of
> unfeigned, and unceasing tears, may be termed an expiation. — All the excuse I have to
> plead is my knowledge of the merits of the object of my affection—His virtues were his
> own. His faults were fortunes! — if exquisite sensibility — refined sentiments — warm
> affections — strength of understanding—seriousness of mind — and symmetry of form,
> could render a man amiable — My Eccles, was so! For those were all his own.[18]

Anticipating criticism from female readers, Hays predicts that "they may on
perusing my letters with the cool, unprejudiced eye of reason, find many
expressions exceptionable." She defends herself by arguing that the sincerity of her
emotions pre-empted the gendered proscription that women conceal their feelings
to entice a man's: "All the defense which I shall make is a frank avowal," she
writes,

> that I ever had a dislike to the affected prudery, and insincerity which is generally
> instilled into our sex, from the most ingenuous motives—that of supposing that the more
> cold ... their conduct is to the man, to whom they intend to give their hand, the more
> desirable they render themselves to him.—Mistaken notion! How contrary to the artless
> simplicity, and winning softness, which ought ever to be the characteristic of a woman.[19]

With lines from the "Spring" section of Thomson's *The Seasons* (1730), Hays buttresses her argument against "affected prudery": to be sincere or not is the central tension of the document. She warns her readers not to expect conventional forms of female behavior or belief, particularly the hypocrisy that a woman should mask her desire for a man. The Hays of the letters refuses to imitate the mythic Daphne's deliberate inaccessibility: "What happiness can we expect with that man, whose tenderness we despair of retaining, unless like Daphne, when pursued by Apollo, we are ever flying before him."[20] To the figure of woman-as-withholder, she contrasts "those joys of virtuous love" described by Thomson, in which "thought meeting thought, and will preventing will/With boundless confidence; for nought but love/ Can answer love — and render bliss secure!"[21] Here is the gist of the conversation that follows between Eccles and Hays's textual selves. The discussion is deepened by her knowledge of Pope's poem, "Eloisa to Abelard," a source for Thomson's work as well.[22]

Hays is a willing co-conspirator with Eccles at the outset of their illicit correspondence. On 29 July, she writes to ask if he will join her in a moonlight walk the next evening, "at a little after eight o'clock — it is rather too late an hour, but I cannot come sooner, besides a walk by moonlight has a thousand charms. It inspires a pleasing melancholy, a delightful sensation." Even as she writes, Hays hears how her words may sound to Eccles. "You smile! — I own I am a little romantic girl! My Mamma often tells me 'I am in a fairy dream'. May the keen hand of adversity never awake me from the pleasing delusion."[23] Hays includes these lines in her "book," knowing how prescient they will ring by its end. The narrative she constructs is based on the evidence of the letters that, in turn, links them coherently.

After proposing a tryst, in the next breath, Hays expresses her concern about "Prudence," a subject that torments her: "I fear I have too often swerved from the rules which [prudence] dictates. I should like to know your real sentiments on the subject. Why should we sacrifice sincerity to politeness?" Hays's remarks suggest abandoning reserves of speech, but also that she and Eccles have experimented with some degree of physical intimacy. Her ambivalence about her own sensual reactions and John's takes the form of teasing: "But how I run on, I shall certainly tire you with my *scribbilation* — that last word is not English, I believe, but ladies have a right to coin you know, 'tis a privilege they have held since creation." Hays speaks lightly, but making words up is a way of compensating for the dearth of codified language to express female vacillation. Like Eve—and Eloisa—she has transgressed against parental commandments, nibbling at the apple of sexual intelligence. A final remark reveals her fear that Eccles may translate her defiance against their parents into a willingness to grant him more sexual freedoms: "You must not keep me more than half an hour to-morrow evening, and must promise to behave with the strictest decorum."[24] Hays questions the authority that insists on female propriety, but at this point in her life feels compelled to warn Eccles and the reader that she nonetheless respects it.

Their "final" meeting takes place in Mrs. Hays's presence the next day. As Hays describes it in a letter to Mrs. Collier, both young people are nearly insensible with emotion. But in her next letter to Eccles on 31 July, she is sufficiently recovered to work out a plan for message, and a somewhat arch rationale:

> If you request it, I will correspond with you; the letters need not come to the house, but may be conveyed to me by Mr. S—, or any other way you may think safest. This is perhaps going too far, but I cannot help making the sacrifice, as we may never see each other again, and I flatter myself it may contribute a little to your peace of mind (perhaps I only imagine so).[25]

Hays represents herself as torn between decisive action and her recurring need for reassurance that she is not too bold in either her judgments or her assumptions.

She also proposes a change in the ground rules for their alliance. "I think I have heard you lament that you had no friend to whom you could unbosom yourself, — make me that friend, I will look upon you as a brother, and as a sister endeavor to give you consolation under every disappointment."[26] In the absence of physical proximity, they can be confidants, under no social pressure to initiate, respond to, or reject sexual relations. As she invites him to confide in her, she confesses her repugnance at worldly pleasures, fantasizing the possibility of a nun's existence, like Heloise. "Had I been a roman catholic, with what pleasure should I have flown to a cloyster, and dedicated my hours to that Being who formed me."[27] But she is still, in part, a sheltered girl who can easily imagine with a mental shudder how lost she would be "should I be deprived of my Mamma (which heaven forbid), I have no asylum — I should be thrown on the world unprotected — on a world I despise and hate."[28] Hays presents herself as an outsider early in her life, presuming that as a rarified soul, Eccles will understand and join her.

Once she has assumed the role of his "third sister," Hays questions whether Eccles's attachment to her can withstand their current deprivations. "I mean not to fetter you," she writes, in a tone of apparent objectivity. "Perhaps some other attachment may afford you more happiness than this has done."[29] Eccles's reply focuses on the pleasures that their correspondence will afford.

> I have been reserved to you, and with some reason, but can now converse freely with you; can ask any questions, and you shall solve them. You shall be my friend, my counsellor; I will do nothing without your advice. This intercourse, the only means left to us, will surely be a source of great happiness.[30]

Yet he is tempted to come see her; so far he has resisted, but will not be

> answerable for my conduct, only it will be difficult for me to know who is with you, —
> lay a book against the window, and then, if I can assume the courage, I will come; if not,
> I will pass by about 9, and if you will write me a few lines, shall be glad to receive them
> from Miss Betsy

—who, it turns out, is waiting for the message he is presently writing.[31] In reply, Hays proposes a meeting on Thursday. "The family are going out to spend the day — any time in the afternoon that suits you — the place I leave to your choice likewise. You see the confidence I put in you, Mr. Eccles, — let me not repent it, I trust in your honor."[32]

Hays attempts to define the gendered differences between the sphere men inhabit, and that of women. Women, she muses, are trained to be more faithful than are men, "by nature ... education and the stillness and privacy of their lives improves this happy disposition, besides their attachments being of a purer, sublimer nature, an exalted species of friendship independent of passion, renders them more lasting. Confess! am I right in my opinion."[33] She tests Eccles's fidelity by echoing traditional notions about women and men. In doing so, Hays also sounds a poignant, albeit ironic, note that expresses her awakening sense of the relativity of socially constructed differences. Nurture and cultural expectations, rather than nature, may produce the apparent discrepancies between the experiences and responses of women and men. Therefore, she suspects that these may be susceptible to modification. "I will own to you, that in general I have but an indifferent opinion of the natural capacities of your sex; had the women half your advantages, depend upon it they would make more shining figures in the world of literature." She concludes, "There are exceptions on both sides, and perhaps I think you are one!"[34] She is sufficiently sincere to acknowledge that Eccles, like her late father, seems to be an enlightened man.

Eccles takes up Hays's theme that women are innately more constant than men both by nature and education. He judges that male and female lives are so different that a woman, necessarily, feels more deeply than a man.[35] For Eccles and Hays, the suspension of coquetry allows for straight talk that a man seeking sexual acceptance, and a woman needing economic security, would never risk face-to-face.[36] In the limbo of their texts, Hays and Eccles may write as brother and sister, equal but not at risk, sincere and open without fear. Both, however, recognize that the differences between women and men, whether natural or artificial, usually produce uneasy alliances. "I have always considered you as truth herself," Eccles writes, "whatever I know, you shall know ... I am happy to think I have met one to whom I can speak with freedom; this seldom happens between two of different sexes."[37] Hays agrees, alluding to Henry Mackenzie's popular novel about sensibility: "The unreserved manner in which I write, the frankness with which I have avowed my esteem, might expose me to the contempt of a coxcomb; but on the man of feeling, the man of sense, it will have quite a contrary effect."[38] Her honesty may prove to be a social liability in the larger world. In the intimacy of their letters, she can speak her mind to him.

Regardless of how closely Eccles meets this standard, the great divide between the limitations of female education and the expanse of male erudition separates them. Hays soon feels secure enough to express a wish that Eccles teach her.[39] "In the course of our correspondence," she writes,

> I shall have a thousand cases to put to you; I love to hear your definitions; I promise myself improvement as well as pleasure from them; by this innocent intercourse, we shall be able to form a right judgment of each other's sentiments and characters ... my thoughts, my heart shall be laid open to you;

then, hearts aside, she cautions him, "The lover must be forgot in the monitor."[40] The "innocent intercourse" between their texts, unlike the dangerous bodily skirmishes when they are face-to-face, holds the promise that he will share what he knows as a man without harming her as a woman. Unknowingly, Hays echoes Huguenot Poullain de la Barre's assertion that "the mind has no sex,"[41] and plays at being Eccles's academic equal. "Don't you think I have a *quantum sufficit*?" she writes, "I shall be a Latin scholar in time, I verily believe, — will you undertake to teach me?"[42] This is Hays's fervent female fantasy.[43]

Hays's request suggests Eccles is nonchalant about his privileged study of the Classics. He makes casual references to Horace and Ariosto, wonders whether to turn to his Petrarch or a letter to her, compares her favorably to Laura, and uses the occasional French phrase. When he sends some verses he has written for her, Hays replies that he has been trained to imitate classical poetry, but she has not.

> Were I an equal favorite with Apollo, you might expect some pretty, poetical compliment on your cleverness, but as that is not the case, you must be content with my telling you in plain prose, that I am always pleased with what you write ... a very meek, good sort of girl, am I not?[44]

Her rhetorical deference points to her sense of deficiency. On a few occasions, she reminds Eccles that she has read widely. "Your reflections on women were illiberal — even Virgil does not think them so mutable, — his Dido is a proof to the contrary; she dies a victim to her love."[45] Elsewhere, she playfully chides him: "You grow such a pedant with your languages, that I shall expect your next letter in Greek or Hebrew perhaps, and must be obliged to have recourse to an interpreter."[46] Eccles reminds her that he is acting in accord with her request as if she were his equal. "I had rather you was here, *in propria persona*," he writes, "(you cannot call this pedantry, because you set me the example of writing in Latin, consequently I have a right to suppose you understand it)."[47]

Other conflicting forces undermine their collegial exchanges: Eccles's sexual demands on her when they meet, and Hays's sense that, as the woman, she is responsible for dictating erotic limits. "The very high opinion I have ever entertained of your honor and understanding," she tells him,

> has induced me to sacrifice many of those punctilios which seem necessary to be observed between the sexes ... I had been taught to imagine that fidelity and disinterested affection amongst the men existed only in the legends of romance, that they are "by nature false, dissembling, cruel and inconstant."

—a line from Thomas Otway's *The Orphan* (1783).[48] Their physical relations agitate her:

> I am covered with confusion when I think of our adventure this morning! Why will you act so indiscreetly? You know not who may see you, and what constructions may be put on your conduct, or my character, by the malicious and the vulgar,— such are always ready to view everything in its most unfavorable light; besides the honor of a woman is of so delicate a texture, that the slightest aspersion may prove an irreparable injury to it.[49]

At least on paper, Eccles echoes Hays's concerns.

> Will not these tales affect *you* most? Will not the reflections of the world be more severe against you than me? What can I think of it? The generality of people are more bitter in their censures on the conduct of your sex than ours; perhaps ... because they think you unable to take any revenge on them.[50]

The reality is women are not equal with men in education or power or the larger world.

Gradually, Hays exploits the neutral medium of their letters to express the complexity of her reactions to him in the flesh: Eccles must not manipulate her feelings for him to demand "freedoms which I dare not allow, and that are not consistent with the delicacy I owe to my sex and character, and which I am sure you expect in the woman to whom you wish to be united. Tell me sincerely, should you not?" Marriage is the great prize according to the world and the common wisdom is that men do not marry women who give themselves sexually before wedlock. Hays speaks not of abstractions here but rather of actualities. "There have been some little improprieties in your conduct lately, that I wish to check you for, but with gentleness, I could not bear the idea of treating you with severity, lest I should offend instead of reform; but let not the mildness of my reproofs give you cause to suspect their reality."[51]

After another rendezvous, she writes, "On perusing this letter, I am almost ashamed to give it you. — I don't know how to regulate my conduct, — one moment I am afraid of disgusting you with my forwardness, and the next of

offending you by my shyness."[52] On occasion, Hays experiments with the
independence her invisibility provides: "Don't you think I have a fine spirit?
Beware! I am a little proud slut, — but remember I gave you warning!"[53] Hays
chafes at the commandment that a woman must be silent about and compliant to
imposed constraints on her sexuality. In turn, Eccles plays cat-and-mouse with her,
reiterating the need for her to negotiate between genuine emotion and prudence
because some men will take advantage of too much sincerity. "I know, I feel, your
delicacy," he writes,

> it has a thousand charms in it. Diffidence in your sex, always raises you in the eyes of a
> man of honor. But remember, love claims a distinction between indifference; there is a
> tenderness due in return, which insures your power, far beyond the arts of reserve
> generally practised by your sex. Yet ever be reserved till you perfectly know your
> man.[54]

Hays is sincere in the private sphere of text, but she never forgets that even with
Eccles there is peril in critiquing the customary balance of power. Occasionally,
Hays is frightened that she has gone too far, ever conscious of her own lack of
physical allure. "Every appearance of a slight alarms my fears; conscious of my
demerits, and that the only charm I possess is a heart faithful and sincere, unstained
with coquetry, incapable of dissimulation, I cannot help sometimes doubting my
ascendancy over you."[55] Eccles hastens to reassure her: "You have released me
from every difficulty, and I am *free* again ... I still remain your *willing* slave."[56]
Even as they banter, Hays presses the larger issue that resonates with the current
political struggles between loyalists to the Church and Crown and the Dissenters.

> What lordly creatures you men are! I am sure your wives ought to practise the doctrine
> of non-resistance, and passive obedience, if they wish to live tolerable happy. You are
> enough to make one shrink back like the sensitive-plant at the thought of matrimony;
> many of my sex annex the idea of freedom to it, because they get from under the
> jurisdiction of their parents; but matrimony and liberty are a — girlish connection — too
> well you know your power. My frankness of disposition has betrayed me into an error;
> wise by experience, I advise the ladies never to let the reins go out of their hands; men
> are not generous in these cases. Yet still you are dearer to my soul than — finish that
> sentence for your Maria.[57]

Hays uses the terms "non-resistance, and passive obedience" with reference to the
serious debate about the American rebellion against King and Parliament that still
rages in 1779.[58] At meeting house, she and Eccles have heard arguments by
Rational Dissenters about the loyalist position articulated in "On Civil Liberty,
Passive Obedience, and Nonresistance" (1775, 1797) by Jonathan Boucher (1738–
1804) and George III's attempts to enforce these.[59] Hays reminds Eccles that even
while loving, she listens and learns. She uses the lexicon of political theory to
compare matrimony with the imbalance of power of the American colonials under

British rule. Marriage, Hays advises, seems to offer women relative freedom, but only from parental control; in wedlock women trade one form of tyranny for another. Wives, Hays suggests, must feign acquiescence to their husbands' commandments, doing just enough to give the appearance of obedience, while at the same time finding ways to sabotage that authority. If not, then like the American rebels, women will live in a state of warfare. She, too, lives in a state of uncertainty because she fears that he will withdraw his love. For now, Hays bids Eccles, "Good night, — may you taste that peace which you so often deprive your Maria of."[60]

Hays is never relieved of her sense of the censorious world always watching, even if unseen. She debates with Eccles on the limits of her sexual freedom, demanding that he, too, recognize the published cultural codes that bind her:

> What shall I say to your argument for freedom of behavior? You seem to think my conduct needs a defence. I must confess I was rather shocked at an observation I met with today in looking over an old magazine; I will here transcribe it, I tore it out on purpose: "The fervor of a man's love is preserved by a proper opposition to his passion; the easy yielding female soon damps the flame which she had raised. By keeping men at a prudent distance, women stand the fairest chance of keeping them in their service." — What think you of it? It has made me rather serious. I own it is mean and ungenerous in a woman to behave capriciously to a man of sense and character, who makes honorable addresses to her, and whom she really prefers in her heart ... but there is a medium to be observed between caprice and forwardness.

In response to public proscriptions on female behavior, Hays attempts to restrict Eccles's sexual demands that "hurt me on the recollection; it seems as if, secure of forgiveness, you took advantages which — don't be angry, — I wish not to offend, but I am fearful lest you should think me tinctured with levity or immodesty." This is the great tension between them: she reciprocates his desire, but fears to express her own sensuality and encourage his because he, like the world, will afterwards accuse her of improper behavior. He has reminded her that some men are dishonorable; she reminds him that they can also be manipulative, testing a woman's virtue by seeing how far their sexual advances will take them. Hays knows herself to be virtuous,

> but we are not proper judges of our own conduct ... if we fall — Alas! they leave us to lament our folly! Yet surely such conduct would be the height of cruelty to us the weaker, the frailer sex? Are they not engaged by every law human and divine to support us when tottering or sliding into errors? not precipitate us into the precipice of guilt, and plunge us into endless remorse?[61]

Hays echoes the rhetoric of the meeting house and the mainstream ladies' magazines and novels that also reflect male Dissenters' traditional assumptions about "the weaker, the frailer sex," despite their heterodox attitudes on other issues. In the real world, as opposed to the artificial realm of texts, Eccles and Hays are not equal: sometimes, despite their mutual affection, they find themselves adversaries rather than allies. Sitting uneasily on the seesaw of propriety and yearning, Hays asks that Eccles shoulder his equal responsibility in their sexual encounters so that she is not left alone to be the gatekeeper. He must consider her feelings, not just his appetites: "Do you wish me to forfeit my own esteem at least, if not yours?" she demands,

> When you are present, I have not courage to resist you; and when you are absent, I am continually uneasy lest your affection should be weakened by my (what shall I say?) want of delicacy. — I love you — (too well you know it) more than all the world besides; can I then act so as to sink in your opinion? Oh no, not for empires.[62]

The vicious cycle of alliance and animosity wearies her. And when her own temerity threatens to overwhelm her, Hays asks for Eccles's tolerance for both her boldness and her equivocations: "Is not your Maria a little moralizing girl tonight. She knows you look with an eye of indulgence on her scribbles, which encourages her to give full licence [sic] to her pen."[63] Writing is exhilarating and dangerous. Sometimes, she says too much.

They are in complete agreement, at least, about the satisfactions of their correspondence. Eccles observes that writing to her is a positive delight. He imagines they are together as he composes his letters. The real difference is that he can make her answer as he wishes. "I can talk to you and make you answer as I please; with a thought I can instantly make you smile, and assent to everything I say," he writes. Then teasing her about her strong will, "'tis charming not to be contradicted!"[64] When Eccles bemoans their plight, Hays comforts him.

> Still shall we have this consolation of conversing on paper; and next to the satisfaction which the company of a friend gives, is that of writing to them. It is now become so habitual to me to take up my pen and scribble to you at every leisure hour, that I don't know whether I could live without it.[65]

They also agree on the primacy of being "generous" in their daily lives, using the word in its contemporaneous connotation as "magnanimous, noble-minded." Eccles remarks on Hays's sense of solidarity with other women: "You are quite unlike the ladies of the *ton* [society], — so far from being a slanderer of your own sex, you are one of their best advocates. I love you the better for it; it discovers a generous spirit."[66] This is an arena in which Hays can instruct Eccles about the errors in male conceptions of women's competition with each other. "I imagine you think me a true woman, — pleased to be flattered at another's expense," she writes in response to his criticism of one of their female acquaintances. "Indeed, I am half angry with you; could you not compliment me, without detracting from

Mrs.—?"[67] Hays observes that men expect women to compete with rather than support one another.

Generosity of spirit and behavior holds the promise of mutuality. For Hays, the basis of a happy alliance between a man and a woman is the union between "kindred mind[s]" that combines respect and love. This, she enthuses, can produce "the most perfect state of sublunary happiness."[68] Men need to be deliberate and sensitive in their behavior to their wives. Eccles provides a useful insight into the differences between men like himself and the others to whom she alludes. "With the generality of the coxcombs of the age," he writes, "I allow it: but the generous man, the man of delicacy, must feel additional warmth of passion from that knowledge."[69] The presence of "generous men" who seem to support her unconventional aspirations and behavior is an idea that buoys Hays through times of crisis during her life.

For now, Eccles proposes that they elope. "I will conduct you to the temple of Hyman *sans ceremonie* [unceremoniously]."[70] Hays recoils, advising that she is "cowardly and timid … by nature."[71] Instead, she proposes, it may be best to break with each other completely because Hays cannot impose any longer on her mother's credulity, or risk the shame of being discovered in her clandestine correspondence and meetings with Eccles. She dramatizes their situation, writing that if she has to give him up, "my life should prove the sacrifice." Hays speaks of herself as the heroine of a romance: "Why was I formed to feel everything in the extreme? ... When things go wrong, I feel myself very rebellious, and am ready to arraign providence, and tax my creator with cruelty."[72] Hays asserts that she rues her highly sensitive nature, but, in reality she prides herself on being one of the elect who feels deeply. Hays conjoins responsiveness and rebellion, signifiers of the culture of sensibility. She is aware of and intrigued by her own responses; later, she will investigate the material basis for her own consciousness in the new science of mind in the character of Emma Courtney, heroine of her first novel who resembles the Hays persona of the "Love Letters."[73]

In July 1780 with a rush, it appeared that Eccles would be given a partnership in a business. But even as the lovers are ready to rejoice, Eccles was taken ill with a fever. At the local doctor's suggestion, Eccles returned to his family's home in Fordingbridge. In relating her last parting from Eccles, Hays wrote to Mrs. Collier that, visibly unwell, he had sent for her to sit with him in his rooms. "I immediately complied with his request (though I had never before been at his lodgings)"—she feels compelled to add.[74] In the "Love Letters" Hays excerpted a letter from a relative of Eccles that describes his last hours. In the midst of successive convulsions, Eccles

often called on the name of his dear Miss Polly Hays with great eagerness, and seeming to clasp her in his arms in great ecstasy, would be satisfied for a moment … Sometimes he would attempt to sing a line or two of a hymn, at others would repeat the words —

but not with the least seeming sensibility. He expired just at twenty-five minutes after twelve at noon.[75]

Eccles's will, in the version Hays includes, was written the previous autumn and acknowledges the importance of the love letters. "Few, yet invaluable are the treasures I possess; they are contained in letters and other papers; to my dear Miss Hays I bequeath them all."[76]

"Ah my dear Madam!" wrote Eccles's sister in response to a letter from Hays requesting further details, "let us derive comfort from the assurance that he is happy; landed safe on the blissful shore, where he is singing the praises of redeeming love."[77] In return, Hays rose to the requisite rhetorical pitch. "[F]or [Eccles's] sake I will love you — if you will permit me to do so? ... his sisters shall be my sisters, and his father mine!" At home, Hays felt she had prevailed upon "the best, the most indulgent of parents" who "has permitted me to put on mourning for my beloved; 'tis a dress I never intend to quit!"[78] Mrs. Hays's assent in allowing an unmarried maiden to wear widow's weeds suggests how lenient she was with her grieving daughter. Two weeks later, Miss Eccles wrote to invite Hays to travel to Fordingbridge, in the company of the senior Mr. Eccles who would be in London. Hays accepted and wrote to prepare the family for her lack of physical appeal. "I have a thousand anxious fears lest my dear Miss Eccleses should esteem me less when known than they do at present; I sincerely assure them that I have no external charms to prepossess them in my favor."[79] Like a virgin widow, she recites to Mrs. Collier the vow Eccles made that "bound his soul in love and fidelity to his Maria! ... Do not chide me, my friend ... 'tis true he was not my husband, but could a ceremony have added anything to an attachment like mine?"[80] Hays mimics Heloise's social defiance in the name of love. She bears her tragic loss of Eccles as a banner of identity: she is a woman alone but a good man has loved her.

The Consequences

For the next year, Hays wore mourning. Even after she shed the black clothes that signify her ambiguous position, Hays continued to grieve for the life she might have led. In its stead, she lived increasingly through the written word. In time, the deprivation she had experienced became the vector for intense introspection. She rued the loss of both matrimony and passion; reconstructing the "innocent intercourse" with Eccles she realized that as a result of her own acquiescence to the conventions of female chastity, she had squandered the opportunities for personal fulfillment that he had offered her. Yet, in embryonic form, the "Love Letters" express Hays's intimation of her vocation as a writer. Even amidst the turbulence of their relationship, Hays was able to thank Eccles for the effect of his love on her understanding, telling him, "I was a stranger to the sensibility of my soul, till you called forth all its powers."[81] For much of the rest of her protracted life, thinking, learning, and writing would be inextricably tied up with men she believed, rightly or wrongly, supported her in these activities.

In the decades to come, the mature Hays will call upon her relationship with Eccles to question the confines of her gender. Without the spur of financial duress, Hays would bide her time at home until 1795, when Wollstonecraft would show her the reaches of female freedom. From the vantage point of subsequent feminist history, Hays's early and continuing expressions of the dilemma of female autonomy are more representative than Wollstonecraft's of the legions of ambitious women, on whose behalf widespread enfranchisement of education, professional training, and, by the turn into the twentieth century, suffrage, that women claim in the conversation about gender that Wollstonecraft initiates and which Hays advances. Following Wollstonecraft, Hays would assert her right to that knowledge which single women are denied, demanding physical intimacy outside marriage with at least one man as part of her understanding of "the idea of being free."[82]

The "book" Hays constructed of the correspondence with Eccles provided her with the opportunity to explore a variety of textual forms that she later deployed in her career as a published writer. In telling her private drama of passion, despair, and appeal to posterity, Hays drew upon her extensive reading to experiment with the techniques of autobiography, memoir, epistolary fiction, poetry, reportage, and the personal essay, techniques that anticipated her ground-breaking efforts in several genres to represent the growth of a woman's mind. The "Love Letters" presaged Hays's later, public representations, in which sexuality, gender, and Dissent would be newly allied.

Notes

1   The term "Rational Dissenter" was used frequently during the 1770s to refer to those Dissenters from the Church of England who exercised their belief in the responsibility of Christians to interpret the Scriptures according to their own reason. This "right to private judgment" produced heterodox interpretations of Christianity: Rational Dissenters distinguished between themselves and other "orthodox" Dissenters in their rejection of Calvinism and sympathy with belief in the divinity of Christ, but as a subordinate agent of God ("Arianism)"; or rejection of Christ's divinity while adhering to his teachings as the most perfect human being ("Socinianism"), G.M. Ditchfield, "'How Narrow will the limits of this Toleration appear?' Dissenting petitions to Parliament, 1772–1773," *Parliament and Dissent*, eds Stephen Taylor and David Wykes (Parliamentary History Trust, 2005), pp. 91–106.

2   See Gerald Newman's discussion of "sincerity" as a national trope, *The Rise of English Nationalism: A Cultural History 1740–1830* (New York, 1997), pp. 131–45.

3   Anne K. Mellor, *Romanticism & Gender* (New York, 1993), pp. 309–12.

4   See the informative background on Southwark and the family business, *CMH*, pp. 7–10.

5   N.H. Keeble, describes seventeenth century Puritan interest in self-reflective "*Heart accounts*," the record of one's spiritual struggles against external adversity, *The Literary Culture of Nonconformity in Later Seventeenth-Century England* (Athens, 1987), pp. 204–8. See also J.R. Watson, *The English Hymn: A Critical and Historical Study* (Oxford, 1997).

6   Anne F. Wedd, Hays's collateral descendant and first twentieth-century editor, reported that Mrs. Hays disapproved of Eccles because of his uncertain financial status, while the senior Mr. Eccles withheld support because Eccles refused to continue in the family business. See Wedd, "The Story of Hays," *The Love-Letters of Mary Hays 1779–1780* (London, 1925), pp. 1–14.

7   For a reading of Hays's earliest extant correspondence, see Gina Luria Walker, "Hays's 'Love Letters,'" *Keats-Shelley Journal*, LI (2002): 94–115.

8   *L&E*, "No. VII.," pp. 95–6. Hays advised that she read *Clarissa* "repeatedly in very early life, and ever found my mind more pure, more chastened, more elevated after the perusal of it. The extreme youth and beauty, fine talents, and exalted piety of the heroine, render her character, I allow, something like the fine ideal beauty of the ancients ... The characters are well preserved, and the epistolary style of the several writers marked with peculiar distinction. It is generally (and perhaps not without reason) thought too prolix, but I own, I ever felt myself more interested from this minuteness, and perceived, in the nicer shades and touches, the hand of a master."

9   Letter VII, 31 July 1779, "Love Letters."

10   Wedd subsequently abridged and published the manuscript "Love Letters" in 1925 as *The Love-Letters of Mary Hays 1779–1780*. Wedd had the complete two-volume set at her disposal, as well as autobiographical materials that no longer exist. Volume One of the manuscript "Love Letters" is now included with other Hays documents in The Carl H. and Lily Pforzheimer Collection of Shelley and His Circle, New York Public Library. Volume Two has not been located. Wedd assumed that Hays's older friend Mrs. Collier transcribed the "Love Letters," although she gives no supporting evidence. Brooks conjectured that the extant letters are in Hays's handwriting. The letters were carefully copied over; I agree with Brooks that the handwriting is Hays's. *CMH*, p. 31.

11   Theophilus Lindsey, "*A SERMON* preached at the Opening of the Chapel in Essex House, Essex-Street ... April 17, 1774," *Conversations on Christian Idolatry* (London, 1791), unpaginated.

12   Letter I, 12 February 1779, "Love Letters."

13   Letter LXXX, 27 October 1779, "Love Letters."

14   Wedd, "The Story of Hays," p. 2.

15   Letter LXXXI, 28 October 1779, "Love Letters."

16   Wedd's edition of the love letters does not include the introduction. See *CMH*, pp. 31–4.

17   Mary Hays, "Introduction," "Love Letters," unpaginated.

18   Ibid.

19   Ibid.

20   Ibid.

21   James Thomson, "Spring," *The Seasons* (Yorkshire, 1970), 52, ll. 1040–1042.

22   See Thomson, "Commentary," in James Sambrook (ed.), *The Seasons* (Oxford, 1981),
      l. 1123, pg. 339.
23   Letter IV, 29 July 1779, "Love Letters."
24   Ibid.
25   Letter VII, 31 July 1779, "Love Letters."
26   Ibid.
27   Hays's fantasy of herself as a Roman Catholic may reflect what G.M. Ditchfield
      describes as "a marked decline" in anti-Catholicism in the 1770s after Theophilus
      Lindsey, "in theoretical defiance of the law ... founded the first avowedly Unitarian
      chapel at Essex Street, London" in 1773. Unitarian worship was not legally tolerated
      until 1813 in Britain. "'Incompatible With The Very Name of Christian': English
      Catholics and Unitarians In The Age Of Milner," *Recusant History*, 25/1 (May 2000):
      52–73.
28   Ibid.
29   Letter VII, 31 July 1779, "Love Letters."
30   Letter VIII, 1 August 1779, "Love Letters."
31   Ibid.
32   Letter X, 1 August 1779, "Love Letters."
33   Ibid.
34   Letter XCVIII, 18 November 1779, "Love Letters."
35   Eccles writes, "By second nature I suppose so too; their educations are so different,
      and their occupations and habits so opposite to ours, that it is impossible but that the
      ideas of a woman must be of a more delicate texture than those of a man;
      consequently the attachments of a woman of fine sentiments and polished education,
      are softer and more deeply rooted, and likewise secured by a more lasting cement than
      those of a man." Letter XII, 4 August 1779, "Love Letters."
36   This interchange is similar to the conversation that Jane Austen constructs between
      Anne Eliot and Captain Harville in *Persuasion* (1818), on the question of gendered
      differences in romantic fidelity (New York, 1984), pp. 110–207.
37   Letter XXIII, 19 August 1779, "Love Letters."
38   Letter XXIV, 21 August 1779, "Love Letters."
39   Precedent existed for Hays's request. Marjorie Reeves has described how in a
      provincial group of families in the southwest of England through the eighteenth
      century, "the real education of intellectual young women was fostered by the men in
      their social environment." "Eighteenth-century young women: How were they
      educated?" *Pursuing the Muses: Female Education and Nonconformist Culture,
      1700–1900* (London, 1997), pp. 18–29.
40   Letter X, 1 August 1779, "Love Letters."
41   François Poullain de la Barre, "On the Equality of the Two Sexes: A Physical and
      Moral Discourse Which Shows the Importance of Getting Rid of One's Prejudices," in
      Marcelle Maistre Welch (ed.), *Three Cartesian Feminist Treatises*, trans. Vivien
      Bosley (Chicago, 2002), pp. 49–121.
42   Letter XXXVIII, 8 September 1779, "Love Letters."
43   See Siep Stuurman's illuminating discussion in "The Deconstruction of Gender:
      Seventeenth-Century Feminism and Modern Equality," in Sarah Knott and Barbara
      Taylor (eds), *Women, Gender and Enlightenment* (Houndsmill, 2005), pp. 371–88.
44   Letter XXXIV, 2 September 1779, "Love Letters."

45   Letter XXX, 31 August 1779, "Love Letters."
46   Letter LXI, 5 October 1779, "Love Letters."
47   Letter LI, 24 September 1779, "Love Letters."
48   Letter XXIV, 21 August 1779, "Love Letters."
49   Letter XL, 10 September 1779, "Love Letters."
50   Letter XXV, 21 August 1779, "Love Letters."
51   Letter XL, 10 September 1779, "Love Letters."
52   Letter XXXVI, 6 September 1779, "Love Letters."
53   Letter XX, 17 August 1779, "Love Letters."
54   Letter XL, 12 September 1779, "Love Letters."
55   Letter LVIII, 31 September 1779, "Love Letters."
56   Letter LXIX, 2 October 1779, "Love Letters."
57   Letter LXVI, 11 October 1779, "Love Letters."
58   See James E. Bradley, *Religion, Revolution and English Radicalism: Non-conformity in Eighteenth-century Politics and Society* (Cambridge, 1990).
59   Hays writes to Eccles on 9 November 1779, "You mistook the question that was to be debated at Coachmaker's Hall; it was this, 'whether considering the badness of the present time *in a political view*'" a single or a married state was most conducive to happiness? Hays interrupts her letter to observe a press-gang passing by her window and writes Eccles, "these are the shocking calamities that are ever attendant on war and this incident may furnish the *debaters* with an argument." See *CMH*, ftnte 331, p. 185 and ftnte 337, p. 187.
60   Ibid.
61   Letter LV, 27 September 1779, "Love Letters."
62   Letter LXXXII, 30 October 1779, "Love Letters."
63   Letter V, 27 September 1779, "Love Letters."
64   Ibid.
65   Letter XLVI, 18 September 1779, "Love Letters."
66   Letter XXVIII, 29 August 1779, "Love Letters."
67   Letter XLIII, 14 September 1779, "Love Letters."
68   Hays borrows and revises this idea from *Emily Montague* (1769) by Frances Brooke (1724–89), also author of *The History of Julia Mandeville* (1763). Marilyn Brooks points out that Hays incorporated text from Brooke approximately 30 times in the love letters, *CMH*, pp. 20–1 and subsequent references. Hays refers to Frances Brooke by name in her letters (Brooke may have been a friend of Mrs. Collier) but did not identify the author or her novel as sources of particular phrases or passages. Hays does this with other works, only occasionally identifying the author. Plagiarism was a matter of continuing debate in Hays's time, and there seem to have been more elastic definitions in use. See Richard Terry, "'In Pleasing Memory of All He Stole': Plagiarism and Literary Detraction, 1747–1785," in Paulina Kewes (ed.), *Plagiarism in Early Modern England* (Houndmills, 2003), pp. 181–200. In addition, Hays may have fantasized authorship, but likely did not anticipate that her handwritten text would have such a long shelf life.
69   Letter LX, 4 October 1779, "Love Letters."
70   Letter LXXXV, 3 November 1779, "Love Letters."
71   Letter LXXXVI, 4 November 1779, "Love Letters."
72   Letter CXX, 11 July 1780, "Love Letters."

73   G.J. Barker-Benfield writes, "'Sensibility' signified revolution, promised freedom, threatened subversion, and became convention. The word denoted the receptivity of the senses and referred to the psychoperceptual scheme explained and systematized by Newton and Locke. It connoted the operation of the nervous system, the material basis for consciousness." "Introduction," *The Culture of Sensibility: Sex and Society in Eighteenth-Century Britain* (Chicago, 1992), p. xvii.

74   Letter CXXVIII, 13 September 1780, "Love Letters."

75   Ibid.

76   Letter CXXV, 24 November 1779, "Love Letters."

77   Letter CXXVII, 6 September 1780, "Love Letters."

78   Letter CXXVIII, 13 September 1780, "Love Letters."

79   Letter CXXX, 7 October 1780, "Love Letters."

80   Letter CXXII, 9 & 10 November 1780, "Love Letters."

81   Letter LXXXVIII, 5 November 1779, "Love Letters."

82   Hays to William Godwin, 13 October 1795, *Pforz.*, MH 8.

Chapter Two

An Age of Controversy

"This is an age of controversy, and all who love truth must rejoice in seeing the spirit of freedom and enquiry universally disseminated."

Mary Hays, *Cursory Remarks*, 1791

It took Mary Hays nearly a decade to recover from the shock of John Eccles's sudden death, or so she represented. In the early 1790s, Hays entered the public fray, embraced Unitarianism,[1] may have written sermons for Dr. John Disney at the Unitarian Essex Street Chapel,[2] read widely, and began the study of mathematics and French. The autobiographical materials Wedd consulted have vanished, but the texts that do survive attest to Hays's ongoing quest for knowledge and concomitant ambivalence about her own ambitions. Such equivocation compromised Hays's success in gaining recognition; discerning readers quickly sensed the element of self-doubt and dependence that she expressed in both public and private. What follows is an account, based on extant sources, of the next, crucial phase in Hays's intellectual growth, from John Eccles's death in 1780 to her first public appearance in print in 1791. During this time, she prepared to participate in the republic of letters through self-study that was advanced by her extraordinary tutelage with Robert Robinson. Robinson's eccentric religious convictions, political activism, autodidactism, and textual production help situate Hays's idiosyncratic intellectual genealogy. Chapter Two includes a summary of Robinson's work to provide the context for Hays's long career as thinker and writer, and to demonstrate the ways in which she built upon his beliefs.

Though she remained in her mother's home until 1795, when she was in her mid-thirties, Hays was mentally adventurous. Sheltered in the half-life of her ambiguous state as maiden widow, she began the relentless effort necessary to transform herself into a learned lady—like Héloïse—a role that, unknown to her, had a long and honorable history.[3] Over time, her idiosyncratic education metamorphosed her pledge to John Eccles of "Triumphant Constancy," modeled on Prior's "Emma," heroine of *Henry and Emma, or the Nutbrown Maid* (1708), into an experiment with what she subsequently described to Godwin as "the idea of *being free.*" The humiliations and achievements of her first forays into public life shaped her radical understanding of what both Hays and Wollstonecraft later imagined as "the magic circle" of gender. In the process, Hays quietly discovered that chastity, enforced or voluntary, might serve as a vehicle for autonomy.

After Robinson's death in 1790, Hays initiated contact with some of the tutors at New College Hackney, the newest and most politically radical Dissenting academy, where she sought access to late Enlightenment learning. Stimulated and supported by the *philosophes* she encountered there, Hays was emboldened to publish a pamphlet, *Cursory Remarks*, in which she took on the formidable and irrepressible scholar Gilbert Wakefield on the issue of communal worship. The textual skirmishes that followed between Wakefield and Hays, soon joined by Joseph Priestley, Anna Barbauld, and other Dissenting leaders, brought Hays approbation and, unexpectedly, attentions that she wrongly judged romantic from the Cambridge reformer, William Frend. The stage was then set for the next act of her life, engagement with leading radicals in the post-1789 ferment in Britain and publication of her experimental texts, *Letters and Essays, Moral, and Miscellaneous* (1793), followed by her best known work, *Memoirs of Emma Courtney* (1796). The novel established Hays's equivocal reputation and underscored the tensions that weakened her authority and her reputation, already evident as early as *Cursory Remarks*, between her compelling ambition to be recognized as a woman intellectual and her fear of exposure in the glare of public attention.

Intellectual Beginnings: Eccles and After

Theological inquiry among the Dissenters provided the catalyst for Hays's search for erudition. The Baptist meeting house the Hays family attended was the venue in which Hays made important intellectual, social, as well as spiritual, connections. Hays attended meeting house services once, sometimes twice, each week, where listening to sermons and religious political debate familiarized her with learned forms of thought. Within the safe epistolary medium with John Eccles, she judged that one minister was not qualified to teach; apparently she had a basis for comparison with other men she regularly observed.[4] She lived among people considered as subversives[5] who conducted their own schools, printed their own texts, and formed their own republic of letters. But much as young Mary Hays was avid to learn what Eccles knew, she lived the incongruities between the search for knowledge male Rational Dissenters[6] advocated and their obliviousness to female aspirations. She absorbed the exhortation to think for herself, but even with Eccles's encouragement, there was no formal, sanctioned route to higher training in doing so for women.[7]

In the aftermath of Eccles's sudden death, Mary Hays wrestled with the anomalous state in which she now found herself. Although there was no public language to express this, she had experienced sexual intimacy—at least, to some degree, according to her protestations in the love letters—with Eccles, without social and religious sanctions. Now family and friends expected her to spend the rest of her life grieving at the loss of domestic status and interest that marriage would have provided. Her rarified sensibilities would seem to conspire with the expectations of family and community to immure her in the past.

Hays paid lip service to what society expected of her, even as she discovered her own persistent, restless curiosity that first surfaced in her correspondence with Eccles. Like many of her female contemporaries, she pursued a vicarious life through reading, mainly novels, but this was insufficient to satisfy her. Almost immediately, the tenacity of Hays's ambitions to learn and be heard compelled her to seek out other men from within the Rational Dissenting community. In her quest for education, the only viable alternative was tutelage by men in the form of informal apprenticeships that concealed her aggressive ambitions. Confronted with Hays's determined attentions, erudite men extended themselves to mentor her. They were in no peril of being slandered by sexual interests as Hays admitted she was a plain woman. Moreover, they were high-minded and disciplined; Hays described those men who provided her informal support during this period, including Robert Robinson, Joseph Priestley, Hugh Worthington, John Disney, and Theophilus Lindsey, as "Gentlemen not only of the *first literature*, but of the most *distinguished virtue*."[8] Their correspondence reveals that she exercised the freedom to move from one to another to satisfy her intellectual hunger. These men served as mentors, editors, guides, defenders, and agents; often they provided her with the tools of the trade: texts that, without university and professional venues, were otherwise inaccessible to her.

At the same time as Hays began to pursue serious study, she contributed to the feminine culture of Sensibility. Several of her early "exercises of fancy" met with success. She tried her hand at poetry, and wrote "The HERMIT. An Oriental Tale," modeled on Samuel Johnson's *The History of Rasselas, Prince of Abyssinia* (1759), which was published in the *Universal Magazine of Knowledge and Pleasure* in April–May 1786, reprinted in the *Hibernian* later the same year and again in the *Edinburgh Review* in 1793. The tale is an allegory of the consequences of excessive passion. The effect of extreme sensibilities was a subject Hays visited often throughout her career and was to become the focus of her most controversial work. "Polished society" applauded her conventional accomplishments, but Hays soon aspired to make contact with the Enlightenment debates she heard each week at meeting house. These were not merely polemical: they were about the ideas and practice of citizenship, rights, education, livelihood, and tolerance, all of which mattered to her. *Letters and Essays, Moral, and Miscellaneous*, her first published book, engages with a wide range of authors and texts, including Shakespeare, Milton, Pope, Dryden, Rousseau, Goethe, Voltaire, Lavater, and the English novelists and essayists. Her reading encompassed philosophical, historical, and political works, including those of such Nonconformist luminaries as David Hartley, Priestley, Richard Price, and Anthony Collins. Like many women before and after her, Hays was an autodidact, structuring an idiosyncratic curriculum, learning as she could. A kindly widow, perhaps Mary's older friend, Mrs. Collier, responded to Hays's predicament as a melancholy but aspiring single woman and introduced her to local intellectuals.[9] But, Hays also found help for herself.

First Mentor: The Awakener of My Mind

The principal influence on Hays's development during the 1780s was the Reverend Robert Robinson (1735–90), to his admirers distinguished by "his earnest love of truth, and laborious search after it," as well his espousal of "unlimited toleration."[10] Even in comparison with the other larger-than-life reformers Hays knew between 1780 and 1790, Robinson exuded an iconoclastic courage that set him apart.[11] He was politically active on behalf of the same reforms as the Unitarian path breakers who were his contemporaries: repeal of the Test and Corporation Acts that kept male Dissenters less than full citizens, support of the American War for Independence, expanded parliamentary representation, universal male suffrage, abolition of the Slave Trade. Yet, for the most part Robinson acted alone with a few adherents, neither of nor with the Rational Dissenting community.[12] We get a vivid sense of Robinson's anomalous status in the turbulent religious politics of the time at the moment in March 1790 when Edmund Burke attacked him as a palpable threat to the status quo in a speech to Parliament. Responding to Burke, a Unitarian spokesman argued that Robinson was too eccentric to be taken seriously by the Dissenting interest. In this instance, Burke was shrewder than his opponent: he recognized in Robinson's published works the subversive force of ideas whose time had nearly come.

Burke's attack on Robinson suggests that he had read at least some of Robinson's 40-odd published works; he knew Robinson's provocative *A Political Catechism* (1782), which Burke denounced as positive proof of the Dissenters' intent to undermine Church and King.[13] In his speech, Burke responded to a causal view of the past propounded by Robinson that linked current events in revolutionary France with earlier civil strife between Protestants and Catholics. Burke discerned the subtext of Robinson's historiography: in his translations of Huguenot polemics, Robinson identified the principle of toleration as the crux of the French religious wars of the fifteenth and sixteenth centuries, fleshing out his argument with chronologies, biographies, moral judgments, and predictions for the future that ran counter to Burke's most deeply held beliefs.[14]

This was the backdrop against which Hays pursued her own unconventional ambitions to become learned. Hays first heard Robinson preach in London in 1781 after he was invited by a committee of metropolitan Baptists to collect material for a history of their sect, using the resources of the British Museum where one of the Baptists was a librarian. Robinson agreed to come to London for ten days a month from Cambridge where he led a flourishing congregation, to collect materials for his history and to preach at various locations. In selecting Robinson as her first mentor, a maverick even among the Rational Dissenters, Hays responded to both his public character and to the private man who educated his daughters as he did his sons.

In their communications, Robinson responded seriously to Hays's theological and philosophical inquiries, fostering her independence while extending her contact with Enlightenment ideas. In Robinson's published and private representations, Hays found hospitable variations of religious and political tolerance that permeated his texts that she read as his life. His translations of the works of the Huguenot theologians Jean Claude and Jacques Saurin were part of this endeavor. Two thinkers of *Le Refuge*, the second Huguenot exodus following the Revocation of the Edict of Nantes (1685),[15] Claude and Saurin participated with other exiles in the proliferation of early modern liberal ideas such as toleration, the right to private judgment, separation of church and state, and engaged citizenship. Robinson's translations of the Huguenots' works, in combination with his own texts, exposed Hays to unique expressions of general toleration.

Robinson proved to be a crucial first mentor for Hays in several respects. He was a political activist whose remarkably democratic opinions informed his every action. He was a dissenter among Rational Dissenters, and caused other Nonconformists discomfort because his protean views adhered to no established sect or theology. He possessed enormous personal charm and generosity, although his sometimes brutal candor startled many. As importantly to Hays, he was an autodidact who built upon a few years of early schooling in Latin and French to produce a substantial number of published works that engaged fearlessly with the most controversial issues and advanced learning of his time. Robinson demonstrated to Hays that experience galvanized learning, that ideas had meaning, not in the abstract, but as they could be lived. Long before meeting Wollstonecraft, Hays gingerly applied Robinson's teachings to the condition of women.

Eight manuscript letters and one fragment from Robinson to Hays survive that attest to Robinson's matter-of-fact acceptance of Hays's intellectual ambitions, Hays's uneasiness with his genuine egalitarianism, and Robinson's conviction that dissent was the right of every human being.[16] The first letter, 13 November 1782 from Walworth, indicated that the two have previously met, and that although Robinson was busy, he would visit at her mother's home at Gainsford Street the next day. The following January Robinson wrote from his home in Chesterton. In the interim, Hays had provided him a "narration" of herself that Robinson described as "a miniature portrait of a lady in danger and distress, the work of an exquisite artist calculated to touch the heart. Happy for you and your friends it is an *historical* portrait of what *was*." This "*Heart account*,"[17] modeled on the spiritual autobiography of the nonconformist Richard Baxter (1651–91), expressed Hays's rage at God and her religious doubt. Her despair was not entirely the result of her disappointment in love, for even in her letters to Eccles, Hays revealed a propensity for rebellion and skepticism. Robinson replied directly to her spiritual distress by assuring her that grief made her susceptible to doubt, but that true belief would accompany her return to health.

With characteristic bluntness, Robinson chafed at the extravagance of Hays's flattery, demurring at her unrealistic expectations of him and encouraging her to meet him as an equal.

> I am obliged to be silent on all that part of your letter, which [concerns?] myself, only I must take the liberty to say that you have adapted that mode of instruction, which the priests [for the] princes of Egypt formerly did, that is they ascribed to them such virtues, not as the princes had but as they ought to have. Some of them took the hint and refined their manners. I wish I could do so, and be the man you describe. If ever piety was rendered amiable by an insinuating manner of describing it, it must be so by the use of your elegant pen.[18]

Robinson offered Hays a dose of genuine equality for which she was unprepared. She wanted him to be her teacher, as he was to the young men she knew he mentored. She was intent on establishing the conventional dynamic between master and student; what he heard and rejected was her supplication to him as a superior. "No, you are not my pupil, but my friend," he insisted,

> and if there be objections, which I can say anything towards removing, I shall always be extremely happy to contribute all in my power to so good a work, yet give me leave to say if Miss Hayes expects to meet with a correspondent equal to herself for fine sense, and delicacy of stile, she will be disappointed in her poor, dull, impoverished Robt Robinson.

Hays likely resorted to obsequiousness to camouflage her intellectual aggression. Her exaggerated compliments may have been intended to give the appearance of womanly deference to deflect attention from her unladylike situation in which celibacy was the price of freedom. She continued to mask the intensity of her quest to learn from Robinson and subsequent men from whom she wanted training with that textual coquetry that later irritated both Wollstonecraft and Godwin. She may also have tried to conceal her ambitiousness from herself. She began at cross-purposes with Robinson. He was a wise, as well as learned man, a public figure of both originality and independence, kind as well as generous, and accessible; she persisted, as he did. They were connected by their common membership in the insular, self-protective Rational Dissenting community. He had met her mother and extended family; she knew his wife. Early on, Robinson warned her of the danger of idealizing men. Through her long life, this is one lesson she increasingly disregarded: she never failed to be shocked to discover that men she had trusted were fallible. By June 1783, when he wrote again, Hays had been sick, and in her weakened physical state, she expressed anxiety over her behavior towards him during their latest meeting in London. She revealed the insecurities she had expressed to Eccles about being too demanding, a burden, in the way. Robinson hastened to assure that she had never distressed him, adding that he believed her incapable of bothering anyone. Hays knew herself better; but, at a distance, she could hide the extreme symptoms of her interpersonal awkwardness. In answer to her question about when he would be in London, Robinson proclaimed an exuberant faith as he prepared for his "dissolution": "Now," he wrote Hays, "I snatch an hour, or steal a moment, and hover between religion and the world like a needle between two loadstones, then I shall be, I humbly hope, for ever with the Lord."[19] In the hymns he composed, the sermons he preached, the causes he championed, and the younger minds he nurtured, Robinson expressed his sense of the divine in this world, and the next world, as a palpable inevitability.

Robinson's reassurances point to Hays's sense of already being an unappealing encumbrance that Godwin, Wollstonecraft, and others of their circle were to contend with in the 1790s. When he wrote again in March 1785, he could not resist admonishing her:

First, give me leave to tell you, yea to threaten you that, if you do not leave off complimenting me, as soon as I can write, I will spoil a quire of paper, and stretch every power I have to try to out compliment you. Would not that be an edifying correspondence?

Robinson rejected her flattery, but not her friendship. He expected to see her soon again in London.

He next turned to questions that arose out of the course of study she was pursuing on her own. He responded to her reading of his translation of Jean Claude's *Essay on the Composition of a Sermon*, pointing her to a footnote that articulated his belief in both the divine plan and free will, although for Robinson only God could reconcile the apparent contradiction.[20] The theological position Robinson articulated here was decisive to Hays's feminism. She took his assurance about "man's free agency" to signify human potential that was valid for *woman's* agency, too. In correspondence with her later male mentors, she continued to worry over the apparent collision between free will and divine intention.

Robinson referred to his translations of the sermons of Jean Claude (1619–87), a minister of the *Refuge* who subsequently led the exiled Huguenot community in the Hague.[21] Robinson's interest derived from Claude's assertions of the rights of individual conscience and the autonomy of congregational communities. Claude's *Essay on the Composition of a Sermon*, which Robinson explicated for Hays, was intended to strengthen the heuristic differences between "preachers of the Church of Rome" and Calvinists.

Robinson also addressed Hays's frustrated efforts to obtain copies of his translations of the sermons of Jacques Saurin (1677–1730), the distinguished Walloon pastor who scandalized public opinion from 1728–31 for publishing a dissident scriptural analysis on the subject of "beneficial lies." Saurin posed the question, Does God lie for the good of humankind? Saurin's heterodoxy led to ecclesiastical and state charges against him, making it a test of the limits of early modern toleration and freedom of press in the Netherlands.[22]

However menacing Robinson was judged by conservatives, however marginal by Rational Dissenters and Unitarians, he was central to Hays's continuing cognitive development. She acknowledged this after a lifetime of experience and observation in a letter written shortly before her own death in 1843, in which she described Robinson as the "awakener of my mind."[23] Trained by Robinson in the virtues of heterodoxy, Hays cut her Nonconformist teeth on books he gave her, including a full set of his translations of Saurin and Claude, Robinson's own sermons, and other books. In this way, Hays came in contact with ideas of what Jonathan Israel characterizes as the "Radical Enlightenment" that refused to compromise with the past.[24] Hays would have read with special attention Robinson's translation of Saurin's "Repentance of the Unchaste Woman" and his fiery *Slavery Inconsistent with Christianity* (1788) that promoted the equal humanity and claim on God's justice of the fallen woman and the African slave respectively.

Robinson's interest in Saurin's work was enduring. His first translation was followed by four other volumes of translations of Saurin's sermons published between 1771 and 1777. Robinson represented Saurin as a pathfinder for British Nonconformists. In Volume II of his translations of Saurin, Robinson provided a short biographical sketch, based in part on interviews with older Dissenters who knew Saurin during his sojourn in England. This journalistic technique imbued the history of intolerance in France with a rhetorical immediacy that connected the present tribulations of Rational Dissenters and Unitarians with the terrors of civil strife in sixteenth-century France. History was thus a living, changing expression of human recognition of the working out of the divine plan on earth. Hays learned at Robinson's hand history as moral example, life-writing as "perfect history,"[25] and the existence of an international community of believers that participated in the virtual dissident republic of letters.

But where, in these grand designs, was there some thought of women? Gender, of course, was implicated in theology, and revising traditional understandings was part of the lesson Robinson, by way of Saurin, taught Hays, deliberately or not. Little literature exists either by women or about their place in Huguenot thought, although precedent existed for consideration of women's condition.[26] Hays's familiarity with Saurin's work provides some explanation for her early and continuing rebellion against the historical commandment that chastity is the preeminent virtue for women.

"The Repentance of the Unchaste Woman" is based on a text from *Luke* vii. 36–50. Jesus is invited to the house of one of the Pharisees to eat. An unidentified woman known to be a sinner recognizes Jesus, and wets him with her tears. Simon the Pharisee thinks to himself that if Jesus were a true prophet he would see that the unchaste woman is not fit to touch him. Jesus answers, as if he could read Simon's mind, with a question, in the form of a parable: who loves him the most, the man Jesus forgave for owing him five hundred pence or the man who owes him 50? When Simon answers that it is the one to whom he forgave the most, Jesus points out that the woman's attentions to him have revealed that her love for him is greater than Simon's. Jesus then turns to the woman and forgives her, telling her that her faith has saved her; he has forgiven her many sins, and bids her go in peace.

Hays likely interpreted the sermon idiosyncratically, following Robinson's example. She would notice Saurin's empathy with the woman's experience of her situation and his refusal to condemn her.[27] Saurin describes the tears she shed that express her perpetual sorrow and, at last, her courage in repenting. He considers what she felt on being absolved by Jesus. Though he describes the woman in conventional terms, Saurin refuses to pass sentence on her without further inquiry. If she is an adulteress, he asks, how does she judge herself? This was a central question for Hays, allowing her to connect the moral struggle against intolerance with the constraints imposed on women because of men's ignorance of female experience. In the next decade, Hays would join Wollstonecraft in creating alternative explanations to conventional assumptions about the sociology and psychology of female behavior.

When Simon the Pharisee would dispense rough justice, Saurin warns him not to judge hastily, without considering the woman's humanity, and her specific circumstances. Saurin proposes an elaborate, pragmatic process in which all facts and conditions are considered in determining wrongdoing, even in the case of an unchaste woman. In the 1790s, realistic portrayals of the oppressive conditions of women's lives appeared in Hays's *Emma Courtney* and *The Victim of Prejudice* (1799), Wollstonecraft's unfinished *Wrongs of Woman* (1798), and Eliza Fenwick's *Secresy* (1795). Such depictions might inform men about the multiple forces that provoked women to acts of social defiance. Saurin asserts in the sermon, "*An idea of the mercy of God is not particular to some places,* to any age, nation, religion, or sect." Hays may have wondered whether women were included in God's merciful embrace. Does God's mercy extend to those who have been sexually wronged? Does God's understanding incorporate intolerance based on gender? How deep into the private sphere of women does divine tolerance reach? Emboldened by Wollstonecraft's example, Hays subsequently posed these questions and posited some public answers in various genres—essays, novels, and, especially, life-writing. She ultimately advocated that Robinson's ideal of "universal toleration" be extended to real women in her memoirs of contemporaries, including Wollstonecraft, Catharine Macaulay, Charlotte Smith, and Manon Roland, as well as earlier victims of prejudice like Marguerite de Navarre and Anne Askew.

The sermon concludes with a statement about the invisibility of the unchaste woman's repentance. "Her joy was not a circumstance that came under the notice of the historian," Saurin writes. "In the heart of this frail woman converted and reconciled to God lay this mystery concealed." Here, perhaps for the first time,

Hays discerned the potential in Rational Dissenting theology to apply heterodox scriptural exegesis to the female condition. The unnamed woman's crisis might not interest male historians, but Hays and Wollstonecraft soon exerted themselves to reveal the mystery of her common humanity.

In the last years of his life, Robinson advanced Hays's nascent iconoclasm as he continued to explore new versions of unlimited toleration. Racism was so entrenched in British culture that it required courage to identify and address it.[28] Robinson accepted the challenge. In a letter to Hays describing the death of a beloved daughter, Robinson enclosed a copy of his sermon, *Slavery Inconsistent with the Spirit of Christianity*, a contribution to the coalescing movement to end the Slave Trade.[29] The sermon was based on a passage from Luke x. 18, "*The Lord hath sent me - to preach Deliverance to the Captives.*" Robinson thinks through the slaves' harrowing experiences in the sermon, marshaling biblical, classical, and historical examples; contemporary accounts; psychological and economic analysis; and his interpretation of God's active grace, to demonstrate that slavery in any form is indefensible by Christian believers.

In this sermon, Robinson elucidates how Jesus planned to subvert slavery.[30] He describes the agency of each individual's feeling in the reformation Jesus called for, drawing upon a long tradition within Nonconformity. For Robinson, Christianity teaches that belief is strong enough to attack injustice and cruelty manifested as corrupt passions; the lust to own another human being is such a feeling. The individual's responsibility is to feel Christ's influence in order to resist the seductions of enslaving others. Robinson connects personal responsibility and public action: the Slave Trade is collective, a "national sin" which the legislature endorses. Moral education must connect reason and passion, private individuals and the citizenry. Children should be taught "the natural connexion between civil and religious liberty, and the indispensable obligation fostering both. Let us shew them where encroachments on natural rights begin, and whither they tend." "Christianity," he proclaims, "is ... *a perfect law of liberty,* and its natural and genuine produce is universal justice, or, which is the same thing, universal freedom."

For Robinson, Jesus adumbrated how all Christians had spiritual affinity with African slaves, but Hays recognized that woman's affinity was even more subversive than that. Others of her female contemporaries drew comparisons between the female condition and that of African slaves; Hays's exposure to this sermon of Robinson's locates the genesis of her understanding of the nexus between gender and the existential condition of enslavement that is threaded through her works. Hays was thus inculcated in the most radical of Robinson's beliefs: feelings *and* ideas have political consequences, and thought and sensation are equally important in human consciousness. Our actions are most effective when they reflect the combined energies of all our faculties.

Robinson's unorthodox teaching continued to the end of his life. In March 1789, he wrote appreciatively of Hays's attentions to his two daughters, recently relocated to London. He took the opportunity to express his dismay at his daughters' reports of the metropolitan preachers' commandment, "Do not *criticise*." Robinson pointed to the dire effects of such ministerial self-importance: "Thus they murder free inquiry." His children, he told Hays, were encouraged to question, "that is, [to] Take nothing for granted."[31] Robinson feared that his younger daughter, whom he raised as "a child of liberty," might become gullible and submissive in her new environment. "Such tame believers are not at all to my taste," he wrote Hays, "I love the inquisitive, the reasoner, who never takes mysayso, and who wants to know the why, and the wherefore." His words were potent: Hays had become his spiritual daughter, assuming nothing, doubting everything, yet like Robinson, believing in the ongoing transformation of this world in anticipation of the next.

Robinson died in June 1790 while on a preaching visit to Joseph Priestley's meeting houses in Birmingham and was buried there. In his eulogy, Priestley praised Robinson for his determination to educate his daughters as he did his sons, teaching them learned and modern languages himself, engaging tutors to instruct them in mathematics and philosophy. Priestley elucidated Robinson's understanding of Lockean materialism that at birth all human beings have an equal capacity to learn. "Certainly," Priestley insisted, "the minds of women are capable of the same improvement, and the same furniture as that of men, and it is of importance that, when they have leisure, they should have the same resources in reading, and the same power of instructing the world by writing, that men have."[32]

Priestley's eulogy was published some months later, and caused a stir within Rational Dissenting circles for declaring Robinson a convert to Unitarianism[33] who led his congregation to this position in the last months of his life. Robinson's Cambridge parishioners, supported by his survivors, protested so loudly that Priestley had to withdraw the assertion. Thus Robinson remained mired in controversy even after his death. His earlier biographers—George Dyer, Benjamin Flower, and William Robinson (no relation)—attempted posthumously to pigeonhole Robinson as an adherent to one sect or another. They all failed in their efforts, in the end confirming his refusal to avow any but his own beliefs.

Entering the Fray: The Wakefield Controversy

Hays now directed her grief at the loss of Robinson towards new sites of knowledge, as she did after John Eccles's death. She actively extended her contacts in the wider world of Rational Dissent, inserting herself into the doctrinal and political debates that continued to roil the republic of letters in reaction to events taking place in revolutionary France. In 1786, a group of prominent Dissenters gathered in London to plan and construct a new Dissenting academy. Among the supporters and financial advisors of the aptly named "New College" were Theophilus Lindsey, Rochemont Barbauld, Joseph Johnson, Josiah Wedgwood,

John Disney, and John Aikin, brother of Anna Barbauld. Among those who served as tutors during the first years of New College were Richard Price, William Enfield, Thomas Belsham, Hugh Worthington, Andrew Kippis, and Gilbert Wakefield.[34] This enlightened circle benefited from continuity with the academic cultures at Warrington and Daventry[35] to which the tutors and their friends were connected.[36] Hays's association with the New College tutors emerged organically from her tutelage with Robinson. Female learning, Priestley and his colleagues asserted, even if informal and pursued only after a woman had fulfilled her domestic duties, was, like the training of men, intended to be returned as public good.

As she made her way among a new, more politically visible group of Rational Dissenters, Hays was stirred to participate in Dissenting politics for the first time. The occasion was a public blast against Rational Dissenting religious practices, such as required evening services, from former New College Tutor Gilbert Wakefield. The Rational Dissenting and Unitarian leadership saw Wakefield's position as a dangerous breach of loyalty. They had enough to contend with without having a flank exposed. Hays was secure in her knowledge of the inspirational possibilities of religious worship as Robinson exercised them, especially the cumulative force of transcendence when true Christians gathered together, that gave lie to Wakefield's grumbling. Hays reflected on her years of informal training: listening to meeting house debates between learned men, reading accounts of Puritan travails, and studying Huguenot texts in Robinson's translations. She was also ready to exercise those ambitions for a public career that Robinson had helped her hone for nearly a decade. When Wakefield took exception to the scriptural precedents for and contemporary practices of collective worship, Hays took advantage of the crisis. Hays was establishing a pattern in which grief galvanized her into action.

In 1790, Wakefield, a friend of Robinson's from Cambridge, was engaged as Tutor in Classics at New College. Although originally an Anglican and a graduate of Jesus College, Cambridge, Wakefield left the Anglican Church in 1780 when he declared himself a Unitarian. He taught Classics at Warrington Academy and translated the New Testament for use at the Essex Street Chapel. Wakefield was a brilliant iconoclast, devoting his energies to scholarship and to pamphleteering for civil and religious liberty. But he proved a mixed blessing to the New College community. He reorganized studies in the Classics there, but became disgusted by what he observed elsewhere in the curriculum and incensed by their emphasis on religious rituals. Lucy Aikin, familiar with the interpersonal conflicts at New College, described Wakefield as an entirely self-contained thinker, an independent if insulated critic, who stood apart from what might be supposed to be his religious cohort.[37]

Wakefield initially voiced his strenuous objections to what took place at New College in conversations with other tutors. He judged his colleagues and students according to the standards of his own training in comparative linguistics. As self-appointed arbiter, he found them all wanting. He was righteous in his opinions as scholar and theologian, Lucy Aikin attested, and "incapable of thinking one thing and practising another." He stopped attending any public services.[38] His conspicuous absence alarmed other tutors because Wakefield was popular with his students. In the summer of 1791, Wakefield left New College. Later in the year, he broadcast his disaffection in *An Enquiry into the Expediency and Propriety of Public or Social Worship*, adding the insult of publicity to the injury of disloyalty in his former colleagues' eyes.

Wakefield's *Enquiry* was a scholarly attack that assumed his readers' familiarity with Greek and Latin, and was directed to his learned male colleagues. He protested not only what he saw as the corrupt practice of enforced public worship, but also the rituals of his colleagues. He objected to what he considered the quasi-Anglican rites required of tutors and students. If such practices could be faulted in an academic setting, he asked, what rationale could there possibly be for devotional rites within the bosom of certain private families? His position was that all enforced ceremonies were as antithetical to the spirit of Christianity as those demanded by the Church of England.[39]

Wakefield did not spare the basic values or the customs of the New College Dissenters: rational inquiry, individualism, the spirit of open dissent, scriptural exegesis, the lecture-room style of their meetings, all came under his attack. He refused to soften his criticism: Wakefield warned his former colleagues that they must try harder to practice what they preached, to reflect on whether their own conduct attested to their public assertions about liberality, knowledge, and love of truth.[40] The tone of Wakefield's pamphlet is occasionally exclamatory and provocative. For example, he collapses public and private and seems to compare the Dissenting leadership at New College with a lactating woman. "My *nursing-mother*," he exclaimed, "does not owe me many obligations; and therefore I should be uncandid and injurious indeed, if I did not bear her this testimony, that she enjoins and practices no ceremonies in any degree so absurd and contemptible"[41] as those at New College.

Several leading Rational Dissenters and Unitarians responded to Wakefield— Priestley, Disney, and others among Wakefield's critics answered promptly in sermons that were subsequently published in 1792,[42] as they circled their wagons against the apostate. Their concern was intensified by increasingly severe governmental and majority reactions to religious and political heterodoxy in the wake of the French Revolution.[43] There were conflicting views about specific theological points, but the primary concern was to restore the public unanimity that Rational Dissent and the embattled Unitarians attempted to represent to a skeptical world. Textual skirmishes erupted with missives flying between Wakefield, Priestley, Anna Barbauld, and Disney, but the first published response seems to have come from Hays. What prompted Hays to speak up is not clear, but she may have been aroused by the explicit threat to her own experience of collective worship since theology, politics, and erudition had been made accessible to female as well as male worshippers in the hands of a minister like Robinson. Hays saw an opening for herself into the republic of letters to which Robinson had introduced her, and on a subject which a pious woman might appropriately have opinions.

Cursory Remarks (1791), her maiden publication, was apparently safe in both its subject and tone, and announced the direction she determined to take in her public career. Hays boldly chose to write under the guise of "Eusebia," a Greek word that means "piety," and with connection to the historical roots of Unitarianism.[44] The pen name was rarely used in English publications;[45] it would suggest to many of Hays's readers the "good Eusebia" in William Law's popular and influential *The Serious Call to a Devout and Holy Life* (1728). Significantly for Hays, Law's Eusebia is a learned widow representing "*the spirit of a better education,*" in his chapter that expounds on the present deplorable superficiality of female education and the pressing need for improvement. Law insisted on the importance of resisting the temptations of fashion and social conformity usually encouraged by parents; he advised that, whether married or single, a woman whose mind and spirit had been trained to humility, piety, and the pursuit of truth, could have as much good effect on those around her as a man—particularly in the amelioration of other females. Importantly, Law did not privilege the married over the single state. "Eusebia" suggested that Hays had emerged from the chrysalis of disconsolate maiden widow into an aspiring female Christian teacher-preacher with particular interest in the education of women, a concern that she later made more explicit in *Letters and Essays, Moral, and Miscellaneous.*[46]

The title of the pamphlet, however, reveals Hays's hesitancy, suggesting that the writer is speaking informally rather than as an authority. Her self-deprecation was genuine, but ingenuous, too, as an attempt to distance herself from the critical machinery of the public sphere where not every man was supportive of intellectual women like Robinson or avuncular like Hugh Worthington. In *Cursory Remarks ... by Eusebia*, Hays offered the distaff perspective on public or social worship, the point of view of the woman who sits with her needle stilled, listening to learned men.

Anna Barbauld was the only other female Rational Dissenter to reply to Wakefield. She drew upon her significant, if informal, authority as daughter, sister, and wife of Rational Dissenters, with an established reputation as an acclaimed poet and author of devotional children's stories. Mary Hays spoke out because she was nearly ready to be noticed. The reasons for Eusebia's modesty were obvious— her youth and ignorance, offset, she hoped, by her love of truth and virtue. Unlike Barbauld, Eusebia labored under the feminine handicaps of having no institutional credentials, even if, like Barbauld, by proximity. Eusebia was ignorant of Greek, Latin, Aramaic, Hebrew, and the training in disputation that translating and parsing original texts provided; and she acknowledged her limited, because gendered, feminine understanding. She was therefore an example of those uneducated Christian souls who needed collective worship to inform their comprehension and elevate their belief. "Should Mr. Wakefield take the trouble of perusing the following pages," she began,

> he will probably charge the writer with great presumption; a woman, young, unlearned, unacquainted with any language but her own; possessing no other merit than a love of truth and virtue, an ardent desire of knowledge, and a heart susceptible to the affecting and elevated emotions afforded by a pure and rational devotion.[47]

Eusebia's critique simultaneously revealed her uncommon education and Hays's ambivalence about displaying her learning in public.

Nonetheless, like Law's Eusebia, Hays presented the *bona fides* that would be recognized by every like-minded reader. She was intellectually and spiritually ambitious; moved both mentally and emotionally by the force of ideas *and* faith; she had willy nilly secured basic training in the lexicon of Nonconformity. Hays attested here to the duality of her public role: uneducated by traditional masculine standards, nonetheless she had struggled to learn what she could by reading scriptures, comparing these with doctrinal arguments of various sects, attempted to keep an open mind and, a crucial part of her legacy from Robinson, to divest herself of prejudice. In other words, like the men she most admired, Eusebia now spoke out with the intention of "pursuing and embracing truth without partiality and without prejudice, wherever it may be found."[48]

Hays, as the pious woman, assumed the authority to join the Christian Enlightenment enterprise.[49] But she equivocated about this, too. Eusebia acknowledges that she is hardly a fit challenger for Wakefield. In the same breath she expresses a sense of her right to answer him, albeit not as an equal, because of her individual pilgrim's progress in searching for the truth and acting on it. Her education, she confesses, has been impeded by female disadvantages she has encountered along the way, "disadvantages, if I may be allowed so to speak, that would have been almost insuperable to a mind less active, and less in earnest in the research." Enlightenment is her primary pursuit because for her it is the sole "source of exquisite intellectual entertainment and moral improvement."

Eusebia refers to her intimate history of disappointed love as thwarting her search for truth. She emphasizes how hard she works to be enlightened. She recognizes that she will never be a legitimate preacher with public authority, but, like any Christian, she exercises the right to speak her mind. Eusebia challenges Wakefield's presumption that he stands at the apex of a moral, academic, and intellectual hierarchy that decides who may and who may not seek enlightenment. Eusebia admits to being initially startled by Wakefield's novel position in his pamphlet, but is well-trained enough to resolve "to suspend my opinion, and seriously consider the arguments adduced in support of an hypothesis, which appeared to me so singular and extraordinary." She knows Wakefield's reputation for upright character. His tract invokes in her "reverence for his understanding and genius." But his outstanding qualities as scholar, theologian, and philosopher make him a poor judge of the religious capabilities of the rest of the world. If Everyman resembles Wakefield, then each individual might seek eternal truth alone, without any need for encouragement or discipline. "But alas!"

The "alas!" is a rhetorical sigh. Hays describes the world as it is in her time, when the majority of human beings are still infantile in their understanding. Therefore, they are "not yet ripe for a religion purely mental and contemplative." Wakefield may object to those aspects of Rational Dissenting worship that savor of evangelical effusions or showy Anglican rites, but, except for the advanced few like himself, most people experience belief through participation in the spectacle of worship. Eusebia is aware that Rational Dissenters, and particularly the Unitarians, are frequently portrayed as cold and overly rational. Christianity, in general, she avers, "by becoming a science, too frequently appears sour, haughty, and contentious." But, Wakefield is guilty of perpetuating the very sins he protests: he provokes sectarian debate rather than acknowledging common spiritual feelings. For all his disdain for unseemly histrionics, Wakefield magnifies the differences between his beliefs and other Dissenters by charging them with Evangelical exhibitionism and Church of England artifice.

Eusebia has no pretensions to scholarship like the multi-lingual Mr. Wakefield, but she has studied her Bible well enough to refer to several passages in which the apostles speak of collective worship. In fact, the 18 examples she identifies are from Wakefield's own translation of the New Testament. Is this not sufficient authority, she asks, for the conduct of the followers of Christ in all ages? Later in her pamphlet, she adds the Last Supper and the baptism of John to the list. The precedent for communal worship extends to private devotion. To demonstrate the ubiquity of this practice, Eusebia quotes the "elegant language of a modern Deist," which she identifies as Rousseau, in a passage from his *Emile*. Even the arch skeptic Rousseau supports regular worship. Eusebia reminds her readers that while devotion cannot influence divine intentions, communal worship may be a link in the great natural chain of causes that have beneficial effects.

Eusebia insists that the Lockean laws of necessity and materialism mandate the habits of worship by inculcating early associations in the minds of the young, and reaffirming these patterns in their elders. Moreover, domestic affection is enriched by communal prayer in Eusebia's female vision of the Christian community, a family bound by feeling rather than reason, for which God is the ultimate source of enlightenment. Domestic or public, worship with others provides emotional satisfaction and mental improvement. Wakefield asserts that the true Christian has no need of a priest or minister. Eusebia replies that she does not agree that a clergyman is necessarily in charge of another's soul. The true minister is as Rousseau represents in *Emile*, a passage Eusebia quotes for its affective power. Rousseau's Catholic pastor ministers to the poor people in his region, and preaches the gospel without concern for religious forms. He welcomes Protestants to his congregation. He encourages members of his congregation to love and respect each other as believers on their own terms, a tolerant practice that Wakefield appears to dismiss in his insistence on solitary worship. Public or social worship celebrates the diversity of individual faith within a community of the faithful.[50]

Cursory Remarks nearly ends on an enthusiastic, even visionary, note. "This is an age of controversy," Eusebia explains, "and all who love truth must rejoice in seeing the spirit of freedom and enquiry universally disseminated." Impartial discussion where nothing is taken for granted is the only way to ensure that the ongoing search for religious and moral truth will be sustained. Imposition over another's conscience, Eusebia proclaims, violates the basic principle of Christianity. Eusebia offers an invocation to ineluctable progress as Robinson might have, affirming her faith that God's divine plan will ultimately be accomplished, although at present, she can only see part of the unfolding. Finally, she rhapsodizes, "In a future system, where our faculties will expand, neither bounded by time, nor darkened by frailty; we shall, I trust, penetrate to the heart of things, and become true philosophers, without any danger of mistake or hazard." She looks forward to the time when the divine Intelligence will be manifest and men's minds will apprehend the truth—and women's, too.

But for all the implicit homage to him in Hays's text, Robinson would have been disappointed by the timid tone, self-deprecation, and, especially by the weak conclusion. As if in response to Eusebia's lyrical effusions, Hays undercuts herself throughout, retreating to gendered reality, ending, almost as a ventriloquist might, by offering an apology for her female puppet's ineptitude and impudence. "I feel as if I had ventured beyond my depth; I am unequal to the management of controversial weapons, and have perhaps, though influenced by the purest motives, displayed in the preceding remarks my weakness only, and incapacity for the discussion." Here, Hays fails to meet the benchmark for human responsibility that Robinson established: she desires to assume the voice of public authority, but, at the final moment, plays the card of womanly disability in a bid for sympathy. The ambitious act of writing and publishing *Cursory Remarks* contrasts with its rhetoric: Eusebia as the pious woman assumes the natural right to speak out in defense of that religion which instructs women, as well as men, in the sacred right to private judgment. Eusebia moves that imperative forward by predicating her case on study of the scriptures and personal observation, projecting her interior experience onto the larger stage of public debate. But, at the same time, Eusebia reflects Hays's ambivalence about her own competence to withstand the glare of public disputation.

Wakefield, by contrast, was a hardy public combatant who relished controversy and rarely overlooked an opportunity to incite or engage in textual conflict.[51] Had Robinson been alive to read *An Enquiry*, he might well have discerned some truth in Wakefield's criticism of Rational Dissenting compromises to the faith of the Apostles; he would recognize that Wakefield's disappointment fueled his attack. Robinson knew what it was to be a dissenting Dissenter. Wakefield read the first several replies from defenders of the New College tutors, including Eusebia's. He shot back a second edition in which he addressed his several challengers in turn, focusing on hers. From a letter Wakefield wrote to Cambridge Unitarian William Frend, we know that he assumed that Eusebia was a man hiding behind the identity of a woman. Therefore, in answering Eusebia in his second edition, Wakefield debased the idea of intellectual battle with this female impersonator to that of a sexual encounter, expressing mock terror and awe at confronting "so mysterious an adversary."[52] He compares their textual collision to fear-inspiring natural phenomena that defy understanding; quoting the *Book of Proverbs,* Wakefield alludes to "three things, which are too wonderful for me; yea four, which I know not. The way of an eagle in the air, the way of a serpent upon a rock, the way of a ship in the midst of the sea, and"—in capital letters—"THE WAY OF A MAN WITH A MAID"[53]—thus dismissing the entire idea of intellectual debate. In mocking Eusebia, Wakefield also dismisses the idea of such disputation with an actual woman.

Wakefield sometimes teased his opponents when jousting in print. Hays, as she pointedly explained to Godwin later, never appreciated humor.[54] Eusebia's nascent persona was too fragile to laugh off public embarrassment. Hays may have felt that Wakefield threatened the integrity of her chaste independence by eroticizing her role as debater, calling attention to her anomalous status as a self-taught and unmarried woman. Hays solemnly replied to Wakefield in her second edition of *Cursory Remarks*, admitting that his "ludicrous sally" had offended her, correctly pointing out that he had not addressed the substance of her comments, but had resorted to a diversionary distraction. She described herself as "abashed and wounded" and walked away from the controversy with Wakefield, declaring herself unequal to the demands of this public debate.[55]

There was much private consternation among Unitarians at Wakefield's airing of doctrinal differences. Theophilus Lindsey shook his head over the tone of Wakefield's second polemic, noting to a correspondent that Dr. Priestley had praised Anna Barbauld's response to Wakefield.[56] As the dispute escalated, Lindsey worried that Wakefield's reputation as an inventive scholar and sensible man had been obscured by his provocation about public worship.[57]

New evidence reveals that unknown to Hays, William Frend took Wakefield to task for his foolishness in a private letter to Wakefield, probably prompted by the concern of Lindsey, Priestley, and other leaders. Frend, like Wakefield, was a recently professed Unitarian, affiliated with Jesus College, Cambridge. He knew of Eusebia's identity from mutual acquaintances, including George Dyer and Michael Brown, minister of the church Hays attended at Gainsford Street. Frend had provided books from the Cambridge libraries for Robinson's researches in the *History of Baptism,*[58] and was his parishioner. His loyalty to Robinson extended to Hays as Robinson's spiritual daughter.

Frend's letter does not survive, but Wakefield's answer does. "You must lower your opinion of me," Wakefield wrote Frend in self-defense, for you seem to suppose, that I have the gift of Prophecy: otherwise how was it possible for me to know, without any Means of knowing, that the Author of that Pamphlet was a Lady? There is no Artifice more common ... and so often complained of by Reviewers, as that of assuming a female Name to escape the Lash of Criticism. Had I known who it was, I certainly wd by no Means have thought of such a Piece of Levity.[59]

A man writing as a woman, Wakefield alleges, is an easy way to avoid the rigorous standards of consensual male expectations. Wakefield promised Frend that he would omit the offending text in subsequent editions, but insisted that the lady needed educating. The information that his detractor was a woman would modify his manners, but not his understanding or his standards. Like Robinson, Wakefield believed in *human* responsibility; if a woman entered the public arena she would be judged, at least by him, according to the same criteria as any man. Wakefield was blunter than many of his colleagues: here and elsewhere he expressed the pervasive, private view that since women were not educated equally with men, they should stay out of public debate for which there existed masculine precedents and procedures.[60] He was also ambivalent: in the heat of battle Wakefield denied the possibility that women might be trained to enter such lists, although he was an intellectually generous father to his several daughters and tutored them himself.

Wakefield issued another reply to all his critics,[61] introducing his "opponents in the order of their march to the attack ... led on by their expert and accomplished general Dr. DISNEY." He gave special attention to the "amazonian auxiliaries"— Anna Barbauld had joined Eusebia in the fray.[62] Wakefield extended the military conceit to his female critics: he quoted a Greek epigram in which Pallas, armed, meeting Venus, unarmed, challenges her to fight. "What occasion have I?" asks Venus, "for the shield or spear? If I could vanquish you with my native unadorned beauty, how much more, if I put on armour?"

Joining the twin classical figures of Venus Amatoris and Venus Imperatoris,[63] Wakefield implies that women's real, indeed only, weapon is their naked sexual allure. Women are ill equipped in mental contests with men because they are without cognitive training or armor and, therefore, should not attempt to engage in intellectual controversy.[64] Wakefield's display of classical erudition had the effect of trivializing his female critics, as well as camouflaging his resistance to addressing the content of their criticism. His swipe resonated with the snickers of a schoolboy translating salacious Greek and Latin texts in the classroom, more reckless than intentionally cruel.

Sympathetic and conciliatory, Frend wrote to Eusebia soon after hearing from Wakefield. In his letter, Frend introduced himself, praising her pamphlet, and appealing to her to continue as peacemaker between sectarian men, for "the aid of the fair sex" might be needed again "to soften the animosity and fervor of disputation."[65] Frend, a devoted brother to an unmarried younger sister, likely smarted at the inappropriateness of Wakefield's references to female sexual powers in his answers to Eusebia and Barbauld. Unlike Robinson, Frend used the courtly language between gentlemen and ladies, although he was aware of Hays's unconventional intellectual interests. Regrettably, this was also the diction of romance, and had inadvertent effects that Frend never intended. He judged that as a studious, plain woman known to many of his associates, Eusebia would expect only an intellectually collegial relationship with him, too. This was a serious, if understandable, misjudgment, and so the seeds for the explosive narrative of Hays's later fiction, *Memoirs of Emma Courtney*, were set in motion.

Frend's letter mingled chivalry with current political religious struggles and focused on the unwavering search for truth among Robinson's followers like themselves. Frend addressed Hays as she presented herself in print, as John Eccles had done, in this instance as the sagacious widow Eusebia, instead of saucy "Polly" or "Maria." Frend named Michael Brown as their common friend and identifier of the real author of *Cursory Remarks*. He represented himself and Hays in gendered terms: he as the learned but battle-weary soldier, "one who has been under the necessity of listening to the wranglings of contending parties & been wearied with ineffectual struggles against the power of interest & prejudice," alluding to the fallout from his public declaration of Unitarianism; she as Eusebia, happily offering him reactions unsullied by sophistry or sectarian posturing. He praised her untutored but genuine eloquence, contradicting Wakefield's criticisms of her performance.

Frend acknowledged Hays's training with Robinson, as well as her growing involvement with the Unitarian community. He expected that sectarian strife was unlikely between them; Frend discerned from her pamphlet that they seemed to agree in most points of Unitarian belief. He looked forward to the pleasure of hearing her thoughts on the character of Christ, a contentious subject among Unitarians, and asserted that he would be guided by her assessment of his own convictions. That he looked to her views on the knotty questions of Christology was recognition indeed.

Hays's reference to Rousseau, always a litmus test of a reader's degree of tolerance for heterodox points of view, intrigued Frend. The son of a prosperous Canterbury wine merchant, Frend had traveled among the Savoyards when he needed to take some distance from the furor his confession of Unitarianism had provoked at Cambridge. He told Eusebia that he had witnessed the rural worship that Rousseau described firsthand. Frend painted an idealized scene for her, in which a patriarchal minister engages his congregation on the question of mortal sin, posing questions and eliciting answers from them. Leaving the church, Frend reported, he was overtaken by one of the parishioners whom he questioned about the pastor's teachings. To his surprise, Frend heard the peasant answer clearly and cogently about his faith. This was the pure, natural piety Rousseau promoted in which man was free from imposed social constraints to embrace God. Frend regretted that he had never had the chance to worship in such a peaceful setting. But Rousseau's enthusiasms were notoriously contagious, particularly to women.[66]

Here, Frend instructed Hays, was the lesson to be learned by readers of Rousseau: excesses of sensibility must be controlled by reason. And, pointing to a weakness in Rousseau's Alpine fantasy, he asked Eusebia, did such men as the Savoyard minister actually exist among Dissenters and Anglicans, on the pure model of Christ and his apostles?[67]

Frend expected that Eusebia would reflect on his concerns about following the Deist Rousseau as her religious guide. His letter, as gesture and instruction, intimated that he might be willing to serve instead, unknowingly arousing in Hays the fantasy of Frend as St Preux teaching and loving her in the guise of Julie, or, even perhaps Heloise. On rereading Frend's letter, Hays likely imagined that Abelard, in somber Dissenting garb, had come to call.

Notes

1   E. Kell, "Memoir of Mary Hays: With some Unpublished Letters addressed to Her by Robert Robinson, of Cambridge, and Others," *The Christian Reformer*, XI/CXXIX (September 1844): 814.

2   There is conjecture that Hays's influence may be seen in John Disney's "Defence of public or social worship," published in 1792 and reviewed in *The Gentleman's Magazine*, LXII, pp. 242–3. However, Hays in her second edition of *Cursory Remarks*, notes that had she known of Disney's reply to Wakefield earlier, she never would have written her own.

3   Myra Reynolds, *The Learned Lady in England 1650–1760* (Gloucester, MA, 1920: reprinted 1964); Siep Stuurman, "The Deconstruction of Gender: Seventeenth-Century Feminism and Modern Equality," in Taylor and Knott (eds), *Women, Gender and Enlightenment* (Houndmills, 2005), pp. 371–88; *Women and Literature in Britain 1500–1700*, ed. Helen Wilcox (Cambridge, 1996), Jacqueline Pearson, "Women reading, reading women," pp. 80–99.

4   Letter LIX, undated, "Love Letters."

5   The term "Rational Dissenter" was commonly used to repudiate heterodox believers. "Rational Dissent" itself was "increasingly portrayed as a subversion of spirituality, a repudiation of fundamental Christian beliefs, the sort of unhealthy speculation that led to deism and infidelity," G.M. Ditchfield, "'How Narrow will the limits of this Toleration appear?' Dissenting petitions to Parliament, 1772–1773."

6   Ditchfield notes, "Joseph Priestley in his *Free Address to Protestant Dissenters, as Such* (1769) described 'those who are called *rational dissenters* as advocates for 'the cause of truth and liberty'; in the enlarged 1771 edition of this work he went further and declared that rational Dissenters were those who would 'speak and write with the simplicity and fearless integrity of a Christian, openly asserting the great doctrines of the proper unity of God ... in opposition to what is in reality Tritheism.' Priestley used the term to encourage those of his own persuasion to become more self-aware and distinctive," Ibid.

7   Ruth Watts, "Part One: 1760–1815," *Gender, Power and the Unitarians in England 1760–1860* (London, 1998), and Kathryn Gleadle, *The Early Feminists: Radical*

Unitarians and the Emergence of the Women's Rights Movement, 1831–51 (New York, 1995), have documented that disparities endured "between the urbane liberalism professed by Unitarians, and the conservative, patriarchal tenor which overshadowed their personal relationships and codes of etiquette," p. 8.

8   Anne F. Wedd, "The Story of Mary Hays," *The Love-Letters of Mary Hays 1779– 1780* (London, 1925), pp. 1–14.

9   E. Kell, "Memoir of Mary Hays: with some unpublished letters addressed to her by Robert Robinson, of Cambridge, and others," *The Christian Reformer*, XI/CXXIX (September 1844): 943–4.

10   In *Arcana*, Robinson expressed his basic creed: "There is neither Jew nor Greek, bond nor free, Prince nor subject. The right of one argued from his nature is the right of all. Whether men forfeit this right in a state of society is another question." Robinson had no doubts about separation of church and state, the primacy of the individual's rights of conscience, or freedom of the press. He equated civil with religious liberty, predicated on the "inviolable" principle that all power originates in the people, including the power to create civil governors and ordain Christian ministers. Repeatedly, he cautioned, "religion ends when persecution begins," Robert Robinson, "Letter III. On The Right of Private Judgment," *Arcana, or, The principles of the late petitioners to Parliament for relief in the matter of subscription: in VIII letters to a friend* (Cambridge, 1774), p. 35.

11   George Dyer, Robinson's assistant minister and first biographer, described this phase of Robinson's career as unfolding in a "new theatre." Acknowledged in Dissenting circles as a prolific writer, in London he was unknown as a preacher, a role in which he was "more conversational than oratorical, reasoning from the scriptures, teaching, pleading, persuading, delighting," demonstrating "a singular rapport with his hearers; a gift for speaking the needs of each and everyone," as well as "an impish delight in puncturing pomposity" and "a sense of humour, a flash of satirical brilliance and a touch of comic genius that scandalised those who thought ministerial dignity depended on carrying about everywhere the preternatural solemnity of a perpetual funeral." Robinson's message soon proved too radical for the majority of his audiences, Dyer, *Memoirs of the Life and Writings of Robert Robinson*, (London, 1796), p. 218.

12   For more specifics about Dissenting interests, see "An ARRANGED CATALOGUE of the Several Publications which have appeared relation to the enlargement of the Toleration of PROTESTANT-DISSENTING-MINISTERS; and the Repeal of the Corporation and Test acts: with reference to the Agitation of those Questions in Parliament, from the Year M.DCC.LXXII, to M.DCC.XC, Inclusive." The catalogue was compiled by Lindsey's assistant minister, John Disney, and published by Joseph Johnson, St. Paul's Church Yard, unpaginated.

13   In perusing the work, Burke reported, he could find no religious principles, only political ones. These political principles inveighed against the established monarchy and church. In short, he thundered, accentuating Robinson's use of the theological term, "[I]t was a catechism of misanthropy, a catechism of anarchy, a catechism of confusion! grossly libeling the national establishment in every part and passage." Even worse, "these catechisms were to be put into the hands of Dissenters' children, who were thus to be taught in their infancy to lisp out censures and condemnations against the established church of England, to be brought up as a rising generation of

its determined enemies, while, possibly, the dissenting preachers were themselves recommending the same sort of robbery and plunder of the wealth of the church as had happened in France, where some men were weak enough to imagine a happy revolution had taken place; but where [Burke] knew the most miserable system of Government at this moment prevailed that ever disgraced the annals of Europe." *The Parliamentary Register; or, History of the Proceedings and Debates of the House of Commons*, vol. XXVII (London: J. Debrett, 1790), p. 180.

14   See Robert Robinson, "Memoirs of the Reformation in France," V/X (Cambridge, 1784).

15   John Christian Laursen, "Imposters and Liars: Clandestine Manuscripts and the Limits of Freedom of the Press in the Huguenot Netherlands," *New Essays On the Political Thought of the Huguenots of the Refuge* (Leiden: Brill, 1995), pp. 73–108.

16   The *Christian Reformer* reprints nine of Robinson's letters; the Pforzheimer Collection has eight letters and a fragment of the ninth.

17   Keeble describes the Puritan belief in the "duty of introspection" and the practice of writing "*Heart accounts*," in which an individual Christian narrates for others' contemplation her own spiritual struggles, pp. 207–8.

18   Robinson to Hays, 11 January 1783, *Pforz.*, 2154.

19   Robinson to Hays, 16 June 1784, *Pforz.*, 2157.

20   These "inquiries," he judged, "discover, as everything you write does a wise and virtuous mind bent upon the acquisition of truth." "You are pleased to say, you have examined Claude's Essay," he wrote. "I flatter myself if you will turn to Vol. ii. Pag. 152 Note 6th abd Oag, 155, Bie 9- you will find the best answer I can give to your questions. I believe *both the divine decrees* and man's *free agency*. In my opinion it is extremely difficult to deny either, and there is no difficulty in believing that the *reconciling* of them is possible to God, though far above our comprehension."

21   Luisa Simonutti describes Claude as "the chief interpreter of contemporary Huguenot ideals," in "Between Political Loyalty and Religious Liberty: Political Theory and Toleration in Huguenot Thought in the Epoch of Bayle," *History of Political Thought*, XVII/4 (1996): 535; see also Jean Claude, *Cruel Persecutions of the PROTESTANTS in the Kingdom of France*, first American reprint of the English translation ... (Boston, 1893), pp. 168–9. See the dramatic account of this that quotes Professor Henry M. Baird in the introduction, "Claude and His Masterpiece," by Narcisse Cyr, pp. x–xii.

22   John Christian Laursen, "The Beneficial Lies Controversy in the Huguenot Netherlands, 1705–31: an unpublished manuscript at the root of the *cas Saurin*," *Studies On Voltaire & The Eighteenth Century*, 319 (1994): 96.

23   Hays to Henry Crabb Robinson, April 1842, *DWL*.

24   See Jonathan Israel, *Radical Enlightenment: philosophy and the making of modernity, 1650–1750* (New York, 2001).

25   According to Francis Bacon, "writing lives" of individuals is a form of "perfect history": "Lives," Bacon asserts, "if they be well written, propounding to themselves a person to represent in whom actions both greater and smaller, public and private, have a commixture, must of necessity contain a more true, native, and lively representation." The University of Oregon, "The Advancement of Learning: Book Two (1605)," *Renascence: An Online Repository of Works Printed in English Between the Years 1477 and 1799*, <http://darkwing.uoregon.edu/~rbear/adv2.htm>.

26   Ruth Whelan argues that the three Cartesian proto-feminist treatises by Huguenot
      Poullain de la Barre (1684–1723) —*On the Equality of the Two Sexes* (1673), *On the
      Education of Ladies* (1674), *On the Education of Men* (1675)—demonstrate Poullain's
      innovative thinking as a feminist theologian, and implicitly connect him to the larger
      theme of toleration. Ruth Whelan, "'Liberating the Bible from Patriarchy': Poullain de
      la Barre's Feminist Hermeneutics," in Allison P. Coudert, Sarah Hutton, Richard H.
      Popkin, and Gordon M. Weinter (eds), *Judaeo-Christian Intellectual Culture in the
      Seventeenth Century* (Dordrecht, 1999), pp. 119–43. For a less sanguine view, see
      Michèle Le Doeuff, *The Sex of Knowing*, trans. Kathryn Hamer and Lorraine Code
      (New York, 2003), where she contends that in his work "the very question of
      women's access to an intellectual life seems to be limited from the outset, unable to
      find its own terms, or discussed against a background of constraining, tacitly accepted
      but unexamined principles that undermine the very effort to open the world of
      knowledge to women ... [Poullain conceives of] a conditional access to knowledge for
      women,"
      pp. 23–4.
27   John Christian Laursen, personal communication, 7 April 2000.
28   Marcus Wood, "William Cobbett, John Thelwall, Radicalism, Racism and Slavery: A
      Study in Burkean Parodics," *Romanticism On the Net* 15,
      <http://users.ox.ac.uk/~scat0385/thelwall.html>.
29   As founder of the Cambridge Constitutional Society and actively involved with
      several like-minded young men at Jesus College, Robinson's subsequent
      Parliamentary Petition called for total abolition.
30   Robert Robinson, *Slavery Inconsistent with the Spirit of Christianity*. 1786.
      (Baltimore: Abner Neal, 1819).
31   Robinson to Hays, 4 March 1789, *Pforz.*, 2160.
32   Joseph Priestley, "Reflections on Death. A Sermon, on Occasion of the Death of The
      Rev. Robert Robinson, of Cambridge, Delivered at the New Meeting in Birmingham,
      June 13, 1790, and published at the Request of those who heard it, and of Mr.
      Robinson's Family." (Birmingham: J. Belcher, 1790), p. 419.
33   In Chapter Two and thereafter I use the terms, "Unitarian" and "Rational Dissenter,"
      to identify those figures that identified themselves publicly as belonging to either
      group. After Theophilus Lindsey established the first Unitarian chapel in 1773,
      Unitarians evolved a dogma of their own that distinguished them from the larger
      cohort of Rational Dissenters. Unitarians believed in the unity of God, the humanity of
      Jesus Christ, the supremacy and right to individual interpretation of the Scriptures,
      denial of the atonement and original sin, and an optimistic view of human nature and
      the possibility of material and moral improvement that promoted activism. Some
      Rational Dissenters became Unitarians; so did some Anglicans. For cogent
      discussions of these theological and historical complexities see R. K. Webb, "The
      Emergence of Rational Dissent," in *Enlightenment and Religion: Rational Dissent in
      Eighteenth-Century Britain*, ed. Knud Haakonssen (Cambridge, 1996), pp. 36–41; R.K.
      Webb, "Religion," *An Oxford Companion to The Romantic Age: British Culture 1776–
      1832* (Oxford, 1999), pp. 93–101; G.M. Ditchfield, "'How Narrow will the limits of this
      Toleration appear?' Dissenting petitions to Parliament, 1772–1773," *Parliament and
      Dissent*, eds Stephen Taylor and David Wykes (Parliamentary History Trust:
      Edinburgh University Press, 2005), pp. 91–106.

34 Along the theological spectrum, each of the men was a staunch Rational Dissenter or Unitarian, see *Hackney New College Sermons and Reports* (London, 1786–91), unpaginated.

35 Daventry was founded by Reverend Phillip Doddridge (1702–51), and was until 1789 a respected and liberal Dissenting Academy that Priestley attended.

36 J.W. Ashley Smith, "Tutors Constructing their own Curricula," *The Birth of Modern Education: The Contribution of the Dissenting Academies 1660–1800* (London, 1954), pp. 129–87; Watts, "Ideals into Practice: Unitarians in Education," *Gender, Power and the Unitarians in England 1760–1860*, pp. 56–63; for a trenchant history of pedagogy at the academies, see David L. Wykes, "The Contribution of the Dissenting Academy to the Emergence of Rational Dissent," in Knud Haakonssen (ed.), *Enlightenment and Religion: Rational Dissent in eighteenth-century Britain* (Cambridge, 1996), pp. 99–139.

37 Lucy Aikin (1781–1864) was the daughter of John Aikin, M.D., brother of Anna Barbauld. Lucy Aikin, also a social historian, wrote biographies of both her father and aunt. See her *Memoir of John Aikin* (London, 1823), vol. I, p. 262.

38 Ibid., p. 264.

39 Jane Austen may have taken a leaf out of Wakefield's pamphlet in her descriptions in *Mansfield Park* (1814) of piety enforced solely for propriety's sake for both family and servants at decadent Sotherton Abbey.

40 Gilbert Wakefield, *An Enquiry into the Expediency and Propriety of Public or Social Worship* (London, 1791), p. 13.

41 Ibid.

42 Joseph Priestley, LL.D., *Letters to a Young Man, occasioned by Mr. Wakefield's Essay on Public Worship* (London, 1792). Anna Barbauld's response was also published that year.

43 Edmund Burke singled out the New College students' support for the French Revolution for special notice, denouncing the college as the "new arsenal in which subversive doctrines and arguments were forged," quoted in Matthew Mercer, "Dissenting Academies and The Education of the Laity, 1750–1850," *History of Education*, 30/1 (2001): 53.

44 See M. Phillips and W.S. Tompkinson, *English Women in Life and Letters* (Oxford, 1926), pp. 180–81. I appreciate Miriam Wallace's observations that Eusebia was the second wife of the Roman Emperor Constantius II who was associated with the "Arian controversy," or the roots of Unitarianism, personal communication, July 2003.

45 COPAC, the merged online catalogue of the members of the Consortium of Research Libraries in the UK, lists only a few "Eusebias" as authors.

46 William Law (1686–1761) believed that female role models represented an ideal of ascetic Christian life. He was educated at Cambridge, felt compelled to declare himself a nonjuror (one who remained loyal to the Stuarts and refused to acknowledge George I as his monarch), and served as private tutor in Edward Gibbon's household. He was ordained as an Anglican priest, wrote *A Treatise upon Christian Perfection* and *A Serious Call*, and then founded a school for girls based upon his convictions. Dale A. Johnson writes that Law's ideas of a Christian community required seclusion from the worldliness of contemporary life; in his view, more likely for women than for men. Law was concerned that the gendered social expectations for women

encouraged the belief that women possessed "little and vain minds." Although he
accepted that women should be active only in private life, Law's critique of female
education "contributed to the growing recognition that traditional expectations did not
take women very seriously." See Dale A. Johnson, "Women in English Religion,
1700–1925," in *Studies in Women and Religion* (New York, 1983), vol. 10, pp. 22–31.
Isabel Rivers discusses Law's continuing influence on John Wesley, who edited
Law's texts, including *A Serious Call* (1744). See Rivers, *Reason, Grace, and
Sentiment: The Study of the Language of Religion and Ethics in England 1660–1780*,
(Cambridge, 1990), vol. I, pp. 210–18.

47   Norma Clarke advises that "by 1791 the persona of a 'woman, young unlearned' was
a cultural artefact," made familiar to readers in Fanny Burney's first novel, *Evelina*,
that linked the young author with her heroine, *The Rise and Fall of the Woman of
Letters* (London, 2004), p. 327.

48   "Cursory Remarks on *An Enquiry into the Expediency and Propriety of Public or
Social Worship*: Inscribed to Gilbert Wakefield, B.A., Late Fellow of Jesus-College,
Cambridge. By EUSEBIA" (London, 1792, second edition), p. 1. The pamphlet in
DWL in London bears Theophilus Lindsey's signature, and is the copy Hays sent him
as a gift.

49   Helena Rosenblatt, "The Christian Enlightenment," in Timothy Tackett and Stewart
Brown (eds), *The Cambridge History of Christianity, vol VII: Enlightenment,
Revolution and Reawakening (1660–1815)*, (Cambridge, 2005).

50   Jean-Jacques Rousseau, "The Creed of A Savoyard Priest," *Emile*, ed. P.D. Jimack,
trans. Barbara Foxley (London, 1993), pp. 274–383.

51   Henry Crabb Robinson later remarked that Wakefield had "the pale complexion and
mild features of a saint, was a most gentle creature in domestic life, and a very
amiable man; but, when he took part in political or religious controversy, his pen was
dipped in gall."

52   Gilbert Wakefield published "An Enquiry into the Expediency and Propriety of public,
or social Worship" in 1791 (London: J. Deighton; a second edition, subtitled "A New
Edition," was published after 29 February 1792, by Deighton). Wakefield's response
to "Eusebia" is from the "Appendix," p. 59.

53   Ibid.

54   "You accused me, of not seeming to participate in the hilarity of the circle on Sunday
… I have no great relish for what is term'd wit & humour, I never had," Hays to
Godwin, [January 1796], *Pforz.*, MH 24.

55   *Cursory Remarks*, "Postscript," pp. 23–4.

56   Lindsey remarked, "I should otherwise however have rather questioned her writing to
very general approbation on the subject of prayer, unless it be treated differently from
what she published some years ago, on devotional Taste, which seemed to me liable to
many objections." Theophilus Lindsey to William Turner of Newcastle, 4 May 1792,
DWL, 12.44 (54).

57   Theophilus Lindsey to William Turner of Newcastle, 14 June 1792, *DWL*, 12.44 (55).

58   T. Knott published Robinson's *History of Baptism* in 1790, according to *CMH*, p. 243.

59   I appreciate permission to quote from this unpublished letter. On the back flap of the
envelope Wakefield added that the same ladies who were so quick to take offense
"very likely go & read bawdy Novels, as soon as the Person to whom the[y] complain,
has turned his Back," Gilbert Wakefield to William Frend, *DWL*.

60   See *Memoirs of the Life of Gilbert Wakefield, B.A...in two volumes. Vol. I. Written by Himself, A new edition, with his latest corrections and notes by the editors, To which is subjoined, An Appendix of Original Letters* (London, 1804). See also Thomas Amyot to William Pattison, 18 February 1795, "Letter 25," in Penelope J. Corfield and Chris Evans (eds), *Youth and Revolution in the 1790s: Letters of William Pattison, Thomas Amyot and Henry Crabb Robinson* (Phoenix Mill, 1996), p. 120. Watts discusses these tensions in "Unitarianism and Women 1760–1815," *Gender, Power and the Unitarians*, pp. 77–96.

61   Gilbert Wakefield, "A General Reply to the Arguments Against the Enquiry into Public Worship," published after 19 June 1792. In this work, Wakefield replied to his critics, including Dr. Disney, Mr. Wilson, Anna Barbauld, Dr. Priestley, Mr. Simpson, Mr. Bruckner, Mr. Pope, as well as "Eusebia."

62   Anna Barbauld published "Remarks on Mr. Wakefield's Enquiry …," (London, 1792). I appreciate Amy Weldon's generous donation of a facsimile of this text.

63 Patricia J. Johnson, "Constructions of Venus in Ovid's Metamorphoses V," *Arethusa*, 29/1 (1996): 125–49.

64 Wakefield, "A General Reply," p. 3. Hays would have known Matthew Prior's rendition of the Greek original in his "Pallas and Venus" (1708), in which Pallas advises Venus that, "Thou to be strong must put off every Dress:/ Thy only Armour is thy Nakedness." Matthew Prior, "Pallas and Venus," *The Penn State Archive of Samuel Johnson's* Lives of the Poets, Kathleen Nulton Kemmerer, http://www.hn.psu.edu/faculty/kkemmerer/poets/prior/pallas.htm.   Coleridge,   too, translated the epigram from the Greek Anthology as a schoolboy or student at Cambridge. His version reads:

On the peaks of Ida, Cytherean Aphrodite was exulting over Athena:
"Now, naked, I am victorious. How, when I take up arms?"
But Athena answered her, laughing:
"Ha! Naked, Cyprian, you have your body fully armed."

"Greek Epigram on Aphrodite and Athena" in J.C.C. Mays (ed.), *The Collected Works of Samuel Taylor Coleridge: Poetical Works I, Poems (Reading Text): Part 1*, (1786–91?), (Princeton, 2001), p. 8.

65   William Frend to "Eusebia," 16 April 1792, *DWL*, HCR 24, 93 (2).

66   For example, in *Thoughts of Jean-Jacques Rousseau, Citizen of Geneva, Selected from his Writings by an Anonymous Editor and translated by Miss Henrietta Colebrook.* (2 vols, London, [1788?]). Colebrook enthuses that Rousseau "speaks from the heart to the heart: he communicates to his readers, as by an irresistible contagion, that enthusiastic love of nature and virtue which glowed in his own breast. The novelty of his own sentiments excites attention; the boldness of his painting fixes them in the memory; and the inimitable dignity and grace of his style and manner, charm and captivate the awakened soul. This great moral teacher traverses the whole field of duty, and in the most familiar and pleasing manner, instructs his readers in all the graces and virtues, as well as all the propriety and decorum of civilized and polite life." Colebrook tempers her enthusiasm with widely held reservations about Rousseau, "It must be confessed, at the same time, that there are eccentricities and errors in the writings of this exalted genius, equally repugnant to the Christian faith

and to sound sense: and well-disposed minds might, perhaps, doubt whether an indiscriminate perusal of all that he has written, might not be followed by dangerous consequences." I appreciate Fiore Sireci's generous contribution of this citation.

67   See James E. Miller's nuanced discussion in "The Forms of Freedom," *Rousseau: Dreamer of Democracy* (New Haven, 1984), pp. 165–201.

Chapter Three

Sewing in the Next World

"I doubt whether there will be any sewing in the next world, how then will those employ themselves who have done nothing else in this?"

Mary Hays, *Letters and Essays, Moral, and Miscellaneous*, 1793

Mary Hays met Mary Wollstonecraft in June 1792, after reading *A Vindication of the Rights of Woman*.[1] Hays heard Wollstonecraft's query as a clarion call, "When do we hear of women who, starting out of obscurity, boldly claim respect on account of their great abilities or daring virtues? Where are they to be found?"[2] Almost immediately Hays took advantage of Wollstonecraft's experience as writer and editor and asked her to comment on the introduction to the manuscript of *Letters and Essays, Moral, and Miscellaneous* that Hays was preparing for publication. Wollstonecraft's response to the piece was famously severe. She admonished Hays for her dependence on the "*shouldering up* of Dr this or that," that is, broadcasting the value of her work on the basis of the private approval of learned men. Wollstonecraft's advice was crucial to Hays's development as a professional woman writer, but she failed to understand the complexity of Hays's project in becoming learned by any means available to a Nonconformist woman.[3]

Wollstonecraft's astute blast signaled the next phase in Hays's education. She had lived for a decade now overstating her gratitude for the kindness of studious men, much of it helpful instruction. Wollstonecraft struck at the heart of Hays's dilemma: to be good and pleasing, or to be honest and useful. Wollstonecraft's warning was directed to Hays as both woman writer and aspiring female professional and likely, to herself as well. Wollstonecraft's reactions were sharper than Hays's textual postures may have warranted. After all, thus far in her own public career, Wollstonecraft too had depended on the help of generous men—Richard Price, Joseph Johnson, James Burgh, Thomas Christie, and even Henry Fuseli.[4] Hays needed the dose of reality that Wollstonecraft provided, but perhaps her new female mentor served it laced with asperity because she recognized in her apprentice's supine postures her own deep desire for recognition from more powerful men. As the future proved, like Hays, Wollstonecraft continued to depend on men who could advance her ambitions, such as publishers, and those who could fulfill her desires as lovers. Wollstonecraft imagined herself the "first of a new genus" of professional women writers, but, as Hays's experience demonstrates, she was not the only one to emerge at this time.[5]

Before she met Wollstonecraft, Hays's tactic in balancing intellectual and gender imperatives was to hover at the periphery of the male culture of teaching and learning. Most recently, she had participated as a shadow student at New College, relishing the unusual attentions accorded her in that male arena. At the same time, she met with gendered obstacles in her pursuit of intellectual attainment, and was conscious of the gendering of the knowledge she sought to attain. Uncertain access to teachers and texts was the chief impediment; when she had direct contact with books, lectures, sermons, and generous men, learning came easily, even joyously, to her. Stimulated by the company of mostly male, erudite Unitarians she hoped to communicate what she learned, both the struggle to achieve and the knowledge attained. She chose as her audience the one most likely to be receptive to what she had to say: other women, perhaps less ambitious but of similar sympathies, like the Unitarian wives and daughters she knew. The more she mingled with Rational Dissenting and Unitarian *philosophes* and the more she read of the republic of letters, the more she became convinced that disadvantages of education and arbitrary cultural expectations, rather than disparities in natural or innate abilities, produced the obvious differences in understanding and achievement between men and women. She studied everything she could that touched on the subject of human cognition to make sense of her own experience, as well as to explain the history and causes of women's subjugation. At the end of 1792, Wollstonecraft as thinker, writer, and woman changed Hays's life. *Letters and Essays, Moral, and Miscellaneous*, Hays's first book, published in March 1793, announced her profession as a radical controversialist and proto-feminist.

Supporter: Hugh Worthington

Hays had turned to Rational Dissenting leaders as the only viable vehicle for her unconventional ambitions. She initiated contact with Hugh Worthington, a former tutor in Classics and Logic at New College, a preacher at Salter's Hall meeting house, as she had with Robert Robinson. After hearing Worthington preach, Hays wrote a letter to him praising his performance. Worthington, an avuncular man and popular minister, responded in characteristically flattering terms, and welcomed Hays with her sister Elizabeth to his congregation.[6] Hays quickly engaged Worthington in discussions of thorny theological issues like the death of Christ that she had raised earlier with Robert Robinson, and exchanged visits with Worthington and his wife Susanna. In the course of their frequent correspondence and meetings over the next two years, Worthington cheered on Hays's self-learning, including her study of Lavater's theories of physiognomy and French. He particularly applauded her determination to learn mathematics, commiserating with her on the difficulties of geometry.[7] The study of mathematics, likely undertaken at the advice of William Frend, was important in several ways to Hays: as a way to share Frend's academic training and interests; as an enlightened, because independent, mental exercise;[8] and as the key to a mystery that formed the basis of other categories of scientific knowledge. Worthington lauded Hays for her exertions at theology and mathematics, remarking that these were not subjects usually studied by women.[9]

Worthington easily adopted the pattern Hays had established first with Robinson, then Disney, providing her with his writings that they subsequently discussed in person.[10] He continued to be gallant, complimenting both Hays sisters for their uncommon interests.[11] Yet for all his attentions to Hays, Worthington also dealt with her as a competent mind. Hays was eager to learn everything, and Worthington helped her as best he could.

When Worthington and his wife came to tea at Gainsford Street in early July 1792, he urged Hays to teach and instruct others on the basis of her performance in *Cursory Remarks* and ongoing studies. Here was the opportunity she had been preparing for. After their visit, Hays wrote to ask if he were in earnest. She explained demurely that whatever learning he credited Eusebia with was originally garnered in the hopes that she would be equipped to fulfill the duties of a wife and mother. These hopes, she explained, were tragically cut short by John Eccles's death. Disingenuously, she assured him that when she began to study and write, she never imagined assuming the public title of "authoress," quickly adding she did not "denigrate" it. If Worthington were serious in his suggestion, she proposed to show him some short pieces she had already written, works that she deemed "more affecting" than fiction because "drawn from truth." If Worthington judged that Hays's pieces were not sufficient to make a book, her sister Elizabeth might also have some texts to contribute. Her only stipulation was that he read her manuscript as she wrote; her willingness to move forward rested on his continuing estimation of her talent.[12] Whether this was rhetorical or real dependence is unclear. Hays seized the moment. In the next weeks and months she sent Worthington the introduction and other sections of her manuscript for his review and comment.

Worthington proved to be a sympathetic, if uncritical, supporter. In August of 1792, he wrote Hays to discuss the progress of her project. The plan for her to write and for him to read and comment was already in process. He remarked in glowing terms on what he had read, especially commending the introductory piece.[13] Buoyed by his attentions, Hays continued to gather existing pieces and write new ones to complete her manuscript, a work that would attest to her deepening commitment to the vital connections among religious freedom, political struggle, and women's need for instruction on these crucial issues.

Mentor: Mary Wollstonecraft

George Dyer took on the long distance intellectual nurturing that Robinson had provided Hays. When Wollstonecraft's *Vindication of the Rights of Woman* appeared in 1792, he gave a copy to Hays, knowing that she would respond to it passionately. Hays tore through the *Vindication*, marking certain passages and sharing the book with her sister.[14] She then wrote an enthusiastic letter to Wollstonecraft, praising her for courageously raising the neglected issue of women's natural rights. Hays also requested a personal interview, intrigued to learn more about the author who announced herself as a female critic of the gendered status quo. Hays likely also considered whether and how Wollstonecraft might help further Hays's public ambitions. Wollstonecraft, busy with her own professional and private affairs, made time to meet Hays, first at Joseph Johnson's convivial shop in St Paul's Churchyard, and later at her own place at Store Street, Bedford Square. When they met, Hays immediately recognized Wollstonecraft as a genius, as one unique person among ten million others. Hays described the feelings that Wollstonecraft evoked by her presence: "fear and reverence, admiration and esteem."[15] This impression coincided with Wollstonecraft's presentation of herself as fiercely independent, self-confident in her public authority, and already seasoned in the hurly burly of London publishing under Johnson's aegis. The dynamic between the two women was established: Wollstonecraft, the trailblazer as female mentor, Hays the devout if curious woman as her apprentice.[16]

Wollstonecraft prepared to leave for Paris in late 1792. Hays asked her to read *Cursory Remarks* before she left, as well the manuscript of *Letters and Essays*. Worthington's soothing flow of assurances about her manuscript continued to buoy Hays. Wollstonecraft's reactions contrasted sharply with his. After reading *Cursory Remarks*, Wollstonecraft fired back a short note giving Hays a lesson in female professionalism in crisp prose. Her initial impression was that Hays's pamphlet displayed fewer of the stylistic sins of exaggeration commonly committed by lady writers of light publications than Wollstonecraft expected, a topic of particular interest to her.[17] Wollstonecraft commented on the lack of clarity in Hays's prose, but assured her that practice would improve this fault.[18] Thus Wollstonecraft refused to cosset Hays just because she too was an anomaly, a woman who aspired to contribute to the republic of letters.[19]

Hays then sent Wollstonecraft the manuscript of *Letters and Essays* with the request that she read the work and show it to Johnson for possible publication. Wollstonecraft promptly replied that Johnson had agreed to consider Hays's project, and had asked to review the contents. Wollstonecraft cautioned Hays that the decision to publish or not was Johnson's, and that she would make no attempt on Hays's behalf to persuade him. In a sharp aside, Wollstonecraft reproved Hays for stooping to banal flattery in having spoken of the honor it would be to have Johnson publish her work, presumably in the note she had enclosed for Wollstonecraft to give him. Wollstonecraft was adamant that a woman professional should not behave like a serving maid waiting on her master's favor.

Wollstonecraft reacted even more vehemently to the preface to *Letters and Essays* that Worthington had praised. Wollstonecraft rejected Hays's pet defenses of her own work, particularly as they shifted responsibility for her errors to the disadvantages of female education. Wollstonecraft thundered back that this provided no excuse for inferior writing, much less publishing; if a writer did not possess the competence and will to overcome such difficulties, then common sense directed that writer to leave the work to others who could and did. Wollstonecraft's perspicacity derived perhaps from her own complex responses to exposing the female self in public. She condemned Hays's "false humility," as if Eusebia, the respected religious matron, had masqueraded as a girlish, subservient neophyte. Wollstonecraft reserved her severest criticism for the last paragraph of Hays's preface, skewering Hays for its vanity. She punctured Hays's fantasy that representing herself as the overly grateful acolyte of eminent men would somehow neutralize the brutal realities of gender and publicity. "Your male friends will still treat you like a woman," Wollstonecraft barked, predicting that even Priestley would think twice about publicly approving such a display of female erudition.

Worthington, too, commented on the emerging note of narcissism, even self-congratulation, in Hays's communications. Writing in September 1792, he replied to her concerns that after a recent severe illness, her "beauty had consumed away like a moth."[20] Worthington did not provide details about the illness, but vanity about her appearance was new to Hays, now perhaps a reflection of her growing sense of self-worth at becoming a professional writer and her expanding contact with some of the most stimulating people of the day. Worthington questioned whether her complaint about her looks arose from current humility, past complacency, or the reverse.

Hays also asked Frend and Dyer to review her manuscript. That autumn, Frend was consumed with the fallout from publication of his *Peace and Union Recommended* and getting ready for his University trial.[21] In his obliging way, Dyer served as messenger for Hays. Dyer included a short note in the parcel of her papers that Frend was about to return to her that included Frend's editorial comments and changes. Dyer reported Frend's overall pleasure in the manuscript. Dyer offered to read proof sheets if Hays desired, assuring her sympathetically that he had suffered the want of a friendly eye to catch the errors in his own texts before publication.

Joseph Johnson decided not to publish *Letters and Essays*; instead, the bookseller Thomas Knott, who had published *Cursory Remarks* two years before, agreed to take it.[22] Shortly before the book appeared, Hays described her pre-publication jitters to Worthington, who responded in his usual, consoling manner, predicting that if some readers criticized it, many more would sing its praises.[23] Worthington accurately predicted the response of liberal readers, but proved wrong about more conservative ones.

Letters and Essays, Moral, and Miscellaneous

Letters and Essays, Moral, and Miscellaneous was directed to a friendly female audience, mediated through the prisms of predominantly male scholarship and pedagogy. The book was published in March 1793, and dedicated to John Disney,[24] who had recently gained greater prominence by succeeding to the ministry of Essex Street Chapel on Theophilus Lindsey's retirement. Hays capitalized on historian Catharine Macaulay's *Letters on Education* (1790) and Wollstonecraft's *Rights of Woman* to break new ground by appropriating the female conduct book that hectored women,[25] transforming it into a dynamic vehicle for instructional curricula for them, adapted from the male education at New College. Hays had listened carefully to discussions about both pedagogy and academic substance at this newest Rational Dissenting academy, one that had benefited from tutors' previous experiences at elite academies such as Daventry and Warrington. Her efforts were solitary, compared with the *philosophes'* collective deliberations about curricula at New College. But Hays followed the tutors' leads in explaining abstruse, if politically charged, concepts for women. *Letters and Essays* functions as a primer of Rational Dissent for female readers, as well as a palimpsest that reveals the growth in Hays's understanding and her concomitant anxiety, as she reformulates what she had recently learned.

Letters and Essays brings together several elements of Hays's previous education—rational faith, Rational Dissenting skepticism, the poetry and fictions of Sensibility, philosophical study, Materialism and Necessity—in the context of Wollstonecraft's critique of gender, but newly applied to the realities of female life that Hays knows firsthand. The narrator is a woman teacher/preacher instructing an imagined female audience in imitation of Robinson and Wollstonecraft. Like *Cursory Remarks*, *Letters and Essays* opens with an apology, one that is immediately transformed into a vindication of the writer and her method, Hays advises her readers that the various pieces are sketches rather than finished works. Thanks to Wollstonecraft's teachings, Hays can explain why. The profound defects in cognitive training for women, and the consequent lack of knowledge and skills among intellectually curious women continue to render them ignorant, ineffectual, and frustrated. Therefore, practicing unaccustomed restraint, Hays offers an apology to the critical reader (Gilbert Wakefield, perhaps?), who may fault her efforts as illogical or inconclusive.[26] If this sounds like special pleading, then Hays accepts that it is so. Women are not educated like men, and therefore they cannot be judged by the same standards, but if similarly trained, women might surprise men with their competence in every human enterprise.

Hays's first statements reveal the sea change she experiences from earnest novice to hopeful public woman intellectual. She makes a case for the effects of gender instead of echoing Eusebia's expression of hurt feelings at Wakefield's sexual innuendos. Nonetheless, her feminine sense of insuperable disabilities persists. She quotes Wollstonecraft on the insufficiency of female education to produce women with vigorous intellects or clear judgment. In the absence of such improvements, Hays acknowledges with "a mixture of indignation and regret" that *Letters and Essays* exposes her own deficiencies in reasoning and writing that better-trained readers (Wakefield again?) may "censure as unconnected, or inconclusive."[27] She claims that improvements in women's education are in the interest of all humanity. She responds to the historical anxiety that learning distracts women from their appropriate reproductive and domestic duties with the argument that it is rather socially imposed ostentation and social competition, "not the acquirement of knowledge, [that] is the most likely to take women out of their families."[28]

For Hays, female enlightenment derives from Wollstonecraft's stark insights into the realities of the inequalities between men and women. Early in *Letters and Essays* Hays pays public homage to Wollstonecraft, adapting her mentor's words to Unitarian principles. Hays lauds Wollstonecraft's courageous advocacy of women's mental competence and her piercing analysis that female weakness is the result of social conditioning, not innate limitations.[29] Hays identifies the rights of woman, "founded on nature, reason, and justice," as the basis of her personal feminism.[30]

The narrative voice throughout *Letters and Essays* is strikingly more assured than in *Cursory Remarks*, due partly to Wollstonecraft's influence, and partly to Hays's independent reading and writing. *Letters and Essays* conveys her appetite for leadership, as well as scholarship, the former whetted by the latter, and vice versa. If she could not be trained with the male students at New College to be credentialed and work as a tutor and teach, she could at least construct her own virtual academy where, though on her own, she was in control.

Letters and Essays reveals the breadth of Hays's autodidactism in the early 1790s and her purposeful, if idiosyncratic, intellectual genealogy. Like archaeological strata in an excavation, the allusions to and quotations from specific works and their dates of publication suggest a hypothetical chronology of Hays's contact with particular sources and cultural currents. Hays quotes extensively in *Letters and Essays* from the poetry of Sensibility she read as an adolescent, as she did in the love letters: James Beattie, Mark Akenside, William Shenstone, Robert Blair, Isaac Watts, James Thomson. She includes excerpts from the English authors, poets, and moral essayists that she studied as a middle class young woman of "polished education."[31] Hays refers to and quotes from Continental works available in English translation, including Rousseau and Goethe.[32]

Hays alludes to serious historical books, some in English translation from the originals: Voltaire, Rollin (perhaps recommended by Frend[33]), Hume, Sully, Stuart, Wraxall, and several histories of Christina, Queen of Sweden. There are allusions to lighter texts: *The Art of Cookery, Made Plain and Easy; Which far exceeds any Thing of the Kind ever yet Published* (1747), which Hays refers to by its popular name, "Mrs. Glasse's Art of Cookery,"[34] English and Scottish ballads, and the then recently published poetry of Robert Burns.

Hays deliberately cites works that identify her as a theological and political radical to establish her credentials among her intended audience.[35] She is explicit in her advocacy of the right to private judgment, the need for increased toleration, and the consequent separation of church and state.[36] Echoing the cadences of

Robinson's earthly faith, Hays writes, "So long as Christianity is kept distinct from civil polity, it will fall like a rich dew, fructifying and fertilizing the human character."[37] She cannot resist the temptation to disparage Roman Catholic "priestcraft," as in Huguenot France, that seeks to yoke church and state together to impose a rigid, universal system of belief that keeps God at several removes from the individual. This is a tactic she learned from Robinson's texts: use the errors of the past to alert Nonconformists to the perils in the present.[38]

Like her radical associates in 1793, Hays felt compelled to comment on the cataclysmic events that took place in France in the summer and fall of 1792, particularly the September massacre and the abolition of the monarchy.[39] In "Thoughts on Civil Liberty," she confesses that she quails at the idea of revolution because suffering for the benefit of others inevitably leads to martyrdom. Unlike her more zealous associates, Hays voices an equivocal blend of republicanism and fear at the turbulence in France. She acknowledges that unrepresentative political institutions will prove unstable, and that feudal structures are ripe to fall. Like Robinson, she associates political currents in France and England, expostulating "that all monarchical and aristocratical governments, carry within themselves the seeds of their dissolution,"[40] a view derived from Part Two of Thomas Paine's *Rights of Man,* published in 1791–92. Repression leads to rebellion, Hays argues, because institutions, "when they become corrupt and oppressive to a certain degree, the effects must necessarily be murmurs, remonstrances, and revolt." So it was in France. She predicts it could be so in Britain, like her fellow Jacobins reversing dire conservative warnings about the contagion of imminent revolution. Change must come; the question is whether it will be deliberate and gradual or explosive.

However, the recent eruptions in France give Hays pause about the general diffusion of radical political knowledge. In a change of mind, she points to the ongoing violence in the aftermath of the Revolution as a demonstration of the danger when conflicting interests claim those rights in the name of constituencies that refuse to find common ground. Hays doubles back on herself, remarking in a footnote to this passage that, "The above observations were written while the public mind was agitated with the account of the massacres and popular insurrections in Paris,"[41] events, she observes, produced by temporary public passions that are manipulated by republicans concerned about counter-revolution. Perhaps the original passage provoked comment from Frend when he read Hays's manuscript and she modified her opinion to reflect his. Frend and many of his colleagues saw the French Revolution as the gateway to unprecedented possibilities for greater dispersion of human freedom.[42]

Hays's concluding view in this letter, like that of her English Jacobin confederates, is that in an enlightened nation, such violent eruptions are temporary, and should not be confused with the principles that produced them. Though no advocate of the French royal family's cause, she pities them as individuals. Hays thus distances herself not only from the exaggerated rhetoric Burke used in denouncing Richard Price's elation at the Revolution, but also from Wollstonecraft's critique of Burke's manipulative representation of current events in his *Reflections on the Revolution in France* (1790). Hays takes the long view of the turbulent present, borrowing a page from Robinson's history of the Huguenots. She expresses sympathy for the French king and his dependents; like everyone else, they are the products of early prejudices and associations; the royals' minds have not been trained to deal with adversity. Hays insists that thoughtfulness teaches toleration, not exoneration. Even justice must be softened with empathy.

If she seems to equivocate, Hays represents her position as objective and philosophical, taking in all points of view. She concludes the letter by comparing the European body politic to the human body, struggling to rid itself of ill humors, yet vulnerable to the remedy that may destroy the organism it attempts to cure. She quotes David Hartley's apocalyptic prophecy that the "vice and impiety that over-runs every state in Christendom" will inevitably end in "all the forms of government that subsist at present in the Christian countries of Europe," a more dire expectation than the millennial optimism of Robinson and Priestley.[43]

Letters and Essays is filled with Hays's interest in the new science of the mind, applying it to herself and others, and even to the French royal family. She makes frequent use of new principles of mental classification to organize her reading and thinking. Two recent books were useful to her: Lavater's *Essays on Physiognomy*,[44] and William Enfield's translation from the Latin of Brucker's magisterial *History of Philosophy*, published by Johnson in 1791.[45] Both referred to Priestley's brand of optimistic materialism, which had a profound effect on Hays, as it did on many of the people she read and studied with. Roy Porter explains that following Locke, Hartley, and Priestley, British radicals like Hays understood the self "as a dynamic, interactive development of the human powers, the flesh bodying forth consciousness and consciousness turning the being from something low and self-regarding into a higher entity." Hartley, Porter advises, hypothesized that "within God's providential plan, man thus made himself: self or personality was not a given but a potential, something which in every way developed."[46] Hays recognized this potential as the engine of female freedom.[47] Hartley posited mind and body were integral parts of the human whole with an innate moral sense as the hinge between the two.[48] External human expression could be interpreted to signify internal states and casts of thought, as well as outer appearances.

Johann Caspar Lavater (1741–1801) erected his theories of physiognomy on this conceptual groundwork. He claimed that through careful observations physiognomy could explain the inner being from its external manifestations.[49] Even a "raw adventurer" in mental science like Hays could confidently deploy physiognomy as a helpful aid in understanding the human mind. Hays did more than parrot Lavater's system. She adapted it for her own uses in her early attempts at life-writing (See Chapter Four). Hays applied the system inward to her own perceptions, intuitions, emotions, ideas, and, at the same time, outward to those of other people. Hays knew herself to be powerfully responsive; instead of passively experiencing the play of external sensation on her like an Aeolian harp, here was a set of tools with which she could construct meaning out of the welter of others' reactions to her and her reactions to these.

Physiognomy, as Lavater theorized, offered Hays mental taxonomy for lived experience. By contrast and as complement, Enfield's adaptation and translation of Brucker's *History of Philosophy* supplied classifications for understanding the history of ideas. Intended by Enfield for lazy male students who would not read the original in Latin, his English translation allowed Hays to survey the sweep of intellectual history in nicely ordered fashion for the first time. Enfield modified Brucker's treatise for his own theological and temperamental purposes.[50] But Hays could not tell the difference, having read neither Brucker in Latin, nor the texts in the original languages that Brucker translated and Enfield then adapted. Like any attentive tourist what she could do with Enfield's guided tour was to peer knowingly at the landscape of the past to distinguish the landmarks of progressive enlightenment. "Look back through the history of the world," she directed her readers, "from its golden days of infancy and innocence, to the maturity of the present times, and you will discern various truths, first dawning like the sun."[51] Ideas, in common with those who conceived them, evolved as part of the providential plan. Hays was quick to use Enfield's text to credential herself as a public intellectual. With his book in hand, she became knowledgeable about the history of the history of ideas, familiar with philosophic terms and figures, and, like her male associates, could compare and connect the present with the past. She felt free to experiment with the content, as well as the categories, of Enfield's work.[52]

In *Letters and Essays* Hays combined the psycho-perceptual dynamics described by Locke and Hartley with Rousseau's ethical pedagogy to convince women that their first responsibility was to educate themselves and their daughters. "Letter No. VII.," "to Mrs.____ on reading Romances, &c." addresses that most difficult maternal task—of supervising the enthusiasms of an adolescent daughter. It began reassuringly, tempering Mrs.____'s alarm at the interest her young daughter, Elizabeth, demonstrated in novels and romances.[53] Even in dealing with a girl on the cusp of womanhood, authority must not be arbitrary. The wise mother, Hays wrote, should read and discuss books with her daughter, respecting her choices and opinions, rather than dictate to her. Like Wollstonecraft, Hays preached that a mother must be mindful that she was educating a future teacher of the young, "train[ing] [her] to virtue,"[54] a reference to Rousseau's *Emile*. In contrast to Wollstonecraft and Worthington,[55] Hays endorsed novel reading for women where enthusiasm could foster associations that strengthened the mind.[56]

Hays prefaced a recommended course of reading for Elizabeth with an appeal that made reference to an afterlife where the mind had no gender. "Remember you were born for immortality," she counseled, "not merely for the solace of man, but for those regions where there will be neither marrying, nor giving in marriage."[57]

She informed her reader that disdain for women's complicity in their own mental subordination and deliberate dependence on men provoked Christina, Queen of Sweden, to distance herself from other women. Hays quotes an infamous line from Christina, "I would become a *man*," "but it is not that I love men because they are men, but merely that they are not women."[58] Hays's reference to Christina attests to her advocacy of idealized feminine authority, universal tolerance, and unblinking skepticism. As queen, Christina was renowned for being tough but fair, encouraging learning and the arts, intervening for good and ill in the careers of learned men and women. She abdicated the throne to be free herself, left Sweden, dressed, walked, and cursed like a man, and converted from Lutheranism to Catholicism. She possessed wit, learning, courage, ambition, and, Hays added in the interests of truth, vindictiveness. Mothers and daughters might be intrigued: this was hardly a boring dead man from a musty history book.[59]

Hays advises Elizabeth's mother to encourage her daughter's intellectual transition from reading fiction, which she sees as arousing adolescent fantasies without benefit (perhaps echoing Worthington) to the essays of Addison and Steele that entertained as they instructed, to biography, to history, and from these to philosophical, political, moral, and religious truth. This progression was Hays's amendment of Priestley's didactic progression for men, proposed here in gendered terms for a female student. In doing so, she emphasizes the study of individual lives as they reveal the complexity of human character, the imperative of moral choice, and the sufficiency of human reason.[60] She selected particular titles from Priestley's syllabus for study of the past, ancient, contemporary, and local.[61] In the aftermath of the French Revolution, women, too, she judged, should have information that improves their minds and "liberalize[s]" their understanding by "tracing the fate of nations, and the rise and fall of empires."[62]

Letters and Essays includes four letters to "Amasia," a biblical name[63] that suggested feminine erudition based on the sharing of knowledge between two women, with respect to which Hays takes the lead. In these texts, Hays treats major philosophical and theological concepts—Materialism and Necessity, Authority and Hierarchy, the Calvinist concept of original sin, separation of church and state, the next world, theory of dreams, the presence of evil—in a meditative rather than zealous manner, referring to various sources: Rousseau, Goethe, Voltaire, Lavater, Price, Priestley, Hartley, Montesquieu, Locke, Sterne, Pope, Wollstonecraft, the Bible, and her own experience. She insists that her understanding has not been acquired, and is not the product of that feminine intuition historically attributed to women in the absence of masculine powers of reason.[64] "I do not pretend to *intuitive* genius, or knowledge by inspiration"; she advised, "my ideas are the result of having had leisure for reading and inquiry."[65] Current restrictions on female education have produced gendered differences in intellectual achievement, but not in human potential, or women's willingness to work hard to attain knowledge. The female mind can reason as well as intuit and enthuse. Hays demystifies learning, making transparent how she thinks through an idea. For example, she takes exception to Amasia's practice not to consult books for others' views on important subjects because, Amasia judges it is "plagiarism to adopt the opinions of others: pardon me, if I presume … to differ!" Hays insists that the accumulation of knowledge is part of the providential plan, and that every man and woman has the responsibility to participate in the process that otherwise is retarded. "How slow would be the attainments of the most ingenious and acute unassisted mind!" Hays describes the method by which she learns, the mental twists and turns by which understanding is achieved, and demonstrates that the female mind can be trained equally with the male. "Did we not avail ourselves of (though not servily copy) the wisdom and labour of past ages, arts and sciences would be ever in their infancy, and we should scarce ever rise above savage life." Learning is integral to collective improvement. "Everything is progressive: it is not in nature to produce perfection at once; and all that dignifies, adorns, and elevates life, has been the result."[66] Freethinkers are able to tolerate disagreement; ignorance makes us afraid of those who differ from us. Revising Wollstonecraft's exhortation, Hays urges, "Let us have the courage to trace our ideas, as far as we have the ability through their whole train of consequences; this can afford the only test of truth." She points out that even the revered scholar Erasmus was patient with his opponents. He remarked "that his most virulent enemies were among those, who had the least acquaintance either with him, or his writings," a reference to Enfield's *History*.[67] Hays is the object lesson from which other informally trained women might catch encouragement to learn how to learn.

Remarks in *Letters and Essays* display Hays's personal contact with several of the *philosophes* whose texts she incorporated, as well as her newfound sense of intellectual independence from her teachers. "Letter No. XV.," "To Amasia, on a future State," finds Hays thinking out loud about her uncertainty over the precise nature of the next world. She speculates, for example, on the possibility of an afterlife for both animals and humans. Much as she feels herself in Priestley's debt, she takes exception to his notion that life after death will be much like life in the here and now. Her own belief is that human desire for perfection reflects the individual's search for divine eternity.[68] At this speculative elevation, Hays describes her own experience of earthly paradise in which intellectual pleasures provide the only genuine and lasting happiness. As for the next world, Hays rhapsodizes that it will be the fulfillment of Unitarian visions: "I cannot conceive of greater happiness, than in the enjoyment of a society consisting only of the wise and virtuous; where there will be no jarring interests, no sordid passions, no narrow prejudices, nothing little, mean, or vile; add to this immortality, and what remains to be desired." She envisions an afterlife spent among idealized beings like Robinson, Frend, Priestley, Price, Lindsey, Disney, and Wollstonecraft, where she will join "the society of the just made perfect!" Surely, this would be Unitarian heaven.[69]

Hays subverts the classical epistle form, written from man to man about weighty subjects, by appropriating it to educate women in philosophy and theology. She finds philosophical justification for enlightened feminism in Priestley's version of "philosophic necessity" that rejected Cartesian duality, advocating that objective causal relations must obtain for mental experience just as Newton had demonstrated they did for natural phenomena. Hays notes that a male correspondent, perhaps Worthington, who read the philosophical essays in manuscript, had objected that she taxed her female reader with abstruse subjects. In response, she admonished him that God was critical of those who "wrap their talents in a napkin." St Paul's authoritative example validates those who do not hesitate to present "things hard to be understood ..." Hays insists that women, too, have a sacramental duty to expand their minds.[70]

Hays resists the historical imperative of women's hand work, the insistence that all women in every culture produce textiles, the very mark of confinement to the domestic realm.[71] Women's work is the justification for keeping them ignorant of anything else, fixed in behavior, and pursuing a socially sanctioned vanity, interested only in fashioning their appearance to please men. In "Letter No. IV." Hays situates her narrator in the privacy of the domestic enclosure where she expresses her sense of claustrophobia at the tedium of women's work, work that stifles the ambition to live the life of the mind. "I confess I am no advocate for cramping the minds and bodies of young girls," she writes, "by keeping them for ever poring over needlework." She gives an existential cry at observing young women still being required to learn intricate repetitive patterns in "the tapestry and tent-stitch of former times." She laments their "waste of eyes, spirits, and time ... nor do I think it so very important a part of female education as has generally been supposed."[72] Even in the familial domain, earthly existence is preparation for the divine, and women, too, must be elevated mentally and spiritually as preparation for paradise. Enlightenment should change women's work. "Surely the covering of the body ought not to be the sole business of life," Hays insists. She then shrewdly asks, "I doubt whether there will be any sewing in the next world, how then will those employ themselves who have done nothing else in this?"[73]

Hays identified in *Letters and Essays* with the ultra-progressive lineage of freethinkers—Priestley, Price, Hartley, Anthony Collins, extending back to Locke. Hays argues that women, too, might aspire to a vigorous intellect that is trained to resist constraints. "The emancipated mind," she wrote, "is impatient of imposition, nor can it, in a retrogade [sic] course, unlearn what it has learned, or unknow what it has known."[74] She couples this fierce declaration with avowals of the certainty of a benevolent Creator, misquoting from *Paradise Lost*, Book V, the Archangel Raphael's rapture to God.[75] Hays's creed was based on the doctrine of Materialism, the belief that all causes and effects happen within the physical world. She adhered to the complementary principle of Necessity or determinism that all causes and effects can be explained by pre-existing conditions. Under the laws of Materialism and Necessity the result follows inexorably from the cause. Hays explains that we are the creatures of a divine artist's fashioning from the matter of the physical universal, according to the necessity of his wise plan.[76] She explains that a necessarian—a believer in philosophical Necessity—would never sink into absolute despair or attempt suicide. Hays emulated Robinson's effusions, incorporating the work of other writers in her own to orchestrate a final chorus of hallelujahs to God's perfection in the light of current struggles.

For all the quotations from the work of other writers, *Letters and Essays* is noticeably barren of references to Hays's female writing contemporaries, except for Wollstonecraft. By 1793 Charlotte Smith, Mary Robinson, and Helen Maria Williams had all published. Most surprising of all is that Hays never alludes to or quotes from the substantial body of work of Anna Barbauld, the leading female Rational Dissenter of the time, except when she cites Dyer's encomiums on female lovers of liberty. The paucity of allusions to other women writers suggests Hays's ambivalence about sharing the spotlight with them and presages her later competitiveness with them, particularly Elizabeth Hamilton, which would recoil against her.

Reviews

Only men's assessments of *Letters and Essays* survive. Lindsey wrote to thank Hays for her gift of a copy,[77] applauding an achievement that raised his estimation of Eusebia even higher. He particularly liked her treatment of philosophical matters, including "the scarecrow doctrine of Necessity [that] you have known how to strip of the horrid form, and familiarize and make it easy, and I think to vindicate its truth, to those who will read and make use of their understandings." He praised her, as had Robinson and Worthington, for her pious energy that sought to serve God and inspire others to do so, too.[78] This was high praise from Lindsey, and there was more to come. Hugh Worthington wrote jovial congratulations to Hays for the style and sense of her book, thanking her for the gift of an inscribed copy.[79] *The New Annual Register*, a progressive publication, complimented the book as "correct and elegant."[80] Dyer had spoken on Hays's behalf to Joseph Johnson about a notice in his progressive periodical, the *Analytical Review*, where Wollstonecraft was an editor and reviewer; the September issue included an encouraging discussion of *Letters and Essays* that was the first to identify it as a woman-centered work. Hays was praised for successfully advancing the rights of women initiated by "an enlightened female philosopher"—that is, Wollstonecraft. The reviewer applauded Hays for transcending gender restrictions dictated to women writers by "the tyranny of example and custom," and for leading her female readers beyond the accustomed frivolity of fiction to philosophy, politics, metaphysics, and theology. The critic judged the style not as elegant as other women's, but concluded Hays compensated for this with her observations on morals, and her ability to explain speculative debates to her female readers.[81] The review identified Hays as a translator of and commentator on other people's ideas rather than as an original thinker, and included a long excerpt from "Letter No. VII.," "On reading Romances."[82]

The reviewer for the *Critical Review* took a more conservative view of the book. He acknowledged Hays as an advocate of the liberal "Priestleian [sic] school" and praised her comprehension of philosophy and theology, quoting from her letter on salvation. But the critic could not endorse what he characterized as Hays's "sneering" at woman's traditional work, particularly cooking. Here the critic felt compelled to

> confess ourselves touched in a tender point; for though women, who are more like angels, may be above these low gratifications, men are not; and we freely acknowledge that the delicacies with which our good ladies have occasionally regaled us, have given us a great respect for the said Mrs. Glasse, and as, unfortunately, we are not possessed of the skill to make ourselves the various good things they treat us of, we do hereby enter our protest against her treatise being left out of the library of any female, be she Unitarian, Trinitarian, Arian, or supra lapsarian.[83]

The critic for the conservative *English Review* disagreed on every count with his more liberal colleagues. He warned female readers about the book's dangerous sentiments that threatened existing social, religious, and domestic hierarchies. A letter to Hays from John Evans, also a Rational Dissenting minister, undated but obviously sent sometime in 1793, included a copy of the review. Evans maintained that "the malignity" of the review was "beneath her notice."[84] Evans prefaced the excerpts he had copied with the disclaimer that the reviewer was clearly prejudiced against Wollstonecraft and her disciples as representative of Jacobin sympathies. Evans noted that the worst attacks were directed at the sections in Hays's book that advocated improved education for women and that the critic linked her advocacy of improved female education with her radical political views. Evan accurately assessed the review.

The conservative critic's opinion of *Letters and Essays* merged the person of the unattractive author and her thinning hair with her nasty ideas in a cunning pun, exploiting her opening apology by suggesting that she might have spared herself the trouble of producing such trash. Evans's transcription read, in part: "These are sketches and outlines but the question is whether the public is indebted to this Lady for them — perhaps a mere whisper from Mary Hays may be gratifying to the public ear — the baldest disciple of Mrs. Wollstonecraft." The wretched literary performance, the critic asserted, was consistent with the unnatural ambitions of the female author and her immaturity, and, like all abominations against nature, failed. "These performances have all the marks of youth ungifted by genius and unformed by taste," he wrote. The reviewer was particularly harsh about Hays's first essay on the controversy with Gilbert Wakefield over public worship: "In the first number Miss Mary Hays conceives but her conceptions are an indigested heap and the whole of this paper is an abortion." He was particularly contemptuous of Hays's pretensions to knowledge, as he was of her assumption of authorial authority on learned subjects. "We despise," he wrote, "dogmas that originate in affected wisdom, and we are disgusted by flippancy and frivolousness that betray all the conceit of an half-educated female – such are the crude effusions of Mary Hays." He took especial offense at Hays's unfeminine hubris in trying to explain philosophical concepts to other women, which merely revealed her stupidity and demonstrated how deviant her ambitions were. "Female philosophers," he advised, "while pretending to superior powers carry with them (such is the goodness of providence) a mental imbecility which *damns* them to fame." The threat to domestic peace, he concluded ironically, was rather absurd than real. He particularly called attention to Hays's perverse disparaging of woman's work, opposing this with the argument that "even to mange her needle with dexterity (though there be no sewing in the next world) may be as rational a mode preparing herself for hereafter, as to weave the web of sophistry, in attempting to disprove the existence of an immortal soul!" "Soon," he predicted, "it will appear that to be a skillful housewife just as well accords with the female character as to be a quibbling necessarian."[85]

Hays had succeeded in making her voice heard in the ideological war between reformers and conservatives with each side parsing her book in predictable ways. The conservative reviewer recognized subversion in the cluster of radical ideas and thinkers she espoused. His response to *Letters and Essays* struck a new note among establishment opinion makers that reverberated through the decade and colored Hays's reputation for the next 150 years. The serpent of misogyny had now reared its ugly head, contaminating female aspirations with its venom. The Enlightenment dream that the mind was neither sexed nor gendered, a dream promoted and practiced by Hays and Wollstonecraft, was provoking increasingly vituperative public responses in the context of the "Reign of Terror" in France and its military conflict with Austria, Prussia, Holland, and Spain. In coupling the natural rights of woman with the Rational Dissenting right to private judgment and in appropriating Lockean psychology in defense of a rigorous education for women, Hays had achieved what she sought, as well as what she feared.[86] She had chosen sides in the emerging gender wars and she had learned that as in love, all was fair.

Notes

1   According to Anne F Wedd, in June 1792 George Dyer gave Hays a copy of Wollstonecraft's recently published *A Vindication of the Rights of Woman*.
2   *VRW*, "Observations on the State of Degradation to Which Woman is Reduced by Various Causes," p. 173.
3   Wollstonecraft to Hays, 25 November 1792, *Pforz.*, MW 35.
4   Helen Braithwaite writes, "Becoming a writer and earning a full-time living by her pen was not Mary Wollstonecraft's own idea. It was first suggested and, then,

repeatedly impressed upon her by close male friends and it was largely owing to the sympathetic support of men that she was encouraged to try and write her way to independence ... at St Paul's Churchyard, MW met and conversed with male intellectuals, exchanging ideas which filter directly into her books and gained intellectually, if not always emotionally, from her encounters ... She had almost certainly looked at male-authored works which touch sympathetically on women's issues, such as James Burgh's *Dignity of Human Nature*. In turn, young male writers of her generation — Thomas Christie, George Dyer and Thomas Cooper — all come into contact with her and/or her ideas, which they positively refer to in their works." Personal communication, 1 December 2004.

5   See Mary A. Waters's cogent argument in "'The first of a new genus:' Mary Wollstonecraft, Mary Hays, and the *Analytical Review*," *British Women Writers and the Profession of Literary Criticism, 1789–1832* (Houndmills, 2004), pp. 86–120.

6   Hugh Worthington to Hays, 16 June 1791, *DWL*, 24, 93 (9).

7   Hugh Worthington to Hays, 17 January 1794, *DWL*, 24, 93 (18).

8   In his essay, "What is Enlightenment?" (1784), Immanuel Kant's definition included the use of "one's understanding without direction from another," in Isaac Kramnick (ed.), *The Portable Enlightenment Reader* (New York, 1995), p.1.

9   Hugh Worthington to Hays, 4 November 1791, *DWL*, 24, 93 (10).

10   Ibid. Worthington, like Robinson, argued for the benefits of multiple religious perspectives: "I resemble Dr. Price in one thing (would I did in 100 more) in being free from ye rage of Proselytetism [sic]; I wish all to think for themselves, & esteem ye circumstance of making them my Disciples, a very small matter compared with their being ye Disciples of Goodness."

11   Ibid.

12   Mary Hays to Hugh Worthington, 3 July 1792, in private hands.

13   Hugh Worthington to Mary Hays, 17 August 1792, *DWL*, uncatalogued.

14   Hays's copy of Wollstonecraft's text is part of the Pforzheimer Collection. Hays wrote her name in the volume, and the pages are covered with exclamations and brief notes.

15   Wedd, "The Story of Mary Hays," *The Love-Letters of Mary Hays 1779-1780* (London, 1925), p. 5.

16   Waters, "The first of a new genus," p. 88.

17   See, for example, Wollstonecraft's earlier review of Hester Lynch Piozzi's *Observations and Reflection, made in the Course of a Journey through France, Italy and Germany* (1789), in which Wollstonecraft judges that "From a lady who has had so many advantages, and whose knowledge of a dead language is so frequently displayed, we naturally expected more purity of style; yet we find in her journey all the childish feminine terms, which occur in common novels and thoughtless chat, sweet, lovely, dear dear, and many other pretty epithets and exclamations," *Analytical Review*, IV (1789): 127.

18   Wollstonecraft found "[f]ewer of the superlatives, exquisite, fascinating, &c, all of the feminine gender, than I expected. Some of the sentiments ... are rather obscurely expressed; but if you continue to write you will imperceptibly correct this fault and learn to think with more clearness, and consequently avoid the errours [sic] naturally produced by confusion of thought," Wollstonecraft to Hays, undated.

19   "In the [rhetorical] tradition of Catharine Macaulay Graham," Tania Smith argues, "Wollstonecraft advises that a female author behave as if the social equality she

promotes were already in existence. 'Let me remind you,' writes Wollstonecraft to her pupil, 'that when weakness claims indulgence it seems to justify the despotism of strength'. The ethos that Wollstonecraft describes, and Hays learns to practice, is itself a form of indirect persuasion to change the ways in which men and women, writers and publishers, speak and write to one another." "The Rhetorical Education of Eighteenth-Century British Women Writers," (unpublished Ph.D. diss., The Ohio State University, 2002), pp. 267–85. From another perspective, Waters identifies this as a crucial stage in the interactions between the two women. Wollstonecraft's professional position and "commissioned work as a staff writer reveals that she also stands as a landmark" in a new degree of professionalism for women writers, and her "role as a professional mentor, offering expert guidance to Hays, marks the first time in the history of British letters that such a relationship between two women writers can be traced," Waters, "The first of a new genus," p. 88.

20   "When thou with rebukes dost correct man for iniquity,/ Thou makest his beauty to consume away like a moth:/ Surely every man is vanity," Psalms 39:11.

21   Frend published *Peace and Union* in February 1793. He was charged with sedition for urging conciliation with rather than war against France to the British government.

22   Thomas Knott published Robert Robinson's *History of Baptism* (1790), as well as other Baptist and Rational Dissenting and Unitarian authors, including John Disney.

23   Hugh Worthington to Mary Hays, 9 December 1792, *DWL*, 24, 93 (16).

24   D.O. Thomas comments, "In addition to his clerical duties and his own publications J[ohn] D[isney] was generous in helping other authors, including Priestley and Lindsey," "Preface and Introduction to John Disney's Diary," *Enlightenment and Dissent*, 21(2002): 31.

25   Pam Morris provides a useful overview and recent critical assessments of more conventional late eighteenth-century conduct books for women, "General Introduction," *Conduct Literature for Women 1770-1830* (London, 2005), vol. 1, pp. ix–xxxvii.

26   Hays rearranges Wollstonecraft's text from Chapter II, "The Prevailing Opinion of a Sexual Character Discussed," *A Vindication of the Rights of Woman*, pp. 130–31. The passage actually reads: "This contempt of the understanding in early life has more baneful consequences than is commonly supposed; for the little knowledge which women of strong minds attain, is, from various circumstances, of a more desultory kind than the knowledge of men, and it is acquired more by sheer observations on real life, than from comparing what has been individually observed with the results of experience generalized by speculation. Led by their dependent situation and domestic employments more into society, what they learn is rather by snatches; and as learning is with them, in general, only a secondary thing, they do not pursue any one branch with that persevering ardour necessary to give vigour to the faculties, and clearness to the judgment."

27   *L&E*, "Preface," pp. 9–10.

28   Ibid., p. viii.

29   Hays characterizes Wollstonecraft as "the woman who has courageously and brilliantly attempted to rescue the female mind from those prejudices by which it has been systematically weakened, and which have been the canker of genuine virtue; for purity of heart can only be the result of knowledge and reflection," Ibid., p. vi.

30   Ibid.

31 Hays refers to Shakespeare's plays, Milton's *Paradise Lost* and *A Mask*, or *Comus*, Otway, Dryden, Samuel Johnson, Sterne, Fielding, Richardson, Charlotte Lennox, Steele and Addison, The Letters of Sir Thomas Fitzosborne (William Melmoth, the Younger), *The History of Lady Julia Mandeville* by Frances Brooke (1763), and Henry Mackenzie's *The Man of Feeling* (1771), reprinted in numerous editions, including the most recent in 1791.

32 A story by La-Roche in the *Mirror*, Voltaire's histories of France, *Persian Letters* by Charles de Secondat, baron de Montesquieu; *The Life of Petrarch. Collected from Memoires pour la vie de Petrarch* [by J.F.P.A. de Sade], trans. Susanna Dobson; Jean Francois Marmontel, *Le Diable Boiteux* (1707), by Alain René Le Sage; Goethe's *Sorrows of Werter* (1774); and, of course, Rousseau's *Emile* and *La Nouvelle Héloise*. In "Letter No. IV.," Hays adds a comment in a footnote: "Some years ago, when 'the Sorrows of Werter' were a subject of general conversation, from the number of elegant engravings, which it had occasioned, I wrote some observations upon it, which were inserted by a friend in the Universal Magazine, with my name affixed to them. A little time after, I found them to my great surprise (with some additions) at the conclusion of a new edition of the work, without being marked as a quotation, or any acknowledgment being made from when they were taken."

33 Frida Knight refers to Frend's correspondence with his younger half-sister Mary in which he urges her to be disciplined in reading Rollin's histories. Frida Knight, *University Rebel: The Life of William Frend (1757–1841)* (London, 1971), p. 45.

34 Mrs. Hannah Glasse wrote the first cookbook for women to use at home.

35 Locke, Richard Price, Priestley's *An Essay on a course of liberal education for civil and active life. With plans of lectures ... To which are added remarks on a Code of Education proposed by Dr. Brown in a late treatise entitled Thoughts on Civil Liberty (1765), A Philosophical Inquiry concerning Human Liberty. The fourth edition, corrected. [By Anthony Collins.] Republished with a preface, by Joseph Priestley; and A discourse on occasion of the death of Dr. Price: delivered at Hackney, on Sunday, May 1, 1791*, published by Johnson; "Discourse on the character of Judas by Mr. Walker of Nottingham," probably Hays's shorthand for *The Dissenter's Plea: or the Appeal of the Dissenters to the justice, the honour, and the religion of the Kingdom, against the Test Laws.* [by] George Walker, F.R.S., Dissenting Minister at Nottingham (1790); David Hartley's *Observation on man, his frame, his duty, and his expectations. In two parts ...; to which are now added notes and additions to the second part; translated from the German of the Rev. Andrew Herman Pistorius*, published by Johnson in 1791; Dyer's *Poems* (1792); Robinson's *A Political Catechism*, and quotes from his lesser known works and letters to Hays; Wollstonecraft's second *Vindication*; Gilbert Wakefield's recent translation of the New Testament (1791), which Hays referred to in *Cursory Remarks*.

36 Anthony Page suggests that some of Hays's views may have been influenced by her connection with Ann Jebb, "'A Great Politicianess': Ann Jebb, Rational Dissent and politics in late eighteenth-century Britain," forthcoming.

37 *L&E*, "Letter to Mr.____ on the Meliorating and Beneficial Effects of Pulpit Elocution," p. 9.

38 G.M. Ditchfield points out that Baptist Robert Hall (1764–1831), who succeeded Robert Robinson as minister, published *An Apology for the Freedom of the Press, and for General Liberty ...* (London, 1793), that defended the separation of church and

state and freedom of the press: "In the present crisis of things," Hall wrote, "the danger to liberty is extreme," p. xvii.

39   Between 1791 and 1793, most of the liberal thinkers Hays knew, and many she was to meet, published personal manifestos on the issues of liberty and peace: Wollstonecraft's *A Vindication of the Rights of Men* (1790) was followed by the even more militant *A Vindication of the Rights of Woman* (1792). That same year, Dyer published *Poems* on the themes of freedom, peace, and toleration, followed in 1793 by his stirring *Complaint of the Poor People of England.* In February 1793, two ultra provocative works were published: William Frend argued his anti-war, anti-establishment positions in *Peace and Union Recommended* (1793), creating furor among his Cambridge colleagues; and William Godwin's comprehensive critique, *An Enquiry concerning the Principles of Political Justice, and its Influence on General Virtue and Happiness.*

40   *L&E*, "Letter No. II. Thoughts on Civil Liberty," p. 17.

41   Ibid., pp. 17–18.

42   The conservative *English Review* singled out these passages for particular attack: "In vain may Mary Hays exhibits her lucubrations to prove, that 'woman possesses the same powers as man' — that (as she modestly expresses herself) 'there is no sexual character' — and that 'the name of Wollstonecraft will go down to posterity with reverence;' ... Is it for woman (or for man either) — we cannot repress our indignation — to despise authority — to speak evil of dignities — to scoff at priests and kings — to point her sarcasms at the best of sovereigns, 'who, with paternal solicitude (she says) endeavours to guard his people from light and knowledge by royal proclamations' — and, to complete the climax of impertinence and malignity, 'by dragging the usurper to punishment, the victim of his usurpation.'" *The English Review*, 22 (October, 1793, second series): 253–7.

43   Kathryn Gleadle points to Hays's "Thoughts on Civil Liberty" as directed at a discrete and small audience in the culture wars, "British Women and Radical Politics in the Late Nonconformist Enlightenment, c. 1780–1830," in Amanda Vickery (ed.) *Women, Privilege, and Power: British Politics, 1750 to the Present* (Stanford, 2001), p. 139.

44   In English translation by Henry Fuseli, published by Joseph Johnson in 1791, and, in the same year, another translation by Thomas Holcroft, later a friend and critic of Hays's, published by G.G.J. and J. Robinson.

45   William Enfield, *The History of Philosophy: from the earliest times to the beginning of the present century: drawn up from Brucker's Historia Critica Philosophiae* (London, 1791). In a letter to Hays from Hugh Worthington dated 3 September 1792, he advised that she "take another draught of Enfield's excellent Philosophy" to calm her from the effects of her encounters with Wollstonecraft, and the attentions paid to *Cursory Remarks.*

46   Roy Porter, "Psychologizing the Self," *Flesh in the Age of Reason* (London, 2003), p. 360.

47   Isaac Kramnick points out that "materialist psychology, by eliminating the mind-body distinction, provided a scientific basis for the widespread belief that social and moral behavior could be changed by bodily discipline – by the application of pleasure and pain." Isaac Kramnick, "Joseph Priestley's Scientific Liberalism," *Bourgeois Radicalism and English Dissent: Political Ideology in Late Eighteenth-Century England and America* (Ithaca, 1990), p. 92.

48   Hartley, *Observation on Man*, pp. 30–31.

49   Ibid., p. 32.

50   For a publication history and commentary on Enfield's polemical interpretations, see John Christian Laursen, "Brucker in English and the Uses of the History of Philosophy in the Revolutionary Era," paper presented at Construction of the Past in Modern Political Philosophy, The Conference for the Study of Political Thought, Colorado Springs, 9–11 November 2001. I appreciate Professor Laursen allowing me to read his essay in manuscript.

51   *L&E*, p. 13.

52   Hays adapted Enfield, for example, in her crisp rendition of his lengthier description of Antisthenes, founder of the Cynic sect, in "Letter No. I." She also refuted Wakefield using an anecdote related in Enfield's *History of Philosophy* concerning Antisthenes, p. 299.

53   *L&E*, p. 86.

54   Ibid., p. 9.

55   Worthington spoke about novels in a fundraising address for New College that Hays may have heard. Worthington pointed to twin poles of study that produced no good: "Justly have we a mean opinion of them, who spend their time in nothing else than reading romances; but very little better ought we to think of those, who, having acquired the best knowledge, never make use of it to regulate their conduct." His belittling of novels and their readers anticipated Wollstonecraft's critique in *A Vindication of the Rights of Woman* the next year, and Jane Austen's ironic defense in *Northanger Abbey* (1817).

56   Hays "value[d] novels," like Richardson's *Clarissa*, as Miriam Wallace astutely comments, "as the natural beginning place for female education." Miriam Wallace, "Mary Hays's 'Female Philosopher,'" in Adriana Craciun and Kari El Lokke (eds), *Rebellious Hearts: British Women Writers and the French Revolution* (Albany, 2001), p. 241.

57   Hays echoes Wollstonecraft's invocation of this phrase from Luke at the end of her first novel, *Mary; A Fiction* (1788).

58   *L&E*, p. 92.

59   See Hays's account in *Female Biography, III*.

60   *L&E*, pp. 92–3.

61   Hays recommended, in translation when necessary, *History of Charles XIIth, King of Sweden/ translated from the last Geneva edition of M. de Voltaire, by W.S. Kenrick; to which is added, the life of Peter the Great*, trans. J. Johnson, M.A. (1780) and *The Age of Louis XIV; Ancient History* by Charles Rollin; *Memoirs of the Duke de Sully*, trans. Charlotte Lennox; the portrait of the "unfortunate" Mary of Scots in Gilbert Stuart's *The History of Scotland*; and *Wraxall's Memoirs of the Kings of France of the race of Valois*.

62   *L&E*, p. 97.

63   There are several Scriptural references to the name. "Amasia" was a geographical name for a city in ancient Asia Minor, according to James Orr, M.A., D.D. General Editor. "Entry for 'PONTUS.'" "International Standard Bible Encyclopedia." 1915. <http://www.searchgodsword.org/enc/isb/view.cgi?number=T7020>. Hays's use of the name may be derived from "Amasa, sparing the people," or "Amasai, strong" or "burdensome." "Amasi" was also the name of four men in the Old Testament and a

warrior in King David's army. Roswell D. Hitchcock, "Entry for 'Amasa.'" "An Interpreting   Dictionary   of   Scripture   Proper   Names."   1869. <http://www.biblestudytools.net/Dictionaries/HitckcocksBibleNames/hbn.cgi?number =T179>.

64   Michèle Le Doeuff, "Cast-offs, 1. How Intuition Came to Women," *The Sex of Knowing*, trans. Kathryn Hamer and Lorraine Code (New York, 2003), pp. 1–10.

65   *L&E*, p. 187.

66   Ibid., p. 174.

67   Ibid., p. 171.

68   Ibid., p. 203.

69   Ibid., p. 205. For an illuminating discussion of the theology of Lindsey and Disney, see D.O. Thomas, pp. 1–41. Thomas comments, "Lindsey's theodicy follows in the lines made familiar by Leibniz. God is omniscient, omnipotent and benevolently disposed to mankind," "Preface and introduction to John Disney's Diary," *Enlightenment and Dissent*, 21(2002): 23.

70   Ibid., p. 173.

71   See Elizabeth Wayland Barber's *Woman's Work: The First 20,000 Years* (New York, 1994).

72   *L&E*, "IV. Letter to Mrs. ____ with a Sketch of the Family of Sempronia," p. 33.

73   In "Letter No. IV" Hays tells the story of Sempronia and her daughters. Hays reiterates her view of the connection between female education and political theory that she noted in a letter to John Eccles. Sempronia, Hays writes, inculcates her daughters conventionally by "early train[ing] with unrelenting rigour to the duties of non-resistance and passive obedience," p. 34.

74   *L&E*, p. 16.

75   Milton, *Paradise Lost*, Book V, ll. 154–9:
      "Almighty! thine this universal frame,
      Thus wondrous fair: Thyself how wondrous then!
      Unspeakable! who sitt'st above these heavens
      To us invisible, or dimly seen
      In these thy lowest works; yet these declare
      Thy goodness beyond thought, and power divine."

76   D.O. Thomas quotes from Lindsey's *Conversations on the divine government* (1802), "There is nothing of which we can be so absolutely certain, or which is so clearly demonstrable to us as that there is an intelligent God and benevolent Creator of all things," p. 22.

77   The volume, with Lindsey's signature, is at *DWL*.

78   Lindsey wrote that the book attested to a "mind, turned to virtue and to God, and ardent to inspire others with the same sentiments and engage in the same pursuits." Theophilus Lindsey to Hays, 15 April 1793, *DWL*, 24, 93, (1).

79   Hugh Worthington to Mary and Elizabeth Hays, 21 May 1793, *DWL*, uncatalogued.

80   *The New Annual Register* (London, 1793), p. 275.

81   "Article LXIL," *Analytical Review*, XVI (May 1793): 464–5. The review included a lengthy excerpt from "Letter VII, On reading Romances."

82   See Penelope Deutscher's discussion of the historical marginalization of female "commentators," in "'Imperfect Discretion': Intervention into the history of

philosophy by twentieth-century French women philosophers," *Hypatia*, 15/2 (Spring 2000): 160–80.

83 *Critical Review*, vol. 8 (August 1793, second series), pp. 433–5.

84 [John] Evans to Mary Hays, [1793?], *Pforz.*, 2202.

85 The reviewer continued, "We have been sedulous to bring forward into full view every female politician and philosopher that meet us in the paths of literature; since to render these characters conspicuous, is, generally speaking, to expose them to the contempt and ridicule which they deserve, by detecting their affectations, their vanities, and their follies. And thus the pupils of Mrs. Wollstonecraft actually invalidate, by these specimens of themselves, the very doctrines which they are labouring to establish. Proudly to vaunt their intellectual powers, and to exhibit, at the same instant, the most 'damning proofs' of mental imbecility, has (providentially, we had almost said) been the fate of these literary ladies!" *The English Review*, 22: 253–7.

86 See Barbara Taylor, "Feminists Versus Gallants: Manner and Morals in Enlightenment Britain," *Representations*, 87 (Summer 2004): 127. See also Katherine Binhammer, "Thinking Gender with Sexuality in 1790's Feminist Thought," *Feminist Studies*, 28/3 (Fall 2002): 667–90.

PART TWO
Promises

Chapter Four

Electrical Sympathy

"There is in some minds a certain attraction … a recognition of souls, which glows in the features, and moves the heart with a sort of electrical sympathy. Many I believe will not understand me: but this I cannot help."

Mary Hays, *Letters and Essays, Moral, and Miscellaneous*, 1793

Intellectual ambition fueled Hays's efforts to gain the attention of erudite men. As she surveyed the field of men she now met, Hays privately considered a crucial question, unasked and unanswered since John Eccles's death: could she yet construct a meaningful life with a man willing to take her on her own unconventional terms? By 1792 she had become well known within the Rational Dissenting community as pious Eusebia who confirmed the misogynist stereotype that an unmarried "learned lady" was by default unalluring. She knew that conventional wisdom proscribed women from possessing both breasts *and* brains. But now she imagined that William Frend had beckoned her to a wider world, one more substantial than the one she had studied vicariously through Robert Robinson. Here she saw men and women drawn to each other because of shared feelings and beliefs that informed their marriages with the same caring optimism as did their religious creeds. As Hays stood poised at the threshold of Unitarian culture, she knew she was no Venus: she was short, unlovely, and careless about her dress and hair, nearly middle-aged at 33. Gradually she conceived a hope for Frend's love as well as his learning; she allowed herself to believe that marriage might be another medium of enlightenment for them both. She engaged in the public-private sphere of religion and politics that also gave her latitude to create opportunities, and simultaneously camouflage, for her courtship of Frend. It remained to be seen whether in time to come intellectual beauty and strong will, fired by desire, could realize her fantasy of conjugal life with him.

Eusebia's prompt response to Gilbert Wakefield's attack on Rational Dissenting practices at New College and his offensive rejoinders caught the attention of other prominent Nonconformist heroes within the heterodox Dissenting community in addition to Frend. John Disney, Theophilus Lindsey, Joseph Priestley, and Hugh Worthington welcomed her to chapel services and social gatherings. In this new milieu, Hays expanded her cognitive reach by interacting with what John Eccles had termed "generous men," able and willing to introduce her to fresh intellectual territories. Her affective range deepened, too, as did her sense of purpose.

Hays was now initiated into an energetic, closely knit, progressive culture, inhabited by vivid characters, one that was physically closer than Robinson's "nunnery" in Cambridge. This was a community in which a woman's right to autonomy was taken as a matter of course by men committed to the idea, if not the wider social practice, of universal egalitarianism.[1] The marriages Hays observed fostered independent women who chose to participate in their husbands' pioneering work. As part of her informal education, Hays had the opportunity to examine a different kind of marital interplay from more conventional relationships, one based on perceived Christian principles understood to promote friendship. These relationships reminded Hays of her high-minded expectations for a life with John Eccles, in stark contrast to the showy *tableaux* of "romance" between ladies and gentlemen, relationships that Wollstonecraft had warned invariably produce gendered tyrants and slaves.

Hays got to know some of the Rational Dissenting and Unitarian wives, Jane Disney, Hannah Lindsey, Mary Priestley, Susanna Worthington, because of her frequent contact with their husbands. She saw or heard about others such as Catharine Cappe, Ann Jebb, and Anne Wakefield as part of the daily give and take in a community caught up in doctrinal and political issues. These wives formed a cohort that influenced the direction of Hays's feminism and public career as well as her private ambitions. Here were married women who matter-of-factly created vocations for themselves, albeit unofficial ones, as teachers, strategists, advisors, advocates, polemicists, philanthropists, writers, healers, and organizers. Some reared their children, kept house, ministered to their husbands and their congregations, maintained correspondence, and still managed to participate in the sectarian tussles of the day. Others, including Ann Jebb, Anna Barbauld, and Catharine Cappe, who were childless, and therefore had more discretionary time, exerted even greater energy for the common good. In contrast to William Law's "Eusebia," they played a part in contemporary life, neither secluded from the world, nor cosseted by wealth, underlings, elite status or security. Hays's contact with vital Unitarian women extended into the next generation. Professionally, Hays's observation of the Dissenting wives in their public representations and as wives and mothers suggested to her an emerging market of serious female readers. She aimed her publications over the next 30 years at stimulating and providing for just such readership. Personally, these marriages offered Hays a range of models for a future with William Frend: from these she could imaginatively mix and match, combine and rearrange, elements of actual relationships to suit her fantasies. Philosophically, Nonconformist marriage pointed to a higher form of love, more Platonic and sympathetic than earthly, in which mutual values in the service of God trumped or transformed sexual magnetism based on physical appeal.

Hays determined to make a career for herself in the radical republic of letters in the late 1780s and early 1790s. The primary concerns of British Dissenters during this period were their concurrent efforts to repeal the Test and Corporation Acts, reform parliament, and sustain momentum for advances in the natural and the moral sciences.[2] These ambitions were played out against the backdrop of the concept of "America" as a geopolitical entity that charged the air as did new discoveries about electricity. Like her male associates, Hays responded to the strong currents of political, theological, and scientific inquiry. Her contribution was to apply such markers of Enlightenment progress to a new vision of gender relations in which she was influenced by the religious leaders whom she knew and just as significantly, by their wives.

Even after his death, Robert Robinson continued to serve as Hays's primary mentor as she strove to further her ambitions as a public female intellectual. She parlayed the contacts she had made through Robinson to extend her education by expanding her social network. She also stayed in touch with at least two of Robinson's daughters, the unmarried Ann, and her recently married sister, Mary Brown, wife of a London wine merchant. Ann communicated with Hays as one "sensitive plant" to another, supporting each other's finely tuned responses to life, with the shared conviction that their exquisite reactions rendered them different from and better than people of steelier natures: "I can readily acknowledge your remark relative to the 'extreme sufferings of a susceptible heart,'" Ann wrote in response to Hays's characterization of her own sensibilities.

> [H]ere indeed I can again sympathize with you, for it ever has been my misfortune to be too soon, perhaps, aware — this disposition of mind has caus'd me many a heart-ach, yet I would not willingly (were it possible) relinquish it for one of a more flinty nature: there are certain exquisite emotions unknown to persons whose nature is that of steel; emotions which I should be sorry to be a stranger to! Forgive my speaking of myself — this part of your letter excited the idea.[3]

Mary Brown assured Hays that her unique role as spiritual daughter to Robinson was not forgotten, even among the Rational Dissenters Hays did not know. "They know of you," Mary wrote, of the aunts and sister she and her husband visited while traveling outside the metropolis, "and regard you, they say because my father loved you." In this way, Hays's reputation as Robinson's student was perpetuated, as was her continuing membership in a select society of advanced thinkers who simultaneously encouraged one another to feel deeply.

Hays also corresponded during this time with George Dyer (1755–1841), a young man with the kind of checkered early origins that appealed to Robinson. Robinson had taken Dyer into his home variously as boarder, tutor to the Robinson children, and assistant minister. Dyer had been the object of Anna Barbauld's generosity as well; with her support, he matriculated at Emanuel College, Cambridge, where he and William Frend became fast friends. Dyer remained close to Robinson's children after their father's death while he worked on Robinson's biography, sometimes conveying messages from them to Hays on his frequent trips between Cambridge and London. Later, he served as go-between for Hays and Frend.

Growth of a Woman's Mind

New College Hackney

Beyond the circle of Robinson's intimates, including Frend and Dyer, Hays now concentrated on the New College tutors. For a brief time, New College was a magnet for some of the most brilliant and activist Rational Dissenters and Unitarians. Hays's connection with the New College tutors emerged organically from her tutelage with Robinson. At Robinson's funeral in June 1790, Joseph Priestley famously praised Robinson for educating his daughters equally with his sons.

The example of Robinson's daughters' erudition, combined with Priestley's avowed support for female education, encouraged Hays to seek further training from the tutors at the New College at Hackney. From 1786 to 1796 New College was the most innovative Dissenting academy. Here, Hays hovered at the periphery of the final flowering of Dissenting pedagogy, as the tutors invigorated education designed for men, building on what they had learned at other academies, producing new textbooks, incorporating the literature of living languages and modern history into the traditional curricula, and encouraging free inquiry into current controversies, all in deliberate contrast to Cambridge and Oxford. New College was closely allied with the Essex Street Chapel in London, founded by Unitarian Theophilus Lindsey (1723–1808). As Lindsey declared in his inaugural sermon, Unitarianism's rigorous creed promoted the ongoing search for wisdom through knowledge as a Christian duty. Hays reacted to this mandate more intensely than others among her female Dissenting cohorts; Anna Aikin, later the distinguished Mrs. Barbauld, for one, had direct contact to the life of the mind during her girlhood at Warrington Academy where she studied informally with her father and Priestley, but responded equivocally to her own gifts and subsequent eminence.[4] Like her male Nonconformist contemporaries, Hays decisively embraced the mandate to learn as part of her evolving theology. Over time she went further, pressing Unitarian enthusiasm for inquiry and knowledge beyond conventional limits to investigate every facet of female life, even such apparently irrational impulses as love and sex.

Free inquiry was the engine that fueled New College, and Hays sought access there to the unmediated roots of knowledge by studying informally, attending sermons, and reading tutors' publications. When tutor William Enfield's translation from the Latin of Brucker's magisterial *History of Philosophy* was published in 1791,[5] Hays now found herself able to study the history of ideas from the ancients to the moderns in English and assess the absence of women in this system. She deepened her understanding of the materialist epistemologies of British freethinkers derived from Locke by reading Priestley's edition of Anthony Collins's *A Philosophical Inquiry Concerning Human Liberty* (1790) and his abridgement of David Hartley's *Theory of the Human Mind, on the Principles of the Association of Ideas* (1749, 1791). Hays drew on these readings to develop an unconventional, personal program of self-improvement. Almost immediately, she modified her earlier focus on traditional feminine piety to devise a uniquely female vocation to extend enlightenment to other women. Such study bore fruit later in her mature texts on the presence of learned women throughout history.

Hays found rationales for her pedagogical convictions in Priestley's *Essay on a Course of Liberal Education for Civil and Active Life. With Plans of Lectures* (1765, 1788). This work had added history, government, and economics to the traditional curricula because, Priestley wrote, contemporary geopolitical circumstances required new and different information.[6] Priestley quoted Hume in expressing the hope that women might learn from the study of history that "love is not the only passion that governs the male world;" Priestley himself acknowledged that history was "calculated for the use of persons of both sexes."[7] Hays incorporated both views in her curricula for women.

Hays's personal contact with Nonconformist luminaries brought her additional stimulation. The crisis of the "Priestley" or Birmingham Riots from 14–17 July 1791, in which Priestley's laboratory, home, and library were burned by an angry mob in response to his confrontational support of the French Revolution and his publicly avowed Unitarianism, brought Priestley to New College as a tutor. There he sought asylum with the expectation that he might also take over the ministry of the Gravel Pit Meeting in Hackney from his friend Richard Price (1723–91), Rational Dissenting leader, mathematician, colleague of Benjamin Franklin's, and generous supporter of Wollstonecraft in her early attempts to run a school in Newington Green.[8] Hays found the doctrinal views that Priestley, Worthington, and Disney espoused coincided closely enough with her own evolving theology to turn to them for further instruction. She questioned Worthington, an avuncular man, about theological points in his sermons, particularly the thorny question of Christ's resurrection that Frend had raised with her. She read Priestley's works, heard him preach at the Gravel Pit Meeting when he assumed leadership after Price's death in late 1791, and saw him in company with Dyer and Frend before his self-exile to America in 1794.[9] Disney provided her with books detailing previous reformist challenges recent enough for Lindsey, Disney, and others Hays knew to have been participants. These included a series of personal accounts of doctrinal and political struggles by and about those who had lived them: *The Life of Thomas Hollis* (1780) by the Anglican Francis Blackburne (father-in-law to Disney and Lindsey), an account of the heterodox Dissenter who early supported the American colonists' resistance to British rule; Priestley's *An Appeal to the Serious and Candid Professors of Christianity* (1770); and Disney's life of his Cambridge tutor, the Unitarian reformer John Jebb.

Hays attended sermons at New College and read tutors' publications, some of which included actual lectures and curricula. She read Priestley's tome *The History and Present State of Electricity* (1767). This work stimulated her to further research with its useful concepts and literary tools. In his book, Priestley extended Hartley's arguments about the world's materiality. Priestley explained that pursuit of scientific truth was second only to the love of God. Heaven itself might be glimpsed in the history of the study of electricity. Priestley opined that electricity, in particular, was the field of investigation that offered the opportunity, even for "raw adventurers" (his term for untrained entrepreneurs), to make discoveries and earn a living. According to Priestley, the road to human happiness depended on an individual's sense of purpose, and the intensity with which that purpose was pursued. Moreover, personal energy was best expended on pursuits of one's own choosing, rather than in conformity to those arising from conventional ones. Personal fulfillment, Priestley preached, depended on an individual's honest, even courageous, willingness to strike out on an autonomous path to enlightenment.[10] This was a crucial idea for Hays from which she extrapolated an idiosyncratic concept of empirical research based on actual experience and gained confidence to choose as her subject what most interested her. Priestley's hypothesis, closely based on Benjamin Franklin's theories,[11] about the unseen but omnipresent "electrical fluid" in all matter provided Hays with useful metaphors to express Enlightenment excitement that free inquiry could reveal the otherwise hidden operations of the natural world and as importantly of human nature.[12] Hays shared with others among her associates belief in the marvelous confluence of reason, feeling, and faith that presaged a female version of Romanticism. In *Frankenstein; or, the Modern Prometheus* (1818), Mary Shelley deployed electricity as both literal and allegorical force to express what Anne Mellor identifies as the "feminine Romantic ideology ... grounded on a belief in rational capacity and equality of woman" that included access to modern scientific advances.[13]

Priestley was known for his compelling lectures and Hays sought him out. She was now introduced to new cognitive terrain: the history of philosophy; experimental as well as natural science; advanced theology; mathematics, particularly Euclidean geometry; theories of physiognomy; and French. In an attempt to integrate the several parts of her expanding universe into a new, more egalitarian version of "sociability,"[14] she invited the Priestleys, the Disneys, the Worthingtons, as well as bachelors Dyer and Frend, to the Hays home at Gainsford Street, in Southwark.[15] Beneath her mother's watchful eyes, Hays appeared to be entirely caught up in this next, exciting phase of her education, extending the stimulating discourse of chapel, lectures, and books to domestic gatherings.

At the same time, Hays made occasions to see Frend among a group of couples sympathetic to his religious and political views. When in London, he would not refuse an invitation to a genteel party at Gainsford Street if the men and their wives who were strong supporters of his personal convictions and public behavior were to be present. How else was Hays to gain access to him? Moreover, proximity to Frend in the company of his backers offered direct exposure to progressive marriages at close range. Hays hoped Frend might be persuaded by example.[16]

Progressive Marriages

In *Letters and Essays* Hays expressed a buoyant faith in the divine design in human affairs. "Our nature is progressive, and every thing around us is the same. Wise and benevolent plan!"[17] Matrimony, she recognized, was also part of the providential plan. Hays came to trust what she observed in marriages between heterodox Dissenters. Her own father's early death had left her mother with seven children to support, leaving little opportunity for adult romance, enlightened or otherwise. Little is known of Hays's older siblings' relationships with their spouses, although in later years Hays depended on the advice of her brother-in-law John Dunkin. Hays's first experience with the daily life of an unconventional marriage came about through her acquaintance with Robert Robinson and his wife Ellen Payne Robinson (1733–1808). Hays saw Ellen Robinson when she accompanied her husband on preaching and research trips to London from their farm in Chesterton where they lived with their 12 children.

Robinson's letters reveal his unconventional involvement in domestic minutiae with his wife and children. With customary candor, Robinson described to his brother his participation in the uncertain prelude to childbirth, the need for him to minister to his wife in the absence of an adequate number of servants, and his attentions to his daughters beyond their academic instruction. In 1772 Robinson confided to his brother that, instead of busying himself with scholarly pursuits, he was on alert for his wife's tenth delivery. The baby was not due for another three weeks, but Mrs. Robinson had been so uncomfortable that her husband had been responding to the demands of the household, which included caring for their nine children in residence and his aged mother while continuing with his public duties as minister. He confided that he was so exhausted that, "I am now fit to sleep on the floor" and thus asked his brother not to "omit praying for us."[18] Some months later, he reported that his wife felt better, although he remained on duty at home, ministering to everyone in the household. "And I, poor I," he wrote, "all day forced to find eyes and see, and thought for all."[19]

In his later correspondence with Hays, Robinson described how he and his family lived contentedly together, expressing his active pleasure in domestic life. "You must know," he wrote in 1788,

> my eldest daughter is married, and to her husband I have put off my farm, and all business, so that now I have no employ of that kind except to keep my house in repair, to cultivate my garden, to keep my pleasure boat in trim, to watch my bees, and to pur [sic], like old pup by the fire, to my wife and family. We are a sort of nunnery concealed by brick walls and high trees, guarded in front by the river; out back to the town and our prospect the fields, and we have no ideas of solitude. Had Mrs. Robinson her health, all would have a zest.[20]

After his death, Ann Robinson shared her proto-feminist inklings with Hays, alluding to her parents' happy, if not fully egalitarian, relationship. "I do not give the [masculine] sex credit for too much," she wrote in discussing another sister's fiancée, "but where a woman meets with a man of sense and a friend in her husband I think she must enjoy the full happiness allotted for mortals."[21] Like Hays, Ann Robinson had time to reflect on the ideals and realities of men and matrimony, and viewed friendship, rather than romance, as essential for a woman's happiness in marriage.[22]

Contemporaries of various religious and political persuasions pointed admiringly to this new phenomenon: marriage in which spouses were friends as well as lovers and colleagues. For example, somewhat later, Hannah More (1745–1833), Evangelical arbiter of morals, commented in her *Strictures on the Modern System of Female Education* (1799) that the "profession of ladies" was to fulfill their domestic roles and therefore they should be trained to execute these as much as men are trained for public professions. In common with her declared enemy, Wollstonecraft, More advised that sensible men want companions for wives, not ornamental objects. A man, More instructed, wants "a being who can comfort and counsel him; one who can reason and reflect, and feel, and judge, and discourse and discriminate; one who can assist him in his affairs, lighten his cares, sooth his sorrows, strengthen his principles, and educate his children."[23]

Relationships between late eighteenth-century Rational Dissenting and Unitarian husbands and wives pointed towards an advance on the kind of marriage that More recommended because of the spouses' intense intellectual connections, and genuine regard for each other as human beings engaged in common work.[24] Of the newly widowed Ann Jebb, her contemporary Thomas Brand Hollis opined that she felt her loss extremely and differently from other wives. "Poor Mrs. Jebb! I dread to inquire concerning her; her loss is beyond the conception of common minds. 'Tis not merely of a husband, a partner in a common interest; but her guardian and protector, her guide, philosopher and friend. For the diruption [sic] of such an intimate union, what adequate name can be found?"[25] Another observer commented, "[Jebb's] excellent consort, whose masculine mind understood and was in unison with all his principles, is pre-eminently distinguished by her loss." From Hays's perspective, the several Unitarian wives she saw in action offered different facets of marital possibility. Jane Disney (1745 or 46–1809),[26] for example, with whom Hays now spent considerable time, was the oldest daughter of the Archdeacon Francis Blackburne, and combined literary and musical competence with the "generosity and ardour" of her character.[27] Theophilus Lindsey, married to Jane's stepsister, and John Disney's senior at Essex Street Chapel, noted with approval Mrs. Disney's efforts in producing a new edition of the well loved hymns of Dr. Isaac Watts, which she "corrected and improved."[28]

Hannah Elsworth Lindsey (1740–1812), whom Hays would have seen at Essex Street services until her husband retired from the ministry in 1793, was esteemed by her contemporary male biographer for her responsiveness to the training she received from her mother's second husband, Archdeacon Blackburne. Hannah Elsworth demonstrated exceptional ability to learn and a prodigious memory even as a young child. Blackburne trained her in both the scriptures and the tools for free inquiry, so that she, too, could exercise what he saw as the sacred right to private judgment, even against prevailing opinions.[29]

Hannah Lindsey's husband jettisoned a promising career in the Anglican hierarchy in 1774 after much internal struggle. When he finally decided to leave the Church of England, his farewell to his congregation expressed his sense of how much he had renounced in order to exercise the right of private judgment against the advice of those close to him, including Priestley.[30] Nonetheless, he explained, the moral imperative of his changing theology left him no choice. In his *Farewell Address to the Parishioners of Catterick*, he acknowledged:

> To leave a station of ease and affluence and to have to combat with various straits and hardships of an uncertain world, is but a dark prospect. But we must willingly submit to this hard lot, when not to be avoided without deserting our duty to God and his truth.[31]

He was not alone in either his decision or its results. For Hannah Lindsey, his young wife, the rupture made for uneasy relations with her mother and stepfather, as well as theological, practical, political, and economic distress.[32] Mrs. Lindsey, by her friend Catharine Cappe's account, proved to be the perfect partner for her husband, although others regretted that he had not married a more compliant woman. Hannah Lindsey acknowledged privately to Cappe that she possessed a harsh temper.[33] Cappe held that for Theophilus Lindsey to achieve the providential reforms he believed God had assigned him, he required a wife who could withstand public and private censure and provide counsel as his willing helpmate.[34]

Lindsey was lauded as a pathfinder of Unitarian creed and practice; Hannah Lindsey was acknowledged in the Unitarian pantheon as his spiritual peer. G.M. Ditchfield, editor of Lindsey's voluminous correspondence, describes Lindsey's acknowledgement of his wife's fellowship:

> The support and encouragement which Lindsey received from his wife is impossible to quantify. She brought to their marriage a medical knowledge for which she was well known, and a gift for the niceties of day-to-day administration, which she subsequently placed at the disposal of the various Unitarian societies which Lindsey established. He himself described her as "one of the best of women, and a grounded rational christian and strict Unitarian, inferior to none."[35]

Hays would have known of Catharine Harrison Cappe (1744–1821) because of her erudition and activism.[36] Like Hays, young Catherine Harrison was determined to be well educated, and as the daughter of an Anglican clergyman, she had opportunities to read her father's theological books.[37] Like Hays she was distressed at the inferior education available to young women,[38] but she received more formal training than Hays at a girls' seminary in York. Harrison pressed for and finally won the privilege to have private tutors teach her arithmetic and French at school. When she was forced to leave the seminary and return home, she suffered when her female relations advised her that needlework was her only appropriate task.[39]

Harrison saw that her only alternative to a conventional female education was disciplined autodidactism, reading her way to knowledge. This proved to be a life-long pattern. Almost immediately her aunts opposed her reading, particularly of periodicals like the *Gentleman's Magazine* and the *Monthly Review*, for fear that it would make Catharine Harrison socially unacceptable in her role as a learned lady.

Catharine Harrison differed from Hays in her sturdy sense of self and early participation in a progressive marriage. In her quest for intellectual training and purpose, she found attention, support, and stimulation at the home of Hannah and Theophilus Lindsey. Her frequent visits to their happy household in the vicarage of Catterick became her delight and inspiration. When Theophilus and Hannah Lindsey left the Anglican Church, Catharine Harrison followed. In later years, she judged this to be the determining decision of her life.

Her experience may have demonstrated the relative unimportance in a progressive marriage of good looks, a telling matter for Hays. As a young woman, Catharine Harrison contracted smallpox. The disease permanently disfigured her, much to the chagrin of her mother and grandmother. She subsequently married the Unitarian minister, Newcome Cappe, who was 20 years older and in poor health, a widower with six adult children. Newcome Cappe functioned as his wife's teacher, "guide, counselor and friend." Catharine Cappe served as her husband's editor and interpreter and learned on the job. After her husband's death in 1790, she came into her own as a thinker, eventually judged by the Unitarian *Monthly Repository* in 1811 to be an important Christian scholar and writer.[40] Cappe went on to even greater visibility and influence as a philanthropist, reformer, and advocate for women;[41] in private, she was a trusted friend and correspondent of Hannah Lindsey and Mary Priestley, both of whom supported Cappe's pioneering career.[42]

Progressive marriages supported independent wives; it also fostered male/female fellowship across marital lines. Priestley, for one, found encouragement from Hannah, as well as Theophilus, Lindsey; late in his life, Priestley repeated in a letter to Mrs. Lindsey Dr. Doddridge's belief that "there would be more women in heaven than men."[43] Priestley's demographic expectation for paradise was based on earthly experiences with living women, including Mrs. Lindsey, but especially with his wife, Mary Wilkinson Priestley (1744–96). Priestley's assessment of his wife after her death reflects his respect and affection for her. "A noble and generous mind," he described her, "feeling strongly for others, little for herself, through life," and of their marriage, "a happy union to me for more than thirty-four years." He acknowledged her efforts to leave him free from all domestic cares so that he could devote himself to his work; he considered the marriage to have been "a real partnership; his helpmate was both 'Mary' and 'Martha.'"[44] After the "Priestley riots" in 1791, Mrs. Priestley wrote to Mrs. Barbauld of her readiness to try "a fresh soil."[45] She got her wish when the

Priestleys immigrated to America in 1794, where she died in 1796. Priestley's biographer commented on Mary and Joseph's "felicitous union," lauding Mrs. Priestley for supporting her husband's multiple efforts to realize God's plan.

Hays was likely especially interested in the successful combination of learning, love and limited money in the marriage of Ann Jebb (1735–1812) and John Jebb (1736–86). Hays knew that Frend looked to John Jebb as a model of courageous activism; he had publicly praised Jebb in his *Thoughts on Subscription and Religious Tests* (1788).[46] Hays sought out the widowed Ann Jebb, perhaps as a female mentor.[47] She may have imagined a particular kinship with Mrs. Jebb, who was considered homely, had passionately loved a zealous Unitarian reformer, and by 1793 was widowed like the good "Eusebia," although still as much in the religious political world as her poor health would allow.[48] According to her biographer, Mrs. Jebb had stirring memories to relate: as Ann Torkington, she and John Jebb met at a ball, and quickly fell in love.[49] They married in 1764 when Jebb obtained an Anglican living, while still a tutor at Peterhouse College at Cambridge. During their Cambridge years, the Jebbs provided an early example of "radical sociability," informal discourse between men and women that showed a new equality in which conventional social forms were transmuted into enlightened intellectual exchanges. Her biographer notes that at private parties, the great Cambridge tutor William Paley treated Mrs. Jebb with the same humorous informality as he did his male students, questioning her arguments and parrying with her verbally, all of which she took in stride. The lady and the scholar shared a biographer; he was in a position to judge that Mrs. Jebb had early on discerned the relative liberalism in Paley's support for abolition of the Slave Trade, as well as informal resistance to the continuing University requirement that candidates for degrees must subscribe to the Thirty-Nine Articles of the Church of England. Later, both Jebbs were disappointed when Paley, an adherent of philosophical expediency, publicly endorsed subscription.[50]

Ann Jebb held her conversational own with the best Cambridge academics; she read their works, and formed and expressed her opinions independently. When John Jebb demanded that the University reform its academic practices, Ann Jebb actively defended her husband's call for university-wide annual examinations in international law, chronology, history, classics, mathematics, metaphysics, and moral philosophy—a list that included subjects that some of the colleges did not teach.[51] Assuming the pen name "Priscilla,"[52] Ann Jebb published articles in the *London Chronicle* from 1772–74 that championed academic reform in the University. She pointedly attacked powerful University figures William Powell, Master of St John's College, and Samuel Hallifax, Professor of Civil Law, both of whom had opposed John Jebb's reformist efforts. Priscilla's success at publicizing the controversy and poking holes in the arguments of her husband's opponents provoked Paley to outspoken admiration for the power of her writing.

The Jebbs offered proof that a progressive marriage could survive adversity. When John Jebb became a Unitarian, his parents disapproved of the abrupt end to a

promising career as an Anglican minister and cut off his financial support.[53] His
continuing efforts at reform cost Jebb academic status, income, and good health.[54]
Independence from the need to conform to Anglican mores emboldened Ann Jebb.
Without any of Eusebia's subsequent apologies, she joined the bitter debate over
repeal of the Corporation and Test Acts, war with the American colonies, and
reform of Parliament itself. The Jebbs shared Unitarianism's benevolent, activist
values; together they advocated the end of the Slave Trade. The Jebbs remained
constant in their common convictions and mutual esteem. John Jebb died in 1786
at age 50. Ann Jebb survived him by 26 years during which she sustained social
contacts, political interests, and maintained her own opinions. For Hays, Ann Jebb
may have represented female autonomy within a supportive marriage,
demonstrating that a wife might speak out on her own in public and still be loved
by her husband.[55]

Anna Aikin, who became Anna Barbauld (1743–1825), established the high
water mark for female intellectual agency among Rational Dissenting women.
From Hays's perspective in the context of progressive marriages, Barbauld, a
Presbyterian, was likely most important for the contrapuntal elements in her own
life and texts: her intimate interactions with generous men; her teaching career, in
partnership with her husband Rochemont Barbauld; her equivocal expressions
about female education and learned ladies; her willingness to engage in strenuous
debates with men—fiery Gilbert Wakefield and her erstwhile mentor, the great
Priestley; and her moving representations of female solidarity, particularly with
Mary Priestley.[56] Although they moved in the same Dissenting circles, Hays left no
comment about either woman.

George Dyer was passionate about "personal and gender equality."[57] He
welcomed accomplished women as well as men among his associates, perhaps as
much from private generosity as from principle. His poem, "On Liberty" (1792),
catalogued a "who's who" of heterodox Dissenters and their forerunners and Hays
included some of Dyer's verses in her *Letters and Essays, Moral, and
Miscellaneous* published the next year. Dyer drew gender lines, not to provoke
strife between the sexes, but rather to establish equitable representation among
lovers of freedom. At least in literary form, marital status mattered less than shared
values: Dyer's array on the male side included John Milton, Hartley, and Algernon
Sidney as spiritual forebears, and Disney, Jebb, Lindsey, Priestley, and Thomas
Paine among the living. Dyer dedicated the volume in which "On Liberty"
appeared to Frend. In the poem he praised him as an intrepid freethinker and
reminded his readers in a footnote of Frend's conscientious stand and its
consequences.[58]

The women's contingent in Dyer's poem included Jebb and Barbauld, shoulder
to shoulder with Hays, Wollstonecraft, Helen Maria Williams, Catherine
Macaulay, and Charlotte Smith. The poem described American Paine in the
Priestleyian metaphors of electricity and feeling, calling on Paine to arouse his
enlightened British comrades' love of liberty. Dyer bids Liberty, "sweet

enthusiast!," to acknowledge the female lovers of freedom who have advocated her cause in their publications.

> Then will I from my Jebb's fair pages prove,
>   That female minds might teach a patriotic throng;
> Or 'on the Loire's sweet banks' with Williams rove;
>   Or hear the warble in Laetitia's song…
>   Or I will hear thee, fair Melpomene,
>   In my own Charlotte's pensive notes complain.

Dyer provided explanatory footnotes for the cast of characters he assembled, starting with Wollstonecraft as author of *A Vindication of the Rights of Woman*, emphasizing Wollstonecraft's denunciation of the tyranny of both gendered social conventions for women and the limitations of female education. Dyer identified Ann Jebb as Dr. Jebb's widow, and noted the range of her published works and his admiration for it.[59] Dyer's footnote for Hays curiously omitted mention of *Cursory Remarks,* noting only, "Miss Hays, an admirer and imitator of Mrs. Charlotte Smith," a reference to Hays's earlier poetry rather than her recent appearance in print as Eusebia.

Dyer was explicit about the gender implications he represented: compared with the heroes of Nonconformity, Rational Dissenting women were likely to be more zealous about necessary change because they were discriminated against both as women and as Dissenters. Hays incorporated Dyer's view of this issue in a discussion of Wollstonecraft's feminism in *Letters and Essays*.[60]

Drawn from Life

Letters and Essays, Moral, and Miscellaneous showed the imprint of Rational Dissenting and Unitarian relationships. In "Letter No. IX., To Amasia," Hays synthesized her observations of working marriages in the Ciceronian figure of Hortensius and his feminine counterpart, Hortensia.[61] Hortensius represents Hays's gold standard for enlightened men. He resembles Frend: good-looking, mentally equipped from strong training in the liberal arts, and "a citizen of the world"[62] as a result of his foreign travels. Like Robinson and other intrepid Rational Dissenters and Unitarians, Hortensius is open-minded and flexible, and, most importantly, follows truth wherever it might lead him, his integrity intact despite the blandishments of ambition and financial gain. Like most of the Unitarian men Hays knew, Hortensius had occasion to sacrifice public honors. His friends and enemies might wonder at his choices, but imbued with the examples of others' greatness and goodness, he has no self-consciousness about resisting conventional glory.[63] This might describe Frend, Theophilus Lindsey, John Disney, John Jebb, and Joseph Priestley. Hortensius's manner of interacting with others is elegant and straightforward, while his quality of mind is reflected in his direct and virtuous conversation.

Like Hays's male associates, Hortensius believes that understanding comes after impartial examination and unrestricted freedom of thought. He combines love of solitude and social affections with duty; he has the knack of correcting those less enlightened without hurting their feelings. He modifies his manner appropriately towards others in his various roles as husband, parent, master, and friend. Like Robert Robinson, his *bona fides* include his egalitarian attitude towards the education of his sons and daughters who are trained to judge the differences among prejudice, opinion, and principle. He sees beyond the "absurd notion" that "nature has given judgment to man, to women imagination."[64] Hays emphasizes the countervailing effect of his attitudes and actions to gender prejudices, "sexual distinctions in intellect and virtue, [that] have depraved and weakened the human species."[65] In her portrait of Hortensius, Hays demonstrates that everyone loses when bigotry is tolerated, a moral to be drawn from the contrast between working and more traditional forms of marriage and parenting.

Hortensius is not without flaws. But Hays insists that his failings should not obviate the generosity of a great soul. Hays likely draws on the less attractive personal traits of some of her colleagues: Lindsey's readiness to argue,[66] Disney's occasional impatience, Frend's pigheadedness, and Jebb's propensity, according to a contemporary, to make himself "obnoxious."[67] Hays tells us that Hortensius's very faults—an uneven temper, fastidiousness, and zealotry—have rendered him observant, more humble, and more honest because they arise from his virtues. Even earthly flaws, Hays urges, tend towards providential goodness.

Like the Rational Dissenting and Unitarian wives Hays observed, Hortensia, Hortensius's wife has adjusted herself to his character and interests, reflecting and refining on his virtues. Hays argues that in a progressive marriage, kindred minds are capable of a marital harmony that physical attraction, earthly wealth, and worldly power cannot produce. She bolsters her assertion with a quote from Wollstonecraft's refutation of Rousseau's depiction of woman as a mindless, pretty toy. Hays represents female autonomy in Hortensia, modeling her likely on Ann Jebb. Hortensia shares her husband's intellectual interests, as well as his amusements, but not as cipher or follower: her presence intensifies and improves such activities. Hortensia and Hortensius do not compete with each other: they strive to be reasonable, and their reciprocal affection enables them to keep momentary difficulties in perspective. They behave deliberately towards each other, rejecting either formality or familiarity; they are friends and colleagues in the work of their lives, as well as lovers. They do not argue in public: they are frugal and cheerful and their genuine hospitality compensates for the absence of affluence in their mode of living. To Hays these are scenes drawn from life, an idealized composite of actual relationships that Hays saw around her, embellished by Ann Jebb's memories of her marriage.

In "Letter No. V.," the "History of Melville and Cecilia," Hays pays special homage to Robinson in a representation of America that reflects his view that it was the "happiest of countries!"[68] Other Dissenters shared Robinson's sympathetic view of the embattled colonies.[69] Hays brings together multiple strands of her experience of Robinson in this piece: his earthy enjoyment of life; his rejection of sophistry and affectation; his idiosyncratic representations of Huguenot history and theology; his spiritual and intellectual tutelage of young men, particularly Frend, and of women like herself and his daughters; and his emblematic role as a Christian minister who ameliorated the lives of his congregation, not by tyranny, but by educating them about their birthright of freedom. She draws on her impressions of Frend, and more crucially creates a romanticized vision of herself as tall, assured, and beloved for her learning. Hays thus imagines her rightful place in Enlightenment discourse, and as importantly her role in an enlightened life. This is her fantasy for a future with Frend. Hays also experiments with a new version of gender relations based on her reactions to the several progressive marriages she observed and on her own idiosyncratic education with Robinson to portray an agricultural Elysium where "the feast of reason/ and the flow of souls" coexist in an earthly paradise.

"Letter No. V." continues the story of Melville, a young man who earlier made a hasty and incompatible first marriage, the subject of "Letter No. IV." Melville travels to America when his luck runs out in England. He is released from the prison of his marriage by the death of his wife soon after he reaches the New World. With an unexpected expanse of personal freedom before him, Melville decides to settle in New York state, spending his time in business and study.

Melville's autodidactism leads him to works by Voltaire that dazzle him and by Hume that rattle him with their sophistry. Melville becomes melancholy and skeptical about the mechanistic universe the Deists such as Voltaire and Hume portray. One day, seated in the woods, amid the untamed American landscape, he is inspired to address God directly about his doubts. He confesses that he cannot accept as truth any longer the teachings of revelation. Instead, he proposes to embrace "the religion of nature." As he utters these words, he sees a man approaching him. It is Theron, an older man who preaches to a simple but numerous nearby congregation.[70]

Hays's *tableaux* portray fruition and harvest. Theron begins his clerical life as an Anglican priest in England, then sees the light of Unitarianism, resigns his living, and retires to New York where he farms and preaches to his neighbors, much as Robinson did in Chesterton. Melville is instantly charmed by Theron, and listens as the minister explains Christianity with startling clarity. Theron invites Melville to visit his farm where the Anglican finds that "the amiable mind of the owner of the fields seemed to pervade every object, and the very air to breathe virtue."[71] Just as Frend (clearly the model for Melville) discovered among the real Savoyards, observing a good man at work as farmer and minister is to witness God's shaping hand, whatever that man's sectarian creed.

Hays describes in detail a "small gothic hermitage" near a waterfall on Theron's property, which draws Melville to reflection and melancholy. Hays inserts lines from Thomas Gray's "Hymn to Adversity" (1753) that speak of the power of nature to heal the wounded heart. Near the grotto, Melville hears a woman's voice reciting lines from Dr. Beattie's "The Minstrel." It is Cecilia, Theron's niece, who is mourning the loss of her mother. At this promising moment, Hays enters center stage as the idealized heroine of her own romance. Cecilia is no conventional fictional figure; she is noteworthy not for beauty, but for the responsiveness of her face and the play of her mind: "[G]race and expression irradiated her features, and, to the discerning observer, compensated for the want of exact regularity; penetration and intelligence beamed in her eyes, and her looks varied with every sentiment of her heart." The short, frumpy Hays designs Cecilia to be a better self, although not young, "of the middle height, inclining to tall" with a "light and elegant" figure. She appears to be 27 and her maturity only increases her attractiveness: "[I]f time had faded the first bloom of youth, the mature graces and dignity of womanhood rendered her not less interesting; at least Melville thought so." Melville is Hays's ideal of Frend, possessed of an enlightened male gaze that privileges spirit and intellect over youth and loveliness, because "moral sentiment entered into his ideas of beauty." Unlike her creator, Cecilia's "manners are frank and elegant, full of spirit, delicacy, and good sense; mixed with some degree of pride, or rather elevation, as conscious of her own worth," a feminist quality straight from Wollstonecraft. Like Hays, Cecilia is accustomed to look and speak her heart.[72]

Hays weaves together multiple strands of meaning here: Cecilia is counter-heroine to prevailing expectations for women's fiction. She is neither beautiful nor wealthy nor young. In contrast to Fanny Burney's Cecilia,[73] Hays's Cecilia is who she seems to be: a sensitive woman, unvarnished by pretension, well educated, and active. Her true inheritance is her spiritual and academic wealth, endowed and encouraged by her uncle. Although she is an orphan in a new country, she quickly takes root, achieving authority as teacher, thinker, and guardian of cultural capital, especially poetry. She is no longer nubile—one thinks of heroines to come, like Austen's Elinor Dashwood, or Anne Elliot—or physically alluring. In Melville's eyes she can be seen as she is and seems to be: womanly, wise, beneficent, learned, and radiant with spiritual and intellectual beauty.[74]

Hays takes the opportunity in this letter to think out loud about conventional romantic love and compare it with the new kind of relationships she observed in progressive marriages. She calls upon her understanding of electricity to calibrate the differences between superficial attraction and the intense spark of recognition between soulmates.

> Those emotions which we feel at the first sight of an object that pleases us, cannot perhaps with propriety be called love. This is an idea that has generally been ridiculed as romantic and absurd, and not without reason: for how very unworthy are those transient

sensations of passion, which are sometimes excited in the giddy of both sexes, from the bloom, of a cheek, or the sparkling of an eye, or other advantages equally adventitious of the sacred name of love![75]

She bolsters this devaluing of romantic love with a quote from Frances Brooke's popular novel, *The History of Emily Montague* (1769): "It is sensibility alone can inspire love," that is, ennobling associations wrapped around intense feelings.

Hays situates the relationship between Cecilia and Melville in the new republic, representing her characters' interactions in terms of the new, progressive, experimental science, electricity, which provides her with a metaphor for vital forces that cannot be seen, but are revealed through enlightened inquiry. Electricity serves as metaphor in another sense: as a way for Hays to connote sexual attraction, female eroticism, and psychological interplay—everything she experienced for which there was no codified language.[76] In Hays's Eden, electricity kindles understanding that transcends reason.[77] "It is certain," she explains, "there is in some minds a certain attraction, a congeniality – were I not a materialist, I should say, a recognition of souls, which glows in the features, and moves the heart with a sort of electrical sympathy. Many I believe will not understand me: but this I cannot help."[78] The capacity for powerful feeling refined by enlightened values signifies the spiritually elect among lovers.[79]

In her philosophical research, Hays goes Priestley and his scientific colleague Benjamin Franklin one better: she applies Priestley's hypothesis that electricity is everywhere to the realm of emotions, and beyond, to the uncharted psychological realm which a century later Sigmund Freud would locate in the unconscious.[80] Later, in *Memoirs of Emma Courtney*, she would call upon her own philosophical researches as an amateur scientist to report those "energetic sympathies of truth and feeling — darting from mind to mind … with electrical rapidity," to express the web of associations and "Newtonian vibrations" that were her fantasies of sexual and intellectual love.[81] Indeed, in another context, Roy Porter has hailed Hays as an early harbinger of modernity in which "truth was subjectivized, and Eros became the idiom of the modern."[82] Hays uses the language of experimental science to identify the experience of love at first sight in *Letters and Essays*, as the material foundation of moral, intellectual, and sexual engagement. Hays depicts a progressive America where a new kind of romance, a new kind of female beauty, and a fuller explanation of "the feast of reason and the flow of souls" seems possible. Hays emphasizes the "freedom of the Will," Jonathan Edwards's term, and the title of one of Robinson's favorite books,[83] to imagine personal liberty and the potential for mature, as opposed to youthful, love. In the American Eden where Cecilia and Melville meet, women are supposed to speak their minds, and do. They are allowed to be as they are: contemplative, bookish, unfashionable, even appropriately melancholy, but still loving, lovable, and loved.

Hays concludes her fable when Theron dies a peaceful death and Cecilia marries Melville and brings his children by his first wife from England to join their

growing and accepting family. Presumably, she lives happily ever after as a
Unitarian wife. Although she was 34 when *Letters and Essays* was published in
late 1793, for Hays this was a vision to live by. Hays sustained a faith that
misogyny, like every other species of intolerance, need not obliterate a deep
connection between soul mates. Progressive marriage signified to her the liberal
confluence of the human impulses for love, sexual pleasure, and moral
perfectibility, in which women and men chose each other freely and fully in the
sight of God.

Notes

1   Contemporary theologian Rosemary Radford Ruether opines, "It was in the
     philosophy of the Enlightenment that [the] identification of patriarchal social order
     and the order of creation was broken ... However ... universalist egalitarian theory
     was not, in fact, applied to women, nor to the servant and nonpropertied classes, in the
     liberal revolutions of the late eighteenth and nineteenth centuries," *Women-Church:
     Theology and Practice of Feminist Liturgical Communities* (San Francisco, 1985), p.
     50.
2   For a discerning discussion of Unitarianism's equation of religious reformation with
     political reform, see G.M. Ditchfield, "Theophilus Lindsey and the Cause of
     Protestantism in eighteenth-century Britain" (London, forthcoming, 2006).
3   Ann Robinson to Hays, 8 May 1792, *Pforz.*, 2204.
4   Recent commentary on Barbauld includes Lucy Newlyn, "Case Study (3): Anna
     Barbauld," *Reading, Writing, and Romanticism: The Anxiety of Reception* (Oxford,
     2000), pp. 134–169; Anne Janowitz, "Amiable and radical sociability: Anna
     Barbauld's 'free familiar conversation,'" in Gillian Russell and Clara Tuite (eds),
     Romantic Sociability: Social Networks and Literary Culture in Britain 1770–1840
     (Cambridge, 2002) pp. 62–81; Deidre Coleman, "Firebrands, letters and flowers: Mrs.
     Barbauld and the Priestleys," in *Romantic Sociability*, pp. 82–103; Daniel E. White,
     "'With Mrs. Barbauld it is different': Dissenting Heritage and the Devotional Taste,"
     in Barbara Taylor and Sarah Knott (eds), *Women, Gender, and Enlightenment*
     (Houndmills, 2005), pp. 474–92; William McCarthy and Elizabeth Kraft,
     "Introduction," *Anna Laetitia Barbauld: Selected Poetry and Prose* (Peterborough,
     2002), pp. 11–32.
5   William Enfield, The History of Philosophy: from the earliest times to the beginning
     of the present century: drawn up from Brucker's Historia Critica Philosophiae,
     (London, 1791), 2 vols. For a publication history and commentary on Enfield's
     polemical interpretations, see John Christian Laursen, "Brucker in English and the
     Uses of the History of Philosophy in the Revolutionary Era," paper presented at
     Construction of the Past in Modern Political Philosophy, The Conference for the
     Study of Political Thought, Colorado Springs, 9–11 November 2001. I appreciate
     Professor Laursen allowing me to read his essay in manuscript.
6   Joseph Priestley, "An Essay on a Course of Liberal Education for Civil and Active
     Life," in Ira V. Brown (ed.), *Joseph Priestley: Selections from His Writings*
     (University Park, 1962), pp. 79–100.

7   Joseph Priestley, "Lectures on History and General Policy," *Selections from His Writings*, pp. 102, 111.
8   Jenny Graham, Revolutionary in Exile: The Emigration of Joseph Priestley to America 1794–1804 (Philadelphia, 1995), p. 23; see also MH, pp. 59–61.
9   Dyer to Hays, 28 February 1794, *Pforz.*, 2107.
10   Fulfillment, Priestley declared, "depends chiefly upon having some object to pursue, and upon the vigor with which our faculties are exerted in the pursuit," especially "those pursuits wholly our own" rather than those "when we are merely following in the track of others." Joseph Priestley, *The History and Present State of Electricity: with original experiments* (London, 1767), p. 200.
11   Jessica Riskin comments, "Knowledge and virtue were inseparable; physics and moral understanding must improve together or not at all, the perfection of each being necessary to the advancement of the other … [Franklin] gave sentimental empiricists, seeking a moralized understanding of nature … an empiricist sentimentalism, a naturalized approach to the moral world," *Science in the Age of Sensibility: The Sentimental Empiricists of the French Enlightenment* (Chicago, 2002), pp.71–2.
12   Patricia Fara advises that "Electricity was the greatest scientific invention the Enlightenment" and "of all the branches of natural philosophy that would eventually become modern scientific disciplines, the most popular was the study of electricity," *An Entertainment for Angels: Electricity in the Enlightenment* (Cambridge, 2002), pp. 2, 19.
13   See Anne K. Mellor, *Romanticism & Gender* (New York, 1993), p. 33. See also Irene Tayler and Gina Walker, "Gender and Genre: Women in British Romantic Literature," in Marlene Springer (ed.), *What Manner of Women – Essays in English and American Life and Literature* (New York, 1977), pp. 98–123.
14   See the discussion of "radical sociability" in Margaret C. Jacob, "Sociability and the International Republican Conversation," in Gillian Russell and Clara Tuite (eds), *Romantic Sociability: Social Networks and Literary Culture in Britain 1770–1840* (Cambridge, 2002), pp. 24–42.
15   See Gillian Russell and Clara Tuite, "Introducing Romantic Sociability" in Gillian Russell and Clara Tuite (eds), *Romantic Sociability: Social Networks and Literary Culture in Britain 1770–1840*, pp. 1–23. I do not identify Hays's experiments with sociability as necessarily "romantic," but, rather, as emerging out of her engagement with quasi-egalitarianism in the Rational Dissenting community.
16   In a letter to Godwin that she incorporated into *Emma Courtney*, Hays refers to her hopes for a relationship with Frend that would have wider social consequences, "I cou'd have encreas'd the felicity & improvement of a small circle of individuals __ & this circle, spreading wider & wider, wou'd have operated towards the grand end, general utility." Hays to Godwin, 9 February 1796. *Pforz.*, MH 13. Brooks comments that "10 January 1796 is written on the letter but it is clearly postmarked 9 February," *CMH*, ftnte 249, p. 431.
17   *L&E*, p. 13.
18   Select Works of the Rev. Robert Robinson, of Cambridge, Edited, with Memoir, by the Rev. William Robinson (London, 1861) [1772], p. 186.
19   Ibid., p. 187.
20   Robert Robinson to Hays, 15 July 1788, *Pforz.*, 2158.
21   Ann Robinson to Hays, 8 May 1792, *Pforz.*, 2204.

22   See Barbara Taylor's discussion of Wollstonecraft's views on companionate marriage in historical context, in "Eros and Equality," *Mary Wollstonecraft and the Feminist Imagination* (Cambridge, 2003), pp. 116–142.

23   Hannah More, *Strictures on the Modern System of Female Education* ed. Gina Luria (1799; reprinted 1974), vol. I, p. 98.

24   Pam Morris comments that "the ideal of companionate marriage developed largely within the wider discourse of sentimentality" and "derived from belief in the biological gendering of bodies," *Conduct Literature*, pp. xxix.

25   In a letter from Thomas Brand Hollis, Esq., regarding the death of John Jebb, written 12 March 1786, included at the beginning of *The Works Theological, Medical, Political, and Miscellaneous of John Jebb, with Memoirs of the Life of the Author by John Disney* (London: T. Cadell, J. Johnson, J. Stockdale, 1787), 234–8.

26   I am grateful to G.M. Ditchfield for his generous contribution of Jane Blackburne Disney's birthdate, Parish Records, Richmond, Yorkshire (North Yorkshire County Records Office, Northallerton), PR/RM 1–5.

27   G.M. Ditchfield has generously provided the references in Lindsey's correspondence to Mrs. Disney's work. In a letter to Russell Scott dated 25 September 1787, Lindsey notes "printed for Marshall by Dr. and Mrs. Disney." On 1 October 1787, Lindsey wrote to William Tayleur of Shrewsbury, "Watts's hymns, which Mrs. Disney had very well corrected and got printed, were a great improvement and have been useful."

28   For an informative account of the Lindseys and Disneys and their circle, see D.O. Thomas, "Preface and introduction to John Disney's Diary," *Enlightenment and Dissent*, 21 (2002); 1–41; see also "John Disney's Diary: 1 January 1783–17 May 1784," ed. D.O. Thomas, *Enlightenment & Dissent*, 21 (2002): 42–127.

29   "The Christian Character Exemplified in A Discourse occasioned by the death of Mrs. Hannah Lindsey, and delivered at Essex Street Chapel, January 26th, 1812; by Thomas Belsham" (London), p. 10.

30   Thomas writes, "Lindsey's action in throwing up his preferment and leaving the Church was courageous, heroically so for many of his friends disapproved of what he did, notably his father-in-law, the Archdeacon. Moreover he was poor … and when he moved to Essex Street he lived in somewhat straitened circumstances, having had to sell portions of his library," "Preface and introduction to John Disney's Diary," p. 33.

31   Theophilus Lindsey, *A Farewell Address to the Parishioners of Catterick* (London, 1774), p. 12, quoted in G.M. Ditchfield, "Friends of Dr. Williams's Library 51st Lecture: Theophilus Lindsey: From Anglican to Unitarian" (1998), ftnte 20.

32   Thomas comments, "When Lindsey threw up his preferments in the Church of England [Blackburne] did not approve; he maintained that the reformers should fight for what they sought from within the Church … When J[ohn] D[isney] threw up his preferments he too met with the same disapprobation," "John Disney's Diary," p. 43, ftnte 7. Disney published *Reasons for resigning the rectory at Panton and the vicarage of Swinderby, in Lincolnshire; and quitting the Church of England* (London, 1782).

33   Catherine Cappe, Memoirs of the Life of the Late Mrs. Catherine Cappe (London, 1822), p. 100.

34   Ibid.

35   Ditchfield, "Friends of Dr. Williams's Library 51st Lecture: Theophilus Lindsey: From Anglican to Unitarian," p. 13.

36 The Unitarian community maintained close contact throughout England, even extending to America.

37 Letter from G.M. Ditchfield, personal communication, 12 October 2003.

38 Helen Plant, Unitarianism, philanthropy and feminism in York, 1782–1821: the career of Catherine Cappe, Borthwick Paper No. 103 (Borthwick, 2003), p. 3.

39 Ibid., p. 4.

40 Ibid.

41 See Ruth Watts's discussion of Cappe, "Women, philanthropy and class relations," *Gender, Power and the Unitarians in England 1760–1860* (London, 1998), pp. 70–76.

42 Catharine Cappe's marriage provides an intriguing contrast to George Eliot's representations of the stifling dynamic between Dorothea Brooke and the Reverend Mr. Causabon in *Middlemarch* (1871–72).

43 H. John McLachlan, "Mary Priestley: A Woman of Character," in A. Truman Schwartz and John G. McEvoy (eds), *Motion Towards Perfection: The Achievement of Joseph Priestley* (Boston, 1990), p. 251.

44 *Life and Correspondence of Joseph Priestley, LL.D., F.R.S.*, &c., ed. John Towill Rutt (London, 1831), vol. I, pp. 48–9.

45 Ibid., p. 260.

46 Helen Braithwaite, Romanticism, Publishing and Dissent: Joseph Johnson and the Cause of Liberty (Houndmills, 2003), pp. 84–5.

47 A reply from John Disney to a letter from Hays in early 1793 attests to Hays's interest in visiting Ann Jebb, *DWL*. Mss. 24.93.f.3. Anthony Page notes that Disney scheduled Hays's visit, perhaps one of several, a few days after Ann Jebb's two pamphlets on the French Revolution were published anonymously by T. Knott, who also published *Cursory Remarks* and *Letters and Essays*, "A great politicianess."

48 Anthony Page reports that Theophilus Lindsey judged Mrs. Jebb the thinnest person he had ever beheld. Young Abigail Adams, writing in 1785, observed equivocally that Ann Jebb was "a great Politicianess, which consequently pleased Mamma. The American War, [and] Present dispute with Ireland furnished this woman with subject of conversation," While her mother found Ann's company engaging, the young Abigail seems to have been less impressed: "Were I to attempt a description of Mrs. Jebb, I should find myself unequal to the business. Perhaps you never saw such a looking Woman," *John Jebb and the Enlightenment Origins of British Radicalism* (Westport, 2003), p. 179. Mrs. Jebb, like Hays, represented to a girl the perils of being brainy but not pretty. George Wilson Meadley, *Memoirs of Mrs. Jebb* (London, [1812]), p. 265; Disney to Hays, 31 January 1793, *DWL*, 24.93.3.

49 Rutt, "Biographical Sketch by Capel Lofft, esq.," p. 246.

50 Frida Knight, *University Rebel: The Life of William Frend* (1757–1841) (London, 1971), p. 24.

51 D.A. Winstanley, Unreformed Cambridge: A Study of Certain Aspects of the University in the Eighteenth Century (Cambridge, 1935), pp. 318–9.

52 Ann Jebb's pen name was a learned reference to a scriptural figure: Priscilla was a recent convert to Christianity and knew Paul in Corinth where she and her husband preached the gospels as equals.

53 Page, John Jebb and the Enlightenment Origins of British Radicalism, p. 40.

54 Ben Ross Schneider, Jr., *Wordsworth's Cambridge Education* (Cambridge, 1957), pp. 125–6.

55　Kathryn Gleadle writes that Ann Jebb expressed her activist role as "political wi[f]e" by "launching herself fully into the fray of fierce public debate." Gleadle points out that public association of Mrs. Jebb's views with her husband's seems to have spared her the ignominy heaped on her contemporary Catharine Macaulay who held similar ideas to Ann Jebb's, but stood entirely on her own in public, "thus, illustrating the subtle web of barriers and prejudices which could (but did not invariably) constrict female political involvement in even these liberated circles," Kathryn Gleadle, "British Women and Radical Politics in the Late Nonconformist Enlightenment, c. 1780–1830," in Amanda Vickery (ed.), *Women, Privilege, and Power: British Politics, 1750 to the Present*, (Stanford, 2001), pp. 136–7.

56　See Lucy Newlyn, "Case Study (3): Anna Barbauld," pp. 134–169; McCarthy and Kraft, "Introduction," pp. 11–32.

57　Jacob, "The International Republican Conversation," *Radical Sociability*, pp. 39–40.

58　Such too is Frend *,
　　a gen'rous name,
　　Glowing with freedom's sacred flame;
　　Who, ardent still in vigrous youth,
　　Climbs up the steep ascent of truth.
　　"* Late tutor of [Jesus] College"

59　"This lady is well known, [Dyer explained], to possess an understanding in political matters exceeded by few. During my writing the above ode, it was my good fortune to read several writings of Mrs. Jebb's, which appeared in the public prints between the years 1780, and 1785, on Annual Parliaments, the Right of Universal Suffrage, Mr. Fox's India Bill, Ship Money, the Liberties of the Irish Nation, and American Independence. When at Cambridge, this lady published a letter to the Author of the Observation on the Design of establishing Annual Examinations at Cambridge; and in the opinion of some of the best judges of the controversy, confuted Dr. Powel and his party. For a reason hinted in a former note, as well as from personal esteem, I pay this tribute of respect to female merit." George Dyer, "On Liberty," *Poems* (London, 1792).

60　*L&E*, pp. v–viii; Ibid., "Letter No. III., On the Influence of Authority and Custom on the Female Mind and Manners," pp. 19–30.

61　Hays's use is likely suggested by Macaulay's addressee, Hortensia, in her *Letters on Education* (1790).

62　Capel Lofft described John Jebb after his death as "Theologian, Orator, Patriot, and Citizen of the World!" in a poem published in 1811.

63　See Ditchfield, "Theophilus Lindsey and the Cause of Protestantism in eighteenth-century Britain," p. 5; see Thomas, "Preface and introduction to John Disney's Diary," pp. 27–9.

64　*L&E*, p. 120.

65　Ibid.

66　Ditchfield quotes Francis Blackburne's description of his son-in-law, "Friend Lindsey can talk, and even dispute, on horseback," "Theophilus Lindsey and the Cause of Protestantism in eighteenth-century Britain," p. 5.

67　Page, John Jebb and the Enlightenment Origins of British Radicalism, p. 146.

68　Robert Robinson to the Reverend Daniel Turner, Chesterton, 22 June 1784, Dyer, *Memoirs of the Life and Writings of Robert Robinson ...* (London, 1796).

69 D.O. Thomas notes that on 13 November 1783 John Adams and John Jay, then in London to represent America in peace negotiations with the British, visited The Society of Antiquaries, an organization which counted Disney and Benjamin Franklin as members. Franklin called the group "The Club of Honest Whigs." "Preface and introduction to John Disney's Diary," p. 30.

70 Hays chooses the same name, meaning a native of Theron, France, and also "height or plateau," for the Robinson-like character that Dyer earlier used for Robinson in his "Monody on the death of a Friend," (1790). Dyer's verse captures particulars of Robinson's character that the two "Therons" share. The French name also alludes to Eusebia's invocation of the Savoyard priest in Rousseau's *Emile*, and William Frend's account in his letter to her of the "'vicaire savoyard' of Rousseau," whom he praised as a benevolent man making his peasant congregation happy. Dyer's "Theron" loves to mingle with the village young people to whom he "strew'd the flow'rs of sacred truth/ With all a pastor's love, with all a patriot's zeal." The verses emphasize Robinson's fierce pursuit of freedom, his extensive learning, and his role as "bishop of barns and fields." They also speak to his effect on his congregation: "Contentment smil'd at poverty;/ Labourer would welcome pain, and hail/ The rising sun of liberty," workers would cry, "Still let me toil, still not inglorious toil,/ In Freedom's happy plains,/ In Britain's sacred Isle." The poetry is bad, the syntax confused and confusing, but the meaning is clear.

71 *L&E*, "Melville and Cecilia," p. 50.

72 Ibid., pp. 54–5.

73 Frances Burney, Cecilia, or Memoirs of an Heiress, By the Author of Evelina (Ondon, 1782).

74 Hays does not use Wollstonecraft's phrase from *The Vindication of the Rights of Woman*, but Cecilia embodies the qualities Wollstonecraft describes.

75 *L&E*, "Melville and Cecilia," pp. 55–6.

76 Patricia Fara notes that modern "commentators now view metaphoric thought as an essential cognitive tool for coping with novel situations," *Sympathetic Attractions: Magnetic Practices, Beliefs, and Symbolism in Eighteenth-Century England* (Princeton, 1996), p. 174.

77 Riskin comments, "Franklin's chief propagandist, Priestley, agreed that 'analogy is our best guide in all philosophical investigations' and hoped his *History and Present State of Electricity* would persuade electricians to follow Franklin's example in part by 'deducing one thing from another by means of analogy' ... Along with the epistemological and moral virtues they discerned in Franklinist physics, sentimental empiricists associated a social virtue, an openness to the influence of others," *Science in the Age of Sensibility*, pp. 96, 98.

78 *L&E*, "Melville and Cecilia," ibid.

79 Fara comments, "Writers increasingly applied ... magnetic images not to divine attraction but to the attraction between people ... magnetic power operated specifically ... it carried traditional sexual associations [to represent] the relationship between a particular couple," *Sympathetic Attractions*, p. 190.

80 In her poem on the bluestocking community, Hannah More described the interactions among the women in electrical images, "But sparks electric only strike/ On souls electrical like;/ The flash of Intellect expires,/ Unless it meets congenial fires," "Bas Bleu, or, Conversation, Addressed to Mrs. Vesey," (1786).

81   G.J. Barker-Benfield, The Culture of Sensibility: Sex and Society in Eighteenth-Century Britain (Chicago, 1992), p. 367.
82   Roy Porter, Enlightenment: Britain and the Creation of the Modern World (London, 2000), p. 294.
83   Robinson to "A Dissenting Minister," 2 May 1771, *Selected Works of the Rev. Robert Robinson*, p. 183.

Chapter Five

The Idea of Being Free

"It has been asked me … what benefits I propose to reap from this eccentric step? Shall I reply, a kind of, I know not what, satisfaction in the idea of *being free* … a desire of strengthening my mind by standing alone."

Mary Hays to William Godwin, 13 October 1795

Mary Hays sought and feared independence. Her desire for personal autonomy strengthened dramatically between 1793 and 1796, although the exercise of independent judgment in religious and political matters, individually and collectively, became increasingly perilous as war raged with France.[1] Three leading radicals played crucial roles in Hays's developing conception of personal freedom, both as activist models and close associates: William Frend, William Godwin, and Mary Wollstonecraft. Each of the three emboldened Hays to test her own capacity for living her idea of personal freedom, as they did. Each supported her in these efforts, at least initially, although their own experiences demonstrated the hazards of freedom. Hays's intense interactions with Frend, Godwin, and Wollstonecraft and their responses to her proved to be the crucible in which she forged her first major work, and established the direction of her future life. The drama that now engrossed Hays was mental, what Godwin termed "the collision of mind with mind," and unfolded in a subculture that encouraged new, more relaxed forms of sociability betweem men and women.

William Frend

Before he was forced to leave Cambridge, William Frend was a source of anxiety and pride to Unitarians for his prominent role in the ongoing religious and political print wars. Like the maverick Robert Robinson, Frend made his convictions public, no matter the result. Like John Jebb, Frend jousted with the powers at Cambridge University over enforced subscription to the Thirty-Nine Articles that excluded Dissenters. But Frend was even more provocative than the earlier Nonconformist crusaders: when Louis XVI was executed in January of 1793, England and France declared war on each other. Frend openly condemned the British government and justified the regicide. In the tense days of early 1793, Frend's pamphlet, *Peace and Union Recommended to the Associated Bodies of Republicans and Anti-republicans*, strained the conventional boundaries of British press freedom beyond public endurance, bringing down on him the combined retaliatory might of university, church, and state.[2]

Frend's pamphlet included an appendix, "On the Execution of Louis Capet," that he tacked on at the last minute before sending the manuscript to the printer. The body of the pamphlet had assumed a moderate, even conciliatory tone on contentious issues: free speech, expanded parliamentary representation, maintenance of the constitution, repeal of the Test Acts and poor laws, and modified taxation. But British nationalism ran high before the French king's execution and the declarations of war. In publishing the appendix, Frend chose not to heed the warning signs of loyalist sympathies around him: in December 1792, at a crowded meeting of town and gown at the Cambridge Town Hall, a resolution was passed prohibiting publications that urged sedition against University authorities and the government. At the end of the month, Thomas Paine's effigy was burned by a mob on Market Hill in Cambridge.[3]

Frend's analysis of the French equation of regicide and participatory republicanism included his opinion that no Englishman need be alarmed by the execution of one Frenchman even if a king: once the will of the French people turned to republicanism and against monarchy, Frend argued, the French king became a commoner. The will of the majority, Frend contended, rather than hereditary claim, must decide a nation's leadership and direction. If every European monarch were executed, he urged, it was no concern of the British people. Not surprisingly, many of Frend's readers saw sedition in his text. Two days after his pamphlet was published Frend was charged under the new Cambridge anti-sedition law. Six weeks later the Fellows of Jesus College voted seven to four to expel him; in the rush to judgment the number of Fellows required for a valid vote of expulsion did not convene. The University authorities accepted the College's decision, despite the fact that the University rules had not been observed.[4]

The Jesus College gate was chained against Frend.[5] He was allowed to appeal to the University Senate, and his trial began in May 1793, dominating University life, and riveting Unitarian and national attention.[6] Frend defended himself. His supporters, including Disney and Lindsey, contributed money and advice. Frend was found guilty of sedition and offered the chance to recant, but refused to do so.[7] His academic career at Cambridge was finished; he could no longer teach, use the libraries, or live in University property. But, given the procedural flaws in his banishment from Jesus College and the understanding of University authorities that they did not have a strong enough case against Frend[8]—he still had his fellowship and would therefore retain his income of £150 annually until he married. Frend was now in the curious position of being paid to remain a bachelor. How Hays responded to this situation is part of the story of the creation of *Emma Courtney* in Chapter Six. In the fall of 1794, Frend resolved to relocate permanently to London and live on his wits as teacher, writer, and reformer.

William Godwin

William Godwin (1756–1836) was the son and grandson of a Dissenting minister. Godwin initially trained for the ministry and attended the Dissenting academy at Hoxton where Andrew Kippis and Abraham Rees were among his tutors. They taught him the same lessons of Rational Dissent and political radicalism that Frend, Dyer, and Hays learned with Robinson, Jebb, Lindsey, and Disney.[9] Godwin was expelled from his congregation in Stowmarket in 1782, a painful if formative period of his life that he rarely mentioned,[10] and left the ministry soon after. However, he maintained connections with most of the important Rational Dissenters and Unitarians. In one of his periodic lists of friends and the years in which he met them, Godwin records that he met Theophilus Lindsey in 1783, John Disney in 1784, Priestley in 1785, and Robert Robinson in 1789.[11] After the French Revolution, which affected Godwin as profoundly as it did his Rational Dissenting associates, he met frequently with leading radicals: Richard Price, Andrew Kippis, Lindsey, Disney, Thomas Holcroft, John Horne Tooke, Paine, and Priestley.

Godwin worked as a professional journalist, writing for the Whig *New Annual Register* and *Political Herald*, publishing political pamphlets, often anonymously. He was recognized as an experienced observer of the contemporary political scene.[12] In 1791 he signed a contract with the publisher George Robinson to write "a treatise on Political Principles" that was published in 1793 as *An Enquiry Concerning Political Justice*. The work made Godwin instantly famous, and quickly became a blueprint for reformist ambitions. *Political Justice* set forth a theory of gradual anarchy predicated on the eventual triumph of reason over prejudice and superstition so that external forms of control, including monarchy, are rendered unnecessary by a collective march towards perfectibility. Godwin advocated the right to private judgment, in his lexicon "perfect sincerity," based on the Dissenting concept of "candour," or the importance of making impartial assessments. Many readers assumed Godwin advocated atheism, although he continued to be deeply influenced by his Rational Dissenting origins, and spoke rather of the "truth" than of God in *Political Justice*.[13]

Political Justice was followed in 1794 by *Things As They Are; or, The Adventures of Caleb Williams,* a novel, and *Cursory Strictures on the Charge Delivered by the Lord Chief Justice Eyre to the Grand Jury, October 2, 1794,* published anonymously in the London *Morning Chronicle*. *Cursory Strictures* played a crucial role in the Treason Trials of 1794, in which leaders of the grassroots Society for Constitutional Information and the London Corresponding Society were arrested, charged on allegations of treason, and tried at the Old Bailey. This was the latest in a series of government reprisals against popular political movements in Scotland and England, triggered by the outpouring of radical polemics protesting the war with France and calling for wide-spread anti-government meetings and petitions. The publisher Joseph Johnson was called as a

Crown witness and asked if he had published the *Rights of Man*. Johnson admitted only to selling, not publishing, it and was dismissed.[14]

Godwin quickly produced *Cursory Strictures*, a work that revealed the rationale for the government's prosecution of the radicals.

> Godwin simply pointed out that the government's definition of the radicals' treason involved a departure from that rule of law which was itself fundamental to the continuing legitimacy of Parliamentary rule. He turned the case for treason into a case of persecution, thereby helped swing the common sense of the English juryman over to the side of the radicals.[15]

When Godwin's strategic role became known at this critical moment in the print war,[16] he was again acclaimed. Conventional Britons saw Godwin as a perpetual gadfly: later in his life the British government considered him sufficiently dangerous to arrange surveillance of the children's bookshop and library he operated.[17] Godwin was the seminal radical political philospher who polarized public opinion as spokesman for Jacobin "modern philosophy" of the 1790s.

Godwin coordinated publication in 1794 of a new preface to *Caleb Williams* with the opening of the October Treason Trials.[18] Hays, like other radicals, in reading *Political Justice* was struck by Godwin's advocacy of the right to private judgment and his optimistic espousal of the "perfectibility" of human existence through the mechanisms of materialism and necessity. Godwin inspirited the Locke-Hartley tradition beyond its accepted precepts that all experience is based on sensory impressions that are associated into ideas. He proposed that not only could experience be manipulated to produce certain results, but that ideas could, in turn, produce experience. What the human mind could conceive, Godwin explained, the human being could achieve. Human reason should play the pivotal role in the course of human events and Godwin assumed that no particular class of men had a monopoly on reason. For Godwin education was the most powerful force for changing individuals and society. Godwin defined education in its broadest sense, acting on his belief that an individual's understanding could be advanced, not only by study, but by enlightened conversation with other seekers after truth. Radical sociability then was an integral part of Godwin's personal ethics, in which men and women would openly and frankly discuss the serious subject at hand, and attempt to do so with strict impartiality.[19] Godwin's interest in the "collision of mind with mind" provided Hays with a unique forum in which to further her education and to experiment as an amateur scientist.

Mary Wollstonecraft

Mary Wollstonecraft's story has been told many times. She was the most prominent woman intellectual of the 1790s. Her profound commitment to personal and political freedom emerged from childhood experiences of her alcoholic father's abuse of her passive mother, and from her strong sense of self, a sense that propelled her to independence. At 15, she later recalled, she determined never to marry for financial security or to become dependent on another person.[20] Wollstonecraft responded to her father's fiscal recklessness by looking for work in the occupations available to women: as paid companion, governess, and teacher in her own school. When each of these efforts failed, she made the great decision to try to live on her earnings as a professional writer, significantly supported by publisher Joseph Johnson. Johnson published her early work, provided a place for her to live in London, gave her the opportunity for professional training at his periodical, the *Analytical Review*, and included her in the congenial and stimulating social circle he presided over. There Wollstonecraft met others of Johnson's authors, William Blake, Henry Fuseli, Paine, Priestley, and Godwin.[21]

Wollstonecraft came to public attention in 1790 when she wrote the first response to Edmund Burke's pamphlet, *Reflections on the Revolution in France*. Here Burke attacked Richard Price, another early supporter of hers, for Price's enthusiastic support of the French Revolution. Wollstonecraft's *A Vindication of the Rights of Men* was followed by *A Vindication of the Rights of Woman* in 1792. Like Godwin, she achieved instantaneous recognition, in Wollstonecraft's case for her incisive political analysis of gender relations.[22]

Wollstonecraft's certainty about the wrongs done to women did not provide her with immunity from the havoc of her own emotional and sexual yearnings. She pursued Fuseli, who was married, and Fuseli's rejection of her was the catalyst for Blake's *Visions of the Daughters of Albion* (1793). When she went to Paris to witness the French Revolution, Wollstonecraft met Gilbert Imlay, an American entrepreneur, began a passionate affair with him, and gave birth to their daughter, Fanny Imlay. Imlay quickly tired of Wollstonecraft. She initially refused to face his rejection. In 1794, Wollstonecraft traveled to Norway, Sweden, and Denmark on business for Imlay with Fanny and a nursemaid. On her return to London from Scandinavia in October 1795, she learned from a servant that Imlay was living with a young actress. For the second time, Wollstonecraft attempted suicide; she was rescued against her will. Her heart was broken; she tottered at the brink of despair, but quickly resumed work. Thereafter, Wollstonecraft's public texts reflected her recognition that the "new language" she envisioned between men and women must incorporate both theory and practice, "the sentiments of passion, and the resolves of reason."[23]

Hays and Frend

Frend's move to London had great personal and professional consequences for Hays. Once he was installed in temporary quarters they met frequently, attending Unitarian services and visiting with the Disneys and Lindseys.[24] Both were active in the same circles of Rational Dissenters and English Jacobins.[25] Frend plunged headlong into the debate about free speech and governmental repression. He joined the ultra radical London Corresponding Society. Since 1792 the LCS had led the vanguard in promoting universal male suffrage and parliamentary reform and, most revolutionary of all, a membership that included growing numbers of artisans. Frend devoted himself to being a full-time reformer. His move to London coincided with the trials for alleged treason of 12 political activists, beginning in early October. Frend raised funds for the legal expenses of the defendants in the treason trials, and wrote for the outspoken *Cambridge Intelligencer*, edited weekly by Benjamin Flower, another disciple of Robinson's. He made new friends: Holcroft, the playwright, one of the 12 charged with sedition, and Godwin, among others.[26] At issue in these trials were many of the concerns raised in Frend's case at Cambridge the previous year: the sacred right of private judgment in religion and politics, relief from subscription to the Thirty-Nine Articles of allegiance to Crown and Church, full citizenship for non-Anglicans, parliamentary reform, and expanded suffrage. While the treason trials were in session, Godwin and Frend saw each other often, and Frend visited the prisoners in Newgate.[27]

Hays maintained that Frend was the great passion of her adult life. Although they corresponded from 1792 to 1796, only Frend's first letter to "Eusebia" survives. Evidence for their interactions once Frend moved to London in 1794 is found in Hays's letters to Godwin, Wollstonecraft's letters to Hays, and Hays's use of excerpts from Frend's letters to her, both in her correspondence with Godwin and in her novel *Memoirs of Emma Courtney*. Secondhand accounts come primarily from Henry Crabb Robinson, from reactions to Hays's first novel, from Elizabeth Hays,[28] and, a decade later, from Hays's brother-in-law, John Dunkin.[29] During the first year of closer proximity, Hays and Frend apparently established an idiosyncratic equilibrium. They worshipped together at Essex Street chapel and elsewhere; at Unitarian homes they met and talked collegially about the great events of the day and their own parts in them. They shared Hays's preparations for a writing career, Frend's success in attracting students, and distress at the rapidly deteriorating situations in Britain and France. No evidence exists that any special notice was taken in company with their Unitarian friends of an affinity between the hero of the Cambridge conflicts and the dowdy little woman who listened raptly when he spoke.[30] Hays believed that Frend reciprocated her feelings, but believed that he had refused to act on them.[31] But while Frend established himself professionally, despite the worrisome economic climate, Hays kept her plans to herself, reminded friends that she wanted work, and perhaps relished the secrecy of her romantic intentions.

By her own account to Godwin, Hays wrote long letters to Frend, in which she expressed her love and sexual desire. Frend sometimes responded or sometimes did not. Hays passed through a "crisis" with him in the early months of 1796 when she confronted him about his feelings and he absolutely rejected her. When she recovered relative equilibrium, she made an impromptu visit to his chambers, accompanied by Wollstonecraft, to apologize for her aggressive pursuit of him.[32] Hays reported to Godwin that on this occasion she put out her hand to signify that the chase was over,

Frend took it, and then she invited him to tea the next week and he accepted. In company with two other friends, Frend and Wollstonecraft took tea with Hays at her apartments. Afterwards Hays wrote to ask Frend to return her letters to him so she could use them in her novel. He never answered, and there is no evidence her letters were ever returned.

Hays and Godwin

Hays initiated this next formative relationship, as she had with Robinson, Worthington, and Wollstonecraft. She knew Godwin by reputation as they shared a common religious heritage of Rational Dissent. His recent publications had addressed political and social concerns that interested her. In the first year that Frend was in London, he continued to play a tutelary role in Hays's life. In their correspondence, Frend recommended Godwin's recently published *An Enquiry Concerning Political Justice*. He had written that Godwin's book might effect as a great a change in British political thought as had Locke's *Treatise on Government* (1690). Hays responded to Frend's enthusiasm in characteristic fashion by setting out to get a copy of Godwin's book. When she learned that the circulating library did not have a copy because the publisher charged £1, 16s for the book, Hays realized she could not afford it either. She wrote directly to Godwin to ask if she might borrow a copy, simultaneously establishing her radical *bona fides* and capitalizing on Frend's more relaxed network of male sociability to appropriate it for her own use.

Godwin kept a daily diary of his social activities and of his reading and writing. Hays kept, collected, and preserved many of the letters from others and those she wrote to them that she judged would be of interest to posterity. Together, these documents shed light on the powerful connection between Godwin and Hays between 1794 and 1797, both as friends and colleagues, and as part of a group that included some of the most compelling figures of their time.

Hays's lengthy letters to Godwin have been mostly ignored by commentators except as they provide information about and contrast with Wollstonecraft's letters to Imlay, or Hays's relations with Godwin.[33] The reading that follows traces Hays's inquiry and understanding through this correspondence and examines her fluctuating sense of power, her self-doubt, her anger, and her occasional impotence and despair at the impossibility of achieving the degree of freedom she saw lived and enjoyed by the men she knew. Hays drew on her growing sense of public authority to establish her credentials in her first letter to Godwin in October of 1794. She noted the climate of opinion that autumn: treason trials, conflagrations in France, siege mentality between and among Rational Dissenters and the Establishment, inflationary prices, pressure for reform, public unrest, fear of change. She set forth her own position on these conflicts, introducing herself by adopting Godwin's standard for enlightened conversation: "Perhaps no apology could be equally proper for a stranger addressing Mr. Godwin, and presuming to solicit a favor, as a plain statement of the truth!" Hays anticipated Godwin would read the final word "truth!" as code for her sympathy with his views on current events. To make certain, she alerted him to her "[disgust] with the present constitutions of civil society." Hays alluded throughout the letter to key radical identifiers: she quoted from Holcroft's novel *Anna St. Ives* (1793), knowing that Holcroft was then awaiting trial in Newgate, and from Godwin's recently published novel, *Caleb Williams*, which she had already read; she referred to the favorable appraisal of *Political Justice* in the *Analytical Review*. To establish her adherence to materialism and necessity, she carefully rejected the Deist view of the human mind as the circumscribed pendulum of a clock; she named Frend as her character reference; and she described herself as a disciple of truth who condemned, as she knew Godwin did, the external constraints that poisoned society. Her final credential was a female version of the Enlightenment quest. She assured Godwin that despite the deficiencies of female education, she loved literature, truth, and genius. She expressed her excitement at the prospect of reading his work, which, she understood from Frend, promoted human perfectibility.

This was a long way round to ask to borrow a copy of *Political Justice,* but Hays intended that Godwin would not be able to refuse. And he did not. Godwin lent her the first volume, then the second. More importantly, he visited her in November of 1794, after attending the trial earlier that day, perhaps the first man she entertained in her own apartments who was not a relation. They may well have discussed the treason trials, and Godwin's conversation with Frend and Disney at dinner the previous evening.[34]

In December Godwin noted in his journal that "Walker and Hayes called." Hays was probably accompanied by the Reverend George Walker, a friend of Gilbert Wakefield and John Aikin, and the author of the *Discourses on the Character of Judas* that Hays referred to in *Letters and Essays*. Walker had been on the faculty of the then-defunct Warrington Academy with Priestley, Wakefield and Enfield, and was best known for *The Dissenters Plea* (1790), in which he enumerated Rational Dissenting views on repeal of the Test and Corporation Acts to the satisfaction of many of his contemporaries, including Wakefield and Fox.[35] That same evening Hays wrote a long letter to Godwin, expressing her enthusiasm for the first volume of *Political Justice*. The events of the day may have prompted Hays's rephrasing of Eusebia's earlier interest in "pursuing and embracing truth without partiality and without prejudice, wherever it may be found" to a more active stance, declaring "I honor the man who dares intrepidly follow truth wherever [he?] thinks it may lead."[36] This was an allusion to Frend's indomitable integrity, to Holcroft, to Godwin, and, more subtly, to Hays's growing readiness to take risks.

Hays intimated that through Godwin she was entering another subculture, different from that of the high-minded Unitarians she knew, in which the basis of alliance was neither sectarian affiliation, place of worship, nor marital status. Godwin's set was a constellation of unmarrieds: Frend, Godwin, and Dyer were all bachelors; Holcroft was a widower with a daughter; except for Mrs. Inchbald and Mrs. Reverley, the women were single. What seemed to count in Godwin's circle of friends[37] was an individual's willingness to participate in freer, more egalitarian give-and-take in the pursuit of enlightenment.

As Hays and Godwin corresponded and met over the next months, Hays observed his commitment to what Pamela Clemit describes as "unreserved social communication," Godwin's "the collision of mind with mind," exchanges in which serious conversation between and among equals was a medium of enlightenment.[38] Hays discovered that Godwin expected robust communication, in which he at least tried to remain objective, reasoning and debating rather than arousing or being aroused by others' opinions.[39] She had been accustomed to decorous discussion with other Unitarians, in which the men behaved towards her as gentlemen to a precocious, odd bluestocking, careful not to provoke or wound, united with her against the common enemies of intolerance and persecution. Godwin was more direct. This was a revelation to Hays, and many personal and philosophical disagreements erupted in the pages of their letters and in their conversation over the next months. However, their relationship remained cordial enough that Hays invited Godwin to a "family dinner" on New Year's Day in 1795 at Mrs. Hays's new home, so that her sister Elizabeth and a brother could meet him.[40]

The correspondence quickly took shape as an advanced tutorial in truth and freedom for Hays. At Godwin's insistence, she wrote to him and he responded in person during his visits. From the outset, Hays deliberately demanded that gender itself be a subject of inquiry. In her letters Hays described Godwin as her "tutelary genius;" in fact, their interactions were more equal than that, producing angry sparks and surprising insights for them both, and at least for Hays, pain, as she was to discover things about herself she might rather not have known.

Godwin was the more socially sophisticated and the better educated, but in Hays he discovered a worthy sparring partner, at times an attentive student, at other times a shrewd if shrill critic. Hays experimented with various rhetorical gambits: the lexicon of Sensibility, literary and philosophical allusions from Enfield and others, pious formulations, quotations, sometimes oratory in imitation of her Unitarian teachers. Godwin complained that her letters were too long: she quoted too much and misrepresented his opinions. He soon discovered that beneath the torrent of words there was a steely will and compelling energy. She wanted to know what Godwin knew, to understand his abstract adumbrations, but she was no longer a novice at debate; indeed, masters had trained her. For the first time in Hays's exchanges with learned men, she insisted that the female condition be factored into Godwin's philosophical speculations; she pointed out that, as women's experiences are different from men's, so the projected outcomes must necessarily be reexamined. At first she backtracked with Godwin, as she had with Robinson, confessing need and womanly debility. Like Robinson, Godwin demurred at her lapses into self-deprecation. But when they discussed substance she stood firm, willing and able to cross swords. She frequently frightened herself into protestations of intellectual deficiency, but she was relentless in resisting what she perceived as his excessive rationality. She was convinced that the search for subjective, situational truth arising from experience and not abstract truth was the business of enlightened minds.

Godwin was the mentor Hays had been preparing for: erudite, brilliant, unpretentious, decisive yet open-minded, courageous, innocent of romance, not interested in her sexually, fully intending to be supportive. This was glorious and liberating. He encouraged Hays to write to him "as to your genius in the moon,"[41] as if like Bishop Berkeley's hypothetical falling tree, her words would not be overheard or judged by mundane standards. Godwin's philosophical interest in arriving at truth through interpersonal dialogue obliged him to try to be objective and frank in his responses to Hays. Mark Philp explains this dynamic: "The rules of debate for [Godwin and his] group were simple: no one has a right to go against reason, no one has a right to coerce another's judgment, and every individual has a right – indeed, a duty – to call to another's attention his faults and failings."[42] Whatever Hays revealed to him, Godwin tried to react impartially. Hays told and asked much, but she refused to play by Godwin's rules or control her passions when aroused. In what Mary Jacobus describes as a process of "proto-psychoanalysis" with Godwin, Hays revealed herself, healed herself somewhat in telling her story, and strengthened cognitively through the mental gymnastics. Like Robinson, Godwin proffered equality to Hays, but as the first person in her experience to be suspected of atheism, he also offered a whisper of license. Hays never ceased to love her God, but now she experienced His limitations and briefly, tentatively questioned the necessity of His divine plan in which men continued to inflict pain on women.[43]

Hays was both attracted to and repelled by the social interactions she observed between Godwin and his many friends. She struggled with her primness about received notions of female propriety that had lain dormant since Eccles's death. "I am not sufficiently french in my manners," she admitted, after Godwin had inadvertently seen her *deshabillé* one day when he called before she expected him, "to admit the gentleman to my toilet, & the etceteras of a woman's dress are not adjusted in a moment, on these subjects I am, perhaps, a little over nice." In *Political Justice* she read Godwin's assertions that human progress would render sexual passion and marriage "obsolete."[44] She disagreed vehemently on both counts.

By 1795, some British radicals had responded to the pervasive sense of siege as the opportunity for sexual experimentation: in Paris Wollstonecraft and Helen Maria Williams crossed the bounds of conventional mores by openly living with men who were not their husbands. Hays exercised the freedom her exchanges with Godwin produced in far more discreet increments. Frend relocated to London in the autumn of 1794; a year later, Hays moved from her mother's home in

Blackheath to 30 Kirby Street in the unfashionable Hatton Garden section of London. Her goal was to be nearer Frend, and Godwin and his circle.[45] For nearly 23 months, Hays tried to establish a beachhead of community independent of her family.

This first home of her own was a set of rooms in the house of a respectable female engraver, a block away from Hatton Garden, the crowded commercial street where Jews, Nonconformists, and other non-establishment types rubbed shoulders. It was a neighborhood of jewelers, with too many strangers passing through for prying questions to be asked or for traditional decorum to prevail. Hays usually wrote in the evenings, likely sitting at her second floor window overlooking the narrow pavement of Kirby Street.

In October 1795, almost one year to the day from her first letter to Godwin, she wrote to him to describe the exhilaration and anxiety she felt at the dramatic changes she had made in her life, in part through his influence and example, although he had already visited her there the day before. Stirred by their conversation, she continued it, identifying the reasons for her move: for the first time she had the promise of paid work writing for *The Critical Review*, a radical monthly magazine. Added to her small inheritance of £70 per year, the independent income provided the impetus to escape from her mother and sister Elizabeth, who had recently moved to Peckham, five miles away.[46] She presented this leap of faith into the future to Godwin for his approval, itemizing the catalysts that had prompted her. He was the arbiter of autonomy she trusted now. Hays briefly recounted the disappointments she had early experienced— John Eccles's death and the expectations of conventional happiness this dispelled. She emphasized her sensitive nature that could not easily withstand further disappointments. For the first time in any of her correspondence, she acknowledged the effect of her temperament on her mother and younger sister, explaining that she had taken the bold step of moving out of her mother's home to live independently in part because of her mother's disapproval of her new friends and their opinions that she had adopted. Her mother had described these as revealing a "dangerous freedom." Hays's provocative friends likely included Frend, Dyer, and Godwin himself.

Hays chose freedom, with all its dangers. Safety, she told Godwin, consisted in living a life of monotonous days that were abhorrent to her because of the mental ennui they produced. As a person capable of deep feeling, Hays wanted to be stimulated and aroused. She confessed to Godwin that when her mother and sister considered moving farther away from London, she had decided to act on the independence she had long contemplated, although the imagined perils of living on her own—loneliness, isolation, censure—had previously stopped her. "And thus have I (as the world would say & as some of my friends say)," she confided to him, "very foolishly thrown myself out of the asylum of my youth, & exchanged a life of what is called easy indolence, that is, one of worldly cares, for one more exposed and less assured."[47]

Mrs. Hays observed the difference in her daughter once Frend moved to London. If Hays was now contemplating sexual activity in the style of Wollstonecraft, she needed to move more in Frend's way and less in her mother's. The prospect of sexual liberation to a highly self-conscious woman writing to a radical philosopher must be couched in code he could comprehend. In her letter Hays posed the obvious question to him which she had been asked by others and which she asked herself: why had she taken this enormous step to autonomy, and what benefits did she hope to reap for herself? Her answer to Godwin and to herself rests on the continuing lure of enlightenment that might lead to freedom and fulfillment, the goals of the intellectual odyssey she had embarked on after Eccles's death. Hays calls upon all she has learned, particularly what she has read on the contemporary science of mind to confirm her experience. "Shall I reply," she writes in answer to her own question, "a kind of, I know not what, satisfaction in the idea of *being free*."

Here, uniquely, is Hays's poignant expression of her quest for personal enlightenment, predicated on her understanding of Lockean-Hartleyian mind-body interactions, and informed by radical enlightenment impulses towards social and sexual fulfillment.[48] The *idea* of such freedom, she has learned, involves shifting her mental habits, breaking the patterns of gendered domestic retirement that threaten to ossify "certain fatal, connected, trains of thinking" that predictably depress her spirits.[49] If all experience is based on physical impressions, then her daily environment has to be changed—or so she reasons. She needs Godwin's approval of her decision because he is the theorist calling for liberty from all constraints, even of family, social expectations, and religion. Perhaps alone among her friends, he can appreciate the powerful impulse she acts on, "the desire of strengthening my mind by standing alone." This degree of freedom encompasses both solitude and honesty: living alone now she will also be free of knowing herself with her "wayward fancies" as a burden on the family she loves. But, where was the potential actual benefit in all this for her? "I will own," she admits, to a "latent hope of enjoying, occasionally, more of the intercourse & conversation that pleases me," rational discourse being one of Godwin's favorite pastimes, or, as he had described it, "If we would ... improve the social institutions of men, we must write, we must argue, we must converse."[50] Hays speaks in code of interaction more generally, intimating romantic love and sexual pleasure with Frend. Hays makes herself available for conversation with Godwin and for intimacy with Frend, opening herself in the most obvious ways she can to meet the possibilities, dangerously free though they may be, of the uncertain future.

Hays recognizes that she acts on the idea of freedom, not freedom itself—its potential rather than actuality. She accepts, at least for the moment, that living on her own for the first time brings with it the loneliness she feels this October night writing to Godwin. In him she now has a sounding board and counselor who she hopes will help her answer the great question she has come to: what is a woman's life to be if she acts on the Enlightenment idea of being free? A self-directed woman needs meaningful work, so that dependence on romance will not be her only occupation; earning money of her own is likewise necessary for emancipation: will he help her with these improvements, too? She believes that he is a living example of his radical theories: he is direct, prompt, punctual, and ready to instruct her mind and to aid her restless spirit. In the spirit of full disclosure to Godwin at this important juncture in her life, Hays admits to a desire to write professionally, not because poetic fires burn in her or because she finds herself in dire financial straits. She wishes instead for a task or activity "that would amuse &, at the same time render my situation easier." She has been preparing herself for the kind of work she imagines she may be able to get, "applying closely to my french to qualify myself for translating." She knows of his professional connections with publishers, editors of periodicals, and other busy writers. She, on the other hand, declares herself "very ignorant of literature, as a business." She is willing to be guided by his judgment in finding work. "My wishes are modest, & my expectations moderate;" more than money or fame, she wants mental stimulation: "[T]he constant exercise of my faculties is necessary to preserve me from sinking into that painful lassitude, that want of the radical principle of happiness (the having something to do, to hope & to fear) which is of all states the most intolerable." Yet for all her voluble deference, Hays is proud, and finds it difficult to ask explicitly for Godwin's help. "Something of all this I had meditated to say to you when I saw you, but I had not sufficient courage."

Why is she frightened by the wish to be actively involved with other people and to contribute to the republic of letters? For one thing, much as she welcomes his presence, Godwin still intimidates her in person; she acknowledges this because of the rule he insists on for their friendship, that he will only respond to her letters in person. She would feel less threatened if he would write his reactions so that she could have time to consider her answers. She is afraid, too, of burdening him with her emotional needs as she has her family. She concludes her long letter with the effusions she had earlier expressed to Robinson, directed now to a man who seems to have the time to teach her. What she offers him is a thoughtful listener, a woman who promises she will not flinch at his exercise of candor in the interests of the "idea of *being free*."

Hays thus communicates to Godwin her hopes, needs, and fears. For now, in Frend's stead, he will be her mentor as professional writer, thinker, and outspoken authority. Hays ends her letter by assuring Godwin that she agrees with him on many, though not all, of the subjects they discuss together. In the next few months they will discuss, debate, argue, and reconcile, and their exchanges will intensify and shape Hays's struggle for intellectual, artistic, and existential independence.

Hays and Wollstonecraft

Hays called on Wollstonecraft in autumn 1795 while she was recovering from a second suicide attempt. The two women now drew close, sharing their intimate histories. Eager to advance her relationship with Frend, Hays sought to learn from Wollstonecraft's experiences with Imlay and Fuseli; she studied the realities of the "fallen" woman's experience. Hays was captivated by Wollstonecraft's firsthand accounts of sexual rapture, betrayal, and maternity. She may have read some of Wollstonecraft's feverish letters to Imlay.[51] The equilibrium between the two women shifted: Hays comforted Wollstonecraft, defending her illicit relationship with Imlay.

Hays was quickly tainted with guilt by association because she continued to see Wollstonecraft and to express vigorous support of her. Within the tiny, self-protective networks of English Jacobinism, Hays kept abreast of Wollstonecraft's movements, and reported to Godwin on her friend's depression, explaining it in the context of her own evolving feminism. Hays told Godwin about a recent conversation she had with a group of women who knew that Wollstonecraft had not been legally married to Imlay, and that her daughter Fanny was illegitimate. Hays's account of the conversation echoes Robinson's translation of Saurin's sermon about the unchaste woman. Hays explained that the women present on the occasion were amiable and sensible, and known to both Wollstonecraft and Hays. Yet, like Simon, Saurin's Pharisee, they were quick to apply conventional rough justice to Wollstonecraft, judging her without considering the actual motives and causes of her behavior.[52] The conversation affected Hays deeply and she would later reflect on other women's intolerance towards herself and Wollstonecraft. She described her own reactions to the "amiable" women's censoriousness and determination to ostracize Wollstonecraft. Hays's response was vigorous, drawing on her training in toleration, while positioning herself as a Rousseauvian outsider. She told Godwin that she had become indignant at the women's bigotry. She had admonished the women that the lack of legality of Wollstonecraft's intimate relationship with Imlay was her own business, and no one else's. Wollstonecraft, alone, would have to deal with whatever discomforts might attend her status as an unmarried mother. Hays declared she would continue to socialize with Wollstonecraft, and commented that anyone might be duped by her imagination as Wollstonecraft had been about Imlay. No one, she averred, not even Wollstonecraft's detractors, could boast of being perfect in her human judgments. Hays's critique struck the women as naïve and theoretical.[53] Hays later heard from a third party that as the avowed admirer of Wollstonecraft she was considered likely to imitate her friend's immoral conduct.[54]

Hays, Godwin, and Wollstonecraft

Despite her own disappointments in love, in early 1796 Hays decided to try her hand at matchmaking. Her motive in bringing Godwin and Wollstonecraft together for tea at her home on 8 January 1796 was to distract Wollstonecraft from her preoccupation with Imlay.[55] The pair had been earlier introduced in 1791 at a dinner at Joseph Johnson's, where Thomas Paine had also been present. Godwin had disliked Wollstonecraft on that occasion for monopolizing the dinner conversation when he wanted to hear Paine speak. At Hays's tea party, Holcroft made the fourth; he had already visited Hays earlier in the month with Godwin. Hays reported to Godwin afterwards that though Holcroft "frightened [her] a little," she was pleased to become his friend.

In her letter to Godwin written a few days later, Hays noted that after the Friday night party, Wollstonecraft had applauded Godwin's sensitivity to Hays's unhappiness, and commented that such considerateness raised him in her esteem. Although Wollstonecraft had been animated at their meeting, Hays reported that her gaiety was superficial, for despite her great talents, she continued to suffer acutely over Imlay. Hays expressed her relief that Wollstonecraft's suicide attempt had been unsuccessful and the depth of her feeling for her. "Happy for her, & happy for me she is yet, preserved!" Hays wrote, "I shall ever love her, for her affectionate sympathies, she has a warm & generous heart!" Nonetheless, despite her excellent friends, Hays confessed, "*I am exquisitely miserable!*" The cause, of course, was Frend's obduracy. Hays also noted the interest Wollstonecraft evinced in Godwin; through the spring and summer Hays sensed the growing intimacy between her two friends, and, though she had set their contact in motion, their mutual happiness exacerbated her own sense of loneliness.

Turmoil and Commencement

Hays's acute sense of isolation was aroused long before her two friends found each other. In the summer of 1795, Hays wrote only once to Godwin, a long letter in which she expressed anger and frustration, not at him, but at the uncomfortable situation in which she had placed herself. Hays took the opportunity in the letter to review her efforts to achieve enlightenment and the apparent disconnection between learning and love. Frend came when invited to tea with others, but he would not reciprocate her feelings, and she was stymied in her personal ambitions. Hays appreciated Godwin's invitation to write to him when her mind is "full of thought," as she would to her "genius in the moon." She had waited to write, she explained, because her mind has been too full of "a thousand wayward, contradictory, ideas & emotions, which I am myself unable to disentangle." She despairs that this is so, because she has sought so hard for mental training to reason her way to happiness. She is angry, as well as despairing, because she finds herself no nearer to her goal of understanding or fulfillment than before.

Hays is discouraged when she compares herself with other women who appear content with frivolity, and who find gaiety in the superficial pastimes of conventional society. She reiterates Wollstonecraft's critique of the mindless, heartless routine of female domestic life, exemplified in such women's vain pursuits as "hanging drapery on a smooth block."[56] There is nothing of the impartial observer in her prose, although she uses the diction of reason to demonstrate to Godwin her ability to examine her feelings. Hays concedes that she is not free from female duties or female vanity. She, too, is the product of gendered education. But unlike the women she despises and envies for their careless existence, she thirsts for more: cultural assumptions about woman's proper sphere, she cries, are "insufficient to engross, to fill up, the active, aspiring mind!" The reformist women who deliberately spurned Wollstonecraft exemplify the internalized, as well as external, restrictions on female freedom. Hays sees herself in much the same position: she is "hemmed in on every side, by the constitutions of society," as she puts it, and, she confesses, by her own adherence to social restraints: "I perceive, indignantly perceive, the magic circle, without knowing how to dissolve the spell!"

Hays writes from an uneasy dual perspective as an aspiring woman intellectual, culturally conditioned like others of her sex, but at the same time resistant to the imposed constraints of gender. She aspires to a life where the mind has no sex, but she sees that knowledge is controlled and produced by and for men and that they exclude women from that arena. She can find comfort nowhere. In her desperation, she invokes the supernatural, that realm beyond the reach of reason antithetical to Frend and Godwin, with the image of the magic circle of gender expectations that she is able to see, but powerless to dispel. She acknowledges the "eccentricities of conduct" attributed to women like herself and Wollstonecraft, the result, she explains, of the disparity between women's ambitions and the lack of any acceptable way to express them. Hays articulates her sense of impotence in even expressing "the struggles, the despairing, though generous, efforts of an ardent spirit denied a scope for its exertions." In this letter, Hays stands on Wollstonecraft's shoulders to summon the private learned woman to her modern incarnation as the public woman of letters. Hays speaks in code, as she had in her earlier letter, of female aspirations for freedom—including sex and power—that, if released, could contribute in original, *female* ways to the common good.[57] But without socially acceptable release, these energies poison, rather than empower. "Strong feelings & strong energies," she insists, "which properly directed, in a field sufficiently wide, might – ah! what might they not have aided?" but that "forced back, & pent up, ravage & destroy the mind that generated them!"

Much of the content of Hays's letters was to be included verbatim in *Emma Courtney*. As the heroine is stimulated to serious thinking by Mr. Francis, the philosopher modeled on Godwin, so Godwin had encouraged Hays in their visits together. During the autumn, he called on her more often; as their friendship deepened, her letters became longer. In November of 1795, she wrote a chatty letter in which she discussed a variety of subjects, including her personal commitment to "perfect sincerity." Earlier in life, she writes, she observed the human practice of concealing faults from one another, a practice she considered "fruitless labour." Resisting such hypocrisy, as a lover of "the beauties of truth," she deliberately confesses her faults, in this way believing that she neutralizes other people's criticisms of her by apologizing first. Pre-emptive confession may produce absolution, but it also enriches her understanding of herself and others as human beings with imperfections that are also the roots of their virtues.

Such introspection leads to her reaction to Godwin's "plan," his suggestion that she set down the thoughts she has communicated to him in her letters in the form of a novel. She responds to his proposal as she had to Worthington's three years earlier. She will try her hand at fiction if Godwin will promise, as Worthington did, to read the work in progress. "Would you allow me to transmit the sheets to you from time to time," she asks gingerly, "that I might avail myself of your observations as I went on?"[58] Godwin's suggestion that she codify her thoughts in a novel validates Hays's sense that, despite her prolixity, he recognizes her observations as worthy of wider attention.

Hays worked hard at her new project into the new year. She sent Godwin the first pages of her novel in March of 1796. In the covering note she writes that she is not satisfied with her draft, nor does she expect he will be. But following Wollstonecraft's example, she finds energy in anguish.[59] "I am solicitous for your opinion of my papers," she writes, "that I may calculate my chances of success." She appreciates the time he takes from his own work to review hers, and assures him that his friendship is "my pleasure and my boast." If he does not reciprocate by reassuring her he is convinced of her sincerity, she threatens to become "proud and saucy again." She even makes fun of her own proclivity to whine: "This is a letter, I believe, without a complaint, I must not end it so, or you will suspect, that somebody has assumed my signature and imitated my writing."

Godwin read her draft quickly. On 8 March he noted in his journal that he received Hays's manuscript and the same evening wrote her a short encouraging note to say that what he read absorbed and pleased him. He advised her to work on fleshing out the story appropriately for her intentions.[60] Two days later, with uncharacteristic impetuosity, he came in her while she was still dressing in front of her landlady's fire, probably eager to talk about her book.[61]

Mary Hays launched the next phase of her career by simultaneously severing her dreams of romance with Frend and intensifying her ambitions for public authority with Godwin's encouragement. In November, her first novel would be published, bringing her some fame, much notoriety, and a little money. Until then, she wrote hard, observing the changing fortunes of her friends, and gestating the text that would be her *Political Catechism*, her *Farewell Address,* her *Peace and Union Recommended,* her cry of conscience, her declaration of independence, her apostasy.

Notes

1   Nicola Watson argues, "In post-Terror England, it becomes harder and harder to authorize the voice of individual feeling as a form of legitimate rational protest," "Julie Among the Jacobins," *Revolution and the Form of the British Novel 1790–1825* (Oxford, 1994), p. 39.
2   See Kevin C. Knox, "'The Revolting Propositions of Newtonian Mechanicks': Natural Philosophy and the Trial of William Frend," *Enlightenment and Dissent*, 17 (1998): 126–53.
3   Arthur Gray and Frederick Brittain, *A History of Jesus College Cambridge* (London, 1960), pp. 124–5.
4   Ibid.
5   Peter Searby, *A History of the University of Cambridge, III 1750–1870* (Cambridge, 1998), p. 419.
6   Ibid.
7   Here was civil disturbance in their midst, resonant with what Ditchfield describes as "one of the fundamental debates of this period, namely the extent to which Cambridge should serve as a predominantly Anglican institution and how far it bore wider responsibilities to an increasingly sophisticated secular society," G.M. Ditchfield, "A History of the University of Cambridge – Review," *English Historical Review* (April, 1999).
8   Gray and Brittain, ibid., pp. 124–5.
9   "The tradition of religious dissent was a tradition also of political dissent. And it was out of this tradition that William Godwin arose," Kenneth N. Cameron, "William Godwin," *Shelley and his Circle* (Cambridge, 1961), vol. I, p. 161.
10   Peter H. Marshall, "The Ministry," *William Godwin* (New Haven, 1984), pp. 46–55.
11   William Godwin, Diary, *Abinger*, Dep. e. 196–227.
12   Pamela Clemit, "Two Pamphlets on the Regency Crisis by William Godwin," *Enlightenment and Dissent*, 20 (2001): 185–93, and [William Godwin], "The Law of Parliament in the Present Situation of Great Britain Considered," pp. 194–225, and [William Godwin], "Reflexions on the Late Consequences of His Majesty's Recovery from His Late Indisposition," *Enlightenment and Dissent*, 20 (2001): 228–48.
13   See Mark Philp's illuminating discussion in *Godwin's Political Justice* (Ithaca, 1986), pp. 34–7.
14   See Helen Braithwaite's account in *Romanticism, Publishing and Dissent: Joseph Johnson and the Cause of Liberty* (Houndmills, 2003), pp. 144–8.
15   Philp, *Godwin's Political Justice*, pp. 117–19.
16   Pamela Clemit, "Introduction," *Lives of the Great Romantics: Godwin, Wollstonecraft & Mary Shelley by their Contemporaries, I, Godwin* (London, 1999), p. xvi.
17   Pamela Clemit, "Philosophical Anarchism in the Schoolroom: William Godwin's Juvenile Library, 1805–1825," *Biblion: The Bulletin of The New York Public Library*, 9/1–2 (Fall 2000/ Spring 2001): 44–70.
18   Pamela Clemit, "*Caleb Williams*: The Paradigm of the Godwinian Novel," *The Godwinian Novel: The Rational Fictions of Godwin, Brockden Brown, Mary Shelley* (Oxford, 1993), p. 36.
19   Ibid., p. 11.

20 Wollstonecraft to Godwin, 4 September 1796, in *MH*, pp. 242, 357.

21 Braithwaite, *Romanticism, Publishing and Dissent*, pp. 164–5.

22 Harriet Jump, "Introduction," *Lives of the Great Romantics Volume 2: Wollstonecraft* (London, 1999), p. x.

23 Mary Wollstonecraft, "Letter XXXVI to Imlay" [Paris, 1793], *The Works of Mary Wollstonecraft*, ed. Janet Todd and Marilyn L. Butler (7 vols, London, 1989), vol. 6, p. 402.

24 In August 1797 the *Monthly Magazine* reported that William Frend, M.A., was offering a "series of lectures in Mathematics and Natural Philosophy" at his chambers, No. 4, Hare-Court Temple, near George Dyer's rooms.

25 Eventually Frend settled into his own chambers at No. 4, Hare-Court Temple, near George Dyer who had moved to London in 1792 and lived at Clifford's Inn.

26 See Nicolas Roe, "'Barricading the road to truth': Wordsworth's Godwin, London 1795," *Wordsworth and Coleridge: The Radical Years* (Oxford, 1988), pp. 186–98.

27 See "Letter 5," Elizabeth Pattisson to William Pattisson, 12 February 1794, which mentions Frend as well as Wakefield among other visitors to the "honourable mansion" at Newgate, Penelope J. Corfield and Chris Evans (eds), *Youth and Revolution in the 1790s: Letters of William Pattisson, Thomas Amyot and Henry Crabb Robinson* (Phoenix Mill, 1996), p. 52.

28 See Elizabeth Hays, Letters to Hays [c. 1796], 4 February 1801, 24 February 1801, 14 August 1803, *CMH*, pp. 481–3.

29 In 1808, the year Frend married a younger woman, John Dunkin commented that Hays had acquitted Frend of ingratitude too easily when he made an advantageous marriage, John Dunkin to Hays, 3 March 1808, 23 March 1808, *CMH*, p. 490. On the envelope of an 1805 letter to Hays from her sister, Joanna Dunkin, the name "Frend" is written in what may be Hays's hand, as well as the letter H many times. Joanna Dunkin to Hays, 7 January 1805, *CMH*, p. 486.

30 Hays confided to Godwin that part of Frend's appeal arose from his role as fearless freethinker and advocate of the right to private conscience in the historical struggle for toleration: "I shou'd never have been attached to Mr.____ had I not conceived his principles & conduct to have been magnanimous, had he not been persecuted for those principles, & a sufferer by that conduct," Hays to Godwin, 6 June 1796, *Pforz.*, MH 22.

31 "The behaviour of the man I sought," she advised Godwin, "was too inconsistent to be entirely the result of indifference," Hays to Godwin, 6 February 1796, *Pforz.*, MH 12.

32 Hays described the scene to Godwin: "guilty of errors, who is free? — I held out my hand — he took it, and replied to me with a degree of cordiality," Hays to Godwin, 8 March 1796, *Pforz.*, MH 16.

33 Mary Jacobus, "Traces of an Accusing Spirit: Mary Hays and the Vehicular State," *Psychoanalysis and the Scene of Reading* (Oxford, 1999), pp. 202–34; *MH*, pp. 174–6; Lyndall Gordon, *Mary Wollstonecraft: A New Genus* (London, 2005); Judith Barbour, "'Obliged to make this sort of deposit of our minds': William Godwin and the sociable contract of writing," *Romantic Sociability: Social Networks and Literary Culture in Britain 1770–1840* (Cambridge, 2002), pp. 166–85.

34 Godwin's journal records, "[Nov] 14. F. dine at Northmore's, w. Frend, Disney, B. Hollis & Sedwick'; [Nov] 15. Su. Newgate; Holcroft, Tooke, Thelwal, Kyd, Richter,

Joyce, Borsville, Frost & col Miles; see J Taylor; call on Miss Hayes [sic]: dine at Lister's, w. Crisp & J Hollis; talk of passions, God and self love."

35   Anthony Lincoln, *Some Political and Social Ideas of English Dissent 1763–1800* (Cambridge, 1938), pp. 249–50.

36   Hays to Godwin, 7 December 1794, *Pforz.*, MH 2.

37   Mark Philp identifies the following as Godwin's associates according to mention in his daily diary in 1795: Amelia Alderson, Anna Barbauld, James Barry, George Dyer, George Dyson, Joseph Fawcett, John Fenwick, John Foulkes, William Frend, Joseph Gerrard, Thomas Holcroft, Elizabeth Inchbald, Alexander Jardine, Henry Constatin Jennings, Joseph Johnson, James Mackintosh, James Marshall, Basil Montagu, Mathew More, Thomas Northmore, Dr. Samuel Parr, Richard Porson, Maria Reveley, Joseph Ritson, George Robinson, William Smith, John Taylor, John Thelwall, John Horne Tooke, Felix Baurghan, Thomas Wedgwood, "Appendix B," *Godwin's Political Justice* (Ithaca, 1986), pp. 241–4.

38   See Pamela Clemit's discerning article, "Godwin, Women, and 'The Collision of Mind with Mind,'" *The Wordsworth Circle*, XXV/2 (Spring 2004): 72–6.

39   Philp, *Godwin's Political Justice*, pp. 125–9.

40   Hays to Godwin, 1 January 1795, *Pforz.*, 3.

41   Godwin to Hays, 7 May 1795, *Pforz.*, WG 217.

42   Philp, *Godwin's Political Justice*, p. 128.

43   Ditchfield notes Godwin's "frequent meetings" with Lindsey, as well as Wollstonecraft, and Lindsey's "subsequent anxiety" at what he perceived to be the rejection of "revealed religion" by Godwin and Holcroft, among others, and Paine's deism. "Theophilus Lindsey and the Cause of Protestantism in eighteenth-century Britain" (London, forthcoming, 2006), p. 5.

44   See Barbara Taylor's trenchant discussion of reformist sexual politics, *Mary Wollstonecraft and the Feminist Imagination* (Cambridge, 2003), pp. 195–202.

45   "I am more in your walks," Hays to Godwin, 1 October 1795, *Pforz.*, MH 7.

46   See *CMH*, "Appendix I: Hays' [sic] addresses," pp. 583–4.

47   Hays to Godwin, 13 October 1795, *Pforz.*, MH 8.

48   Jonathan I. Israel, "Women, Philosophy, and Sexuality," *Radical Enlightenment: Philosophy and the Making of Modernity, 1650–1750* (New York, 2001), p. 83.

49   Hays to Godwin, 13 October 1795, *Pforz.*, MH 8.

50   Clemit, "Godwin, Women, and 'The Collision of Mind with Mind,'" p. 72.

51   There are similarities between the women's writings that are discussed in Chapter Six. A case in point is both women's use of the evocative "magic circle" in their published texts. The phrase does not appear in Wollstonecraft's letters to Imlay. In her 28 July letter to Godwin, Hays used the phrase. Wollstonecraft was first to use the phrase in print some months later in *A Short Residence in Sweden, Norway, and Denmark (1796)*, "Letter 10," in Todd and Butler, *The Works of Mary Wollstonecraft*, vol. 6, p. 294. A few months later, in *Memoirs of Emma Courtney*, published in November of that year, Hays repeated the phrase in two different places. See *MEC*, pp. 66, 116, based on Hays's letter to Godwin, 28 July 1795, *Pforz.*, MH 6.

52   Robinson's translation emphasizes Saurin's empathy with the unchaste woman's experience of her situation and his refusal to condemn her without more information.

53   The ladies advised Hays "that however just might be [...her] reasoning in the abstract, certain situations & circumstances, required certain observances, which [...she] was

only, not aware of from having but little mix'd with society," Hays to Godwin, 20 November 1795, *Pforz.*, MH 9.

54   Ibid.
55   Hays, "Memoirs of Wollstonecraft," *Annual Necrology for 1797–8* (London, 1800), p. 452.
56   *VRW*, "Chapter IX," p. 283.
57   Michèle Le Doeuff writes that in the seventeenth century, "Rather than the right to acquire existing knowledge, what was affirmed was the freedom to extend the boundaries of knowledge and of the freedom to doubt, to challenge past errors or destroy pseudoknowledge," *The Sex of Knowing*, trans. Kathryn Hamer and Lorraine Code (New York, 2003), p. 32.
58   Hays to Godwin, 5 November 1795, *Pforz.*, MH 27.
59   See Godwin's view that after Wollstonecraft began to recover from the rupture with Imlay, "she did not, like ordinary persons under extreme anguish of mind, suffer her understanding, in the mean time, to sink into listlessness and debility," but wrote *Letters from Norway* and an autobiographical comedy, *MAV*, pp. 101–2.
60   Godwin to Hays, 9 March 1796, *Pforz.*, WG 319.
61   Hays to Godwin, 10 March 1796, *Pforz.*, MH 17.

Chapter Six

Hazardous Experiment

"The result of [my heroine's] hazardous experiment is calculated to operate as a *warning*, rather than as an example."

Mary Hays, "Preface," *Memoirs of Emma Courtney*, 1796

Mary Hays spent the first six months of 1796 composing her novel, *Memoirs of Emma Courtney*. This enterprise would prove be the turning point in her intellectual development when she finally exorcised the fawning dependence on the approval of her male mentors and colleagues that Wollstonecraft had discerned. Hays sent successive pages of her manuscript to Godwin, who read and commented as they had agreed; and this set the stage for their ongoing debate. They argued about Hays's sources that included her concurrent responses to Godwin's reactions. Hays discovered how demanding a reader he could be, and how obdurate she was about making changes. They wrangled by letter and in person. In the process, the equilibrium they had initially established as mentor and student frayed, and their battle of wills revealed the fault lines that would permanently rend their relationship in time to come. In the early months of 1796, however, tussling with Godwin was productive as well: the need to defend her text as she wrote sharpened Hays's awareness of what she produced and why; in the process, her work gathered momentum according to her own proclivities. Godwin repeatedly cautioned that the novel's radical defect was that the story unfolded entirely from her self-absorbed heroine's point of view. Hays refused to alter what she saw as the truth of what she wrote because it was based on her personal experience. Such candor and independence came at the high cost of an unhappy notoriety: when the book was published, readers and critics assumed, despite Hays's disclaimers, that author and heroine were one and disapproved loudly of both.

Hays's manuscript and her responsive commentary posited a dynamic in a woman's writing between content and form in which the writer was self-consciously and simultaneously subject and object, artifact as well as artificer. In *The Confessions* Rousseau had served as narrator and subject, but Hays's novel reworked the technique by incorporating letters of real people with close personal relationships to her. Her arrangement of these texts and her use of them to determine the direction of her narrative were new in novel writing. She insisted on making personal experience the subject of her inquiry. This fueled subjective, yet clinically detailed, depictions of female depression, rage, sexual desire and frustration, all as she lived them. As innovative as the experimental form she devised was her discovery that female sexuality was a valid form of knowledge uniquely, if not exclusively, accessible to women.

Readers after Godwin found it easy to misrepresent Hays as a Wollstonecraft *manqué*, a lesser thinker, who failed to achieve Wollstonecraft's powerful status as rebellious reader turned revolutionary writer.[1] Wollstonecraft's intention was to interrupt and explode the fraternal conversation about political theory represented by the canonical continuum of male thinkers.[2] Hays is most cogently read as a lone amateur scientist. In contrast to Wollstonecraft, Hays sought to understand the conversation of her forefathers, not in order to interrupt it, but to learn how to construct a parallel, woman-centered discourse and, perhaps to create an entirely new kind of dialogue. This alternative conversation would focus on cognitive, psychological, and historical concerns rather than explicitly political ones, and reveal the absence of women in the intellectual, social, and political systems created and debated by Hays's male colleagues and their ignorance of female psychology. Hays's first impulse as a nascent scientist without credentials, colleagues or laboratory was to investigate herself. Life-writing provided the vehicle for her experiments.

In 1796 the sentient female self, in its public and private guises, claimed center stage in Hays's textual and existential projects, beginning with the work that Godwin suggested she write. To delineate her heroine's experience, Hays delved into her affective memory to expose successive layers of her own psyche. This was not life-writing as the gathering of external data and "minute particulars" according to Samuel Johnson's dictum in *The Rambler,* or James Boswell's recent illustration of the power of accumulating such intimate details in constructing Johnson's *Life* (1791). Could Hays have read Boswell's journals she might have recognized a kindred raw adventurer in him. But she wanted to learn and write about what she saw as psychological truth. She exploited the confessional tradition derived from Augustine and Rousseau, and appropriated the formal tactics of *Eloisa.*[3] Hays moved beyond received notions about autobiography, biography, and fiction, instead locating her enterprise in an emerging, alternative arena in the contemporary science of the mind.

Investigating the Mind

Exciting discoveries in the new science of the mind proved useful for Hays in her psychological inquiries. Erasmus Darwin[4] was one of the medical pioneers whose anatomical research established that consciousness is located in the brain, that the brain is connected to the body by sensory and motor nerves, and that "mental activity is an organic process that occurs in a physical body."[5] In *Zoönomia* (1794–96), Darwin, physician and fellow of the Royal Society,[6] demonstrated that the brain was composed of "parts or 'organs' rather than, [as previously thought,] an undifferentiated whole." These parts had specific cognitive functions that could be impaired by injury. Darwin diverged from Locke in important ways that would have made sense to Hays, positing an indirect causal relation between "*innate desires*" and behavior, and most importantly, emphasizing "*unconscious* mental processes guided by habit."[7] Hays learned from Darwin that mind and body were not static, isolated faculties, but parts of the indivisible whole of human consciousness. Darwin argued that a person's identity was the product of an idiosyncratic chain of linked thoughts and neuromuscular habits. Education, in the expansive Priestleyian sense of all experience, could modify the brain and, therefore, an individual's identity. Reading Rousseau, suffering rejection in love, even the physical act of reporting one's self-scrutiny in text, all affected consciousness. Here Hays found what she had been looking for since her epistolary persona as "Maria" in the love letters to Eccles: an explanation of her responsiveness that guided her actions more than reason.[8]

The new science of the mind transformed the Puritan "*Heart Accounts*,"[9] an individual's record of spiritual progress against external constraints, that had fueled much of Hays's earlier self-examination into a more empirical dynamic, in which the mind is embodied in the physical circumstances of individual life. As scientific explorers of conscious life, Freud and the American James brothers followed on the heels of this Darwin, as did his grandson Charles. Hays quickly made use of her new understanding that the body was manifested in and organically joined to the mind: in a letter she wrote to Godwin while feverish she was uninhibited about collapsing the Cartesian duality between mind and body. "Do you not perceive," she demanded, "that my reason was the auxiliary of my passion — or rather, my passion the generative principle of my reason?"[10] Hays benefited from the research of Darwin, Cabanis, and Galvani, and Priestley's advances on Hartley.[11] Most importantly, the emerging mental sciences reflected Hays's own finding that physical sensation and reflection were equally important aspects of the ebb and flow of human cognition.[12]

Hays recognized another, radical implication of the new science. Hartley, Priestley, Darwin, and other researchers demanded that knowledge must be based on empirical observation and experience. Hays found in their insistence on Baconian experimentation an epistemological basis for investigating her own sexual desire. Female eroticism, she posited, was a form of knowledge that women had access to, could experiment with, and report on. Emboldened by Wollstonecraft, Hays testified in her novel to her findings in this arena, too.[13]

Hays found support for her convictions in the works of Helvétius, the French materialist. Helvétius affirmed the material basis of thought; he promoted Locke's view that all human beings begin life with equal mental competency. In two influential works that Hays read in English translation, *De l'Esprit* (1758) and *De l'Homme* (1772), Helvétius denied all distinctions made on the basis of birth, race, nationality, religion, sex, or spiritual election, insisting, "Corporeal sensibility is the sole cause of our actions, our thoughts, our passions, and our sociability."[14]

Helvétius argued in common with Condillac and Diderot, also proponents of utilitarianism, that humans were motivated by avoidance of pain and pursuit of pleasure rather than by any inner divine force. Helvétius dismissed romantic love as unimportant compared to erotic desire, and he disparaged the value of chastity. Hays recognized that before 1789 Helvétius called for revolution.[15]

But Hays's dependence on Helvétius has been overstated. She was not a systematic thinker, any more than was Robert Robinson; as she gained in relative confidence, her writing became correspondingly more synoptic on the assumption that her readers would understand her meaning if she just quoted parts of someone else's work. Hays copied and/or misquoted from memory portions of Helvétius's works that struck her as supporting her own arguments. She did not swallow his ideas whole, although she told Godwin that of all contemporary thinkers Helvétius's views struck her as closer to her own: "Had I been any man's disciple, it would most probably have been yours, if the system of Helvétius comes with greater conviction to my mind, it is because it coincides with my experience, & on what other foundation can I rest?"[16] Robinson taught Hays to avoid discipleship to any human doctrine as an imposition on the holy right to private judgment. Hays followed his advice to "take nothing for granted," not even the wisdom of the thinkers she revered.[17]

Hays composed her novel while she engaged in epistolary duels with Godwin. By the time she began writing *Emma Courtney,* Hays had probably read Wollstonecraft's *Letters Written During a Short Residence in Sweden, Norway, and Denmark.*[18] Wollstonecraft likely gave Hays access to her hectic correspondence with Imlay written during her expedition on his behalf.[19] In drawing on these letters to write her book, Wollstonecraft had amended her own excesses of sensibility to transform private reactions into political analysis and lyrical description. Where Wollstonecraft liberated her letters to camouflage and objectify them, Hays plumbed the inner psychological depths to declare her heroine's sexuality.[20] Despite the opposing impulses, both women's epistolary texts exposed the intimacies of female perception to public scrutiny.[21] Wollstonecraft wrote with supreme confidence of her own observations and reactions; Hays was less confident and intellectually brave than Wollstonecraft. She absorbed, appropriated, adapted, and synthesized whatever elements of the thinking of others that might help her understand her idiosyncratic self in the context of the common disabilities of women's external and interior lives.

Writer and Mentor

Godwin was an acknowledged master of lucid prose and logical exposition: he wrote economically constructed, artfully devised works that were compelling reads. Hays knew this firsthand. When she read *Caleb Williams* (1794) it struck her and many of her contemporaries as a riveting suspense story that combined subtle psychological analysis with a rigorous political critique of existing social systems.[22] Godwin may have told Hays what he described decades later: that he carefully plotted the novel "backwards," working hard to produce a fiction that would modify his readers' understanding.[23] Godwin had diligently researched the various factual elements of *Caleb Williams*, drawing on both historical works and contemporary publications, as well as gathering new evidence by interviewing at least one of the treason trial prisoners being held in Newgate for alleged sedition.

Godwin shared with Hays several basic beliefs, especially the supremacy of the right to private judgment that constituted the lynchpin of Dissent. They both agreed with Richard Price's sentiments on the value of good intentions, quoted in Hays's *Letters and Essays,* that "sincerity of heart," the intention by which an individual "faithfully endeavour[ed] to find out, and to practice truth and right, counted for more in the pursuit of truth than justice or rectitude."[24] On the one hand, Godwin possessed all the necessary credentials of a *philosophe*; like the other men to whom Hays looked for support; he shared the reformist goals of the Dissenters.

Initially, Hays was intimidated by Godwin and overly deferential. He was far better at debate than she was. She acknowledged that sometimes his presence made her anxious. She finally asked him to bring her letters with him when he visited to remind her of specific subjects on which she wished to ask his opinion but had forgotten.[25] Well trained as he was, he could persuade in a range of styles, from Ciceronian pronouncements to the language of sensibility.[26] Hays described on occasion being so "dazzled by the force of [his] expressions" in their exchanges that she later recanted what she had said, having felt pressured to agree with him when, in fact, she did not.[27] Moreover, he was famous as well as infamous, well connected with publishers, and attentive to her. She began her novel proposing to follow his direction, even shrewdly intending to dedicate it to him if he liked the finished work.

The intellectual bond between Hays and Godwin was closely linked to their mutual interest in introspection, although his concern was to discover the moral parameters of human character, and hers to discover the psychological.[28] Hays reacted so strongly to Godwin's negative comments and advice to revise her text because she felt he should have recognized that her discoveries were not mere solipsism, but rather her attempts at research in the interests of mental science and her own psychological health. She judged that her writing contributed to the radical project of seeking knowledge through impartial inquiry. She described the basis of what she saw as their shared interest in objective inquiry. "It is because you are a philosopher," she had written to him some months earlier, "that I can unfold my mind without reserve or apprehension: you are able to trace, & to investigate, the sources of its disorders & mistakes."[29] Hays represented her heroine, Emma Courtney, as analysand and analyst, sensate being and inquiring scientist. Her tacit agreement with Godwin provided that, although he held up "a frightful mirror" in which she saw her myriad faults—especially ambition and vanity—he would persevere in improving her.[30] When he disapproved of her text, it seemed to her that he withdrew his support by holding her to the standards of literary convention established by Samuel Richardson, Henry Mackenzie in *The Man of Feeling* (1771), and, most importantly, Rousseau.[31] She judged these masculine models to be irrelevant to her experiments in self-dissection as the *woman* of feeling. Hays insisted on the reality of her representations in the novel, emphasizing the differences between her heroine and Richardson's idealized Clarissa. Male writers might portray female characters that thrilled and instructed readers, but those figures were man-made artifacts. What she presented was the real thing.

Hays regarded Godwin as her "mind's physician,"[32] reporting to him her shifting psychological responses to particular circumstances. For example, she described her good spirits at a large party she had attended where she mingled with Kantian philosophers, military men, fashionable ladies, and musicians. It was, she told Godwin, "the feast of reason and the flow of souls," one of her favorite quotations from Pope. Hays continually calibrated her mental well-being, but whatever her psychological state, she continued to produce text and energetically answer Godwin's objections. Godwin acted as rigorous critic rather than empathetic healer. Hays found Godwin's criticisms of her novel-in-progress less agreeable than his sympathy, but also, she acknowledged, more bracing. From their letters, we can piece together his comments and her reactions, and the portions of the letters to and from Frend that she incorporated into her fiction. These exchanges show that Hays tried at first to respond point by point to Godwin, as she was accustomed to do in their personal conversations. But she was now a writer, not a student; she discovered she could not easily yield to his suggestions about her text. Resistance allowed the flush of a new autonomy; she began to question his authority to counsel her, both as successful writer and preoccupied philosopher intent on improving the general human condition.

In their correspondence between January and late June 1796, Hays held her own, despite his pointed criticisms and recommendations. Godwin claimed that her work lacked ingenuity, credible characters, and invention, and suffered from too much philosophical digression. Hays had drawn on what she had learned from her various mentors, including Godwin, her own intuitions, and her tentative understanding of new theories of the science of the mind. In squaring off with Godwin over the structure, characterizations, diction, and tone of her novel, Hays found herself on the horns of a dilemma: should she depend on his judgments about her work as she had earlier relied on Worthington, Disney, and Frend; or should she practice at last what Robinson, Godwin, and Wollstonecraft advocate, genuine personal independence?[33] Hays determined to find her own way in her ongoing debate with Godwin. In the previous November, Hays told Godwin that she had chosen the epistolary form as the vehicle best suited to her as a writer and reader of letters. She quickly realized that creating imaginary correspondence lacked the stimulating effect on her of writing real letters to real people, especially to her friends. She knew that she required a sympathetic and supportive reader to report on her new research.[34] The fodder for Hays's novel, and, therefore, the debate with Godwin, was a direct discussion of her own feelings and behavior with respect to a particular man, probably Frend, although she never identified him to Godwin.

Behind the debate that ensued about Hays's novel was the real life drama of her experiences with Frend. When she confronted Frend early in 1796, he had made it clear to her that there was no hope for love or a sexual relationship. She likely declared her feelings for him much earlier, perhaps soon after he expressed his admiration for her published performance as Eusebia.[35] In the winter of 1796 and in the midst of her grief at his rejection of her, Hays realized that her letters to Frend and his replies would serve as the engine for the "philosophical romance"[36] she felt compelled to write. And Hays had another purpose: although she represented to Godwin that the man never led her on, nevertheless she smarted because he had spurned her well-intentioned advances. She tried hard to be evenhanded in her representation of her hero, but her text revealed violent feelings that glinted with revenge.[37] She still seethed with the resentment that colored her judgments and as they debated, she admitted to Godwin that she was bitter.

Hays composed her novel by manipulating texts in her possession. She used the literary, historical, and philosophical sources from which she had quoted in her earlier works but now she also used living documents: Frend and Godwin's letters to her and her letters to them. She laid out before her these swatches from life, imaginatively cut and pasted them, and then recombined disparate excerpts that she recopied and sometimes revised. As she wrote, she wove the narrative, not as a conventional plot, but as the glue to hold together the pieces of the mosaic she was creating.

As he read successive pages, Godwin questioned her choices of perspective, plot, and character. He criticized her heroine's narrative dominance in which the story was told exclusively from one point of view,[38] and her self-involvement. Her hero appeared remote, severe, and even unlikable. The story, he insisted, was repetitious; there was little ingenuity, scarce dramatic tension, no hope for resolution between heroine and hero. Hays answered point by point. She chose to write in the first person, deliberately drawing upon her own affective memory for effect, because, she told Godwin, "we never paint well, but when we *feel* our subject."[39] Godwin himself had composed *Caleb Williams* from the first person perspectives of several characters; why, then, should he object to her heroine speaking from her own point of view?

Godwin explained that it was not Hays's use of the first person that he objected to, but rather her heroine's suffocating omnipresence. This issue became a subject of intense contention between them. Early in May he visited her. They argued, and she continued the quarrel in her next letter. His counsel that she drastically alter her text pained her; she knew him to be sympathetic to others' distress. Now she asked him to consider how she must feel after he blasted her latest efforts. He might be able to play critic without reference to her feelings, but she countered that she only considered making the changes he suggested because of their friendship and, she added with some hostility, because of the deference she usually felt for his judgment.[40] He accused her of being "selfish, obstinate, & immov'able," that is, closed-minded about his criticisms. She reprimanded him: she was not being tenacious but resisted his changes because she continued to be ambivalent about her heroine, her story, and herself. She reported that she had "no independence of mind, I am govern'd in all things by my attachments – I act on no steady principles, I am forever the victim of contending emotions." Rather than composing by mimetic precedent in imitation of Richardson, Rousseau, Mackenzie, or even Godwin, she felt her way in writing, as in life. She wished for his approval, but in the end she constructed her fiction to embody herself.

That said, she defended what she had written, starting with the subject of unrequited love. She insisted that unrequited love was not "*in itself*" without interest, linking her story with Petrarch's love for Laura as an example of "a lively & strong imagination, of a sanguine, an enterprising, an ardent, an unconquerable, spirit — It is strength, though ill directed." Moreover she had experienced unrequited love and chose to report on it, even if it was of little interest to Godwin. She acknowledged that this emotional state might not be universally felt, but that "it [...was] congenial to a susceptible and metaphisical [sic] turn of mind" like her own.[41]

Clearly, a deeper issue was in play than the story she chose to tell. Her intention was not to describe the activity—or, in this case, inactivity—of passion, but rather to convey the possible extremities of the experience of *unfulfilled* romantic love from her highly wrought heroine's point of view. As for Godwin's criticism about the "*austerity* of character" she had given her hero, Hays argued that to portray the heightened quality of her heroine's responses in a sublime manner, according to Burke's definition, it was necessary that her hero's behavior be inexplicable and mysterious to heroine and reader.[42] Hays called upon both Enlightenment and Romantic precepts to convey such complex experience;[43] external realism was not her goal, but rather the sensation of psychological propulsion as one obdurate self collided with another: the heroine who doggedly loved, the hero, equally obstinate, who refused to be loved or to love in return.[44]

Hays addressed Godwin's further objections to the hopelessness (and therefore the worthlessness) of her heroine's passion. She countered that the same could be said of her own situation, but neither the futility of the heroine's passion nor the reader's discomfort about it would render the story unrealistic or uninteresting. The romance she depicted was in the mind, she explained, an extended state of aroused sensibilities and associations, and not accessible to revision as either emotion or text. The story revealed itself to her as an imaginatively felt, even supernatural, cerebral drama. Her narrative signified "electrical sympathy," that inexplicable connection between people for which there was barely language to express. Hays reminded Godwin that by his own admission she had not failed completely in her efforts to portray emotional states. Moreover, she argued that he must recognize that the psychological interplay that she represented was empirical, based on the vibrant content of her own consciousness.[45]

Godwin proposed that Hays modify her text to accord more with literary precedent for her reader's instruction and entertainment. She equivocated: if she did change her manuscript—"yet, I do not say, that I will not alter it," she hedged—she would do so "languidly;" a more conventional story might strengthen the twists of plot, but weaken its expressive authenticity. In practical terms, she objected. If she were to follow his recommendations to make the story tighter, to vary the characters and to achieve a conclusive ending, the necessary rewriting would make the greater part of the manuscript unusable. In defense of her existing work, she addressed other specific objections he had raised: whether or not the hero returned Emma's affection must remain intentionally equivocal, implying that this ambiguity existed in her relationship with Frend because at an earlier time he had to some degree reciprocated her love. On this topic she had a confession to make, but Godwin must first promise not to tease: "It is a subject on which I cannot yet, nor I believe ever shall be able to, bear jesting — The wound is too recent, the scar too deep." She wanted him to know that she was aware that she wrote actuated by "private motives." There was subtext as well as context in her pages. She recognized that Godwin, according to his principles of enlightened social interaction, aspired to rational self-control and expected this from others. Having bared to him her inability to similarly restrain her feelings, her idealized regard for Godwin collapsed into regret, shame, even anger. She feared he now saw her vices too clearly: "You see me as incorrigible — yet," in the interests of truth-telling, "I ask no lenity." Then she conceded. She would be "less tenacious" about cutting some of the philosophical digressions in the manuscript, as well as amending the smaller defects. However, she added, "Neither have I *absolutely decided* respecting your *grand* objection"—the overweening presence of her heroine. Contradicting her previous assertion that her hero was not a "rake," she blurted out, "But those appear to me incapable of either love or friendship, incapable of every generous affection, who *coldly & deliberately* trifle with the happiness of another for the mean, the..." The last sentence dangled on the page, incomplete.[46]

What Hays quarreled with most explicitly in Godwin's theory of gradualist anarchy was his apparent disregard for individual affective experience.[47] In a letter to him in early March, she insisted "I am unhappy because 'my occupation's gone'"—that is, the socially approved female vocation, to love and be loved by Frend. She felt the loss of meaningful life work as intellectual, as well as emotional and sensory, deprivation. "When the associations I have so fondly cherished are rudely torn away," she explained to Godwin, "I sink into apathy, because I lose everything that endears life. I abhor indifference, it is the canker of the soul — it is to me sinonymous [sic] with sadness, with death — the death of the mind." According to her understanding of contemporary theories of cognition, the death of the mind was one and the same with the death of the heart: indifference signified stasis of the human ability to feel and reflect synchronously—a form of death, indeed.[48]

Hays offers a poignant example of a woman intellectual trying to apply whatever she knew[49] of contemporary scientific method to the unexplored realm of female consciousness. Of course, she knew very little about how to apply scientific methods. What she did know, she had gleaned from Hartley, Priestley's works, Enfield's history of ideas, conversations with Frend about his mathematical views, and her omnivorous reading of Darwin, Lavater, and others, as such works were published by the writers and publishers she knew. Her presumption, that a Dissenting woman on her own might attempt to replicate the hallowed cultural practices of empirical science as practiced in the late eighteenth century, quickly opened Hays to criticism and satire.[50] What tolerance could there be for Hays's makeshift inquiry into a contentious question at the heart of gendered inquiry: was the female mind as competent to observe, objectify, generalize, and report back as was a man's?[51] Her critics answered these questions with vehement negatives in their reviews and parodies of her pretensions to alleged scientific reporting in her novel.

Hays's mind plagued her with doubts and recriminations. She repented the confidences to Godwin, pointing to the hypocrisy in the practices of the cult of Sincerity that he so valued[52]: "Sincerity," she wrote him, "is a fine theory — I have tried it, but find it impracticable — *I am its victim!*" Yet she was committed to telling the truth as she saw it. She had another confession to make to him: she was uncertain about her part in the failure of her pursuit of Frend. She spat out the humiliating question as almost a declarative sentence: "I have only been the aggressor?" Godwin, by contrast, she described as a "cool looker on — your passions have not been engaged, you therefore are competent to resolve this question." Shame, disappointment, frustration, and depression took their toll. "My mind is no longer the residence of mild & gentle affections — it is agitated by a whirlwind of haughty & contrasting emotions — I wou'd not live always. Life is a tragic farce!"[53] She railed at Godwin, and through him, at Holcroft, for their lack of understanding of her disillusionment and Wollstonecraft's. Despite these distractions, Hays continued writing to Godwin, admitting that the solitude in which she lived made it necessary for her to unburden herself to someone. It flattered her vanity that he, a great philosopher, continued to be interested in her.[54]

Godwin persisted in regarding her heroine's self-preoccupation as her novel's central flaw, a criticism he had made earlier. How, he asked, could others find her interesting if she were only interested in herself? Hays acknowledged the justice of his characterization; she invoked as precedent Rousseau's assertion that sensitive natures, especially those that do not live in the busy world, react more strongly than do worldly ones. She insisted that she neither intended to model her heroine on the perfections of Richardson's Clarissa, nor did she wish to adulterate the character's connection to herself. "I intended this book to be a memento of my own folly or madness, call it which you please!" The larger aim was at once experiential and speculative: to represent the effects of the imbalance of power between men and women on a woman's pursuit of personal fulfillment. Exploring the nexus between private inequality and a corrupt society, in Hays's novel between men and women, was a page taken from Godwin's own books.

The boundaries between private and public, Hays argued, proved necessarily permeable in her tale of the woman of feeling. The story she lived and represented was of a woman scorned who possessed the powers of reason *and* exquisite sensibility. She acknowledged the vital equation between herself and her heroine, and her representation of both in one. "Your remarks on my heroines [sic] 'vanity' made me smile," she wrote Godwin, "you are right, she is vain, &, so am I," and teasingly, "I will try to correct this foible in both."[55]

While Hays worked hard on her novel, Godwin and Wollstonecraft courted erratically, following their reintroduction by Hays in January 1796. Hays sensed their growing attraction to each other. She told Wollstonecraft of her unhappiness[56] and unknowingly served for Godwin as an emblem of the female loneliness and depression that Godwin feared Wollstonecraft might revert to.[57] Although Hays could not share in her friends' intimate happiness, she saw them continually, and depended on them for support in preparing for her next adventure. She was on the threshold of publishing her novel; her vanity and avarice, she told Godwin, remained on the alert, "thirsting after fame & riches! The best method, I believe of quieting one troublesome passion, is to combat it with half a dozen more."[58] Despite his misgivings about Hays's manuscript, Godwin referred her to his friend, the publisher George Robinson.[59]

In November 1796 George Robinson published Hays's fiction, *Memoirs of Emma Courtney*. Many elements of the novel proved to be controversial, beginning with the author's "Preface," which repeated her assertion to Godwin that people on the margins of conventional society were hypersensitive.[60] In the first paragraph, Hays argued that fiction could portray the effect of strong emotions on an individual's life. She bolstered her assertion with quotations from Helvétius, Ann Radcliffe, and *Caleb Williams*. Knowing readers might hear echoes of Wollstonecraft's early novel, *Mary, A Fiction* (1788). There Wollstonecraft had declared her revolutionary intention to fashion a heroine with "thinking powers"— that is, autonomous competence, in contrast to Richardson's Clarissa or Lady Grandison, or Rousseau's Sophie.[61] Hays told the reader that her heroine Emma Courtney had thinking powers, too, but cautioned that these were not strong enough, given the realities of women's lives, to protect her from the tidal pull of her passions. Hays admonished the unsympathetic reader, as she had in her introduction to the "Love Letters" two decades earlier. Then, as maiden widow, young Mary Hays had insisted on her right to active loving rather than coy flirtation; now, as middle-aged *femme philosophe*, she counseled her readers that the dire consequences of her heroine's aggressive pursuit of the hero should serve as a warning about the effects of unbridled passion, not as a guide to recommended conduct.

Hays foresaw how heated readers' responses might be to a first-person narrative by and about a woman who turned the gendered tables on heterosexual romance—woman as pursuer, man pursued. In a preemptive move, she tried to camouflage the combustible missile she had launched with a disclaimer. To distance herself from her heroine, she assumed the guise of preacher-teacher, as she had in *Letters and Essays*, advising that the truth of the story was less important than her heroine's "hazardous experiment" in the delineation of "the phaenomena of the human mind."[62] Hays hoped that readers would read *Memoirs of Emma Courtney* as a mental drama, a story of the growth of a woman's mind as seen through the eyes of Hartley and Darwin and paralleling Hays's own. But readers with some knowledge of the personal lives of those in Hays's radical circle smelled the scandal behind the fiction.

Memoirs of Emma Courtney: Author and Heroine

Like her creator, the heroine of Hays's first novel feels deeply and possesses a philosophical cast of mind. In the opening letter to her adopted son, Augustus Harley, to whom she narrates the facts of his parentage and his adopted mother's life, Emma herself posits the logic of the novel in which observation and analysis of the development of an individual consciousness are the main subject.[63] Hays's effort to integrate sensibility and science proved to be a groundbreaking fictional formula, at least to some of her contemporaries; others found it merely ridiculous. True to her understanding of philosophical necessity and materialism, and following what she saw as experimental methods, Hays carefully delineated the causal chain of specific events in her heroine's early years, emphasizing the circumstances that alienate her from normal society. Among these is Emma's enthusiasm for romantic tales, beginning with the *Arabian Nights*,[64] and continuing with her own inventive fantasies. Like myriad adventurous girls, Emma "hated the needle;" having her strong will opposed made her "vehement, and coercion irritated ... [her] to violence," though "a kind look, a gentle word, a cool expostulation — softened, melted, arrested, [her] in the full career of passion." Emma's education begins at a conventional female boarding school, but reversals of her father's fortunes force him to open the resources of his own library to her instead. Soon he entrusts her with the keys to the bookshelves "through which ... [she] ranged with ever new delight." One day he discovers Emma weeping over Rousseau's *Eloisa*. He snatches the book from her hand and removes the work from the library. "But," Emma tells her adopted son, "the impression made on my mind was never to be effaced — it was even productive of a long chain of consequences, that will continue to the day of my death."[65]

Hays's detailed description of the effect of reading on Emma Courtney refers to the ongoing contemporaneous debate about the allegedly pernicious effects on female readers of a fictional heroine's uncontrolled passions. Hays advances the controversy by representing Emma's "discovery of an intellectual passion" that is unique in women's writing.[66] Hays responds to Hume's challenge that the study of history might teach women that "love is not the only passion that governs the male world." She records an individual female history in which learning *and* love ignite the heroine. Hays tacitly demonstrates that other female autodidacts, including herself, affirm the truth of Emma's experience: like men, women are creatures of education; they too hunger to learn, but their access to knowledge is at best conditional on men's granting such access. *Memoirs of Emma Courtney* traces the trajectory of its heroine's consciousness to expose the lie of Enlightenment, in which even enlightened men privileged feminine loveliness and compliance, and women who would not or could not thus appeal were condemned to be "comfortless, solitary, shivering wanderer[s], in the dreary wilderness of human society,"[67] (with a nod to Rousseau and Wollstonecraft). Hays's critique begins with her hero Augustus Harley senior whose surname links him to Mackenzie's *The Man of Feeling*. Harley is the blood father of Emma's adopted son, and the Frend figure to Hays's Emma. Frend's erudition is disguised, but, through an intricate series of causes, Harley, too, must remain unmarried to receive a legacy of £400.[68] Emma complains to Mr. Francis, the Godwin figure, that "it is not on the altars of love, but of gold, that men now come to pay their offerings."[69] In the actual letter to Godwin that Hays uses for this part of the novel, Hays added, "The man who has sacrificed me, if I am not much mistaken, is a votary at the shrine of Plutus," the ancient Greek god of Wealth, "& has had some struggles to ice his heart & stifle his humanity."[70] She refers here either to Frend's dogged bachelorhood as the price of retaining his income from his fellowship, or the excuse that he may have given her that he could not afford to marry. Emma rages because Harley is free to teach privately, continue his political activism, and maintain his personal independence even if depriving himself and her of revolutionary love. In addition, Hays's knowledge of marriages they both knew of, like Ann and John Jebb's or the Lindseys', gave the lie to Harley/Frend's concerns about money. Had he been willing to live with her unmarried, Frend's £150 and her annuity of £70 would have sufficed for them to live modestly together. His disingenuousness enraged her as it protected him. Hays retaliated by portraying the resolute Frend as the irresolute Harley.

The novel breaks new ground in Enlightenment discourse by representing gendered dissonance in Godwin's appeals to reason in his letters to Hays that Emma rejects as useless. The masculine counterpart to Harley is Mr. Francis, a philosopher who advises the heroine as Godwin advised Hays. Francis counsels Emma to exorcise the demon of unrequited love by exercising her independent judgment, drawing on her hard-earned intellectual resources of philosophy, theology, history, and other systems of rational analysis, to repress her fantasies. Emma's answer goes to the core of Enlightenment hypocrisy about gender: how can a woman seek fulfillment when social expectations and proscriptions thwart her at every turn? "Why call woman, miserable, oppress'd, & impotent," she demands, "woman, crushed & then insulted — why call her to an 'independence' which not nature, but the accursed & barbarous laws of society have denied?" Francis's advice reveals his ignorance of women's condition: "This is mockery," Emma cries. "Even you — wise & benevolent as you are — can mock the child of slavery & of sorrow!"[71] The name "Emma" itself is a comment on the male double standard about women, likely taken from Matthew Prior's popular poem, *Henry and Emma, a Poem, Upon the Model of the Nut-brown Maid* (1709), in which the poet represents an idealized woman who, like Homer's singular Penelope, chooses to remain chaste and constant. Hays defies misogyny by giving the leading female role to her Emma, a woman who cares less for chastity and constancy than for self-fulfillment.

Memoirs of Emma Courtney scandalized readers of every political persuasion because of its almost clinical candor and exploration of new female freedoms, particularly the heroine's intellectual and erotic ambitions.[72] When Harley makes no declaration of love to her at what she judges the appropriate moment, Emma considers making the first move, analyzes her own hesitation, and then condemns society for conditioning her to be fearful about expressing her feelings. "Why should I hesitate to inform him of my affection — why do I blush and tremble at the mere idea? Is it a false shame? It is a pernicious system of morals, which teaches us that hypocrisy can be virtue!"[73] Using excerpts from her letters to Frend, Hays proposes a revised balance of power in heterosexual relations by exposing a real woman's meditations on sex and aggression. When Harley equivocates, Emma goes one better than Heloise by taking the offensive, offering herself to the reluctant Harley outside marriage. Emma tells Harley that her desire for him trumps every other consideration: propriety, reputation, money, and chastity.[74] In the most notorious statement in the book, Hays's apostasy as a respectable woman is mischievously broadcast as she blurts out Frend's name as a homonym: "*My friend,*" Emma cries, "*I would give myself to you* — the gift is not worthless."

To many of Hays's contemporaries, the novel was even blasphemous. Hays incorporated portions of a letter to Godwin expressing the depths of her despair at Frend's rejection. Emma contemplates suicide, although she knows it is morally wrong. Hays's earlier, blanket assertion that a believer in philosophical materialism and necessity could never be a suicide[75] was modified by her intimate knowledge of Wollstonecraft's personal history and her letters to Imlay, which were filled with intimations, threats of suicide and explanations of her failed attempts. In her despair, Emma questions the existence of God.

How am I sure that there is a God — is he wise — is he powerful — is he benevolent? If he be, can he sport himself in the miseries of poor, feeble, impotent beings, forced into existence, without their choice — impelled, by the iron hand of necessity, through mistake, into calamity?[76]

Later, more objective about the depressed state in which she wrote these lines to Godwin, Hays felt constrained to criticize the view expressed in the letter as it appeared in the novel. "This is the reasoning of a mind distorted by passion," she explained to the reader, hastening to neutralize the taint of impiety by acknowledging that, like the reader, she recognized Emma's depression as a symptom, not a recommendation. "Even in the moment of disappointment, our heroine judged better."[77]

The experiments with form, ideas, and genres in *Memoirs of Emma Courtney* reflect Hays's own "hazardous experiment," her attempts to write about something new and her search for a vocabulary in which to do so. The novel is formally experimental: Hays mixes actual correspondence with Frend and Godwin with new text, a technique she had seen Robinson use in his commentary on the Huguenots.[78] She uses this device to explore her interest in Richardson's technique of creating distinct epistolary styles for each of his characters.[79] The novel is thematically bold: the narrator identifies what she describes as "the magic circle" of imposed gender restraints to explain Harley's failure to act on the implications of the radiant reformist ideas he and Emma share.[80] Perhaps using Ann and John Jebb's relationship as a model, Emma hopes these transcendent ideas might transform her, too, so that Harley will desire her despite her lack of physical beauty. Love my mind, love me, Emma demands, because in an enlightened sphere, appearances should not matter. Hays plays with multiple identities of Emma and Augustus and their imagined progeny,[81] invoking the values she and Frend inherited from Robinson, and the children they would never have.[82] When Emma cries, "mine ... is almost a solitary madness in the eighteenth century,"[83] she makes claim to knowledge only she has of Harley's responsiveness to her, at least in the intercourse of their minds, and his refusal to act on his feelings. The romance between hero and heroine is portrayed as platonic based on their intellectual exchanges that Emma's fantasies invest with sexual possibilities.[84] During a halcyon period, Emma describes the season of happiness as Harley teaches her astronomy, philosophy, and the rules of grammar, criticism, and composition. They listen to music, draw, read, converse, and Emma, at least, experiences "the feast of reason, and the flow of souls."[85]

Hays defies existing assumptions about novel-writing by mixing elements from sentimental, romantic, gothic, epistolary, stream of consciousness, suspense, and political texts that are jumbled together to represent the heroine's mental turbulence.[86] Emma pursues Harley to discover the cause of his erratic behavior. He is either silent or absent, shows up unexpectedly and briefly, then disappears again. She is constant in her quest, motivated by that mixture of mental and physical attraction between them that she believes he feels and that Hays described earlier in the romance between Melville and Cecilia in their American Eden.[87]

Emma learns that before he met her Harley contracted a foreign marriage to a woman he now dislikes. In response, Emma goes through the motions of a conventionally gendered life; she marries solely for economic and social reasons, but neither marriage nor motherhood dislodge her first and deepest love for Harley. Emma desires the man; she also desires the expansive life she envisions with him in which Dissenting marital harmony positively affects the larger community. As he dies in her arms, Harley confesses that he has always loved her, and bequeaths her his now motherless son.[88]

Hays's screed is pioneering in its critique of the bankruptcy of male dominated Enlightenment ideas about religion, science, philosophy, politics, and literature that give the narrator no comfort. Gender is beyond public discourse, even among the otherwise progressive English Jacobins and Rational Dissenters. Hays's interest is epistemological as well as sociological and psychological; she argues that separate cognitive training disadvantages women as profoundly as patriarchal laws and cultural expectations.[89] No theory devised by male thinkers of the Enlightenment could yet explain the unconscious accurately enough to improve gender relations; given the ongoing debate about the Trinity and Christ's nature, scientific advances could not even provide indisputable proof of the number of persons belonging to God.[90] Freud, decades later, would first pose the questions Hays implicitly condemns men for being unwilling to ask: What do women think? What do women feel? What do women want? Even the exercise of the vaunted right to private judgment ends badly for women: Hays exercised the prerogative and she was and would be punished romantically, socially, and professionally. Reason unaided by psychological understanding could not ensure that "radical principle of happiness ... the having something to do, to hope & to fear,"[91] which to her signified an enlightened existence. Nonetheless, the novel ends with Emma's prayer that through fearless inquiry by courageous women and men, prejudice will be dispelled, the human mind will be emancipated from superstition, and people will acknowledge that *"true dignity and virtue, consists in being free."*[92]

Initial reaction to the novel was relatively mild, although much worse was to come later. The progressive *Monthly Magazine* took Hays's warning about sensibility at face value, judging the book to reflect "a well cultivated and enlightened mind."[93] The *Analytical Review* similarly praised the author's intellect, but like Godwin wondered about the heroine's persistence, and the wisdom of trying to reason the hero to return her love.[94] The *Monthly Review* described Emma Courtney as a "third Eloisa." It devoted six pages, including excerpts, to the novel that displayed "great intellectual powers," although it, too, questioned some of the principles expressed that criticized accepted codes of female behavior.[95] The *Critical Review* emphasized the influence of Rousseau on the heroine who defied social convention to demand love from Harley.[96] The conservative *British Critic* recognized the author's "respectable talents," but condemned her for forming her opinions from a group of like-minded people, that is, Rousseau, Helvétius, and other unnamed revolutionary thinkers. "A less limited circle of reading and acquaintance," they advised, "would better qualify her to discharge the duties of her sex."[97] The *Anti-Jacobin Review* had not yet been established, so its review did not appear until 1799, a perilous year for anything "Jacobin."

Emma Courtney brought Hays £30 from sales and enduring notoriety. In late 1815 Jane Austen, perhaps aware of the persistent ill repute of Emma Courtney, predicted of her character Emma Woodhouse, "I am going to take a heroine whom no one but myself will much like."[98] In 1856, Flaubert would claim of his Emma, "Madame Bovary, *c'est moi.*" Hays was too ambivalent about herself and her novel to make such declarations publicly, although she acknowledged privately to Godwin that she and her heroine were indivisible. Readers interpreted her silence on the subject as confirmation of their nearly unanimous opinion: when Emma Courtney burst on the scene the public's immediate and lasting belief was that author and heroine formed an unholy one.

Notes

1   For a cogent article that argues against this view, see Katharine M. Rogers, "The Contribution of Mary Hays," *Prose Studies*, 10/2 (September 1987): 131–42.

2   Wendy Gunther-Canada, *Rebel Writer: Mary Wollstonecraft and Enlightenment Politics* (DeKalb, 2001), p. 42.

3   Both Rousseau's *Confession* and *Eloisa* were published in 1761. Hays read them in English translation.

4   Hays makes no reference to Darwin in the novel or in her letters. However, Henry Crabb Robinson, traveling in Germany in early 1802, wrote Hays for "gossip" about her circle of friends and mentioned Darwin along with Godwin and Amelia Alderson, now Opie, in his questions about specific people's current writing projects. Crabb Robinson to Hays, 26 January 1802, *CMH*, p. 552. Darwin was one of the "pro-Woman" members of the Lunar Society, and wrote *A Plan for the Conduct of Female Education in Boarding Schools* (1797) that advocated the addition of geography, civil history, natural history, botany, and chemistry to the curricula for girls. Arianne Chernock notes that he was "deeply committed to liberating *eros*" and published *The Botanic Garden* (1791), extrapolating from the polygamous examples of plants sexual freedom for women and men. "Erasmus Darwin (1731–1802)," *Women, Gender and Enlightenment*, pp. 723–4.

5   James C. McKusick, review of Alan Richardson, *British Romanticism and the Science of the Mind*, *Romanticism on the Net*, 31 August 2003.

6   Nicholas Roe makes a similar point about the influence on Coleridge of John Thelwall's lectures at Guy's Hospital, London, in January 1793. *Samuel Taylor Coleridge and the Sciences of Life* (Oxford, 2001), p. 1.

7   Alan Richardson notes, "Darwin's revision of the Lockean tradition differs significantly … in its physiological and organic commitments and in the optimistic rather than skeptical attitude with which Darwin regards the mind's literal incarnation in the body," *British Romanticism and the Science of the Mind* (Cambridge, 2001). p. 14.

8   Peter Melville Logan notes that writing at the end of the eighteenth century, Hays participated in "the age of physiological psychology" in which "the defining feature of the nervous body was its susceptibility to nervous disorder" that writers represented

according to gender and class. *Nerves and Narratives: A Cultural History of Hysteria in Nineteenth-Century British Prose* (Berkeley, 1997), pp. 6–7.

9   See N.H. Keeble, "Introduction: Reformation Sentiments," *The Literary Culture of Nonconformity in Later Seventeenth-Century England* (Athens, 1987), p. 14.

10   Hays to Godwin, [6 February 1796], *Pforz.*, MH 12.

11   See Thomas Dixon, *From Passions to Emotions: The Creation of a Secular Psychological Category* (Cambridge, 2003).

12   Ernst Cassirer, *The Philosophy of the Enlightenment*, trans. Fritz C.A. Koelln and James P. Pettegrove (Boston, 1964), p. 100.

13   See Anthony Page's illuminating review of Richard C. Allen's "Hartley on Human Nature," *Enlightenment and Dissent*, 20 (2001):126–38.

14   1796 is the earliest date for which there is evidence that Hays had read Helvétius. In a letter from her sister Elizabeth sometime that year, Elizabeth promised that she would follow Hays's advice and "return to Helvétius with new vigour." Both sisters read his works in their English translations, and/or excerpts in *The Cabinet*. Elizabeth Hays to Mary Hays [c. 1796], *Pforz.*, EH 1.

15   David Wooten argues that Helvétius advocates equal inheritance and property rights for women, the right to divorce, and other proto-feminist positions. "Helvétius: From radical enlightenment to revolution," *Political Theory*, June 2000.

16   Hays to Godwin, 1 March 1796, *Pforz.*, MH 15.

17   See Robinson to Hays, 4 March 1789, *Pforz.*, 2160.

18   Wollstonecraft's novel was published by Johnson in January 1796. Hays knew that Godwin had read and responded enthusiastically to it. *MH*, p. 369. Hays may have read Wollstonecraft's work in manuscript.

19   Barbara Taylor points to Hays's appropriation, at least once, of a phrase from Wollstonecraft's book, *Mary Wollstonecraft and the Feminist Imagination* (Cambridge, 2003), p. 190.

20   Taylor characterizes *Emma Courtney* as "a novel of extraordinary daring, offering a passionate yet nuanced defence of female eroticism," and as a "gloss on [Wollstonecraft's] Short Residence … [Hays's novel] makes scandalously explicit the valorization of women's eroticism implicit in Wollstonecraft's later works," *Mary Wollstonecraft and the Feminist Imagination*, pp. 188–91.

21   Mary A. Favret writes that once the personal letter enters the marketplace, it "performs a social act, diffusing the self into the world, making it public property. And that worldly self demands a private reckoning." Wollstonecraft, Favret explains, "wrote the *Letters* to claim possession over her emotional attachments and guarantee movement from personal and sentimental to national and political economies," *Romantic Correspondence: Women, Politics and the Fiction of Letters* (Cambridge, 1992), p.132.

22   Gregory Dart, *Rousseau, Robespierre and English Romanticism* (Cambridge, 1999), p. 76.

23   Godwin, "Preface" to the 1832 "Standard Novels" edition of *Fleetwood* in "Appendix II," *Things as they are; or, the Adventures of Caleb Williams*, ed. Maurice Hindle (London, 1794, reprinted 1987), pp. 347–54.

24   *L&E*, p. 76.

25   Hays to Godwin, 5 November 1795, *Pforz.*, MH 27.

26   Mark Philp, *Godwin's Political Justice* (Ithaca, 1986), p. 166.

27 Hays to Godwin, 6 February 1796, *Pforz.*, MH 12.
28 Richardson, *British Romanticism and the Science of the Mind*, p. 217, ftnte 48. Raymond Williams dates the use of the word "psychological"—"the psychological unity which we call the mind"—to 1794.
29 Hays to Godwin, 13 October 1795, *Pforz.*, MH 8.
30 Hays to Godwin, 5 November 1795, *Pforz.*, MH 27.
31 See Gary Handwerk and A.A. Markley, "Introduction," *Fleetwood: Or, the New Man of Feeling by William Godwin* (Peterborough, 2001), pp. 16–27.
32 On 11 January she appealed to Godwin to continue to be "my good physician."
33 Modern readers of *Emma Courtney* have similarly objected to the lack of a straightforward story or accessible plot, and a hero whose inexplicable actions are lost in the heroine's too frequent declamations. For example, Nicola Watson characterizes Hays's narrative as "Emma's virtual monologue," *Revolution and the Form of the British Novel 1790–1825* (Oxford, 1994), p. 47.
34 Hays wrote, "[T]he epistolary form I conceived the most adapted to my style & habits of composition, but cou'd not please myself – fictitious correspondance [sic] affords me not the stimulus which I ever feel when addressing my friends," Hays to Godwin, 20 November 1795, *Pforz.*, MH 9.
35 The suggestion for this is found in her sister Elizabeth's tale, "Josepha, or the Pernicious Effects of Early Indulgence," in *L&E*, in which the ardent, overindulged heroine in a letter declares her love to the bookish hero, who eventually returns it. Elizabeth seems to have known that Frend was the object of her older sister's passion, and been critical of her behavior in her letters. John Dunkin, Hays's brother-in-law, wrote Hays about Frend's marriage in 1808 to express his opinion that Hays was too tolerant towards Frend. "E. H.," "Josepha, or the Pernicious Effects of Early Indulgence," *L&E*, pp. 138–59. See also Elizabeth Hays to Mary Hays, [c. 1796]; Elizabeth Hays to Mary Hays, 4 February 1801, *Pforz.*, EH 2; Elizabeth Hays to Mary Hays, 14 August 1803, *Pforz.*, EH 3; John Dunkin to Mary Hays, 23 March 1808, *Pforz.*, 2286.
36 Hays to Godwin, 6 February 1796, *Pforz.*, MH 12.
37 Hays wrote Godwin, "I would not wish a certain individual to suppose, that I had the vanity to believe myself beloved – much less wou'd I be thought to insinuate a notion false & injurious to him, that he had sacrificed my peace to cold-hearted & vilely selfish coquetry," [May 1796], *Pforz.*, MH 25.
38 Hays may have modeled her heroine on Godwin's hero Caleb Williams. Hindle argues that Godwin was among "the first of those at the end of the eighteenth century whose focus was shifting from Enlightenment politics and philosophy to Romantic psychology and ideology," "Introduction," *Things as they are*, p. xxvi.
39 Hays to Godwin, [9 February 1796], *Pforz.*, MH 13. Wollstonecraft expressed this view as, "we reason deeply, when we forcibly feel," "Letter XIX," *Letters From Norway*, in *The Works of Mary Wollstonecraft*, ed. Janet Todd and Marilyn Butler, (7 vols, London, 1989).
40 Hays to Godwin, [May 1796], *Pforz.*, MH 25.
41 Hays's diction was more studied than she represented: her choice of words here was likely drawn from Erasmus Darwin's definition of "writers of metaphysics" as those who study "idea, perception, sensation, recollection, suggestion, and association," in his recent *Zoönomia*.

42   Edmund Burke, *A Philosophical Enquiry into the Origin of Our Ideas of the Sublime and Beautiful* (1757).

43   Marshall Brown argues, "Far from being a repudiation of Enlightenment, Romanticism was its fulfilling summation," "Romanticism and Enlightenment," in Stuart Curran (ed.), *The Cambridge Companion to British Romanticism* (Cambridge, 1993), p. 38.

44   In a letter from the Frend figure included in the novel, Harley writes to Emma of "the illusions of the passions — of the false and flattering medium through which they presented objects to our view," *MEC*, p. 118.

45   Emma writes to Harley, "I wish we were in a vehicular state; you might then comprehend the whole of what I mean to express, but find too delicate for words," with a footnote from Hays that refers the reader to *The Light of Nature Pursued* (1768–78), by Abraham Tucker, writing as the Enlightenment philosopher Edward Search.

46   Hays struggled to elucidate the intention of her narrative: "My ms was not written merely for the public eye — another latent, & perhaps strong, motive lurked beneath. — If this in some respects has spoiled my story (for I suspect most of your remarks are just) it has also given to it, that 'energy of feeling, & ardor of expression' which impressed you. No, my friend, my story is too real, I cannot violate its truth by making [my hero] either a coquet or a lover — I have a melancholy satisfaction in presenting to the stubborn heart, which I sought in vain to melt, a just, but far from an exaggerated picture, of its own cruel & inflexible severity — yet tho' 'cruel' he was not 'worthless' — I urged him too far — carried headlong by my own sensations I did not sufficiently respect him. I confess my fanaticism — I anticipate your censures — & I submit to them," Hays to Godwin, 11 May 1796, *Pforz.*, MH 21.

47   "I suspect ... that you do not treat fairly either Mrs. Woolstonecraft's [sic] disappointments or my own, you select, merely, the object, calculate its worth abstractedly, & say it is not deserving a regret ... but you shou'd take into consideration all the associations, habits, & plans, connected with this object ... With women, the connection of [love] with other sentiments is ... more wide & complicated than with men ... their establishment, all their importance in society, yes, their very social existence, is close-twisted with it, it is then necessarily made, with them, a primary pursuit, their whole education has this tendency, & unless you cou'd make them wholly independent of circumstances, you cannot cure the effects which these trains of thinking & acting produce," Hays to Godwin, 1 March 1796, *Pforz.*, MH 15.

48   Hays to Godwin, [14–20 February 1796], *Pforz.*, MH 14.

49   In one of her letters to the Editor of the *Monthly Magazine* in November 1796, "A Woman," likely Hays, writes that the hypothesis that humans are born with no other faculty than that of sensory reception has been argued by Locke, Hume, and Hartley, "names that will be respectable in the annals of science, when superficial essayists are sunk in oblivion," "Letter from 'A Woman,'" *Monthly Magazine*, 2 (November 1796), p. 784.

50   According to J.G. McEvoy, even Joseph Priestley's contributions to the "Chemical Revolution" were seriously weakened in the eyes of his contemporary commentators by his mixing of science, politics, and religion, and by what they regarded as his amateur status because he lacked formal university training. J.G. McEvoy, "Perspectives on Priestley's Science," *Enlightenment & Dissent*, 19 (2000): 63–4.

51   See Londa Schiebinger, *The Mind Has No Sex? Women in the Origins of Modern Science* (Cambridge, MA, 1989).

52   See Gerald Newman, *The Rise of English Nationalism: A Cultural History 1740–1830* (New York, 1997), pp. 131–45.

53   Hays to Godwin, [14–20 February], 1796, MH 14.

54   Hays to Godwin, [29 April/3 May 1796], *Pforz.*, MH 20.

55   Hays to Godwin, 23 March 1796, *Pforz.*, MH 18.

56   Wollstonecraft to Hays, [1796], *The Collected Letters of Mary Wollstonecraft*, ed. Janet Todd (New York, 2003), p. 344.

57   Godwin compared Wollstonecraft to Hays, with whom she had visited the previous afternoon, fearing that Hays's dejection might prove contagious to Wollstonecraft. "Afford, for instance," he pleaded, "no food for the morbid madness, & no triumph to the misanthropical gloom of your afternoon visitor," Godwin to Wollstonecraft, 17 August 1796, *Godwin & Mary: Letters of William Godwin and Mary Wollstonecraft*, ed. Ralph M. Wardle (Lincoln and London, 1967), p. 17.

58   Replacing a negative stimulus with other, energizing stimuli was a Darwinian notion she had recently encountered, Hays to Godwin, [29April/3May 1796], *Pforz.*, MH 20.

59   On 15 September 1797 Wollstonecraft wrote Hays about some titles Hays was reviewing for the *Analytical Review* where Wollstonecraft was an editor, and declared herself "glad to find that you are out of suspense with Robinson," confirming that he had been considering Hays's manuscript and had just decided to publish it, *Shelley and his Circle* (Cambridge, 1961), vol. I, p. 161.

60   The "Preface" was preceded by an epigraph from Rousseau's Eloisa about "the perceptions of persons in retirement" being different from "those of people in the great world." Since her first textual explorations with John Eccles, Hays represented herself as standing apart from conventional society, and longing for still greater solitude. This was hardly the reality of her life: the Hays family was large and closely knit by ties of kinship, religion, and business; Southwark at the time was on its way to becoming a bustling mercantile area. Rather, like much else in Hays's oeuvre, "retirement" is a metaphor for her sense of alienation from the world because of her over-sensitive nature, and her compelling desire for the ideal realm of ideas, that heaven she pictured in *Letters and Essays* where the "just [would be] made perfect," *MEC*, p. 35.

61   Mary Wollstonecraft, *Mary, a Fiction*, ed. Gina Luria (London, 1788; reprinted 1974), p. 3.

62   "Preface," *MEC*, pp. 36–7.

63   "The science of morals is not incapable of demonstration, but we want a more extensive knowledge of particular facts, on which, in any given circumstance, firmly to establish our data," *MEC*, p. 42.

64   There were numerous editions through the eighteenth century of Antoine Galland's translation of the *Arabian Nights*, including *The new Arabian winter nights entertainments: containing one thousand and eleven stories, told by the sultan's of the Indies, to divert the sultan from performing a bloody vow he had made to marry a virgin lady every day, and have her beheaded the next morning ...* [London]: printed for the translator John de Lachieur, and sold by the booksellers at London and Westminster, 1711. See Eleanor Ty's endnote 14, in *Memoirs of Emma Courtney* (Oxford, 1996), p. 200.

65   See Katherine Binhammer's intriguing discussion of reading in Hays's novel, "The
      Persistence of Reading: Governing Female Novel-Reading in *Memoirs of Emma*
      Courtney and *Memoirs of Modern Philosophers*," *Eighteenth-Century Life*, 27/2
      (Spring 2003): 1–22. Nicola Watson argues that "Drawing on the parallel with La
      Nouvelle Héloïse very early on, Hays makes it clear that Emma Courtney's reading of
      Rousseau has been in every sense partial, limited, in fact, to the first one or two
      volumes before the novel was removed by her father. In this instance paternal
      censorship has had the opposite effect to that intended; as a result of her father's
      action, Emma never benefits from the corrective re-insertion of Julie into patriarchy or
      … from the punitive cutting-short of her revived desire," "Julie Among the Jacobins,"
      Revolution and the Form of the British Novel 1790–1825, p. 46.

66   This is George Eliot's phrase, which has a counterpart only in Eliot's history of
      Tertius Lydgate's decision to become a doctor in *Middlemarch* (1871–72). Rosemarie
      Bodenheimer suggests that Eliot's novel is "a full-blown study of young men in
      search of elusive vocations" and reveals "the intense autobiographical charge" of her
      fiction, including her own identification with Lydgate, *The Real Life of Mary Ann*
      Evans: George Eliot, Her Letters and Fiction (Ithaca, 1994), pp. xvi , 220–21.

67   *MEC*, p. 148; Hays to Godwin, 11 January 1796, *Pforz.*, MH 11.

68   Frend continued to receive the £150 annuity from Jesus College, Cambridge, despite
      his banishment, and, by conventional standards of the time, both Harley and Frend are
      unable to support a wife in middle-class style. Wollstonecraft spoke of having "a peep
      behind the curtain" with which Hays cloaked the hero's resistance to the heroine's
      romantic demands because of financial concerns in the novel, Wollstonecraft to Hays,
      Collected Letters of Mary Wollstonecraft, p. 376. Arthur Gray and Frederick Brittain
      note that beginning with a statute of 1559, the Fellows of the College "are to be
      unmarried," a practice that continued for the next 280 years, *A History of Jesus*
      College Cambridge (London, 1960), pp. 48–9. Hays insisted to Godwin of the realistic
      basis of her fiction, Hays to Godwin, 6 February 1796, *Pforz.*, MH 21.

69   *MEC*, p. 73.

70   Hays to Godwin, 6 February 1796, *Pforz.*, MH 12.

71   Ibid.

72   Marilyn Butler notes that Hays's novel "attracted more remonstrance than any other
      individual revolutionary novel," *Jane Austen and the War of Ideas*, (Oxford, 1987),
      p. 117. See also Richardson, *British Romanticism and the Science of the Mind*, p. 96.

73   *MEC*; this is a restatement of the anxiety expressed by Elizabeth Hays's heroine,
      Josepha, when she sits down to write to the man she loves of her feelings, *L&E*, pp.
      132–4.

74   Emma writes Harley that her love "… would triumph, not over my principles, (for the
      individuality of an affection constitutes its chastity) but over my prudence. I repeat, I
      am willing to sacrifice every inferior consideration — retain your legacy … retain
      your present situation, and I will retain mine. This proposition, though not a violation
      of modesty, certainly involves in it very serious hazards — It is, wholly, the triumph
      of affection!" *MEC*, p. 154.

75   See Hays's sentiments that a necessarian could never be a suicide in *L&E*, p. 185.

76   Hays to Godwin, 11 January 1796, *Pforz.*, MH 11; *MEC*, pp. 166–8.

77   *MEC*, p. 167, ftnte n. 2.

78   See Gina Luria Walker, "'The Emancipated Mind': Robinson's History of the Reformation in France and Mary Hays's View of Censorship and Persecution," *Understandings of Censorship and Persecution in the Eighteenth-Century*, International Society for Eighteenth Century Studies Congress, The Clark Library, UCLA, 7 August 2003.

79   In *L&E* Hays commented that in Clarissa "the characters are well preserved, and the epistolary style of the several writers marked with peculiar distinction," p. 96.

80   It is unclear who borrowed the phrase from whom. Mary Wollstonecraft was first to use the phrase in print in 1796, "Letter 10," *Letters from Norway*, vol. 6, p. 294; Hays invoked the "magic circle" in an earlier letter to Godwin. See also *MEC*, pp. 66, 116, based on Hays's letter to Godwin, 28 July 1795, *Pforz.*, MH 6.

81   Nicola Watson reads the generational permutations of the relationship between Emma and Augustus as transforming "the unstable relation of the lovers into the mother-son relationship [that restructures] the original disastrous love-affair," *Revolution and the Form of the British Novel 1790–1825*, pp. 48–9.

82   Hays intimated from his tutelage of her the kind of father Frend would likely be. Events proved her right: Frend was devoted to his daughter, suggestively named Sophia, to whom he taught mathematics and Greek. He was also an attentive tutor to the young Lady Annabella Milbanke, later Lady Byron. See Frida Knight, *University Rebel: The Life of William Frend (1757–1841)* (London, 1971), pp. 215, 238–9; Ruth Watts, *Gender, Power and the Unitarians in England 1760–1860* (London, 1998), p. 72.

83   *MEC*, 173; Hays to Godwin, dated November, but postmarked 6 February 1796, *Pforz.*, MH 13.

84   In an interview with Harley, Emma expresses concern about the life of her mind as well as her heart: "Must we, then, separate for ever — will you no longer assist me in the pursuit of knowledge and truth — will you no more point out to me the books I should read, and aid me in forming a just judgment of the principles they contain — Must all your lessons be at an end — all my studies be resigned? How, without your counsel and example, shall I regain my strength of mind — to what end shall I seek to improve myself, when I dare no longer hope to be worthy of him —," *MEC*, p. 130.

85   Ibid., p. 103.

86   Janet Todd notes that "broken syntax and typographical exuberance mark [the female novels of sensibility], especially the epistolary ones, since the lady of feeling must stress her non-verbal sensibility through emphasizing the limited nature of verbal communication," *Sensibility*, 125. Hays uses this device, but also to make the more general point about the lack of contemporary discourse about gender itself.

87   "I flattered myself," she tells him, "that between us this sympathy really existed. I dwelt on the union between mind and mind."

88   Nicola Watson argues that this "revelation not only unexpectedly vindicates Emma's plot of sensibility, but seems suddenly to enable her as narrator....Emma survives to exact what looks rather like vengeance," *Revolution and the Form of the British Novel 1790–1825*, p. 48.

89   Vivien Jones argues that "Emma (Hays's) sex" requires that the only career open to her is romantic love. "'The Tyranny of the Passions': Feminism and Heterosexuality in the Fiction of Wollstonecraft and Hays," *British Journal for Eighteenth-Century Studies* 20/2 (Autumn 1997)· 183.

90 See Watts's helpful "Glossary" that includes definitions of the various sectarian ideas of the persons of God and Jesus, including Arians, Socinians, and Unitarians, *Gender, Power and the Unitarians in England 1760–1860*, pp. ix–xi; See also G.A. Cole's useful discussion of the controversies in "Doctrine, Dissent and the Decline of Paley's Reputation 1805–1825," *Enlightenment and Dissent*, 6 (1987): 19–30.

91 Hays to Godwin, 13 October 1795, *Pforz.*, MH 8.

92 *MEC*, p. 121.

93 *Monthly Magazine*, 3 (1797): 47.

94 *Analytical Review*, 25 (1797): 177–8.

95 *Monthly Review*, 22 (1797): 449.

96 *The Critical Review*, 19 (1797): 109–11.

97 *The British Critic, A New Review*, (January to June 1797): 314–15.

98 Jane Austen knew about Godwin, of whom she commented that he was "as raffish in his appearance as I could wish every disciple of Godwin to be," 21 May 1801, *Jane Austen's Letters*, ed. Deidre Le Faye (New York, 1995). Austen alluded to or quoted from Prior's "Henry and Emma," as well as from the works of Hays and Godwin's associates Charlotte Smith, Helen Maria Williams, and Elizabeth Inchbald.

PART THREE

The Buried Life

Chapter Seven

Whirlwind and Torrent

> "Like other strong powers of nature, external *constraint* seems to have upon [mental talents] the most dangerous and fatal operation; when pent up and oppressed, the whirlwind and the torrent are not more wild and destructive; they struggle to burst their bounds."
>
> "M.H.," [Mary Hays] "Are Mental Talents Productive of Happiness?," *Monthly Magazine*, May 1797

Publication of *Memoirs of Emma Courtney* signaled the beginning of Hays's increasing alienation from her natural intellectual allies. Such isolation was exacerbated by the positions she advocated, and culminated in the representation of Hays as the ridiculous canting Bridgetina Botherim, anti-heroine of Elizabeth Hamilton's brilliant satirical novel, *Memoirs of Modern Philosophers* (1800). This book ultimately made Hays a laughingstock, resulting in the dismissal or denunciation of her later works because of her reputation as a clownish subversive. But Hays's sense of dislocation had begun earlier. She became increasingly uncomfortable with the controversial public persona she had created as author and presumed subject of her novel. She found herself unable to defend this role in social situations, and became inflexible and unwilling to compromise in her writing and personal relationships. All this provided more fodder for her detractors to represent her as what conservative Reverend Richard Polwhele (1760–1838) christened a freakish "unsex'd female," meaning, as Claudia Johnson argues, "oversexed."[1]

Hays's private pain was a reaction to larger cultural currents. She had chosen the new role of female explorer in her first novel, reporting fearlessly on her self-scrutiny. In this capacity, she prefigured other public intellectuals whose self-absorption was condemned by the general public.[2] Hays also presaged the uncomfortable dynamic between critics and audiences that later women writers would confront whose reputations as errant females would determine the critical and, therefore, financial reception of their works, rather than the merits of each work on its own terms. Polwhele, in one of his lengthy footnotes to *The Unsex'd Females* (1799), hailed the cultural transformation that was taking place in the gendering of criticism because there were currently so many women writers that "a female author" could no longer assume male reviewers would treat her in a chivalrous manner. Women's attempts to gain readers' favor by pleading "comparative imbecility, or a fearfulness at having offended by intrusion" into the public arena, were now routinely chastised. Critics were on the alert to denounce the inappropriate "glow of self-gratulation" by female authors. Despite the crowd of strident women promoting ideas in print, Polwhele concluded that female blushes on the cheeks of timid women were still more appealing than the "sparkle of confident intelligence."[3]

With increasing competition from other women intellectuals, Hays's intense discomfort within and without radical circles led her to experiments in life-writing, the result of her desire to address her female audience directly in the belief that, however they might differ on topical religious and political issues, shared experience of gender constraints gave writer and reader common interest in the as yet untold history of earlier women. Hays at last acknowledged that the gender of a writer affected reception of her work with respect to genre: life-writing was more acceptable from a woman than philosophical debate. Hays turned to traditional literary forms to make money, but also so that her still-radical ideas might be more accessible to intellectually adventurous women.

After *Emma Courtney* was published, Hays never regained the limited public acclaim she enjoyed as "Eusebia," the pious woman at a safe remove from the world, or the more rarified approbation she achieved as the studious female philosopher of *Letters and Essays*. She had been the first to rise to their defense at Gilbert Wakefield's earlier defection, but in *Emma Courtney* she had disregarded the tacit understanding among Unitarians and Rational Dissenters to avoid public discussion of unseemly private matters.[4] She could no longer be trusted to keep faith with her religious associates because she had given palpable form to longstanding predictions that theological heterodoxy would lead to immorality.[5] As author and supposed subject of *Emma Courtney*, Hays had offended readers and non-readers. She became an object of contempt for women and men, Dissenters and Anglicans, radicals and conservatives alike. When not consigned to oblivion, Hays was remembered only for her narcissistic apostasy from respectability as a sexually aggressive woman. Hays found herself alone, unmoored from the communal theological and political harbor she had found among the Rational Dissenters and Unitarians.[6] Instead, as an advocate of new radical philosophies, she experienced the discomfort of being "unattached." [7] Roy Porter explains that individuals like Hays, alienated from affiliation with traditional institutions, developed a new social consciousness that mandated an even more heterodox stance towards society than their predecessors. Porter notes that late eighteenth-century writers and thinkers increasingly "functioned as autonomous individuals, at bottom beholden to none but themselves, the public who bought their writings ... and such cultural middlemen as publishers." Porter cites Hays and Godwin as representative of the emergence of a "free intelligentsia," sociologist Karl Mannheim's term to signify one of the crucial aspects of modernity.[8] Hays's mounting alienation was compounded by the fact that her voluble detractors rightly believed that her ideas were dangerous to the existing social order.

The hullabaloo her novel produced pained Hays. Yet she was mindful of Robert Robinson's teaching that freethinkers, people willing to test their ideas in the search for truth, should embrace controversy as a privilege. Public attention to her work also initially buoyed her at first with a new confidence. Having had her say about Frend and unrequited love, Hays now had more to say about the other issues she had been studying. She continued to press for opportunities to speak out in the liberal periodicals, where the staunchest radicals included her in their circles. Through Wollstonecraft's good offices, Hays reviewed novels and wrote an opinion piece about novel writing in the still radical *Analytical Review*. In the progressive *Monthly Magazine*, she broke new ground by joining the philosophical controversy about women's intellectual capabilities and displaying her knowledge of seminal texts. What she wrote expressed her own hopes and frustrations, which themselves reflected deeply rooted problems in the general condition of women. Her great quandary remained, as she framed it in a short piece in the *Monthly Magazine*, "Are Mental Talents Productive of Happiness?"[9] Part of Hays's dilemma derived from her growing sense of authority and the absence of any validation of this sense in the larger world. In her cathartic correspondence with Godwin, she had taken the initial steps to free herself from the "magic circle" of female obedience to cultural expectations about women. But unlike the men she knew, she could not imagine her next identity: she saw no clear way to build upon her achievements or any feasible model to follow.

Wollstonecraft lived magnificently; she looked and acted according to her own judgments, rather than as a benighted woman and mother of an illegitimate daughter. Wollstonecraft remained unapologetic and apparently surefooted about her actions. According to contemporaneous accounts, Hays's behavior and appearance made it unlikely she would convey a similar kind of dignity, much less the potential for public influence or private romance. She presented herself as frumpy, didactic, and without any personal charms. She quickly became the personification of her critics' combined prejudices about learned women, Rational Dissenters, and English Jacobins.

The combination of Hays's personal shyness and intellectual boldness may have confused those already predisposed to dismiss her by making it easy for them to do so. The questions about gender, education, and intolerance that Hays raised, the positions she took, and the heat of her convictions, increasingly made others anxious and angry. She proved combative in the republic of letters, frustrated that public conversation about women's education invariably turned into a shouting match over woman's cognitive weakness. In this phase of her career, Hays made her own claims to mental competence by connecting them to the larger questions about the nature of the mind, the existence of learned women, and the failures of female education. She met with resistance and hostility, even slander, yet these obstacles stimulated Hays to devise other ways to validate women's intellectual potential and achievements, and implicitly her own.

Reception and Reputation

Assuming that Emma's offer of sex outside marriage to Harley was based on Hays's similar proposal to Frend, readers of every persuasion found the identification of Mary Hays with Emma Courtney titillating and pressed for more information about the real life connection between author and heroine. The novel took on a life of its own, spinning out of Hays's control; as its author she was expected to listen, respond, explain, and defend herself and her heroine to curious readers. Early in 1797 Wollstonecraft invited Hays to tea with the radical novelist Mary Robinson.[10] Robinson admired the novel, but lost sympathy with the story when the hero died, confessing his love for the heroine. Wollstonecraft agreed with Robinson's reaction, but judged that her own response came from knowing the story behind the story, that Frend still lived and would not reciprocate Hays's passion.[11] Amelia Alderson (1769–1853), the physically attractive daughter of a highly respected Norwich physician knew how to think, write, *and* flirt, was aware of Hays's discomfort in her presence, so she shared her opinions about the book with Wollstonecraft and Godwin. She praised it to Wollstonecraft, commenting that in the then current climate of political repression against alleged subversives, she judged it a brave act to be able to admire a work that subverted female modesty. Alderson suggested a reason for the extreme reaction to the book from readers eager to testify to their loyalty to Establishment values.[12] She teased Godwin about Hays's fealty to him, then wittily imitated in a private letter what she took to be Emma/Hays's equivocations about her own self-referential observations and actions. Alderson's mimicry of Hays's supposed adherence to Godwin's views foreshadowed the virulent caricatures yet to come.[13]

Little evidence exists about reactions to the novel among the Rational Dissenters and Unitarians with whom Hays had been so close. Records of only a few opinions from this circle survive. George Dyer wrote to Hays that he admired her book and was curious to see how the reviewers would treat it.[14] In early 1797 Wollstonecraft reported to Hays that at a dinner with the Reverend Rochemont Barbauld,[15] she felt called upon to defend all three—the novel, its heroine, and the author. Reverend Barbauld, Wollstonecraft wrote, "*stigmatized* [Hays] as a Philosophess — a Godwinian." Barbauld charged that Hays had caught the contagion of Godwin's alleged rational atheism and its consequent freedom from all conventional restraints, including what he saw as theological imperatives like chastity. Wollstonecraft felt compelled to assure Reverend Barbauld that *Emma Courtney* did not subvert Rational Dissenting beliefs.[16]

In 1804 Anna Barbauld invoked Hays when she declined an invitation to participate in Richard Lovell Edgeworth's proposal for a woman's magazine. Barbauld made it seem as if an embarrassing odor of moral error still clung to Hays by connecting her to Wollstonecraft, and implicitly to Godwin's inadvertently steamy revelations about her in his 1798 memoir.[17] Even people who had not read *Emma Courtney* were unable to resist joining the controversy. Robert Southey (1774–1843) wrote a friend that Hays had recently published a powerful, provocative novel. Southey's interest in *Emma Courtney* was piqued by the intensity of censure heaped on it by people whom he considered narrow-minded.[18] Thomas Holcroft, Godwin's great friend and sparring partner, was reported to Hays to have criticized her alleged advocacy of sex outside of marriage in the novel. When she confronted him about the rumor, he admitted that he had based his opinions on those of others who had read the book because he had not.[19]

The incongruity between Hays's intellectual ambitions and her social awkwardness deepened. Her career was tightly wound up with Wollstonecraft who greatly benefited Hays both personally and professionally. But this connection also proved detrimental to Hays in obvious as well as subtle ways. Since Wollstonecraft's return to London it was Hays's misfortune to present a striking contrast to Wollstonecraft, who appeared to many as the alluring embodiment of a forthright public intellectual woman. Supporters and detractors alike noticed the physical and temperamental differences between the two women. Wollstonecraft's easy sociability contrasted with Hays's social clumsiness and timidity; her sexual magnetism heightened Hays's lack of physical appeal. Alderson reported to Wollstonecraft that Stephen Weaver Browne, a mutual acquaintance, had commented on Wollstonecraft's voluptuousness, and in contrast described Hays as "old, ugly and disheveled."[20] Despite the fact that Wollstonecraft was known to be sexually active, while Hays was not, the association between the two ironically tarred Hays with the reputation of moral and sexual impropriety.

Although Frend and Hays no longer communicated, Dyer offered advice about bearing up under such intense public scrutiny. Dyer's intentions were sympathetic; he counseled Hays to be less intense, even to play the fool, as if she paid no attention to her detractors.[21] Such advice was pointless: indifference and witty rejoinders were not in Hays's repertoire.

Southey offers a glimpse of Hays as Godwin's puppet that later made Hays an easy target of satire. London in early 1797 allowed women and men of like religious and/or political persuasions to mingle with new freedom. Southey reported on an informal group that gathered one morning that included Dyer, Hays with her friend, the younger poet Ann Batten Cristall,[22] whom Southey liked, and Gilbert Wakefield, whose loud voice and abrasive manner annoyed him. Southey identified Hays through her association with Godwin, but his picture of Godwin was critical. He saw him as a man who took great pleasure in London literary society where he "talks nonsense about the collision of the mind, and Mary Hayes [sic] echoes him."[23] Alderson and Southey's comments convey more than gossip. Their unattractive descriptions come from two people sympathetic to Hays.

Responding

Hays came to general public attention at a time of accelerated and politicized communication and within the context of the government's enforcement of the "Gagging Acts" of 1795 that proscribed seditious meetings and publications. New periodicals opened up the possibilities of continual exchange of ideas among advocates on various sides of any issue and the reading public quickly became fragmented according to ideology. Every reformer took pen to paper on the crucial issues of the day. Southey had come to London to write, as had many others. The radical writers were an intense group, excited by their pioneering role in inventing a middle class republic of letters, if anxious about the consequences of free speech and press. The careers of Barbauld and Wollstonecraft demonstrate that women, too, played a part.[24] But the transition from reader to professional writer proved to be fraught with psychological and interpersonal difficulties for all the women who attempted it. Backed by Wollstonecraft as her mentor, Hays at first acted aggressively on the potential of a writing career. She published in the new periodicals and was invited to join the avant-garde throng at social occasions because of *Emma Courtney.* She was now a player and her continuing notoriety allowed her a degree of equality with other activists that she had been wanting as the pious woman.

Her stint writing for the *Monthly Magazine* in 1796–97 allowed Hays to exercise her informal position as a staff writer for Joseph Johnson, George Gregory, John Aikin, and especially for publisher Richard Phillips, to devise opportunities to write about what interested her. In addition to Wollstonecraft, male publishers, editors, and staff writers for a time supported Hays in her pursuits. The evidence is scanty, but what is clear is that she seized the opportunity to interact with others in print on a variety of subjects.[25]

By the late 1790s, conservatives resisted even more intensely than they had in 1789 radicals' faith in education as the great engine to democratize society. Those loyal to Crown and Church countered with the traditional belief in inborn human characteristics and the divine imperatives of hierarchy and control. The controversy became most intense about the relative influence on women of innate qualities versus education on women. The opposing camps argued in the new periodicals and the print war heightened the differences among them that often took the form of a new kind of attack that was more highly partisan than it had been in the past.[26] A particularly outspoken and short-lived periodical was *The Cabinet: By a Society of Gentlemen*, published in 1794–95 by the vigorous Dissenting community in Norwich, especially the Unitarians affiliated with the Octagon Chapel there.[27] The periodical showcased reformist interests and writers. William Enfield, Alderson, Wakefield, Henry Crabb Robinson, the Plumptre sisters, and possibly Wollstonecraft contributed to it. Articles included "The Rights of Woman," translations of the French materialist Helvétius, and political analyses of "The Present Alarming State of the Country." The identities of the editors and contributors remained secret, for the express aim of the publication was "eternal warfare against tyranny and oppression"—that is, Pitt's government. Under the "Gagging Acts," anonymity for subversive authors was essential.[28]

The Cabinet addressed issues that were central to Hays's interests after publication of *Emma Courtney* and seemed to offer a supportive venue for her to publish in. Gender, the new science of mind, and abolition of slavery were some of the reformist subjects that *The Cabinet* highlighted. Sympathetic discussion of Wollstonecraft's *A Vindication of the Rights of Woman* appeared in two issues of *The Cabinet*, and three short translations from the works of Helvétius, "On Education," "On the Causes that have hitherto retarded the Progress of Morality," and "Abbreviation of the Code of Nature." Helvétius was widely read by his contemporaries in both England and France for his theories that brought together Enlightenment thought and revolutionary action in France. In common with Hays, editors and readers of *The Cabinet* recognized Helvétius as an advocate for progressive legislation to eliminate social and economic inequality, agrarian justice and fair taxation, equality of the sexes, and the primacy of personal happiness and sexual freedom.[29]

Unitarian Thomas Starling Norgate (1772–1859), a contributor to *The Cabinet*, the *Analytical Review,* and the *Monthly Magazine*, was one of a select cohort of men that advocated equal political rights for women as for men.[30] In his two-part article "On the Rights of Woman," Norgate opened with verses juxtaposing natural rights, free inquiry, and access to scientific learning, and feminine virtue against the tyranny of oppressive cultural assumptions that circumscribed the kinds of knowledge women might aspire to:

> But say, BRITANNIA, do thy sons, who claim
> A birth-right liberty, dispense the same
> In equal scales? Why then does custom bind
> In chains of ignorance the female mind?
> Why is to them the bright etherial ray
> Of science veil'd?—
> . . . .
> . . . . . . and can'st thou think
> That virtues, which exalt the soul, can sink
> The outward charms? Must knowledge give offence?
> And are the graces all at war with sense?[31]

The poem and Norgate's discussion of women's rights laid out the vital elements for further consideration among *The Cabinet's* readership. Then the periodical abruptly ceased publication, likely because of the contributors' growing concerns about governmental reprisals for their outspoken positions.[32] Alderson commented on *The Cabinet's* demise, "What a pity it is that *The Cabinet* is dangerous. I should have enjoyed it else so much."[33]

When *The Cabinet* disappeared, the *Monthly Magazine*, Phillips's progressive periodical, sold by Johnson, inherited its interests, contributors, and readers, and continued the public conversation *The Cabinet* had begun.[34] The *Monthly*'s inaugural issue went to the heart of Rational Dissenting concerns about free speech and repression, inborn and acquired characteristics.[35] A column by "The Enquirer," generally assumed to be William Enfield, roused his readers' attentions by pointedly claiming that government should not have the right to silence its critics. Behind "The Enquirer"'s argument was an expectation that readers and contributors adhered to a common set of beliefs in materialism, empiricism, and the right to private judgment. "From the first dawn of reason," Enfield wrote, "man is an enquirer ... Experience alone can put him in possession of truths."[36]

The first issue also ran a letter from "J.T.," a reader taking up Helvétius's assertion that human qualities are entirely the products of education, likely a response to the excerpts from Helvétius in *The Cabinet*. J.T. archly suggested that if Helvétius were correct, then by knowing how Homer and Shakespeare had been instructed as young men, boys from anywhere similarly trained would immediately produce the same number of Homers and Shakespeares. J.T. demanded to know Helvétius's empirical findings to support his claims.[37] Although he defended innate ideas, J.T. recognized that environmental factors also played a part in human development. He did not address the implications of Helvétius's theories for educating women; he implicitly assumed that the relative influences of inborn mental ability and environment mattered only to men and male debaters.

Hays chose this moment to intrude herself in the otherwise all male skirmish with an exercise of intellectual autonomy unprecedented for a woman, perhaps because periodical culture was still so new. Under the pseudonym "Priscilla," Ann Jebb had published her advocacy of the battles John Jebb was waging with Cambridge for greater academic rigor and relief from subscription to the Thirty-Nine Articles, and, later, anonymously, defenses of Rational Dissenting enthusiasm for the French Revolution. She did not directly oppose the erudite philosophical origins of such disputes; her interests were political.[38] Hays now addressed the philosophical origins of contemporary disputes. Writing as "M.H." and subsequently also as "A Woman,"[39] Hays answered J.T.'s attack on Helvétius in the same issue, countering her knowledge of epistemological theories against his.[40] She refuted J.T.'s position as unfounded superstition.[41] Drawing on and demonstrating firsthand knowledge of Helvétius, Locke, Hartley, Collins, Hume, Godwin, and Wollstonecraft, she reasserted Enlightenment claims about the sensory basis of human thought that argued for the importance of environmental influences over inborn qualities in human development. She concluded that J.T. would have to come up with more compelling arguments before dismissing Helvétius's assertions about the primacy of education. By implication she argued for wider educational opportunities for everyone, restating the theories of Helvétius, Hartley, and Locke.[42]

Enfield as the "Enquirer" quickly posed another provocative question in a subsequent issue: "Are Literary and Scientific Pursuits suited to the Female Character?" A cautious man writing in a dangerous time, he did not come to any conclusion. He supported Wollstonecraft's argument that women have the right to be trained intellectually as men are. But he was wary of the heat that even discussing existing gender relations invariably produced. Instead of advocating any particular position, Enfield let his three female characters do the talking in a conversation that represented current, apparently irreconcilable, differences between those who were inspired by Wollstonecraft's *Rights of Woman* to seek knowledge and improve themselves, and others who rejected such revolutionary ideas. Enfield's piece combines reportage and invention: his female debaters include Margaretta, an experienced observer of women, perhaps modeled on Barbauld; Margaretta's two nieces, Sophia (suggesting the Greek word for "wisdom" and the name of Rousseau's passive female foil in *Emile*), a lively, fashionable young lady, perhaps a mischievous portrait of Alderson; and Eliza, a retiring, studious young woman, more interested in enhancing her mind than embellishing her physical or social charms, perhaps a reference to Hays. Enfield left it to his readers to draw their own conclusions, although his female characters hint at his preferences: Margaretta is wise and moderate, Sophia is popular and flirtatious, and Eliza is humorless and ideological. Enfield's dialogue also intimates how the female characters feel about each other.

Enfield explains that the question he poses is part of the historical debate over female mental abilities.[43] He frames his piece by acknowledging that there are few examples from the past of learned women. The scanty historical evidence, he urges, rather demonstrates that virtues with masculine attributes, like intellectual competence, can exist in the female mind. If the emergence of talented women is infrequent, the cause is not innate ability, but the differences in male and female education—that is, gendered and, therefore, unequal environmental factors. Enfield's little drama concludes with the practical caution that even ambitious women must take care lest learning make them repellent.

Enfield's pretty Sophia opens the debate by teasing the studious Eliza that Wollstonecraft's *Rights of Woman* is an inflated piece of nonsense. Eliza retorts that she is proud to identify herself as one of Wollstonecraft's admirers, and by way of explanation offers a capsule summary of Wollstonecraft's arguments. Sophia dismisses the specifics: she tells Eliza that she threw down the *Rights of Woman* in disgust when she read a passage in which Wollstonecraft claimed that there is no difference in cognitive potential between male and female minds—in other words, that the mind is not innately sexed. Sophia is horrified to learn that Wollstonecraft proposes that both men and women should wear the traditional black philosopher's robe from antiquity to signify their equal mental potential. Sophia's rendition of the *Rights of Woman* yokes gender equality to asexuality; to emphasize how arbitrary Wollstonecraft's dictates are, Sophia challenges Eliza to give an honest answer to a direct question: would she rather converse with neutered philosophers than flirt with fashionable young men?

Eliza ignores Sophia's provocative question. She continues her own line of argument based on Wollstonecraft's that there is no proof for the claim that women have lesser mental powers than men. Her detailed response anticipates the caricatures of Hays to come as she invokes Locke, Hartley, Godwin, Darwin, and Priestley in defense of her position, and, especially, as she disregards others' questions about the possible practical effects of "a revolution in female manners" and male reactions to such changes.[44] Eliza points out that learned women of the past and present—Elizabeth Carter, Catharine Macaulay, Barbauld, Wollstonecraft—are proof of female intellectual capacity. Eliza warns Sophia not to succumb to the conventional belief that intellect and grace are incompatible. "Believe me," she urges Sophia, "philosophy is no enemy to the graces; and a cultivated mind may dwell in a charming form." This is a more moderate version of Wollstonecraft's thunderous assertion that women must cease to be only the objects of men's desires.[45] Eliza's refinement on Wollstonecraft perhaps reflects Enfield's own wish that women might somehow devise a way to be learned, but also physically attractive and compliant.

Sophia responds to Eliza by quoting verses celebrating pleasure and fancy by Anna Barbauld, a good friend of Enfield's from their Warrington Academy days. Aunt Margaretta steps in to reprove Sophia's flippancy. She tells Sophia that the poet whose lines she recited is herself a learned woman. Margaretta advises that at present the education of young women receives greater attention than formerly and includes intellectual, as well as social, accomplishments. Margaretta praises the changes in female education, pointing out that women even have the important opportunity to study science which she sees as the basis for all other knowledge. Margaretta endorses Wollstonecraft's attentions to the controversial subject of women's intellectual competence, but warns Eliza that women should not aspire to comprehensive erudition. The object of female study should be appropriate to its usefulness in preparing middle class women for their roles in personal, domestic, and social life. Margaretta's parting comment suggests that too much learning can make a woman less pleasing to others and thus stymied in her search to find happiness and personal fulfillment:

> I must remark to you the natural tendency which philosophical pursuits have to damp the ardour of affection. Women do not always become more amiable exactly in proportion as they improve in knowledge ... Philosophers — especially female philosophers — if they wish to be loved, as well as respected, should cultivate the imagination and affections, and should be careful that, in improving the head, they do not neglect the heart.

The implication is that Sophia is not altogether wrong to fear that study will render her "unsexed;" if they want to be loved, intellectual women—as Hays's life seemed to demonstrate—must remember that they are subject to gendered expectations and constraints that make it unwise to be too learned. Enfield thus ends the debate about the possibility of expanding female education with the warning that women's minds are capable of being enlightened, but that a woman must think long and hard about the personal consequences of rigorous cognitive training and display.

This struck at the heart of Hays's experience. Whether she discussed Enfield's piece with him and/or others in advance or after is not documented. But she felt compelled to respond, albeit indirectly. In her next "Letter to the Editor," Hays avoided the issues Enfield raised. Her comments on life-writing continued the discussion of environmental influences and prefigured her major work to come. She argued that the life circumstances that produced a Newton, a Milton, or a Shakespeare could never be replicated. If environmental conditions are idiosyncratic, it follows that one way to investigate human development is in individual histories reported by the individuals themselves. "Were every great man to become his own biographer," she proposed,

> and to examine and state impartially, to the best of his recollection, the incidents of his life, the course of his studies, the causes by which he was led into, the reflections and habits to which they gave birth, the rise, the change, the progress of his opinions, with the consequences produced by them on his affections and conduct, great light might be thrown on the most interesting of all studies, that of moral causes and the human mind.[46]

Having just functioned as her own biographer in *Emma Courtney* in the interest of scientifically recording her moral and mental growth, she now began to consider her next project as the biographer of great *women* rather than great men. The debate over women's intellectual capabilities and achievement had stimulated Hays to reinvent female biography, in part to bear witness to the as yet unrecognized historical continuum of women's achievements. Hays's comments also signaled her changing view of the relationship between writer and audience in which a more traditional genre might better serve as a vehicle for her ideas.[47]

But the dispute over women's intellectual potential continued with a letter on "The Talents of Women" from an anonymous writer who identified herself as "A Woman."[48] It is likely that Hays was known among her circle to write under both pseudonyms. A Woman restated Wollstonecraft's query about where learned women were to be found, and Hays's own positions, cataloging some of the female achievers of the past who had dared to become erudite despite the prejudices against educating women. The conclusion linked misogyny with all other forms of intolerance, "whether monarchical, aristocratical, feudal, professional, or sexual!"[49] Hays thus invoked learned women of the past as evidence of female potential, a strategy that women writers before her had used.[50] If one such woman could emerge, so might others. A reader, identifying himself as "C.D.," then attacked A Woman. He called her argument "turgid inanity" and dismissed her faith in universal human potential, with the comment that such naiveté was a "cup of consolation for blockheads." C.D. claimed that every known culture assumed that women were inferior to men, and concluded that the prevalence of this assumption was a sure sign that God and nature intended this disparity to endure.[51]

Another male correspondent joined in, proclaiming that there was no law preventing any woman from pursuing any scientific or literary interest if she wished to. Women did not take advantage of such unlimited opportunities, he insisted, because their intellectual powers were obviously inferior to those of men.[52] J.T. weighed in again and referred disparagingly to M.H.'s earlier claims that intellectual abilities could be acquired through education and reasserted his belief in the primacy of nature over nurture.[53] Hays answered as A Woman again several issues later, joining the debates about female cognition and the effects of gendered education on women's achievements. She argued that women were so poorly educated that it was impossible that any could turn out to be a Shakespeare or a Newton. Using a phrase from Godwin, she protested against the masculine "monopoly of mind," explaining that women ask no favors from men, only the justice of equal education. Hays reminded her critics that the idea of education should be understood in its fullest meaning to connote both academic training and the effects of life experiences.[54]

Some months later, Hays wrote to the editor that she was encouraged by the *Monthly*'s publication of her defense of women's competence. In this letter she delineated several arguments that she would use in subsequent works: the need for a universal standard of human expectations applicable to both women and men; the imperative for improvements in female education to render women self-supporting, free to follow their intellectual ambitions and make financially disinterested marriages; and an end to gender differences in moral expectations, particularly "sexual distinctions respecting chastity." Hays invokes Saurin's "unchaste woman," Wollstonecraft, and her own reputation when she writes, "One of the world's maxims ... equally false and pernicious, is, that a woman having once deviated from chastity is to be considered as irreclaimable."[55]

Hays followed up with a letter to the editor that was published under the caption, "Are Mental Talents Productive of Happiness?"[56] Hays broadens her reach in this letter and makes the general assertion that cultures controlled by monarchs and tyrants squelch individual talent. She poses as a question "whether republics may be less inimical to the production, the encouragement, and the reward of mental excellence," but postpones judgment because the "experiments" in America and France are still too new to draw conclusions. She refers to Godwin's recently published *Enquirer* in support of her conviction of the benefits of "every attempt ... to investigate or elucidate the nature and history of mind,"[57] likely thinking of her own attempts in *Emma Courtney*. Hays refers to the cold war Pitt's government was waging against the radicals, but also the particular suppression of intellectual women, a subject that continued to engross her.

There are several possible interpretations of Hays's role in this public debate. She may have planned these exchanges with some of her male colleagues who also functioned as unofficial staff on the *Monthly*, a cadre of like-minded writers to whom editors like John Aikin or Wollstonecraft, and/or publishers like Phillips or Johnson, gave assignments, depending on the contemporary climate of opinion in the outside world.[58] If the exchanges between men who identified themselves only by initials and Hays were deliberate, then this suggests a high degree of camaraderie with her and support for her interests. If instead, Hays responded to J.T. and other public correspondents who were unknown to her, then she knowingly opened herself up to the slings and arrows of controversy. It is also noteworthy that the *Monthly* sustained, at least briefly, an editorial interest in gender and chose to represent the full range of arguments in these, as in other debates.[59]

Reviewing

Additional evidence for the collegiality of the men who wrote for the *Monthly* with Hays is that she continued to be published. By 1797 her closest associates now considered her something of an authority on the contemporary novel. Wollstonecraft still functioned as Hays's professional mentor, and assigned Hays books to review and recommended improvements in her critical technique. In January 1797, Wollstonecraft sent Hays Jane West's new novel, *A Gossip's Story*, to review.[60]

The review by "V.V." of *A Gossip's Story* appeared in the January 1797 issue of the *Analytical Review*. Hays could be stubborn with Godwin, but she responded to Wollstonecraft's counsel with little resistance: in assessing West's novel, Hays included the plot summary Wollstonecraft had recommended. But she was more interested in the moral complexities of the novel than in the story line. In her review, she argues that the combined powers of reason, imagination, and affection in fiction can and should instruct readers. She uses the opportunity to promote her understanding of new theories of the mind that the united power of feeling and reason is more effective than either alone, because feeling has to be aroused before reason can be activated.[61] She then restates the arguments she made earlier in *Letters and Essays* about the heuristic capacity of fiction to educate by stirring the passions, especially in the young, joining psycho-perceptual mechanics and reformist optimism.[62] We can hear the influence of Hays's many teachers here as well as a strengthening of her own convictions about her vocation as teacher and writer.

In the September 1797 issue of the *Monthly Magazine,* she published "On Novel-Writing," taking as her point of departure Dr. Johnson's *Rambler* essay "On Modern Fiction."[63] Hays summarizes and critiques Johnson's view that imaginative, rather than historical, narratives should display only ideal models of virtue for readers to emulate. She refutes Johnson's position, arguing from the evidence of both Richardson's great novels and the humble productions that fill the circulating libraries. She contends that the absence of recognizably human and imperfectly virtuous characters has actually retarded the ameliorative effects of novels on the morals of the present generation.

Hays maintains that Richardson's idealized heroine Clarissa can never serve as the model for human imitation. "It is the portrait of an ideal being," Hays argues, "placed in circumstances equally ideal, far removed from common life and human feeling."[64] The subject gives Hays a chance to defend her very human heroine in *Emma Courtney*, and to educate what she hopes will be her readership in the future. In this way Hays also articulates her rationale in *Emma Courtney* for exploiting personal experience and for stretching Godwin's "perfect sincerity" beyond existing limits of female propriety. Fiction, Hays opines, can serve higher purposes than mere entertainment only by engaging individual passions and self-reflection. Fiction should represent reality as it is and not gloss over the ugly and the difficult. Instead, it should delineate the conditions of actual female experience. In her theory of the novel, Hays responds to specific criticisms of *Emma Courtney*, and maps out the approach for her second novel, *The Victim of Prejudice,* already in progress.[65] In this way, although Hays wrote for money, she used her opportunities to test out her ideas about the effects of the actual rather than the ideal as they might affect the operations of the human mind. Moreover, her commentary on Richardson's idealization of Clarissa formed the basis of her own critical stance in representing women's lives in her subsequent fiction and nonfiction.

Relating

In the aftermath of *Emma Courtney*, Hays tried to interact, at least in public, with men rather than women. She asked Godwin to arrange for her to visit Holcroft with him. "I shou'd like to meet you someday at Mr. Holcroft's when there is not too much company," she wrote, "Mr. H need not trouble himself to procure ladies to meet me, his daughter is sufficient, I am more used to, and therefore more at ease in, the company of men."[66] Hays lived closely among the many women in her family, and depended on her sister Elizabeth who served for decades as her second. But perhaps, like other ambitious women, she yearned to anchor herself in the safe harbor of the wise and worthy, who happened to be men. This may have seemed to her yet again the only way possible to bootstrap her way to recognition.[67]

She continued to revere, perhaps still fear, Wollstonecraft; but otherwise, Hays looked to male rather than female intellectuals for approval. In the emerging culture of public intellectuals, Hays criticized and competed with other women, like Alderson. Hays could not match the academic pedigree of Barbauld, whose early informal education and socialization at Warrington Academy were far superior to Hays's own, and to whose present eminence Hays could only aspire. She possessed none of the beauty, charm or showmanship of Elizabeth Inchbald, Sarah Siddons, or Maria Reveley. Hays chose as her professional female companions less prominent and less socially dazzling women: Robinson's earnest and retiring daughters; the unmarried poet Ann Cristall; later novelists Annabella and Anne Plumptre; and, until almost the end of her life; Eliza Fenwick, improvident, unlucky, and in need of a strong-willed, generous friend.

Hays was happiest in intimate, sheltered interactions in which she was the sole object of attention, with one or a few others like the extended interlude with Godwin while she was writing her novel. She found the crowded goldfish bowl of London intellectuals distressing, uncertain where to place herself. In addition, as women were new to the business of writing, she, like the others, was learning how to conduct herself as a professional. Moreover, as reaction and counter reaction to the French Revolution and the war with France grew more vicious, the periodicals on both sides of the debate promoted condemnation of specific individuals, by what Zeynep Tenger and Paul Trolander describe as "discursive representations of literary personality:" attacks on an individual's character, rather than independent exchanges of information and ideas. Reviewing was commandeered in the war of words and critical impartiality was attacked, particularly in conservative reviews of books that treated philosophical and political subjects from a progressive perspective.[68]

Hays experienced the perils of public identification as a reformist reviewer, and the snares of mixing private and professional codes of behavior. In the October 1796 issue of the *Analytical Review* she published an anonymous review of the first novel by Elizabeth Hamilton, *Translation of the Letters of a Hindoo Rajah* (1796), which satirized both "courtly society and empire" and "courtly-revolutionary politics in England."[69] Hays knew Hamilton through George Gregory, editor of the *Critical Review*; she had recently entertained Hamilton at her apartments with Godwin, Wollstonecraft, and other associates. Hays may have consulted Wollstonecraft and Godwin about the tone to take in her review of Hamilton's novel. The book contains a pointed caricature of Godwin in the figure of "Mr. Sceptic," and burlesques the feminism of the unbalanced character Miss Ardent that may have seemed too realistic to Hays.[70] In her review, Hays acknowledges the work's virtues, praising it as lively and amusing in the style of the Baron Montesquieu's *Lettres persanes* (*Persian Letters*, 1721), George Lyttleton's *Dialogues from the Dead* (1760), and Oliver Goldsmith's *The citizen of the world; Or, Letters from a Chinese philosopher residing in London to his friends in the East* (1762). However, Hays comments that Hamilton's satire is not up to the standards for satirical writing of her male predecessors. Hays admires Hamilton's knowledge of India, but questions whether the author believes the Indian people are better off since the British interfered (Hays's word) in their internal affairs. Trade relations with Britain may be beneficial to India, but Hays opines, "these injured people have merely *changed masters*, and one species of oppression for another."[71]

The bulk of the review focuses on Hamilton's treatment of English culture, particularly its women, and acknowledges the justice of some of the Rajah's satiric accounts. The review concludes by reprimanding Hamilton for ridiculing principles that differ from her own and about which she is ignorant, and chides her for "a fierce ... zeal for Christianity," that takes the form of an "attack upon moral philosophy and metaphysical inquiry." Hamilton, Hays suggests, dismisses free inquiry by others because Hamilton herself sees no reason to doubt the truth of Scriptural teachings.

Within the buzzing networks of London publishing, Hamilton heard that Hays was the anonymous reviewer and had deliberately asked to review the book. Hamilton confronted Hays with the rumor when they saw each other at a social gathering; Hays denied the gossip, and, apparently, also denied having even read the review.[72] In early 1797, Hays wrote to Hamilton to confess that she was the reviewer, but declared that she had done so at the editor's insistence. Hamilton responded angrily to what she judged to be Hays's intentional duplicity in denying her authorship. Hamilton was furious because some months earlier, Hays had confided to her how hurt she was by the negative notice of *Letters and Essays* in the *British Critic*. Hamilton had responded sympathetically, and now Hays had written an unsympathetic review of Hamilton's book that alleged that Hamilton's motives derived from *ad hominem* partisanship rather than from more high-minded concerns.

Crisply, brilliantly, in her response Hamilton describes Hays's premeditated sneak attack on her and her book.

> The task *was not* put upon you. No. With the Ardour of an ancient champion did you volunteer your entrance into the lists, but not with the generosity of an ancient knight did you maintain the combat. Instead of fairly, and openly, pointing out the passages which displeased you, that betwixt you and the author the world might have it in their power to decide. You, in the dark, and with a muffled dagger aimed the blow which was to fix, as far as it is in the power of a review to fix, the fame and character of the person you saluted as a friend!

Hamilton reminded Hays of her earlier, flattering professions of friendship.[73] She accused Hays of unprofessional, self-serving motives in writing the review and of trying to avenge the harm she had suffered at the hands of reviewers by damaging Hamilton in turn. Hamilton argued that her book only poked general fun at absurdity, and not at any particular party, sect or person, although her use of direct quotations from Godwin in *Hindoo Rajah* suggests otherwise.[74] Hays apparently defended Godwin to Hamilton in her confessional letter that prompted Hamilton's reply, setting herself up as his female champion. Hamilton counterattacked in her letter by insinuating that Hays was guilty of believing Godwin to be the "spokesman for all the absurdity of the world," and thus the specific target of her book.[75]

This was not just a catfight between two nervous women whose first novels had been published in the same month by the same publisher. The tensions between Hays and Hamilton reflected their mutual insecurity in the volatile and polarized republic of letters. They shared the nagging consciousness that they lacked the rigorous training of their male contemporaries.[76] Hamilton had advantages of birth, class, and social connections that Hays did not;[77] nevertheless, Hamilton expressed similar private anxiety similar to Hays's about her own intellectual competence and a concern about being judged by better-educated men. In addition, Hamilton had qualms about the propriety of publishing such an ambitious work, particularly on her own and without the protection of her older brother. She recognized, according to Elizabeth Benger, her close friend and biographer, that as the female author of an erudite satire honoring her brother's career in India and his advancement of Orientalism, she would risk the glare of exposure because a "woman, who has once been brought before the public, can never be restored to the security of a private station."[78] Moreover, Hays may have repeated her rush to judgment about Hamilton's book as she had in responding to Wakefield, in that instance assuming the solid support of Rational Dissenting and Unitarian leaders that thought well of her as Eusebia, the pious woman. But in 1796 there was no clear support for Hays's position in defense of Godwin and Wollstonecraft or the new philosophy, no sturdy cohort of kindred spirits to back her as there had been among the Unitarians—quite the opposite. The continuing war with France produced real dangers, heightened for civilians late in the year by an attempt by a French invasion fleet to land at Bantry Bay in County Cork, Ireland.[79] For radicals, the Habeas Corpus Suspension Act passed by Parliament in the autumn signaled the intensifying repression against opposition to the government. In continuing to defend revolutionary ideas Hays became more visible and more alone.[80]

Hamilton took the moral high ground by acting on the Enlightenment precept of daring to initiate controversy—a teaching Hays strove to practice, but with difficulty because of her thin-skinned reactions to being the subject of or participating in public debate. And Hamilton conducted her inquiry with sophisticated humor, an alien mode of communication to Hays. Godwin had earlier cautioned Hays about her narrow-minded responses to the pungent satires of Rousseau, Voltaire, Smollet, Fielding, and Swift. In one of his rare letters to her, provoked by a recent conversation, Godwin commended Swift, "I consider the Yahoo story, alias the Voyage to the Hoynhnms," he wrote, "as one of the most virtuous, liberal & enlightened examples of human genius that has yet been produced."[81] Godwin ascribed Hays's prudery to her religious training and her misunderstanding of the philosophical system of Epicureanism that she had studied on her own in Enfield's *History of Philosophy*.[82] Hamilton was witty, a quality Hays lacked. Hamilton's satire reflected her religious and philosophical background, different, but not so different, from Hays's.[83] There may have been a unique moment when Hays and Hamilton, as representatives of differing, yet not mutually exclusive,[84] Enlightenment feminisms, could have publicly respected one another's differences.[85] If it ever existed, the opportunity was lost in the ideological clashes of larger political realities that forced women, as well as men, to choose likeminded allies and cling ever more tightly to them.[86]

In 1797 Hays still counted on her close relationships with Wollstonecraft and Godwin. She now played the role of supportive spectator to their love affair, although she occasionally expressed her continuing depression to Wollstonecraft that she was excluded from the happiness they shared. Wollstonecraft acknowledged her debt to Hays for her earlier loyalty by treating Hays carefully and urging her to galvanize her considerable resources to be happy despite the loss of Frend. Hays was privy to the secret when Wollstonecraft became pregnant, and may have urged Godwin to marry her before the baby was born.[87] Godwin wrote to Hays as one of the couple's intimates on 10 April 1797 to announce their marriage on 29 March. Godwin's journal for 1797 records numerous visits and dinners in which Hays was included, as well as one on 13 August which suggests that the "Hayses," probably Hays and her sister Elizabeth, had dinner with Wollstonecraft and Godwin shortly before the birth of their child.

Hays soon had occasion to portray the vibrant circle that coalesced around the married couple in which Wollstonecraft's charm and brilliance acted as magnets to a diverse group of high-powered individuals.[88] As Hays later demonstrated in idealized terms, Wollstonecraft at last experienced the fullness of her life after years of lonely struggle: happiness as woman, wife, mother of one child and pregnant with another, friend, public intellectual, and pathfinder. But ten days after the birth of her daughter, Wollstonecraft was dead. Godwin was inconsolable; Hays was bereft. Who would be her radical female teacher now? Wollstonecraft's death signaled the onset of Hays's self-representation as a solitary wanderer.

There were situational and psychological reasons for Hays's increasing social discomfort and deepening alienation. Hays's mounting missteps attested to her emerging identity, although she did not recognize it, as part of a new generation of modern intellectuals, bound by a common educational heritage rather than by birth, status, religious persuasion, profession, or wealth. Like some of her radical contemporaries, Hays positioned herself at odds with establishment culture, critical of, repudiated by, and never at one with it. As a self-taught student of liberal ideas, Hays responded to the possibilities of a new set of loyalties, believing herself to be out of place in her time. "I shou'd have been born a century earlier or later," she told Godwin, "The age of chivalry might have suited me, or the age of reason — but, in the present motley times, I am an alien — an awkward being."[89]

Hays was self-referential, according to her own accounts, because female introspection was a valid application of the Enlightenment imperative, "dare to know."[90] In this way, Hays served as a precursor of later intellectuals who confronted hostile audiences and public criticism for their intense interest in themselves. She was a forerunner of those women writers whose reputation as gender subversives, accurate or not, directly determined whether and how their texts were read, reviewed, remembered, or consigned to oblivion.[91]

By 1800, Hays had experienced alienation at every juncture. If male intellectuals in the late Enlightenment felt rootless and knew the larger society judged them to be irrelevant and/or deviant, how much more so Hays, whose personal style had the effect of marginalizing herself variously as Rational Dissenter, Unitarian, English Jacobin, female intellectual, and intensely self-aware, unmarried woman? On the cusp of the new century, Hays's actions increasingly combined vanity with insensitivity to others, pride with longing for acceptance, disregard for convention with naiveté, and prim judgments with bold gestures. It is no wonder that she soon alienated the dwindling band of her natural allies.[92] Even the alliance with Godwin that had initially seemed so promising backfired. Hays was pilloried as a "Godwinian" at the same time as political repression, personal tragedy, and the withering of their fragile community pushed Hays and Godwin further and further apart. Hays remained fixed in the public's perception as the sensation-seeking dupe of Wollstonecraft and Godwin, although her connection with them had changed dramatically: Wollstonecraft had been silenced and Hays's relations with Godwin were soon to be rent by new whirlwinds and torrents.

Notes

1   *The Unsex'd Females* (1798) was the title of a poem by the Reverend Richard Polwhele that castigated Wollstonecraft and her followers. See Claudia L. Johnson, "Introduction: The Age of Chivalry and the Crisis of Gender," *Equivocal Beings: Politics, Gender, and Sentimentality in the 1790s* (Chicago, 1995), p. 9.

2   Roy Porter, "Lasting Light?," *Enlightenment: Britain and the Creation of the Modern World* (London, 2000), pp. 478–9.

3   Richard Polwhele, *The Unsex'd Females: A Poem, Addressed to the Author of the Pursuits of Literature*, (1798; reprinted, New York, 1974, with an introduction by Gina Luria), p. 16.

4   G.M. Ditchfield comments that "It was not merely that [Theophilus] Lindsey offered a religion of the intellect, but that he reserved the utmost scorn for the most obvious manifestations of the religion of the heart," with obvious reference to Evangelicalism, "Theophilus Lindsey and the Cause of Protestantism in eighteenth-century Britain," pp. 8–9, 15. D.O. Thomas notes that Lindsey and Disney both believed that "those who repent and return to the paths of virtue, God will show mercy," "Preface to John Disney's Diary," pp. 19, 40–41. Hays's *Emma Courtney* may have been seen as too revealing of nonrational experience and not sufficiently repentant for transgressing Scriptural authority.

5   Ditchfield notes that in the 1770s public "concerns that religious liberty could be equated with religious libertinism resurfaced," "'How Narrow will the limits of this Toleration appear?' Dissenting petitions to Parliament, 1772–1773," p. 24.

6   Kathryn Gleadle comments, "because of the opprobrium Unitarians faced for their religious views, they [were] very concerned to adhere to conventional etiquette," *The*

Early Feminists: Radical Unitarians and the Emergence of the Women's Rights Movement, 1831–51 (New York, 2005), p. 30.

7   R.K. Webb points out, "The outbreak of the French Revolution increased the hopes of some in radical and rational circles, and eventually, through frustration, brought a few to extreme positions, but among others the threat the Revolution seemed to pose in England led to defections from the reforming ranks," "The Emergence of Rational Dissent," *Enlightenment and Religion: Rational Dissent in eighteenth-century Britain*, ed. Knud Haakonssen (Cambridge, 1996), p. 40.

8   Like Hays or Godwin, Porter advises, "Intellectuals came to exude the air of a narcissistic bien-pensant coterie writing about each other, surreptitiously propagating the idea that writers and artists were the people who really counted, the true legislators of the world." Roy Porter, "Lasting Light?" *Enlightenment*, pp. 478–9.

9   "M.H." [Mary Hays], *Monthly Magazine*, 3 (May 1797): 358–60. Roy Porter notes that by the end of the century for intellectuals like Hays "the big issue turned from 'Shall I be saved?' to 'How shall I be happy?'" *Flesh in the Age of Reason* (London, 2003), p. 23.

10   Paula Byrne, *Perdita: the Life of Mary Robinson* (London, 2005).

11   Wollstonecraft wrote that Mrs. Robinson was "very much pleased with the main story; but did not like the conclusion … perhaps she is right. I know my sympathy ceased at the same place; but I thought that was owing to having had a peep behind the curtain," Mary Wollstonecraft to Mary Hays, [London, c. January 1797], *The Collected Letters of Mary Wollstonecraft*, ed. Janet Todd (New York, 2003), p. 392.

12   "I am delighted with Miss Hays's novel [!] I would give a great deal to have written it," and referring to the increase in anti-Jacobin repression, commented, "tho' as society now is, it is something to be capable of admiring it," Amelia Alderson to Mary Wollstonecraft (Mrs. Imlay), 15 December 1796, Oxford, Bodleian Library, [Abinger] Dep. b. 210/6.

13   "Upon my word General Godwin, you have a very skillful aide de camp in Captain Mary Hays." "I felt two or three almost irresistible impulses while reading *Emma Courtney* to [tie] up my pen & send her my blessing directly but did not, for I thought it would seem [conceited] — & as if I thought my praise of consequence to her — so I breathed 'blessing not [kind] but deep'" Amelia Alderson to Godwin, 22 December 1796, Oxford, Bodleian Library, [Abinger] Dep. b. 210/6.

14   George Dyer to Hays, 6 February [1797], *Pforz.*, 2170.

15   Rochemont Barbauld was a Dissenting minister of Huguenot extraction who had been educated at Warrington Academy, and became the husband of Anna Barbauld.

16   Mary Wollstonecraft to Mary Hays, [c. early 1797], *The Collected Letters of Mary Wollstonecraft*, Todd, pp. 310, 400.

17   A periodical by and for women, Barbauld insisted, would never succeed because gender ensured no predictable commonality among women writers, any more than it did among men. Barbauld had wrestled with her own ambivalence about being a learned public woman; she alluded to a female moral spectrum with which she assumed Edgeworth agreed, to illustrate the differing views that divided women. She assured Edgeworth, that the conservative Hannah More would not join such a publication because More judged Edgeworth and Barbauld too liberal; she and Edgeworth themselves, Barbauld wrote, would resist collaborating with Hays or Wollstonecraft for the same reason. See Daniel E. White, "'With Mrs. Barbauld it is

different': Dissenting Heritage and the Devotional Taste," *Women, Gender and Enlightenment* (Houndmills, 2005), pp. 474–92. See also Barbara Taylor's detailed discussion of the "Gallic Philosophesses," *Mary Wollstonecraft and the Feminist Imagination* (Cambridge, 2003), pp. 176–202.

18   Robert Southey to Joseph Cottle, 13 March 1797, *Life and Correspondence of Robert Southey*, ed. Rev. C.C. Southey (New York, 1851), p. 95.

19   Holcroft to Hays, 20 September 1797, *Pforz.*, 2006.

20   "Steven [sic] Weaver Browne has been two or three times of our parties here — He talk'd in a very warm manner of you to a Mr. Rigby, who repeated his conversation to me — one of his expressions was 'she is a very voluptuous looking woman!' I stared! not that I dispute the propriety of the epithet as applied to you, but that I was surprized to find him capable of applying it … Upon my word," she continued, "I can see you blush at this distance, n'importe — a blush is very becoming — What would Miss Hays say?" Godwin had likely repeated to Wollstonecraft or to Alderson Hays's earlier remark about her inability to blush; one of them seems to have told her. Even among those who believed themselves more enlightened than the majority of their contemporaries, gossip had currency. Alderson also reported Brown's unflattering comments about Hays. "Would you believe [ ] the falsehearted man calls her old, ugly & ill-clad? — he is no philosopher …" Amelia Alderson to Mary Wollstonecraft (Mrs. Imlay), 28 August 1796, Oxford, Bodleian Library, [Abinger] Dep. b. 210/6.

21   The letter is undated; Brooks conjectures 6 February 1797? as a date, see *CMH*, p. 287.

22   Johnson published Ann Batten Cristall's *Poetical Sketches* in 1795. Little information is available for Cristall. It is likely that Hays met her through Dyer, to whom Cristall addressed her "Ode on Truth" that included the line, "Thou, whom fraternal love and freedom fire," the last phrase associated with Robert Robinson. See Ann Batten Cristall, *Poetical Sketches* Electronic Text Center, University of Virginia Library, http://etext.lib.virginia.edu/subjects/Women-Writers.html.

23   Southey to Cottle, 13 March 1797, Southey, *Life and Correspondence*, pp. 95–6.

24   Mary A. Waters, *British Women Writers and the Profession of Literary Criticism, 1789–1832* (Houndmills, 2004).

25   John Aikin, George Gregory, Joseph Johnson, and Richard Phillips are mentioned in several letters to and from Hays: See [Hays to ?], *Pforz.*, MH 26; Hays to Godwin, *Pforz.*, MH 8; Southey to Hays, *Pforz.*, 2214; Aikin to Hays, *Pforz.*, 2147–51; Crabb Robinson to Hays, 26 January 1802, *DWL*, bundle 6, XIII (g), see *CMH*, pp. 549–53.

26   Paul Keen argues that "conservatives inverted previous assumptions about the nature and aims of literary and critical discourse, often valuing prejudice, partiality and personality at the expense of reason, universality, general nature, and the strictures of benevolence … This volte face on the part of literary reviews and magazines both directly challenged and undermined neoclassical assumptions concerning a unified reading public, and it reconstituted the literary field as a public spectacle (rather than a public sphere)," *The Crisis of Literature in the 1790s: Print Culture and the Public Sphere* (Cambridge, 1999), pp. 280–81.

27   See C.B. Jewson, *The Jacobin City: A Portrait of Norwich 1788–1802* (Glasgow, 1975), p.136.

28   In 1794, Scottish reformers had been transported to the penal colony in Botany Bay for holding mass meetings, and English radicals Thomas Holcroft, John Thewall, and

Horne Tooke in London were tried for sedition, but acquitted. Penelope J. Corfield, "Appendix 3: Contributors to The Cabinet (Norwich and London, 1795)," in Penelope J. Corfield and Chris Evans (eds), *Youth and Revolution in the 1790s: Letters of William Pattisson, Thomas Amyot and Henry Crabb Robinson* (vols 1–3, Phoenix Mill, 1996), pp. 187–95.

29   David Wooten, "Helvétius: From Radical Enlightenment to Revolution," *Political Theory*, 28/3 (June 2000): 307–36.

30   Arianne Chernock, "Champions of the Fair Sex: Men and the Creation of Modern British Feminism, 1788–1800," Ph.D. Diss. (UC Berkeley, 2004), pp. 163, 177.

31   Thomas Seward (d.1790), father of poet Anna Seward (1742–1809), "The Female Right to Literature, in a Letter to a young Lady from Florence," *A Collection of Poems in Six Volumes. By Several Hands. With notes*, ed. Robert Dodsley (London, 1782), vol. II, with a new Introduction, Notes, and Indices by Michael F. Suarez, S.J. (London, 1997), pp. 312–13.

32   Zeynep Tenger and Paul Trolander advise, "The breadth of the audience for liberal periodicals was limited by the successful politicization of the language of philosophical reform by conservatives," "The Politics of Literary Production: The Reaction to the French Revolution and the Transformation of the English Literary Periodical," *Studies in Eighteenth-Century Culture*, 24 (1995): 286.

33   I am grateful to Penelope J. Corfield for her generous advice about *The Cabinet*, and for providing the quote from Amelia Alderson, personal communication, 21 September 2005. Jewson, *The Jacobin City*, p. 61, quoting A.J.C. Hare, *The Gurneys of Earlham* (London, 1895), vol.1, p. 83.

34   "Preface," *Monthly Magazine*, 1 (February 1796): iii–iv. See Paul Keen's trenchant analysis in *The Crisis of Literature in the 1790s: Print Culture and the Public Sphere*, particularly "Marginalia: Masculine Women," pp. 174–204.

35   Tenger and Trolander read this as "directly signall[ing the editors'] political interests," "The Politics of Literary Production," p. 286.

36   Jon Klancher notes that Phillips and Johnson published for the reader who "responded to that loose collection of ideas called philosophical radicalism." Moreover, "the Monthly collected readers and writers as interchangeable participants," an assorted cohort that was transforming itself into a modern "intelligentsia," "Cultural Conflict, Ideology, and the Reading Habit in the 1790s," *The Making of English Reading Audiences, 1790–1832* (Madison, 1987), pp. 38–9.

37   J.T. defended his position with a lengthy quote from *A Treatise of the Education and Learning proper for the different Capacities of Youth*, by Juan Huartes de San Juan (c. 1529–88 or 9), originally published in 1578 as *Examen de ingenios para las sciencias*. Huartes proposed that souls may be equal, but minds are not, some being more naturally competent than others.

38   George Dyer described Ann Jebb as a "lady well known to possess an understanding on political matters exceeded by few," quoted in Anthony Page, "'A great politicianess': Ann Jebb, Rational Dissent and politics in late eighteenth-century Britain," forthcoming.

39   Burton Pollin was the first scholar to identify Hays as both "M.H." and "A Woman" in "Mary Hays on Woman's Rights in the *Monthly Magazine*," *Etudes Anglaises*, 24.3 (1971): 271–82. The several contributions in the Monthly are characteristic of Hays's style and content. In addition, Hays identifies herself when she replies as "M.H." to

express her pleasure that the Editor had published her piece "The Talents of Women" that she signed as "A Woman."

40   During the four years between publication of *L&E* and her contributions to the *Monthly Magazine*, Hays broadened her intellectual range beyond the theological texts and Unitarian histories that informed *L&E* to political titles, especially Godwin, Helvétius, Wollstonecraft, John Aikin, Edmund Burke, and, of course, Rousseau. She kept current with new fiction written by Ann Radcliffe, Thomas Holcroft, Elizabeth Inchbald, "Monk" Lewis, Madam de Genlis, Henry Mackenzie, and recent poetry by Ossian, *CMH*, p. 178; Robert Burns, John Scott, and Mary Robinson, and a variety of historical sources in translation—Jacques Cazotte's *Arabian Tales*, a rendering of the *Hundred and One Nights* by Robert Heron (1792), another in 1794; the plays of Nicholas Rowe. She made fresh use of her stock of classics: Shakespeare, Milton, Pope, Thomson, Sterne, Goldsmith, Frances Brooke, Dryden, Young, Rowe, Akenside, Gray, the Bible, Enfield's *History of Philosophy*, and what Hays described as a curiosity, *The Light of Nature Pursued* (1768–78) by Edward Search [Abraham Tucker].

41   "M.H.," "Reply to J.T. on Helvetius," *Monthly Magazine*, 1 (June 1796): 385–7.

42   Letter from "M.H.," *Monthly Magazine*, 1 (June 1796): 385–6.

43   Enfield alludes to the Cartesian feminism of Huguenot Poullain de la Barre "that the mind knows no difference of sex." See Siep Stuurman, *François Poulain de la Barre and the Invention of Modern Equality* (Cambridge, MA, 2004).

44   Eliza explains, "It has never yet been proved, that woman's understanding, like her stature, is lower than that of the men … If mind be an effect of organization, as the system at present adopted by our most enlightened philosophers, leads them to conclude, it seems probable, that the female, whose organic structure is certainly more delicate than that of the male, is capable of higher refinement of intellect," *Monthly Magazine*, 1 (June 1796): 182–3.

45   Wollstonecraft writes, "A wild wish has just flown from my heart to my head, and I will not stifle it though it may excite a horse-laugh. — I do earnestly wish to see the distinction of sex confounded in society, unless where love animates the behaviour. For this distinction is, I am firmly persuaded, the foundation of the weakness of character ascribed to woman; is the cause why the understanding is neglected," *VRW* (Peterborough, 1997), p. 172.

46   "M.H.," "Reply to J.T. on Helvetius," *Monthly Magazine*, (June 1796): 386–7.

47   Hays's proposal that impartial life-writing could contribute to the new reformist science of mind appeared in close proximity to Godwin's essay "Essay of History and Romance." Each writer's interest in biography and autobiography demonstrated their respective and different goals, *MAV*, p. 13; Hays was concerned with the inner life and its effects on mental and moral development.

48   Amelia Alderson identifies Hays as both "M.H." and "A Woman" in a letter to Godwin, 1 November 1796, Oxford, Bodleian Library, [Abinger] Dep. b. 210/6.

49   "Letter from 'A Woman' on Remarks on A.B.'s Strictures on the Talents of Women," *Monthly Magazine*, 2 (July 1796): 470. This passage echoes the lines Hays gives to Mr. Francis, the Godwin character, in *Emma Courtney* who instructs, "Imposition is the principle and support of every varied description of tyranny, whether civil or ecclesiastical, moral or mental … Obedience, is a word, which ought never to have had existence," *MEC*, p. 82.

50   A salient example is Christine de Pizan, *The Book of the City of Ladies* and *The Treasury of the City of Ladies* (1405), as well as her last poem on Joan of Arc (1429).

51   "Letter from C.D.," *Monthly Magazine*, 2 (August 1796): 526–7.

52   "Letter from A.B.," *Monthly Magazine*, 2 (October 1796): 696–7.

53   "Letter from J.T.," *Monthly Magazine*, 2 (August 1796): 521–3. A new male correspondent, "S.R.," also replied to "M.H." about Helvétius as if she were a man. "S.R." insisted that specific questions about the relevance of the size and shape of the human brain must be proven before asserting that "all men are equally possessed of intellectual powers," "Letter from "S.R.," *Monthly Magazine*, 2 (September 1796): 629.

54   "Letter from 'A Woman' on the Talents of Women," *Monthly Magazine*, 2 (November 1796): 784–7.

55   "M.H.," "Improvements Suggested in Female Education," *Monthly Magazine* (March 1797): 94.

56   "M. H.," "Are Mental Talents Productive of Happiness?" *Monthly Magazine*, 3 (1797): 358–60.

57   "M.H." "Mental Talents," pp. 359–60. Hays continued her advocacy of women's right to education. Her subsequent contributions to the *Monthly* included "Defence of Helvetius," 3 (1797): 26–8, and a brief defense of her friend in "Remarks on Dr. Reid on Insanity," 9 (1800): 523–4.

58   Helen Braithwaite, personal communication, December 2004.

59   Mary A. Waters, personal communication, 9 July 2002.

60   Wollstonecraft to Hays, undated, *Pforz.*, MW 43. Wollstonecraft's references to previous reviews by Hays suggest that Hays kept busy with such work, although it is unclear which reviews may have been hers. At least one prior review of fiction in the liberal *Critical Review* sounds like Hays—a brief discussion of Elizabeth Helme's *Duncan and Peggy: a Scottish Tale; Castle Zittaw. A Verman Tale* by C.R.; and *Susanna; or, Traits of a Modern Miss*, published anonymously. The reviewer takes to task young women subscribers to circulating libraries who read bad novels that compromise fiction's power to teach by portraying women and men in unrealistic, romanticized characters and situations which fail to prepare readers for the reality of male-female relations. *The Critical Review*, XIV/2 (May 1795): 113. Brooks identifies six reviews signed "V.V." in the *Analytical Review* that she attributes to Hays, *CMH*, Appendix VI. In addition, Brooks also attributes two unsigned reviews to Hays, including *Hindoo Rajah*, ibid. This is an area of Hays's oeuvre that requires further examination.

61   Hays, *Analytical Review*, 25 (January 1797): 25–6.

62   "V.V.," *CMH*, p. 58.

63   *Rambler*, 4 (Saturday, 31 March 1750).

64   Mary Hays, "On Novel-Writing," *Monthly Magazine*, 4 (September 1797): 180.

65   Evidence for this comes from Godwin's journal, "[Nov] 23. Th. … Victim of Prejudice, p. 56, [Nov] 24. F. … Victim, p. 110, Call on Hays.[Nov] 25. Sa. … Victim, p. 199, fin." Wollstonecraft also contributed an occasional essay to the *Monthly* in April, "On Poetry, and Our Relish for the Beauties of Nature," *MH*, pp. 424–5.

66   Hays to Godwin, 8 March 1796; *CMH*, p. 443.

67   "The love of distinction," Hays told Godwin early in their correspondence, "is, you say, an universal passion — mine is never so truly gratified as by the notice & esteem of the wise & worthy," Hays to Godwin, 1 January 1795, *Pforz.*, MH 3.

68   Tenger and Trolander, "The Politics of Literary Production," p. 285.

69   See Gary Kelly's informative discussion in "Elizabeth Hamilton and Counter-Revolutionary Feminism," *Women, Writing, and Revolution* (Oxford, 1993), pp. 126–43.

70   In their superb introduction to an edition of the book, Pamela Perkins and Shannon Russell write, "The Amazonian Miss Ardent elopes with Mr. Axiom, an action which fits comfortably with the anti-jacobin assumption that intellectual women are all, at heart, sex maniacs just waiting to be picked up by the first smooth-talking seducer who crosses their drearily spinsterish path," "Introduction," *Translations of the Letters of a Hindoo Rajah*, ed. Perkins and Shannon (Peterborough, ON, 1999), p. 15.

71   [Mary Hays], "Art. XL. Translation of the Letters of a Hindoo Rajah; written previous to, and during the Period of his Residence in England," *Analytical Review*, (October 1796): 429.

72   Elizabeth Hamilton to Hays, 13 March 1797, *Pforz.*, EH 2210.

73   Hays had recently entertained Hamilton with other friends. See Godwin's diary, [Apr] "16. Sa. ... tea Miss Hayes [sic], w. Hamilton, Blake, Cristal [sic], Mrs. Gregory & [Dr.] Crauford," p. 241.

74   Hamilton accused Hays of treachery, but claimed that Hays's treachery had little effect because her arguments were so weak and insubstantial: "That it did not more deeply wound, was not owing to the compunction of the heart which dictated — but to the feebleness of the arm which struck the blow." Elizabeth Hamilton to Hays, 13 March 1797, *Pforz.*, EH 2210.

75   Perkins and Russell describe the book as "a fairly typical anti-jacobin novel," *Hindoo Rajah*, p. 14.

76   Jane Rendall, "Writing History for British Women: Elizabeth Hamilton and the *Memoirs of Agrippina*," in Clarissa Campbell Orr (ed.), *Wollstonecraft's Daughters* (Manchester, 1996), p. 82.

77   Elizabeth Hamilton (1758–1816) came from a Scottish family and was reared after the death of her parents, by an aunt in Stirling, Scotland, where she was inculcated in a specific set of middle-class values that Claire Grogan identifies as "frugality, morality, meritocracy and tolerance," "Introduction," *Memoirs of Modern Philosophers* (Peterborough, ON, 2000), p. 12. Hamilton was educated at boarding school, and remained throughout her life an evangelical Christian, though, like Hays, she resisted sectarian sanctimony, and was quick to oppose the imposition of religious dogma on children. She was introduced into London literary circles by her brother on his return from a military career in India and met George Gregory, the editor for whom Hays worked at the *Critical Review*. Her brother's sudden death in 1792 devastated Hamilton. She expressed her grief, respect, and desire to continue his Orientalist project in the east in a fiction, *Letters of a Hindoo Rajah*. Hamilton, like "Eusebia," prefaced *Hindoo Rajah* with an apology to her readers, partly rhetorical, partly genuine, for publishing "a presumptuous effort to wander out of that narrow and contracted path, which they have allotted to the female mind," ibid., p. 15. The book was well received by other critics.

78	Elizabeth Benger, *Memoirs of the Late Mrs. Elizabeth Hamilton, with a Selection from Her Correspondence, and Other Unpublished Writings* (London, 1819), 2nd edn, vol. I, pp. 129–30. Grogan quotes from Benger's *Memoirs* of Hamilton: "The character of an author I have always confined to my own closet; and no sooner step beyond its bounds, than the insuperable dread of being thought to move out of my proper sphere (a dread acquired, perhaps, from early association,) restrains me," "Introduction," *Memoirs of Modern Philosophers*, pp. 14–15.

79	The attempt to land failed because of bad weather.

80	See Chris Evans's account of William Pattisson's analogous experience of deepening isolation by 1794–5 by which time "the Godwinians were beleaguered even within the Dissenting camp," "Introduction (2)," "From 'Citoyen du Monde' to 'Citizen of Indifference'; William Pattisson and Some Dilemmas of English Radicalism in the 1790s," *Youth and Revolution in the 1790s* (Phoenix Mill, 1996), pp. 21–40.

81	Godwin stoutly advised that he regarded them as "honoured and adorable champions of human nature" who had "doubled the consciousness of all that is valuable in existence to every one of [their] admirers!," Godwin to Hays, 2 September 1795, *Pforz.*, WG 314.

82	"What an insatiable & merciless deity is yours, who requires that I should sacrifice at his shrine all those persons whom I have accustomed to preserve nearest to my heart!," ibid.

83	In her later *Letters on the Elementary Principles of Education* (1801), Hamilton argued against "Contempt for the Female Character" and "sexual prejudice." Kelly argues that *Hindoo Rajah* "embodies a feminism of the Revolutionary decade distinct from and partly rejecting the Revolutionary feminism of Wollstonecraft and Hays, but overlapping with it and drawing on a common intellectual and literary inheritance in Enlightenment and Sentimental culture," "Elizabeth Hamilton and Counter-Revolutionary Feminism," p. 142.

84	See Pam Morris's nuanced discussion of Hamilton's *Letters on the Elementary Principles of Education*, "Elizabeth Hamilton: Letters on the Elementary Principles of Education," *Conduct Literature for Women 1770–1803*, ed. Pam Morris, vol. 3 (London, 2005), pp. 2–18.

85	Jane Rendall notes that Hamilton's determination to improve female education led her to agree with Wollstonecraft on many points. In addition, Rendall argues that in Hamilton's "one work of history—*The Memoirs of Agrippina, the Wife of Germanicus* (1804)—she [explored] the political dilemmas which faced those who sought to shape new roles for British women. In doing so, she also illustrated the difficulties which faced women writers, who like Wollstonecraft herself, were ambitious to transcend the limits of genres judged appropriate for women," "Writing History for British Women: Elizabeth Hamilton and the *Memoirs of Agrippina*," p. 79. See Perkins and Russell's comparison of Hamilton and Wollstonecraft on women's education that argues for their agreement on the social benefits of educating all women "for self-sufficiency and usefulness," and their difference on the desired results of improved female education, "Introduction," *Hindoo Rajah*, p. 17.

86	Penelope J. Corfield characterizes this dynamic as the "turn-by-turn contest for hegemony within the intelligentsia," "Appendix 3," *Youth and Revolution*, p. 188.

87	Godwin to Hays, 10 April [1797], *Pforz.*, WG 321.

88   Hays portrayed Wollstonecraft in the midst of an abundant life, happy at last: "A wife, a mother, surrounded by tender, admiring, and intelligent friends, her heart expanded, her powers acquired new vigour, life brightened, and futurity opened a prospect beaming with hope and promise," Mary Hays, "Obituary of Mary Wollstonecraft," *Monthly Magazine*, 4 (September 1797): 233.

89   Hays to Godwin, 6 June 1796, *Pforz.*, MH 22.

90   Immanuel Kant, "What Is Enlightenment?," *The Portable Enlightenment Reader*, ed. Isaac Kramnick (New York, 1995), p. 1.

91   See Lucy Newlyn, *Reading, Writing, and Romanticism: The Anxiety of Reception*, p. 38.

92   In another context, Angela Keane writes that "wandering women" like Hays, Smith, and Wollstonecraft "belong yet are detached and detachable from national tradition, a condition that makes them intellectually free but culturally homeless," *Women Writers and the English Nation in the 1790s: Romantic Belongings* (Cambridge, 2000), p. 160.

Chapter Eight

I Am a *Woman*

"The manner in which the present attack has affected my health & spirits convinced me that I am a *woman*."

Mary Hays to William Tooke, [1797]

Mary Wollstonecraft's death in September 1797 hastened Mary Hays's withdrawal to the margins of British culture. Hays now became socially adrift, cut off from any community except her patient family.[1] Her growing isolation produced a new sense of autonomy and even public defiance. Hays determined to do what she chose. Her decision produced innovative texts, a rupture with Godwin, a rumored relationship with the unstable Charles Lloyd, and vituperative attacks against her. Her resolve to publish her next two works, *The Victim of Prejudice* and *An Appeal to the Men of Great Britain in Behalf of Women*, signaled a new disregard for the approval of other people, including Godwin, in defending Wollstonecraft's life and works for posterity.[2] These works provoked fierce, carefully targeted, anti-Jacobin reactions from king and church supporters but also, from former allies. Hays recognized that the stunning void left by Wollstonecraft's death had to be filled, although for her to try to do so might well have been suicidal in terms of public reaction. Hays embraced her mentor's fiery feminism and filtered it through her own sense of decorum, which sometimes appeared to observers to be prim rigidity. Hays was not unaware of the impression she produced, but would or could not modify her behavior.[3]

Hays consciously took up the cudgels that languished after Wollstonecraft's death, although she was already a target of propaganda in the mounting reprisals against radicals. She was an easier butt than Wollstonecraft and was represented as a buffoon in print and gossip. The ridicule became more vindictive following the French invasion and violent uprisings in Ireland in 1798 and the government's suspension of the Habeas Corpus Act the same year. Reformists may have sensed a witch hunt, but conservative public opinion singled out Hays as an especially offensive witch. Hays grieved for her mentor and friend, but Wollstonecraft's absence gave Hays opportunities for imaginative release. Hays was emboldened to try her hand at writing other women's lives, beginning with Wollstonecraft's. Throughout this arduous period, she prepared to compose *Female Biography,* her most ambitious work, in order to demonstrate the growth and achievement of women's minds.

Alienation

From 1797 to 1800, Hays was nearly alone in her determination to sustain momentum in the republic of letters about gender issues.[4] Her own sense of alienation reflected larger cultural fissures. Like Godwin and others among the declining group of radicals, Hays anxiously observed the increase in governmental repression intended to curtail dissent. In 1799 Joseph Johnson sold copies of Gilbert Wakefield's *A Reply to the Bishop of Landaff's Address to the People of Great Britain*, an attack on Pitt and his government for continuing the war with France, the additional tax burden it had created on the poor, and the loss of civil liberties resulting from the new treason and sedition laws. Wakefield predicted that the poor might rise up in violent revolt against the existing government, in a repeat of events in France. The government found the text seditious: the publisher followed the author to jail, and the bookseller soon after. While Johnson was ostensibly arrested only for selling the book, he was a prime target of the sedition laws. Johnson had previously published and sold Thomas Paine's *Rights of Man* (1791–92), and his *Analytical Review* continued to publish and promote radical writing.[5] At Johnson's trial, a recent copy of the *Analytical* was introduced as evidence against him. Johnson spent nine months in prison and was fined £50. Wakefield fared worse. He spent two years in prison, and died of typhus contracted during his imprisonment soon after his release in 1801. Hays was among those who mourned him, the wounds from their earliest encounter seemingly forgotten.[6]

Increasing Isolation

For Hays, Wollstonecraft's dying and death proved to be an excruciating rite of passage to a new stage of loneliness and independence. Hays's extreme agitation and depression during this formative time are evident in a prolonged conflict with Godwin, documented in his letters to her, and in the reports and letters of mutual acquaintances. They ultimately reconciled after a serious breach, but the wounds were too deep on both sides to recreate the close bond they had shared earlier. Hays was caught up in the tragedy that began when Wollstonecraft gave birth to a daughter on 30 August, after an 18-hour labor that ultimately had fatal consequences for her.[7] Intimate friends rallied around Wollstonecraft and Godwin, including Hays. On 4 September, Hays, among others, called and was admitted to see Wollstonecraft. She called again the next day and Godwin informed her that there were already sufficient people to attend to his wife.[8] Hays demanded to see Wollstonecraft, but Godwin refused. Their heated exchange was overheard by one of the women taking care of the dying woman. Wollstonecraft died five days later. Hays never saw her again.

The surviving evidence for what actually happened between Godwin and Hays on 5 September suggests the following interpretation as to why a nearly permanent rupture between them ensued. Hays was enraged by Godwin's refusal to let her see Wollstonecraft. In the emergency of his wife's ineluctable deterioration, Godwin did what he judged he had to. Their respective representations of what had transpired contradicted each other: Hays claimed Godwin acted imperiously in keeping her from her beloved friend, whom she believed she had as much right to attend as anyone else. Godwin, believing he had acted judiciously, resented Hays's charge. They continued to bicker, apparently unable to let go either of their grievances against each other or the bond that connected them to a shared past with Wollstonecraft.

For her part, Hays was deeply offended by being turned away at the door. She loved Wollstonecraft; despite her own loneliness she had made the match between her two friends as a generous, even selfless gesture. When Godwin exercised the privileged rights of a husband over those of a female friend and denied her access to her friend, Hays's misery and perhaps possessiveness exacerbated the residue of suppressed resentment she harbored against him. These were the politics of death: loss exposed the incipient fault lines between the two left behind.

Eliza Fenwick, whom Hays may have met for the first time at Wollstonecraft's lying-in,[9] likely kept Hays informed about events at Wollstonecraft's funeral on 15 September. Godwin did not attend: he spent the time at his friend James Marshall's house, from where he wrote to another close friend to express his profound grief and his concern about the two motherless children now in his charge.[10] Hays may not have attended the Anglican service either, although the evidence for this is faulty;[11] there is no way to be sure whether she was present or not. She might have chosen to stay away on account of her extreme anguish, her anger at Godwin, or her chagrin that Anglican rites would obscure Wollstonecraft's idiosyncratic faith. Hays did not write the letter ascribed to her that Godwin allegedly commissioned a female friend to produce informing Hugh Skeys, the widower of Wollstonecraft's great friend, Fanny Blood, of Wollstonecraft's death.[12] The undated letter indicates that the writer, with Eliza Fenwick, attended Wollstonecraft for the last four days of her life, clearly untrue in Hays's case.

Hays did claim authorship of the earliest notice of Wollstonecraft's death in the *Monthly Magazine's* September issue. In her first published life-writing about Wollstonecraft, Hays incorporated all the elements of *her* Wollstonecraft, emphasizing her proud feminism. Hays's Wollstonecraft was a standard bearer of toleration: "quick to feel, and indignant to resist the iron hand of despotism, whether civil or intellectual."[13] When the brief obituary was published without attribution, Hays wrote a correction to the editor, published in the October issue. She explained to the *Monthly's* readers that she had limited herself to several paragraphs because additional information would be forthcoming from another source. Hays may have felt impelled to stake her claim to Wollstonecraft quickly. She knew, perhaps through Eliza Fenwick, that Godwin had almost immediately begun producing two crucial works about Wollstonecraft: his account of her life, and an edition of her unfinished texts. Johnson published both in 1798.[14]

None of Hays's letters to Godwin after June 1796 survive. His extant diaries and letters to Hays offer some evidence of the turmoil between them in the wake of Wollstonecraft's death.[15] As they each wrestled separately with shock and grief, Hays demanded what she believed was hers. Godwin's letters suggest that shortly after Wollstonecraft died, Hays wrote to him and asked him to return all the letters and notes she had written to Wollstonecraft, without reading them, and all her own letters to Godwin. Two weeks later Godwin replied that he had returned all of Hays's letters to Wollstonecraft that he could find. He attempted to write dispassionately, as in the past, but he was deeply offended; in his grief he became judgmental and severe. With cold precision, he emphasized that, as she requested, he had not read them. His anger expressed itself in a hint to Hays that, given the intimate relations between his wife and himself, it was likely that Wollstonecraft had already shared Hays's letters with him.[16]

Godwin expected that once she had some time to calm down, Hays would retract her demands for the letters she had written to him that he had not yet returned. He attempted to rationalize his own actions and hers. In his letters to her about their estrangement, he singled out an aspect of her character that he claimed he was seeing for the first time in Hays and that he blamed for causing the impasse between them: the vanity of a published author who now felt free to exercise her will and expected others, including him, to do as she wished. In this darkest moment of his life, Godwin resisted Hays's impulse to alter the earlier dynamic between them in which he set the terms for enlightened interaction and she, albeit protesting, mostly followed them.[17] Now he chided her for abandoning the frankness and thoughtfulness he had always valued in her. This was likely code for the effect of her demands that pressed on open wounds that he sensed would never completely heal.[18] Despite what he perceived as Hays's regrettable narcissism, Godwin unbent enough to extend an olive branch by inviting her for what he saw as a long overdue visit. With understated pathos, he acknowledged her tacit sympathy for his distress, even though she had not voiced her condolences.[19]

Hays did not visit him. Instead, word came to Godwin, perhaps through Eliza Fenwick, that Hays had complained that some of her letters to Wollstonecraft were missing in the parcel Godwin sent her. Godwin responded even more icily to the report in his next letter to Hays. He had sent what he could find, he assured her, and nothing would change the fact that he could not find any others. He explained that his reluctance to return the letters arose from his feeling that Hays had violated the honesty and trust on which their friendship rested. "… [R]ecalling them," he said, was "a breach of the principles of confidence & cordiality that hold [society] together."[20] Unless Hays withdrew her demand that he produce her letters to him, Godwin warned, he would not read any future letters she might send him. In her sorrow and anger, Hays may have wanted a breach with Godwin. If so, here it was.

Godwin refused to accept responsibility for the stalemate between them; he said the change was in her, and various mutual friends had made similar complaints about her. Godwin had tried to discuss her changed behavior with her, but insisted she had erected a wall of vanity, over-sensitivity, and suspicion that caused her to misconstrue everything he said. He summed up his view of their current impasse: "We are at present twin stars that cannot shine in the same hemisphere. Hays cannot admit of an equal; nor Godwin in this case of a superior." He planned to see her to give her any of the "trifles belonging to your friend, that might happen to be acceptable"—perhaps, in his view, a final gesture. She, Godwin reiterated, had put an end to their close friendship.[21]

Four days later Godwin paid a visit to the Fenwicks. Hays arrived, and to Godwin's surprise, she asked him to read the manuscript of her second novel. The next day he wrote to her, refusing her request, and reiterating his view that her misinterpretation of his every word made open and frank communication between them impossible. Pamela Clemit suggests that Godwin's interactions with Hays at this time were colored by his perception that her request that he not read the letters he returned had violated their friendship.[22] Mutual esteem would remain between them, he wrote, but frank and open conversation was at an end because she had "poison[ed] the very springs of confidence."

Still, her new request had the effect of softening the tension between them. Godwin repeated his invitation to her to come to collect the mementos of Wollstonecraft's he had set aside for her, and to visit him or the children. He reiterated his affection for her: "[T]here are not a great many persons in whose peace I more interest myself than I do in yours."[23] Whatever answer Hays may have made does not survive. She visited Godwin several days later and presumably collected Wollstonecraft's trinkets. In turn, Godwin visited Hays three times in the next week. A week later Hays called on Godwin with Holcroft, having apparently patched up the rift with Holcroft, too. A week later, on separate days, Godwin noted he was reading the manuscript of Hays's second novel in progress, *The Victim of Prejudice*; that week he called on her, perhaps to discuss her work.[24] He never returned the letters she requested. His failure to do so was to haunt her to the end of her life.

Reviving the Flame

Despite their strained private relations in the aftermath of Wollstonecraft's death, Hays wanted Godwin to critique her public work. She expressed no doubts about his professional judgment. She needed him to read *The Victim of Prejudice* because it explicitly responded to his own novel *Caleb Williams*. In this, her second fiction, Hays devised an alternative story for Godwin's character, Emily Melville. Having achieved catharsis, if not success, in rendering the crisis with Frend, Hays revealed in *Victim* how much she had learned from Godwin. Now she sought to represent the vast discrepancies between the domains in which men and women live, and was ready to debate her differences with Godwin.

Hays drew the stuff of her new fiction from her first-hand knowledge of Wollstonecraft. Freed of Wollstonecraft's critical eye on her, Hays was also released from her fear of offending Wollstonecraft.[25] Hays now conceived of Wollstonecraft as an imaginative artifact, representing her as both a victim of cultural prejudices and an indomitable spirit. Hays came to a new understanding of the power of life-writing, even in fiction, to perpetuate the meaning of a woman's individual circumstances and render it instructive for other women. What better subject for a feminist novel than a generic retelling of Wollstonecraft's struggle from Hays's perspective as her protégée, confidante, and now again her defender? Hays's request for the return of her letters to Godwin may have reflected her wish to use them in her new fiction, as she had used her letters to Godwin and Frend in *Emma Courtney*, in order to incorporate her own spontaneous reactions.[26]

Hays apparently had left little unsaid to Wollstonecraft, particularly in the relatively peaceful months between the beginning of Wollstonecraft's liaison with Godwin and her death.[27] In this second phase of their relationship beginning in late 1795, the two women shared intimate histories; and Hays recognized that Wollstonecraft's story linked the historical struggle over unlimited toleration to ancient prejudices against women who had rebelled against society's assumption that they should not be sexually active unless and until married. As Wollstonecraft dared to live freely, Hays observed the multiple punishments that even a modern woman could not escape because of society's apparently unshakable beliefs about "the weaker, the fairer sex."

During their debate in 1796 as she wrote *Emma Courtney*, Hays had complained that Godwin failed to appreciate her character Emma Courtney, although he was aware of her particular affinity with his character, Emily Melville.[28] She had been skeptical that he could express such keen penetration into the human heart in his own novel while demonstrating lack of empathy for her heroine and herself. She had used Godwin as a sounding board to express her views on the devastating effects on men and women of social conventions, particularly the double standard towards sex. Emily Melville, like Godwin's other female characters, tries and fails to combat the male oppression she encounters. To explain Godwin's obtuseness, Hays had focused on the gendering of chastity, applying both the denotation and connotations of the word: the historical commandment that woman be a blank slate, untouchable outside of marriage, and void of erotic desire or ambition.[29] In her view, this produced stunted human beings: violent men, incapable of genuine feeling, and women who sabotaged themselves by becoming the playthings of men who had also been abused by their superiors in the socio-economic hierarchy. Women like herself and Wollstonecraft, Hays had explained, were forced to become caricatures of rational beings, ambivalent about their own competence, paralyzed at crucial moments in their lives by the terrible consequences of acting on their pent-up desires.

From her understanding of this acculturation and its consequences, Hays transformed Godwin's Emily Melville into Mary Raymond, heroine of *The Victim of Prejudice*. Here, for the first time, Hays self-consciously constructs an alternative narrative to a discrete aspect of an existing text. She reworks one of the subplots in Godwin's novel into the subject of her story: in *Caleb Williams*, the villain Tyrrel pursues Emily Melville in private, imprisoning her at home; when he corners her, he believes that she will easily submit to his plans to force her into a marriage with another man whom she despises. But Emily resists Tyrrel. He is startled by her courage, and attempts to overwhelm her with the argument that she is in his power, that he has supported and reared her, that he can legally demand his rights as her creditor, knowing that she has no money. Godwin's heroine asserts an Enlightenment credo that Hays's heroine is to build on: "You may imprison my body but you cannot conquer my mind."[30]

The Victim of Prejudice traces the period of happiness and inevitable fall of the illegitimate daughter of a prostitute, whose spirit and intelligence blossom briefly under the guardianship of an enlightened man. Mary Raymond is the orphaned victim of the title who reads the sad tale of her mother's thwarted life as she narrates her own. Emily's spirited resistance to Tyrrel's tyranny in Godwin's novel inspires the dramatic momentum of *The Victim of Prejudice*. Hays connects the fight for autonomy of Mary, her Emily, to the struggle of all women for freedom. In *Victim* Hays explores successive locations of female subjugation by rewriting Clarissa Harlowe's rape and death, not as chastity and transcendence, but rather as vicious debasement.[31] The novel's tantalizing theme is the potential for the idea of female autonomy, and the impossibility of its realization. Struggle as she does, Mary is ineluctably ensnared in a net of intolerance and persecution.

The ghost of Wollstonecraft hovers over the work. Like Wollstonecraft's unfinished novel, *Wrongs of Woman*, the central motif of *Victim* is woman as fugitive. Hays and Wollstonecraft may have discussed their new novels; whether intentionally or not, their second novels each reverse the movements of their first. Wollstonecraft's heroine is lawfully imprisoned in Bedlam by her manipulative husband. There she turns inward to contemplate a private history that has public dimensions in her commentary on the laws and customs that have led to her incarceration. By contrast, Hays's Mary is an active figure who provides an alternative narrative to Emily Melville's ultimately deadly fight for autonomy. Hays's heroine declares to Sir Peter Osborne, her aristocratic captor and rapist, "I demand my liberty this moment ... No one has the right to control me. Think not, by feeble restraints to fetter the body when the mind is determined and free." [32] Hays's heroine goes further than Emily Melville: "I ask no mercy," she cries to Osborne, "but liberty, the common *right* of a human being to whose charge no offence can be alleged." Her powerful and clever oppressor hurls back the obvious question: if he lets her go, what will she do with her freedom? Her answer is to fly out the door into the wilderness of London, despite the perils that lie ahead, in an act of autonomy that is unprecedented in women's fiction.[33]

Education, as Hays's several mentors preached, can produce progress, even freedom. Hays builds on this idea, giving it imaginative life, for *Victim* is also the story of Mary Raymond's education, detailing her early tutelage under her guardian's progressive practice of educating the sexes together. The fiction advances Hays's project of displaying different possibilities for female cognitive training. In *Victim,* Hays poses the question, if boy and girl are reared together in learning and play, can they develop into man and woman who are neither tyrant nor slave? Unlike Emma Courtney, Mary Raymond is taught French, Italian, and Latin, geometry, algebra, arithmetic, astronomy, and botany[34] by her erudite guardian, the same subjects and in the same schoolroom as two wealthy brothers. She is encouraged to exercise and play with the boys. As a result, she is healthy in both body and mind. She is trained to work hard, to persevere at her studies, and, unlike Emma Courtney, to discipline her emotions and her fantasies. Her education prepares her for a life of terrifying independence. Pursued by Osborn, she remains resilient. In her attempts to support herself selling flowers, Mary tastes independence, if for a moment. Hays gives us a glimpse of female autonomy that cannot be sustained. Yet Mary can imagine enlightenment. She echoes Hays's hope that someday women will realize "the idea of being free." The novel ends with Mary's retirement to the country as an outcast where, like the heroine of Wollstonecraft's first novel, she longs for death and that heaven where there is "neither giving in marriage nor marrying."[35] The world as it is allows women no economic, social, or psychological autonomy. For women, thinking does not guarantee self-determination. In the end, her fate suggests that Mary Raymond has finally learned what Hays was then acknowledging: that the distance between the idea of self-determination and its fulfillment was still too great for any woman to travel with safety or success.

In Mary Raymond's determination to be independent, we can hear an autobiographical echo of Hays's own mature move towards the independence that Wollstonecraft urged. Also discernable is a new consciousness of the importance of deliberate female solidarity. In Wollstonecraft's earlier *Mary,* there is some foreshadowing of the power of female alliance, based in part on Wollstonecraft's deep attachment to her girlhood confidant, Fanny Blood. In *Wrongs of Woman*, it is evident in the unique dynamic between Maria Venables and the female warden, Jemima, one that transcends class.[36] And in their own lives, Wollstonecraft and Hays displayed a deliberate cohesion in their friendship. But in *Victim,* Hays moves this initiative further to envision a common bond among women based on gender that reaches beyond friendship between individual women into community, to the possibility of collective female cooperation that does not rest on family ties or social convention, whether in a madhouse, drawing room, or country garden.[37]

Reviewers judged Hays's new novel in the context of the oppressive political climate and their own ideological leanings. Johnson's still-liberal *Analytical Review* criticized Hays's failure to demonstrate her declared purpose of portraying the double standard men assume in demanding that women be chaste, despite their own infidelities. Nonetheless, the critic complimented the author for her skill in portraying Mary Raymond's psychological development, and praised Hays for "a mind apt at moral description, fertile in sentiment, and considerably skilled in the science of the feelings."[38]

The *Anti-Jacobin Review* critic was likely the Reverend William Heath, a fierce foe of Jacobins and Dissenters who linked the writer's mental ineptitude with her aggressive, unwomanly views.[39] "To your distaff, Mary, to your distaff!" Heath exhorted Hays in his review. The *New Annual Register*'s list of the eight praiseworthy novels of 1799 included *Victim*, immediately following Godwin's *St. Leon*.[40] Hays earned £40 for her second novel.[41]

An Appeal to the Men of Great Britain in Behalf of Women

The Victim of Prejudice did not appear until 1799, perhaps because Johnson was supervising other publications from prison.[42] Johnson published Godwin's memoir of Wollstonecraft and his edition of her posthumous works in 1798. In the same year Johnson also published an anonymous work, *An Appeal to the Men of Great Britain in Behalf of Women*, long attributed to Mary Hays, probably correctly.[43] The text bears many of Hays's hallmarks: feminist claims argued by way of scriptural exegesis like "Eusebia's," attention to queenship as proof of women's mental competence, and emphasis on women's natural rights to cognitive and vocational training. The author is deliberately vague, even misleading about herself. This may have been a ruse Hays and Johnson agreed on in light of his trouble with the authorities over Wakefield's *Reply*, not out of concern for any explicitly seditious prose in the book, but because government agents were preparing to indict Johnson.[44]

Depending on the contemporary reader's political persuasion, publication of the *Appeal* in 1798 was an act of courage or further provocation: feminist concerns were muted after Wollstonecraft's death[45] and reformists were in decline. Yet the author decided that such work must be carried on. She comments that her text was written some years before, but withdrawn from publication because two other titles pre-empted the topic. The first book, a gift from a learned male friend—perhaps George Dyer[46]—was *Letters from Barbary, France, Spain, Portugal, &c. By an English Officer* (1788), a travelogue by Major Alexander Jardine, that described the status of women in the various regions he observed. The *Appeal*'s author notes that Jardine's views on women were egalitarian.[47] Jardine proposed that women be educated like men in order to assume professional roles and political responsibilities. He linked the condition of women in every culture to its degree of civilization, observing that women's potential had hardly been realized, and that everyone would benefit when it was.[48] According to the author, the text that prevented her from completing her manuscript was Wollstonecraft's *Vindication of the Rights of Woman* (1791), sent to her by another friend, and also published by Johnson. He certainly knew the author's identity, as, likely, did many other radicals. When Godwin hurried into print with *his* representation of Wollstonecraft

after her death, perhaps the *Appeal's* author judged that the time had come for her
to take up Wollstonecraft's advocacy of feminist causes.

The anonymous author is more energetic and less erudite in making her
feminist case than Hays was in *Letters and Essays*, as befits the wider audience—
all British women—to whom she appeals. She structures her *Appeal* as a series of
short staccato assertions, perhaps reflecting the influence of Robinson's *Political
Catechism*. She situates her polemic in the ongoing conversation among erudite
men who appeal to God, the Crown, and British law for liberty and justice, like
those made by the Dissenters she knows at New College and others she has read.[49]
Her appeal, like her Unitarian mentors', draws on the theological and legal history
of appeals that invoke a higher authority to challenge existing mores and behavior.
Thus, like previous appeals to men, the *Appeal to the Men of Great Britain* is also
a call to action to the author's female contemporaries. And although uninvited, the
author intends to join the discussion by and for men, not as an Amazon or a fury,
she assures her male readers, but rather as an advisor, friend, and companion. Like
Eusebia, she begins with the roots of Judeo-Christianity to argue from scriptural
evidence against the subjection of women. She makes the commonsense
suggestion that men reread the gospel carefully to discover that the New Testament
represents the savior of mankind as redeemer for women, too. The *Appeal's* author
points to the presence of as many passages supporting women's independence as
those exhorting them to submit to male authority.[50] The exegesis here is precise,
like that in Hays's *Cursory Remarks* (1791).

The author is an advocate of enlightenment, impassioned about the chronic
inequities between male and female education. She argues that until women are
given a fair chance at serious academic training, men, and women themselves can
have no accurate idea of the authentic nature and actual abilities of the female sex.
She focuses on men's attitudes towards women and characterizes this as a lethal
mixture of contempt and indifference. The author accuses men of tyrannizing over
women the same way that masters impose their will on slaves. As long as men
cannot answer women's charges of injustice and subjugation against them, women
will continue to plot secretly against their oppressors. The author then draws back,
like Eusebia, in her opening apology. "Now that I am fairly afloat," she confesses,
"I begin to tremble at my own temerity; for against a host of foes, against man's
apparent consequence, against the accumulated prejudice of the ages! — Insect of
a day! — what am I?"[51] Hays used this same metaphor of feminine insignificance
in her early fable of "The Hermit."[52]

The author is also a student of Enlightenment theories of knowledge: she traces
all women's current ills to lack of proper education. From their earliest years,
women are taught to be irrational by men, thus perpetuating the charges of
weakness and unreliability made against them. Marriage is the greatest evil, for
when women become wives they are expected to give up the right to private
judgment. Wives and husbands rarely live contentedly, because women are not the
inferiors of men, but are taught to be equally, if differently, clever and

manipulative. Once she has hit her stride, the author is as militant as Wollstonecraft. Women's failure to become independent, responsible adults is denial of that liberty which she holds to be "in the moral world, what the very air … we breathe, is to animal and vegetable life."[53] Without liberty, women die morally as well as physically. The way to progress is clear: women, like men, must be granted all the freedom, including sufficient education, which will allow them to realize their own potential. Such freedom requires new laws, no matter the obstacles or prejudices to enacting such enlightened legislation.

The author's gender egalitarianism is clearly stated: given an equal chance, women, too, may prove to be men's equals in politics, as in all other spheres. The *Appeal* marshals evidence for women's competence by identifying female monarchs as the single class of women who have been given ample scope for their abilities and without the usual impediments. This discussion attests to Hays's burgeoning interest in queenship.[54]

But not all women can be queens. The author is not quite certain what women ought to be, except for the obvious moral imperative that they be the "companions and equals, not … the inferiors, — much less as they virtually are … the slaves of men,"[55] a restatement of Wollstonecraft's claim in *A Vindication of the Rights of Woman*. The author commands every woman to feel indignation that man has set himself up as a god, and worse still, to stand as such between herself and her God. Learning does not encourage domestic neglect; women with masculine virtues and abilities are not unnatural. They can and should be trained as physicians to other women, teachers, and highly trained artisans.

Only the most radical periodicals commented favorably on the *Appeal*. Johnson's progressive *Analytical Review* recommended the book highly, not a surprise since he was the *Appeal*'s publisher; the *Analytical* reviewer applauded its militant stance and presented the author's view that the chastity that men profess to value in women is actually hypocritical in view of their own sensual license.[56] The *New Annual Review* hailed the work for its ingenious defense of women's claims to equality in education and public activity. The *Monthly Magazine* acknowledged that the *Appeal* lacked the energy and originality of Wollstonecraft's *Rights of Woman*, while the male reviewer lamented the freedom of 1791 and the repression of 1798, perhaps a reference to Wakefield and Johnson's indictments for sedition, although the wider atmosphere of suppression would have offered numerous examples. He hoped that the cause of women's rights would avoid the fate of oblivion of other liberal interests. The reviewer concluded that the *Appeal's* author was "an amiable, diffident, sensible woman."[57] The conservative *Critical Review* expressed the majority opinion that the *Appeal* was yet another irresponsible polemic from the pens of reformers who attribute the ills of humanity to corrupt government—a smack at Godwin, Wollstonecraft, and their associates, including Hays.[58] The reviewer found the author inaccurate, ungrammatical, and illogical.

Counter Offensive

Marilyn Butler makes the general point that "All the writers of any note associated with the reformist or pro-French publications of the first half of the decade— Godwin, Paine, Priestley, Price, Wollstonecraft, Hays, Coleridge, Lamb and Southey—were ridiculed in the second."[59] The counter offensive against Hays continued with publication of *Edmund Oliver*, a *roman à clef*, in 1798.[60] The author was Charles Lloyd (1775–1839), an unstable young poet with a history of broken friendships with Coleridge and others in his circle. Hays knew Lloyd, probably through Robert Southey, who introduced them in 1797. How much Lloyd and Hays socialized together is unknown, but the next year Lloyd turned on his reformist friends, issuing an anti-Jacobin, anti-Coleridge, anti-Hays blast in his novel.[61] Godwin, whose ideas were also Lloyd's target, read the work in late April 1798, although no written comment of his survives. Hays read it; she could not mistake Lloyd's caricature of her.[62] Lloyd's avowed purpose was to counteract what in his eyes was the unfortunate influence of radical philosophy. His chief objections were its presumed advocacy of illicit love and rejection of marriage, ideas for which he blamed Godwin. Lloyd also condemned what he described as the rejection of traditional values, as well as the irresponsible sexual, political, and religious experimentation of modern philosophers like Godwin, Thomas Holcroft, Elizabeth Inchbald, Wollstonecraft, and Hays.[63]

Lloyd's private views reflected a large segment of public opinion about Godwin and his followers. Coleridge is the model for the hero, a deeply feeling and impulsive character; Hays is Lloyd's female target in the figure of Lady Gertrude Sinclair, who spouts passages verbatim from *Emma Courtney*, documented with footnotes, although Lloyd occasionally provided his own parodies of Emma's jargon.[64] Lady Gertrude believes in freedom, has moral intentions and is intelligent, but has allowed herself to be led astray by others— "unfortunate from error and not from deliberate vice"[65]—in Lloyd's view, a weak and willing victim of Godwin and Wollstonecraft. Identifying Hays as the aristocratic Lady Gertrude, Lloyd suggested that even noble women might fall prey to the seductions of Jacobinism.

Despite Lady Gertrude's elite status, Lloyd's description of Hays as a curious radical type seemed plausible to his readers: enthusiastic, impatient, reckless, resentful, foolish, and inadvertently dangerous.[66] The character corroborated public antagonism against the remaining radicals, and this, in turn, contributed to Hays's deteriorating reputation. Reactionary reviewers applauded Lloyd's performance. Hays's associates quickly recognized Lloyd's caricature of her.[67] M.O. Grenby argues that the anti-Jacobin press frequently attacked Wollstonecraft and Hays in Godwin's stead because as women, they threatened existing gender relations by challenging "the affectional bonds of society." Many of the conservative novelists, Grenby advises, "preferr[ed] to target them than him." Hays, Grenby suggests, was a prime target because "it was she who imbued [Godwin's] principles with an emotional content and who brought much that remained identifiably Godwinian with the compass of the novelist's pen." Lloyd's representation of Hays gave Hays's enemies additional reasons to fear and weapons to attack her.

The next blow was aimed at all the Jacobin women. The Reverend Richard Polwhele published a 68-page poem, *The Unsex'd Females*, also in 1798. Modeled on Pope's satiric *The Dunciad: An Heroic Poem* (1728), the work exuded Polwhele's obsession with sex. It consisted primarily of explanatory footnotes, and offered a succinct catalogue of the main female offenders against orthodoxy and patriotism. Wollstonecraft led the band, followed by Anna Barbauld, Mary Robinson, Charlotte Smith, Helen Maria Williams, and Ann Yearsley. Mary Hays was at the end described as "flippant Hays [who] assumed a cynic leer." Polwhele dismissed Hays as a minor acolyte of the salacious Wollstonecraft, citing passages from *Letters and Essays*, in which Hays was made out to be a religious apostate and an addled commentator on European politics. In Polwhele's view, Hays was a pretentious nobody trying to keep up with her more competent, if infamous, associates.

The *Anti-Jacobin Review* continued to flog Hays. Printed public attacks stung Hays, but now Lloyd's antagonism took a more personal approach with disastrous results. Lloyd matriculated at Caius College, Cambridge, in the summer of 1798. During the one term he spent there, Lloyd became close with his mathematics tutor, Thomas Manning, who had been denied a degree despite being an excellent student, because he refused to take the necessary oaths of allegiance. Manning remained loyal to Lloyd to the end of Lloyd's life, which was disrupted by recurring bouts of epilepsy and mental illness. Manning was the recipient of numerous letters from Lloyd chronicling his complicated affairs, particularly Lloyd's relations with Sophia Pemberton, the daughter of a wealthy family, with whom Lloyd had been in love on and off since August 1797. By January 1799, Lloyd was living in London, uncertain about his future plans concerning either Cambridge or Pemberton.

Hays's loneliness and equivocal self-confidence led her into treacherous circumstances that made her an object of public mockery in an ever-widening social circle. During the first few months of 1799, Hays and Lloyd appeared in company together, corresponded, and became the subject of gossip.[68] On 24 April, Lloyd suddenly married Pemberton. What really happened between Hays and Lloyd before his marriage is difficult to ascertain; all the reports are second- or third-hand, and made by interested parties; Hays's view appears only obliquely. The most dispassionate account was likely Southey's, who spoke with both parties.[69] Southey reported that, according to Hays, she went out one evening with Lloyd and Stephen Weaver Browne, although she was quite depressed. According to Amelia Alderson, Browne had ridiculed Hays's appearance earlier.[70] Afterwards, the men took her home, where Browne's incessant conversation fatigued Hays. He left first, and when she and Lloyd entered her apartments, she burst into tears. Lloyd seemed genuinely concerned and interested.[71] The next day

Hays wrote Lloyd an effusive letter filled with details of her unhappiness. Southey summarized Lloyd's account, too: Lloyd claimed that Mary Hays was in love with him, had sent Stephen Weaver Browne away to be alone with Lloyd, and had cried because Lloyd rejected her advances.

Southey reports that when Hays heard Lloyd's version of events through the gossip mill, she wrote him a second time, criticizing his presumption for thinking she wanted to be alone with him, rather than reproaching him for telling tales about her, because she did not understand the magnitude of his efforts to vilify her. Lloyd wrote back to confess not that he loved her, but that he felt free to slander her because her principles were so immoral that he suspected her conduct towards him. Lloyd claimed that Hays would have had sex with him, if he had wanted to. Then he confessed repentance.

Additional evidence about what transpired comes from Charles Lamb. Lloyd spread rumors that Hays was in love with him, that many people assumed she had offered herself not only to Frend, but to Godwin, that *Emma Courtney* was a pastiche of her letters to both men and that Lloyd had heard allegations about Hays's promiscuity so often that he took them to be true.[72] Lamb condemned Lloyd, but also Hays harshly, for her poor judgment in confiding in Lloyd. Lamb's final word on the subject joked that there was a philosophical question to be considered in the gossip: was sincerity always a virtue?[73] Hays had been wrestling with that question all her life. The difference now was that she mingled with people little known to her, in the glare of London publicity, and as the emblem of a more relaxed sociability between women and men that prejudiced conventional people against her. Lloyd's loyal confidant Manning insisted that Hays was the cause of Lloyd's bad behavior.[74] He was in touch with others in London literary circles to perpetuate the gossip. Coleridge, who disliked Hays and her beliefs, added more details: during the period when Hays and Lloyd corresponded, Lloyd made a practice of reading her letters out loud in company to everyone's amusement, then answered her in similar sentimental fashion, using his younger sister as an amanuensis, in Coleridge's words, "quite à la Rousseau!"[75]

In the wake of these events, the *Anti-Jacobin Review* ran a critique of *Emma Courtney*.[76] The larger issues Hays's novel trumpeted alarmed the reviewer, Reverend Heath,[77] again. Hays's views, he predicted grandiloquently, could damage the very fabric of society. Perverted notions of female education, Heath prophesized, would produce deviant women—heroines, revolutionaries, learned ladies, even women who wanted to be men, rather than submissive Christian wives and daughters.[78] Heath ridiculed Hays's radical notions about the right to private judgment: he quoted passages from *Emma Courtney* that allegedly revealed Hays's rebellion against country, church, and men. "*Obedience,*" he quoted Hays, "is a word, which ought never to have had existence." He characterized *Emma Courtney*'s heterodoxy about female virtue as "strik[ing] at the root of every thing that is ... valuable, in the female character."[79] At risk, according to Heath, was no less than the fate of British gender relations, the nation, the empire, and Hays's soul in the next world.

Hays suspected that Lloyd had a hand in the savage attack on her novel, perhaps by instigating the review. After Heath's critique appeared, she sent it to her friend, the solicitor William Tooke, to ask if he thought there might be grounds for a legal action.[80] If so, and in light of the tense political environment, she asked Tooke matter-of-factly to suggest someone to represent her who was not associated with a particular political party or persuasion. She assumed that Tooke knew her character could withstand even the severest scrutiny, although she was uncertain whether she had sufficient courage to endure the public notoriety that prosecution would inevitably produce. The *Anti-Jacobin*'s assault, with its innuendo and chastisement, she told Tooke, had so deeply affected her that she felt reduced to that female weakness she had struggled against for years. Like her heroines, she was alone and vulnerable, unable to summon the authority to argue her views or contend against her enemies effectively. "The manner in which the present attack has affected my health & spirits," she wrote, "convinced me that I am a *woman*."[81]

Women at War

Hays was the most conspicuous 'unsex'd female' at the century's end, but the cold war at home continued to mobilize other women in whose work she figured as a lightening rod for feminist beliefs. The debate over female education was joined with concern for women's political participation and a philosophical and practical question about wives and mothers as the first teachers and, therefore, the guardians of enlightened culture.[82] In 1799, the redoubtable Evangelical Hannah More (1745–1833), published her contribution to the debate over female education and female adherents of "sexual equality." *Strictures on the Modern System of Female Education, with a View of the Principles and Conduct prevalent among Women of Rank of Fortune* (1799) attacked Hays and Wollstonecraft as agents of the new philosophy who treat marriage as an "infringement of liberty." More alludes to *Emma Courtney* as an unnamed example of the pernicious genre of novels that she characterizes as "a complicated drug," poisonous to Christian women. More issues a detailed attack against Hays's *Letters and Essays* rather than Wollstonecraft's *Vindication*. Chapter VII of *Strictures*, "*On female study, and initiation into knowledge*," refutes specifics of Hays's recommendations for the female reader (Hays had charted a plan of reading for female autodidacts modeled on the curricula for men at the Dissenting New College in Hackney). In contrast to Hays, More denigrates "the swarms of *Abridgments*, *Beauties*, and *Compendiums*, which form too considerable a part of a young lady's library … as an infallible receipt of making a superficial mind," specifically the historical digests by the French historian Charles Rollin (1661–1741) that make the past accessible to non scholars. Elsewhere in her book, More lauds Hannah Glasse's *The Art of Cookery, Made*

Plain and Easy; Which far exceeds any Thing of the Kind ever yet Published (1747), the first cookbook for women who cook at home, that Hays cautions should not be the only text a woman reads.[83] More's book demonstrated that she agreed with Hays and Wollstonecraft in their general defense of women's right to rigorous education. But More, too, found herself under attack from conservative churchmen and politicians because of her entrepreneurial efforts to educate poor children.[84] Like Hamilton, she distanced herself from those female contemporaries who might have been her allies in the struggle to improve female education.[85]

Ailing Mary Robinson, the radical writer with whom Hays had discussed *Emma Courtney,* published two feminist works in 1799: *A Letter to the Women of England, on the Injustice of Mental Subordination*, a polemic, and *The Natural Daughter*, a novel. Robinson initially published *A Letter* under the pseudonym Anne Francis Randall as a deliberate attempt to avoid the "vicious *ad feminam* attacks"[86] that Hays was subjected to. Of particular importance to Hays was Robinson's attention in her polemic to identifying learned women of the past and present, some of whom demonstrated that women's self-determination was not always the result of male education. Robinson appended to her *Letter* a "List of British Female Literary Characters Living in the Eighteenth Century" that included women whose prominence depended on their roles as "mistresses, lunatics, transvestites, or murderers," as well as thinkers and writers.[87] Hays was on the list as a writer of "Novels, Philosophical and Metaphysical Disquisitions."[88] Sharon Setzer points out that publication of this list was daring in a wartime climate hostile to outspoken women, and innovative because Robinson mixed pious and impious female figures in her catalogue.[89] *The Anti-Jacobin* reviewer led the critical assault on Robinson for her membership in the "legions of Wollstonecraft." Only *The New Annual Register* attempted an impartial response: "How far [Letter to the Women of England] contributes to the decision of the question respecting the equality of the sexes, we leave her readers to determine."[90]

Godwin and Hays saw each other with some frequency during 1799.[91] As Hays's situation worsened, Godwin made attempts to console her. He visited her several times in April 1800, despite what he considered her continuing anger and suspiciousness.[92] Personal contact may have provided some comfort for them both from increasing, ever more powerful anti-Jacobin attacks.[93] They and their associates now gained another level of infamy when Elizabeth Hamilton's popular novel, *Memoirs of Modern Philosophers*, appeared that year.[94]

In early 1800, G.G. and J. Robinson published Hamilton's second satire, *Memoirs of Modern Philosophers*. The *Anti-Jacobin Review* devoted five pages, with excerpts and footnotes, to the work that it claimed had so perfectly captured the treacherous absurdities of "Godwinian and Wollstonecraftian" philosophies. Mary Hays was one of the book's main targets. Readers responded so enthusiastically that a second edition appeared later the same year, a third edition in early 1801, and a fourth edition in 1804.[95] The novel's picture of Hays thus widened the audience of her detractors, casting in stone an image of her as ludicrous and pathetic for generations to come.

Hamilton objected strenuously on Evangelical Christian grounds to the radical feminism Hays continued to advocate after Wollstonecraft's death. In her *Letters on the Elementary Principles of Education* (1801), published the next year, Hamilton explained that "By far the greater part of those, who have hitherto taken upon them to stand forth as champions for sexual equality, have done it upon grounds that to me appear indefensible, if not absurd."[96] Her second novel directly attacked Hays as the surviving representative of all that was wrong with contemporary claims by women for gender equity, particularly as Hays made a spectacle of herself in public.[97]

Memoirs of Modern Philosophers ridicules both ideology and ideologues.[98] Godwin, who appeared as Mr. Vapour in Hamilton's *Hindoo Rajah*, is now cast as Mr. Myope, so distracted by the search for perfectibility that he mistakes abstract ideas for reality. Wollstonecraft makes a brief appearance as the Goddess of Reason—seductive, manipulative, and notorious for her sexual hunger rather than her intellectual powers—that is, the perverse antithesis of Reason. Hamilton treats Wollstonecraft's critique of Rousseau in the *Vindication* with respect through her characters' comments.[99] Prolific and sharp-tongued Holcroft is represented as Mr. Glib. Hamilton's representation of Hays as the self-proclaimed heroine Bridgetina Botherim knowingly combines conservative criticism of Jacobin ideas and personalities with a savage parody of Hays's personal and professional behavior and her private morality. Hamilton, like Charles Lloyd and the Reverend Heath, is particularly concerned with the sexual license preached by apostles of Jacobinism.[100]

Hamilton addresses the vital functions of novel writing and novel reading as vehicles for radical proselytizing, deploying the connection between the novel and its female readers to expose the medium by which women are lured to absurd but dangerous beliefs and actions that seduce them into believing that they, too, can rebel. Like Hays's heroine, Bridgetina spouts passages from *Emma Courtney* and endlessly details her personal history. When Bridgetina, her head filled with Lockean-Hartleyian materialism,[101] chooses a man to arouse her passions, she fastens onto upright Henry Sidney to whom she writes long, nonsensical letters. Hamilton criticizes the contemporary rash of first-person memoirs that she sees as seeking to elevate the mundane to the extraordinary: Bridgetina declares her correspondence with Sidney will be published as *The Sweet Sensations of Sensibility; or the Force of Argument*. The *Anti-Jacobin* claimed in its review that "the *gentle* and *tender* original of Bridgetina once thus addressed the author of *Political Justice* — 'Pray Mr. G' — when will the nation be ruined? I want some vivid emotions."[102] Hamilton reduces *Emma Courtney* to bathos, and skewers Hays's attempt to apply the new mental science to her own mind.

Bridgetina is a parody of what a fictional heroine should be. Hamilton plays her against two conventional heroines whom she punishes and rewards as an additional comment on the targets of her satire. Julia Delmond is young, beautiful, and credulous, an easy mark for Jacobin seductions because she is uneducated and spoiled by her father, who lets her read whatever she pleases. Like Wollstonecraft, Julia promotes radical feminism and elopes with a cad, likely modeled on Gilbert Imlay, who seduces her, then abandons her when she becomes pregnant. Their adventure evokes the model of Heloise and Abelard and Rousseau's Julie and St. Preux.[103] Hamilton's real heroine is Harriet Orwell, who represents Burkean values of tradition and self-control, in contrast to Bridgetina's embrace of revolution and self-indulgence.[104] Unlike Bridgetina, Harriet is a model of restraint in her love for the impoverished Henry Sidney, and she is rewarded for her virtues when she inherits a fortune so she can marry the man she loves. Like the Godwin caricature, Mr. Myope, Bridgetina is oblivious to the world around her and to herself. She mistreats her doting mother, pursues Sidney without mercy, is rude to servants, lacks judgment, and does not understand what she reads or the philosophy she parrots.

In *Hindoo Rajah,* Hamilton took gingerly satiric aim at reformist women in the character of Miss Ardent, who aspires to learning while neglecting her personal appearance. In comparison, Bridgetina is grotesque: loathsome and squat, cursed with a squint, "a long craggy neck," with "shrivelled parchment-like skin,"[105] and unruly hair.[106] She wears her wig topsy turvy, drags her skirts through the mud, runs after various male characters, condescends to other female characters (except the Goddess of Reason), confuses *La Nouvelle Heloise* with her own life and letters, and proudly boasts about her lack of humor.[107] Hamilton skillfully deploys literary styles appropriate to her didactic purposes for each of her characters. She illustrates Bridgetina's (and by implication, Emma Courtney's) misuse of the potential of first-person narrative for immediacy and intimacy between writer and reader, quoting from Hays's novel and providing her own parodies; this contrasts with the disciplined speech Hamilton composes for her worthier characters who represent her own values.[108] The conclusion of the novel explicitly attacks Hays. Hamilton makes a mock address to her readers to explain that, unlike the typical heroine of a circulating-library novel, Bridgetina fails to marry at the end. The narrator expresses mock wonder as to why Mr. Myope, the Godwin figure, does not marry her, suggesting that he and Bridgetina might make a good match. Instead, Bridgetina continues to live with her mother, although Hamilton proposes that Mr. Glib, the Holcroft character, would have married her had she been willing.

Readers accepted Hamilton's satire as a well-deserved dressing down of Hays, and Bridgetina joined and in part replaced Emma Courtney as a personification of the unnatural woman who aspired to be a licentious, self-absorbed revolutionary. Hamilton reduced Hays's quest for enlightenment to a pathetic manhunt, and readers, including those far from London's political and literary circles, accepted Hamilton's equation, partly because the book affirmed their conservative opinions. The character of Bridgetina was the source of the image of Hays that was to endure; and it was a far cry from the picture of the daring experimentalist who had produced the *Memoirs of Emma Courtney*. Hamilton provided the conservative witch hunt with a rendition of Hays as the most obnoxious witch.

Away from London, Miss Iremonger, who prided herself on keeping up with the current circulating-library titles, wrote to her friend Mary Heber about Hamilton's superlative novel:

> Bridgettina [sic] is Mary Hays, a Woman of talents of the Godwin School, who wrote a novel called *Emma Courtney* and who, falling in love with Mr. Frend and having imbibed the principle of the New Philosophy — that she had only to pursue her object in order to obtain it — persecuted the poor man to the utmost, but all without effect.[109]

The deterioration of Hays's reputation had culminated in Hamilton's skillful representation, and this view dominated the public perception of Hays for the next hundred and fifty years. By her own account, Hays would henceforth be solitary, with no hope of finding another community of kindred spirits. She began now to draw courage from the imagined presence of learned women from the past. She planned a new work in a new genre for those enlightened female readers whose existence she had believed in since *Letters and Essays*, and who, she hoped, would pay attention to her writing and not her public image. Even in the midst of public disgrace, Hays was already at work on *Female Biography,* constructing an ideal continuum of women's achievements out of the documentary evidence of their lives.[110] She would escape the unhappy present in the creation of female artifacts that, like Wollstonecraft, could endure in the realm of memory.

Notes

1   Hays wrote to Crabb Robinson, "My solitudes against which you kindly warn me, has become more profound, though my intercourse with my family, which I love & in whom I can trust, has encreased [sic] in frequency," 27 February 1802, *DWL*, HCR 1802, 42, *CMH*, p. 556.

2   Harriet Jump writes, "Hays, alone among the women who had known and admired Wollstonecraft, had the courage to defend her publicly," *Lives of the Great Romantics III: Godwin, Wollstonecraft & Mary Shelley by their Contemporaries*, ed. Jump (London, 1999), vol. 2, p. xv.

3   Comparing herself with Amelia Alderson, Hays wrote to Godwin, "I have some unfashionable & obsolete notions and prejudices — I love the retiring delicacy that sometimes shrinks from observation … You laugh at me, & with reason perhaps — I am out of my place," Hays to Godwin, 6 June 1796, *Pforz.*, MH 22.

4   Jump points out that "by the mid-1790s … the excesses of the Terror [in France] led to a conservative, anti-Revolutionary backlash which affected all but the most radical thinkers … The small number of radical feminist texts that did appear after [Wollstonecraft's] death were either published anonymously, like Mary Hays, *Appeal to the Men of Great Britain* (1798), and Mary Ann Radcliffe, *The Female Advocate* (1799), or, as in the case of Mary Robinson's *A Letter to the Women of England*

(1799), under a pseudonym ('Anne Frances Randall'). As the eighteenth century came to a close, Revolutionary feminism effectively ceased to exist," "Introduction," *Women's Writing of the Romantic Period 1789–1836: An Anthology* (Edinburgh, 1997), p. xiv. Other women spoke out on various sides of the issue, including Quaker Priscilla Wakefield (1751–1832), in *Reflections on the Present Condition of the Female Sex; With Suggestions for Its Improvement* (1798); the anonymous *The female aegis: or, the duties of women from childhood to old age* (1798); Sophia King, in *Waldorf; or, the dangers of philosophy. A philosophical tale* (1798); Mary Ann Radcliffe (c. 1746–1810), in *The Female Advocate; or, an Attempt to Recover the Rights of Women From Male Usurpation* (1799); and conservative Jane West in *A Tale of the Times* (1799).

5 Helen Braithwaite points out that Johnson was politically ecumenical in what he published and sold, regularly publishing the work of authors who promoted differing views from each other. *Romanticism, Publishing and Dissent: Joseph Johnson and the Cause of Liberty* (Houndmills, 2003), p. 181.

6 Hays to Henry Crabb Robinson, 27 February 1802, *DWL*, HCR 1802, 42.

7 See Vivien Jones, "The Death of Mary Wollstonecraft," *British Journal for Eighteenth-Century Studies*, 20/2 (Autumn 1997): 187–205. The placenta was not expelled. A male physician was called in at the advice of the midwife whom Wollstonecraft insisted on having. He removed as much of the tissue as he could, but remnants of the placenta remained, raising fears of infection. Godwin believed Wollstonecraft was recovering; on Friday, 1 September, he reported in person on Wollstonecraft's progress to a few of his closest friends: publisher George Robinson, writer William Nicholson, physician Anthony Carlisle, and Mary Hays. On Sunday, 3 September, Wollstonecraft experienced shivering fits that signaled the onset of septicaemia, infection caused by fragments of the placenta that remained in the womb. Eliza Fenwick, wife of Godwin's good friend, John Fenwick, came to help care for Wollstonecraft and stayed overnight on 4 September.

8 According to Godwin, he told Hays "that we felt ourselves much obliged to you for your kindness, but that my wife has already every [attendant] necessary, & that therefore [we] should not find it requisite to trouble you," Godwin to Hays, 10 October 1797: Oxford, Bodleian Library, [Abinger] Godwin Letter-Press Copies, fols. 60–61.

9 Eliza Fenwick was herself in the early months of pregnancy with her second child, a son, who was born in May 1798, according to Isobel Grundy, "Introduction," *Secresy; or, The Ruin on the Rock* (Peterborough, ON, 1994), p. 8. Grundy supports Marilyn L. Brooks's claim that the unsigned review of *Secresy* in the September 1795 *Monthly Magazine* was "probably [by] Fenwick's friend Mary Hays," in which case the two women knew each other before late August 1797, ibid., p. 9.

10 Godwin to Anthony Carlisle, unsigned, 15 September 1797, . Oxford, Bodleian Library, [Abinger] Dep. b. 215/2; "Appendix C: Letters," *MAV*, pp. 161–2.

11 The claim rests on a mechanical copy of a letter from Godwin to an unknown addressee dated 13 September, now positively identified by Pamela Clemit. "William Godwin and James Watt's Copying Machine: Wet-Transfer Copies in the Abinger Papers," *Abinger*, 18:5 (April 2005).

12 Charles Kegan Paul, *William Godwin: His Friends and Contemporaries* (London, 1876).

13   [Mary Hays], "Obituary of Mary Wollstonecraft," *Monthly Magazine*, 4 (September 1797): 233.

14   Tone Brekke conjectures that Hays and Godwin's representations of Wollstonecraft illustrate conflicting "narrative models for examining their different versions of radical sensibility," "Authoring 'the illustrious dead': Godwin's Memoirs as paratext," Godwin conference, Bristol, 24 July 2004. I appreciate Toni Brekke providing a copy of her unpublished text.

15   Four mechanical copies of letters in Godwin's handwriting, but without addressees have been transcribed by Laura Corwin, and with Pamela Clemit's invaluable help, are identified as addressed to Hays on the basis of internal and circumstantial evidence.

16   Godwin to Hays, 5 October 1797, Oxford, Bodleian Library, [Abinger] Godwin Letter-Press Copies, fols. 58–9.

17   Some months earlier, Hays had described him as "at once, kind & cruel, polite & rude, tender & savage, candid & intolerant I cannot describe how paradoxical you appear to me," 29 April/3 May 1796, *Pforz.*, MH 20.

18   Jump writes that "the full extent of Godwin's anguish following the death of Wollstonecraft … can be deduced from what he did not say. His diary, in which he had kept a careful, objective record of the ten days of her final illness, contains simply a date and time, followed by three lines of dashes." Later he wrote "It is impossible to represent in words the total revolution this event made in my existence," "Introduction," *Lives of the Great Romantics III* (London, 1999), vol. 2, p. 17.

19   Godwin to Hays, 5 October 1797, Oxford, Bodleian Library, [Abinger] Godwin Letter-Press Copies, fols. 58–9.

20   Godwin to Hays, 10 October 1797, Oxford, Bodleian Library, [Abinger] Godwin Letter-Press Copies, fols. 60–61.

21   Godwin to Hays, 22 October 1797, Oxford, Bodleian Library, [Abinger] Dep. b. 277/7, fols. "153–6."

22   Pamela Clemit, personal communication, February 2005.

23   Godwin to Hays, 27 October 1797, Oxford, Bodleian Library, [Abinger] Godwin Letter-Press Copies, fols. 78–9.

24   Godwin's journal for these dates records, "[Nov] 23. Th. … Victim of Prejudice, p. 56, [Nov] 24. F. … Victim, p. 110, Call on Hays. [Nov] 25. Sa. … Victim, p. 199, fin."

25   Hays had written a postscript in an earlier letter to Godwin, "NB I did not tell Mrs I-y, that I suspected she did not like criticism — I love her — 'a word in which is comprehended everything that is benign' — It wou'd grieve me to offend her," Hays to Godwin, 8 June 1796, *Pforz.*, MH 23.

26   Hays had earlier written to Godwin, "fictitious correspondance [sic] affords me not the stimulus which I ever feel when addressing my friends," 20 November 1795, *Pforz.*, MH 9.

27   The passage from a letter that Hays quotes in her *Memoirs* of Wollstonecraft, that Todd conjectures was written from Wollstonecraft to Hays, suggests just such intense dialogue between the two women. "Those who are bold enough," Wollstonecraft wrote, "to advance before the age they live, and to throw off, by the force of their own minds, the prejudices which the maturing reason of the world will in time disavow, must learn to brave censure." The reference may be to the savage attacks on Hays and

Emma Courtney, or the disdain of their women friends for Fanny's illegitimacy, Todd, *The Collected Letters of Mary Wollstonecraft* (New York, 2003), #322, p. 410.

28   Hays to Godwin, [6 February 1796], *Pforz.*, MH 12.

29   She expressed this as "chastity having been render'd a sexual virtue," that is, a gendered characteristic. Hays likely also responded to Saurin's demand for more information about the causal events of the unchaste woman's sin in Robinson's translation of Saurin's sermon, Hays to Godwin, [6 February 1796], *Pforz.*, MH 12 in *CMH*.

30   William Godwin, *Things as they are; or, the Adventures of Caleb Williams*, ed. Maurice Hindle, p. 60.

31   Eleanor Ty suggests, as "rooted in the social and the real," Eleanor Ty, "Introduction," *The Victim of Prejudice* (Peterborough, ON, 1996), p. xxiv.

32   Mary Hays, *The Victim of Prejudice*, ed. Eleanor Ty (1799; Peterborough, ON, 1996), pp. 117-8.

33   Female flight resonates with a textual history of continuous efforts to thwart it. In England, an early example is Juan Luis Vives's treatise *On the Education of a Christian Woman* (1523), which instructs that, without proper restraint, a woman and her thoughts are likely to go "wandering out from home," Juan Luis Vives, *On the Education of a Christian Woman: A Sixteenth-Century Manual*, trans. and ed. Charles Fantazzi (Chicago, 2000).

34   The inclusion of science and mathematics in a girl's education suggest Frend's continuing influence, at least on Hays's pedagogy.

35   "But those who are considered worthy of taking part in that age and in the resurrection from the dead will neither marry nor be given in marriage," Luke 20:34-6.

36   Claudia L. Johnson argues that Wollstonecraft's attempts in her second novel "to establish a collective sense of identity inclusive of all women is unprecedented," *Equivocal Beings: Politics, Gender, and Sentimentality in the 1790s: Wollstonecraft, Radcliffe, Burney, Austen* (Chicago, 1995), p. 66.

37   The most striking example of this in Hays's oeuvre is Emma Courtney's care for the servant girl who bears her husband's child.

38   *Analytical Review*, 1 (March 1799): 326-7.

39   Emily Lorraine de Montluzin, "Heath, Rev. William," *The Anti-Jacobins, 1798–1800: The Early Contributors to the* Anti-Jacobin Review (New York, 1988), pp. 106-7.

40   *New Annual Register*, (1799): 276.

41   Henry Crabb Robinson, *On Books and Their Writers*, ed. Edith J. Morley (London, 1938), 1799, p. 5.

42   The *Monthly Magazine* noted that "Miss Hays will speedily publish her long expected 'Victim of Prejudice' which has only been delayed by the printer," VI (December 1798): 456. Godwin seems to have read the entire manuscript of Hays's second novel in late 1797, but no comment of his survives.

43   A twentieth-century bookseller sold a copy of the *Appeal* as a "first edition Mary Hays" on the strength of the information given in the "Introduction," according to the acquisition notes for the Pforzheimer Collection's copy of the book. The original attribution to Mary Hays comes from a later pro-woman work by William Thompson (1775–1833), an early socialist, and his partner, Anna Doyle Wheeler (1785–1848) in their *Appeal of One Half of the Human Race, Women, against the pretensions of the other half, Men, to retain them in political and thence in civil and domestic slavery, in*

reply to a paragraph of Mr. Mill's celebrated article on Government (1825). Thompson noted that he undertook his work because Wollstonecraft and Hays had failed to argue women's rights strongly enough. Thompson criticized them for their weak performances: "Were courage, the quality wanting, you would have shown," Thompson wrote, "that every day's experience proves, that women have more fortitude in endurance than men. Were comprehension of mind, above the narrow views which too often marred Mary Wollstonecroft's [sic] pages and narrowed their usefulness, the quality wanting — above the timidity and impotence of conclusion accompanying the gentle eloquence of Mary Hays, addressed, about the same time that Mary Wollstonecroft [sic] wrote, in the shape of an 'Appeal' to the then closed ears of unreasoning men ... But leisure and resolution to undertake the drudgery of the task were wanting," "Introductory Letter to Mrs. Wheeler, London, 1825" (reprinted, New York, 1970), p. vii. Thompson and Wheeler knew many of the same radicals as Hays and Wollstonecraft, including Eliza Fenwick. See Barbara Taylor, *Eve and the New Jerusalem: Socialism and Feminism in the Nineteenth Century* (New York, 1983), pp. 22–4.

44   Braithwaite, *Romanticism, Publishing and Dissent*, pp. 155–69.

45   Further damage was done to Wollstonecraft's reputation when one of the girls whom she served as a governess in the 1780s eloped with her mother's illegitimate half-brother who was shot dead by the girl's father, Lord Kingsborough. He was tried in the Irish House of Lords and acquitted, but the anti-Jacobin press smeared Wollstonecraft with the scandal, claiming her influence on the girl's disruptive behavior, Jump, *Lives of the Great Romantics III*, vol. 2, p. xiv.

46   Mary Hays, "Advertisement to the Reader," *Appeal to the Men of Great Britain in Behalf of Women*, (London, 1798), unpaginated.

47   Arianne Chernock judges Jardine in modern terms, "at the more radical end of the male feminist spectrum," "Men's Support for Women's Rights in Britain, 1780–1800," Unpublished Ph.D. Diss. (UC Berkeley, 2004), p. 42.

48   Jardine expressed this as, "the rank and consideration of the [female] sex probably always follows the degrees of civilization," Alexander Jardine, *Letters from Barbary, France, Spain, Portugal by a Soldier* (London, 1788), vol. I, pp. 309–11.

49   Priestley wrote several "appeals," for example, *An appeal to the serious and candid professors of Christianity ... / by a lover of the Gospel [i.e. Joseph Priestley]*, 1771.

50   This sounds like Hays, but the Italian and French quotations given without citation or translation, do not. Perhaps Johnson padded the original text with existing pages from others' works, apparently a common printing practice.

51   Hays, *Appeal*, p. 29.

52   Hays, "The Hermit: An Oriental Tale," *L&E*, p. 250.

53   Hays, *Appeal*, pp. 127–8.

54   Clarissa Campbell Orr, "Introduction," *Queenship in Britain, 1660–1837: Royal Patronage, Court Culture, and Dynastic Politics* (Manchester, 2002), pp. 1–52.

55   Hays, *Appeal*, p. 90.

56   *Analytical Review*, XXVIII (July 1798): 24.

57   *Monthly Magazine*, VII (April 1798): 633.

58   *The Critical Review*, (April 1799): 310.

59   Marilyn Butler, "Culture's medium: the role of the review," in Stuart Curran, ed., *The Cambridge Companion to British Romanticism* (Cambridge, 1993), p. 130.

60   Published by Southey's friend Joseph Cottle in Bristol, and in London by Lee and Hurst.
61   Donald H. Reiman, "Introduction," *Charles Lloyd, Poems on Various Subjects* ... (New York, 1978), pp. v–ix.
62   Henry Crabb Robinson, *On Books and Their Writers*, p. 5.
63   Charles Lloyd, *Edmund Oliver* (Bristol, 1798), vol. I, pp. vii–viii.
64   Gertrude cries to Edmund Oliver, the man she desires who resists her, "Are you to forget the indefinite and incalculable benefit that you will be to society by trampling on the rubbish which fills the onward path of man, directing your eye singly to distant horizon of human perfection?," quoted in M.O. Grenby, *The Anti-Jacobin Novel: British Conservatism and the French Revolution* (Cambridge, 2001), pp. 85–6.
65   Lloyd, *Edmund Oliver*, pp. vii–viii.
66   Ibid., p. 7.
67   Dr. John Reid, a Unitarian friend of Hays's, rushed to defend her and perhaps also the Unitarians, with an acrid review of the novel in the *Analytical Review*, 27 (June 1798): 638.
68   Eliza Fenwick alluded to their relationship in a letter written to Hays in early February. Hays may have asked to visit Eliza with Lloyd. Eliza replied, "I wish much to see your wayward friend — bring him if possible ... Charles Lloyd is then at the end of his grand career," a reference to Lloyd's abortive pursuit of a degree at Cambridge. It is unclear whether Eliza referred to Lloyd as Hays's "wayward friend," but that the reference was to Frend seems unlikely, [February 1799], *The Fate of the Fenwicks*, ed. A.F. Wedd (London, 1927), p. 5.
69   Robert Southey to Edith Southey, 15 May 1799, *New Letters of Robert Southey*, ed. Kenneth Curry (New York, 1965), vol. I, pp. 167–9.
70   Amelia Alderson to Mary Wollstonecraft, 28 August 1796, Oxford, Bodleian Library, [Abinger] Dep. b. 210/6.
71   Robert Southey to Edith Southey, 15 May 1799, *New Letters of Robert Southey*, pp. 167–9.
72   Lamb commented that "Lloyd's amours with Mary Hays ... would not form an unentertaining romance," Charles Lamb to Thomas Manning, 8 February 1800, *The Letters of Charles and Mary Lamb*, ed. Edwin W. Marrs, Jr. (Ithaca, 1975), vol. I, pp. 181–2.
73   Marrs, Jr., *The Letters of Charles and Mary Lamb*, p. 185.
74   Thomas Manning, *Letters of Thomas Manning to Charles Lamb*, ed. G.A. Anderson (London, 1925), p. 127.
75   The *Selected Letters of Samuel Taylor Coleridge*, ed. E.L. Griggs (Oxford, 1956), vol. I, p. 563.
76   *The Anti-Jacobin Review and Magazine; or, Monthly Political Literary Censor*, 3 (1799): 54–7.
77   See de Montluzin, *The Anti-Jacobins*, pp. 30, 106–7.
78   Heath wrote, "Setting aside this slang of modern philosophy, the plain question is — Whether it is most for the advantage of society that women should be so brought up as to make them dutiful daughters, affectionate wives, tender mothers, and good Christians, or, by a corrupt and vicious system of education, fit them for revolutionary agents, for heroines, for Staels, for Talliens, for Stones, setting aside all the decencies,

the softness, the gentleness, of the female character, and enjoying indiscriminately every envied privilege of man?," *The Anti-Jacobin Review and Magazine*, pp. 54–7.

79   Ibid.
80   Hays to William Tooke, undated [May 1799?], *Pforz.*, MH 35.
81   Ibid.
82   Caroline Franklin points out "During the war against republican France ... right-wing patriotism became identified with loyalist propaganda, involving the suppression of class and gender conflict for the national good," "Romantic Patriotism as Feminist Critique of Empire: Helen Maria Williams, Sydney Owenson and Germaine de Staël," *Women, Gender and Enlightenment* (Houndmills, 2005), p. 552; Paul Keen comments that "The image of an unstable and inherently transgressive femininity offered commentators a compelling means of understanding the unprecedented historical events of a revolutionary age," "A Revolution in Female Manners," *Revolutions in Romantic Literature: An Anthology of Print Culture, 1780–1832*, ed. Paul Keen (Peterborough, ON, 2004), p. 235.
83   *L&E*, p. 27.
84   More's vocal criticisms of the Mendip clergymen for neglect of their pastoral responsibilities stirred up the "Blagdon controversy" of 1800–1803, pitting More against powerful Anglican church leaders who accused her of preaching "schism, Methodism, and Jacobinism at her schools," S.J. Skedd, "More, Hannah (1745–1833)," *Oxford Dictionary of National Biography* (Oxford, 2004), p. 7. One of her accusers dubbed her the "She-Bishop." The dispute became more momentous when *The Anti-Jacobin Review* joined the issues of Napoleon's threat of invasion with Hannah More's menace to the Established Church. More, a self-proclaimed political conservative, was now identified with Jacobin and Dissenting subversion. More felt "battered, hacked, scalped, tomahawked" by the uproar, Anne Stott, *Hannah More: The First Victorian* (Oxford, 2003), p. 20.
85   See Anna Clark's trenchant analysis, "From Petticoat Influence to Women's Rights?," particularly her discussion of "The Scandal Against Hannah More," *Scandal: The Sexual Politics of the British Constitution* (Princeton, 2004), pp. 126–47.
86   Sharon M. Setzer, "Introduction," Mary Robinson, *A Letter to the Women of England* and *The Natural Daughter* (Peterborough, ON, 2003), p. 20.
87   Ibid., p. 24.
88   "List of British Female Literary Characters Living in the Eighteenth Century," Setzer, *A Letter to the Women of England*, pp. 86–8. Anna Barbauld, Inchbald, Macauley [sic], More, Plumptree, Robinson, Smith, Wolstonecraft [sic] were among those included.
89   For a compelling discussion of Robinson's proposal for women's political participation, see Felicia Gordon's "*Filles publiques* or Public Women: The Actress as Citizen: Marie Madeleine Jodin (1741–90) and Mary Darby Robinson (1758–1800)," *Women, Gender and Enlightenment*, pp. 610–29.
90   Setzer, "Appendix G. Contemporary Reviews," *A Letter to the Women of England*, pp. 324–6.
91   See Godwin's diary for "[Jan] 29. Tu. M Hays & Miss Reid; [Feb] 20. W. call on M Hays; [Apr] 10. W. ... call on M Hays; [July] 5. F. ... Tea M Hays's, w. Fanny, H Robinson & Cristal [sic]; July] 31. W. ... tea Opie's, w. M Hays, H Robinson &

Fenwicks; [Sept] 20. F. ... call on M Hays; [Sept] 25. W. ... adv. M [s or r] Hays;
[Dec] 21. Sa ... Coleridge & L Jna call: meet Batty: evg M Hays's; adv. H Robinson."

92   Godwin to Hays, 18 March 1800.

93   For responses directed specifically at Godwin, see Mark Philp, "The Decline of
      Radicalism," *Godwin's Political Justice* (Ithaca, 1986), pp. 220–30; "Appendix D:
      Critical Reaction," *MAV*, pp. 169–201.

94   Philp notes the fissuring of Godwin's social circle from 1797 to 1799. The people
      Godwin saw, in addition to Hays and Wollstonecraft, according to his diary, included
      Sir Anthony Carlisle, Rebecca Christie, George Dyson, Joseph Fawcett, John
      Fenwick, Eliza Fenwick, Henry Fuseli, Holcroft, Johnson, James Mackintosh, James
      Marshall, Montagu, William Nicholson, James Northcote, John and Amelia
      (Alderson) Opie, James Barry, James Perry, Richard Phillips, Maria Reveley, Joseph
      Ritson, George Robinson, Charlotte Smith, John Stoddart, Taylor, John Tobin, John
      Horne Tooke, Thomas Wedgwood, William Wordsworth, Philp, "Appendix D" *MAV*,
      pp. 249–52. See also Pamela Clemit's careful reconstruction of Godwin's wet-transfer
      copies of his letters between 4 December 1797 and 15 May 1805 for the names of
      additional associates, including Samuel Taylor Coleridge, Capel Lofft, [Miss] A. or N.
      Pinkerton, and Robert Southey, "William Godwin and James Watt's Copying
      Machine: Wet-Transfer Copies in the Abinger papers," *Bodleian Library Record*, 18:5
      (April 2005): 534–5.

95   Grogan, "Introduction," *Memoirs of Modern Philosophers* (Peterborough, ON, 2000),
      p. 29.

96   In her later *Letters on Education*, Hamilton argued against "Contempt for the Female
      Character" and "sexual prejudice," and also condemned the intellectual pretensions
      and unseemly ambitions of Wollstonecraft and Hays and their female associates. "It is
      not an equality of moral worth for which they contend," Hamilton wrote, "and which
      is the only true object of regard; not for an equality of rights, with respect to the
      Divine favour, which alone elevates the human character into dignity and importance;
      but for an equality of employments and avocations, founded upon the erroneous idea
      of a perfect similarity of powers. Infected by the prejudices which associate ideas of
      honour and esteem with knowledge and science, independent of moral virtue, and
      envious of the short-lived glories of ambition, they desire for their sex an admission
      into the theatre of public life, and wish to qualify them for it by an education in every
      respect similar to that of men. Men scoff at their pretences, and hold their presumption
      in abhorrence; but men do not consider, that these pretences, and that presumption,
      have been caught from the false notions of importance which they have themselves
      affixed to their own particular avocations. Taught, from earliest infancy, to arrogate to
      themselves a claim of inherent superiority, this idea attaches itself to all the studies
      and pursuits which custom has exclusively assigned them. These prejudices operating
      likewise on the minds of women, it is not surprising, that those who perceive in
      themselves a capacity for attaining a high degree of intellectual eminence, should
      aspire to be sharers in those honours, which they have been taught by the pride of men
      to regard as supreme distinction" (London, 1801), pp. 171–3.

97   Pam Morris argues that Hamilton's perspective in *Letters* "is much more complex and
      even-handed between the poles of conservatism and radicalism" than as it first
      appears. "Hamilton's gender and social politics can only be ascertained by a careful
      and detailed examination of her language, her stylistic tactics and the generic forms

she utilizes ... She has a determined resistance to any discursive position that approaches partisanship" "Elizabeth Hamilton: Letters on the Elementary Principles of Education," *Conduct Literature for Women 1770-1803*, ed. Pam Morris, vol. 3 (London, 2005), p. 4.

98   Jane Rendall points out that the novel also "endorsed the case for the rational education and the employment of women, especially single women," "'Women that would plague me with rational conversation': Aspiring Women and Scottish Wigs, c. 1790–1830," *Women, Gender and Enlightenment*, pp. 338–9.

99   See Pam Perkins and Shannon Russell, "Introduction," *Translations of the Letters of a Hindoo Rajah* (Peterborough, ON, 1999), pp. 16–19; Grogan, *Memoirs of Modern Philosophers*, p. 19.

100 Jean de Palacio, "La 'Fortune' de Godwin en France: Le Cas d'Elizabeth Hamilton," Revue de Littérature Comparée, 41 (1967): 326–9.

101 Morris judges that in the novel the "careful balance of approbation and criticism [about Godwin and Wollstonecraft] is a practical example of Hamilton's belief that judgment must always be unbiased and non-zealous." Morris conjectures that Hamilton's animus against Hays may have been the consequence of Hays's application of David Hartley's ideas in her novel. "The notoriety provoked by *Emma Courtney* thus threatened a tradition of liberal philosophy that had had a determining influence upon Hamilton's own thinking. In *Memoirs of Modern Philosophers*, as well as ironising the misappropriation of modern philosophy by scheming or foolish characters, Hamilton seeks to redress the damage by associating all the main virtuous characters with Hartley's ideas on human benevolence," p. 3.

102 Grogan, "Appendix C: Reviews of Memoirs of Modern Philosophers," *Memoirs of Modern Philosophers*, Review iii, *Anti-Jacobin Review and Magazine*, 7 (December 1800): 369–76, p. 412.

103 See Claire Grogan's trenchant discussion, "Introduction," *Memoirs of Modern Philosophers*, pp. 4–26.

104 M.O. Grenby argues that Hamilton and the other "anti-Jacobin" novelists never detail their understanding of what modern philosophy is. Grenby points out that Hamilton, like the other writers, assumes that her readers will be sufficiently familiar with the novels she parodies to appreciate her critique.

105 *Memoirs of Modern Philosophers*, p. 101.

106 Bridgetina is caught in "a sudden gust of wind [that] whirled off the high-raised turban, and with it, O luckless destiny! went the flowing honours of her head. The stiff ringlets so well pomatumed, and so nicely powered, which Mrs. Botherim had with her own hands so carefully pinned on, together with the huge knots of many coloured ribbons; all, all were hurried down the black bosom of the remorseless stream!" p. 47.

107 "Me jest!," Bridgetina exclaims, "no one can say that I ever made a jest, or so much as laughed at one in the course of my whole life," p. 211. Claire Grogan comments, "Despite Hamilton's Christian avowal of tolerance and openness, she is bitingly cruel in her depiction of Bridgetina. Although Wollstonecraft is treated with respect ... Hays ... is contemptuously mocked," "Introduction," *Memoirs of Modern Philosophers*, p. 19.

108 Ibid., pp. 21–2.

109 *Dear Miss Heber: An 18th Century Correspondence*, ed. Francis Bamford (London, 1936), pp. 199–200.

110　In December 1798, the *Monthly Magazine* noted that Hays was to produce "a biographical work of great and lasting interest to the female world, to contain the lives of illustrious women, of all ages and nations."

Chapter Nine

All Things Will Become New

"Oppression and proscription, it is true, still linger, but old things appear to be passing away; and, in another century probably, should the progress of knowledge bear any proportion to its accelerated march during the latter half of the past, all things will become new."

Mary Hays, *Memoirs of Queens*, 1821

In her later works Hays constructed a narrative persona that achieved authority made possible by her efforts to represent women of the past. Hays devised a taxonomy of women's ways of pursuing knowledge that argued for an alternative understanding of the female past punctuated by the emergence of learned and powerful women. Beginning with her second life-writing of Wollstonecraft, Hays documented women's lives for future generations to bear witness to the presence, no matter how sporadic, of such women in various cultures and times. In response to the claim that no female Homer, Shakespeare, Bacon, Newton, or Locke could be identified, Hays marshaled abundant evidence to demonstrate that, whatever the obstacles, women participated in the great intellectual and political struggles of their day. Individual women's lives had been previously recorded for posterity, although relegated mainly to the margins of history. Hays reclaimed these individuals by hypothesizing an imagined female continuum that linked together those women who dared to seek education and/or power, and having achieved these, took part in the great drama of civilization. She drew on living testimony to fashion innovative accounts of Wollstonecraft and Catharine Macaulay Graham. She demonstrated her own worthiness to be included in the panorama she constructed by demonstrating her abilities as a historian with a progressive purpose, in the style of Robert Robinson and other Rational Dissenters, and Catharine Macaulay.

Hays demonstrated that the historical records revealed that women can and do learn; some surpass men's efforts. More significant to Hays were the fascinating ways that women pursued their intellectual passions as mathematicians, classicists, scientists, philosophers, poets, teachers, preachers, martyrs, actresses, spies, courtesans, and queens. In her researches, Hays discovered her vocation as female historiographer, a maker of women's history, objectifying and building on her previous, more personal perspectives in *Emma Courtney*, *The Victim of Prejudice*, and the *Appeal*. She maintained her deepest convictions about universal toleration and women's cognitive abilities to the end of her life. And she continued to hunger for recognition of her abilities and the part she played in advancing the idea of women's capacities to discover, learn, and create new knowledge.

Like every reformist writer, Hays's continuing ability to communicate her views to the public depended on the willingness of liberal editors and publishers to support her. Early in her publishing career she depended on personal connections, first among the Rational Dissenters and Unitarians, through George Dyer and John Disney. Hays asked Wollstonecraft to introduce her to Joseph Johnson. Godwin later referred her to George Robinson. After Wollstonecraft's death, the breach with Godwin, and in the waning days of Joseph Johnson's career, Hays negotiated several inventive writing projects with Unitarian Richard Phillips, founder and publisher of the liberal *Monthly Magazine*. Many writers scorned Phillips's stinginess and alleged shady business practices,[1] but those who needed to earn money, desired a public forum and/or sought an entrepreneur willing to take risks, kept on working for him.[2] At least in the business of life-writing, Phillips's interests matched Hays's. This was an emerging genre[3] that proved a boon to publishers, booksellers, and writers of every political persuasion and ability.[4] Hays was one of Phillips's stable of writers as he experimented with the market for biographical forms between 1798 and 1803: Phillips published *Public Characters* about contemporary figures (1798–1810); the short-lived *Annual Necrology for 1797–1798; including, also, various articles of neglected biography* (1800), an ecumenical collection of subjects that included Condorcet, Burke, Lavoisier, Catherine II, Andrew Kippis, and Wollstonecraft;[5] Hays's inventive *Female Biography* in six volumes (1802); and Godwin's authoritative and long *History of the Life and Age of Chaucer* (1803) that earned him £600 and Phillips presumably a good deal more.[6]

Writing Lives: Wollstonecraft

Hays's initial commission for Phillips was a 49-page life of Wollstonecraft. Hays's "Memoirs of Mary Wollstonecraft" represented *her* Wollstonecraft, and sought more expansively to vindicate both women's lives by tacitly defining her friend's claims to posterity in terms of her own. Hays took the opportunity to enlarge on the particular dilemmas of ambitious women that she had initiated with Godwin while writing *Emma Courtney*. Using Wollstonecraft's history as the vehicle to discuss female psychological and mental development, Hays argued that societal constraints affected intellectual women particularly harshly, and posited a damaging causal relationship between anguish and frustrated female creativity. She emphasized the evolution of Wollstonecraft's understanding, proclaiming that Wollstonecraft belonged to a special class of "genius" distinguished by such forceful reactions to external impressions that they are frequently led into error. Hays implicitly referred to her own self-representations in the correspondence with John Eccles, to Eusebia in *Cursory Remarks*, and, particularly to *Emma Courtney*, representations that valorized deep feeling and thinking as an index of moral superiority. In defending Wollstonecraft as a passionate spirit, she vindicated herself.[7]

At the turn of the century, Hays continued to regard Godwin as her standard-bearer, chief critic, and sounding board, although they rarely saw each other. As a younger woman, Hays had looked to Robinson, Priestley, Worthington, Disney, Lindsey, Dyer, Frend, Enfield, and texts by other male freethinkers to situate her own impressions and ideas. Wakefield's erudition and the cacophony of conservative naysayers had served as warning zones on her mental compass. Following their intense dialogue during the composition of *Emma Courtney*, Godwin's intellectual influence persisted: in 1800 Hays answered his *Memoirs of the Author of A Vindication of the Rights of Woman*, published by Johnson in 1798. Godwin's *Memoirs* had aroused a furor among readers of every political persuasion. He was publicly vilified for his rendition of Wollstonecraft with its unprecedented revelations. The *Monthly Review* commented, "blushes would suffuse the cheeks of most husbands, if they were *forced* to relate those anecdotes of their wives which Mr. Godwin voluntarily proclaims to the world."[8] In her *Memoirs*, Hays responded not only to Godwin's account, but also to the backlash against him as his wife's biographer to the representations provoked by Wollstonecraft's texts in Godwin's edition of her *Posthumous Works*, and for his decision to publish her passionate letters to another man.[9]

In her piece on Wollstonecraft, Hays followed the chronology of Godwin's memoirs of Wollstonecraft, concurred with most of the landmarks he identified in Wollstonecraft's moral growth, cited his life-writing as the source of much of her information, and quoted selectively from *Caleb Williams*. She used his "Wollstonecraft" as a jumping off point to compare and contrast with her own. Hays's text spoke to Godwin's, as if their respective writers were still deep in conversation at her apartments in Kirby Street. In her portrayal of Wollstonecraft Hays also continued the debate with Godwin *in absentia* about situational, conditional truth and the vital combined influence of thinking *and* feeling in human experience.

Godwin's publication of Wollstonecraft's *Posthumous Works* gave Hays access to Wollstonecraft's letters to Imlay. Hays used these as a crucial ingredient in her memoir. Hays included great swathes of Wollstonecraft's prose to reconstruct her friend's life out of her belief in the power of text to embody the individual writer. To incorporate Wollstonecraft's letters in her own memoir, Hays took advantage of both the professional collegiality between Phillips and Joseph Johnson and new advances in printing technology to select and include existing text from Wollstonecraft's letters to Imlay already in print, text that charted their tempestuous affair.[10]

For Hays, the power of Wollstonecraft's texts as they emerged from her life vindicated Godwin's decision to reveal in his memoir and his edition of her texts so much about his wife. Hays argues that great lives like Wollstonecraft's demonstrate human truths beyond narrow prejudices expressed by the majority of readers. In addition, the unfettered search for truth should make all evidence welcome. For Hays the details of Wollstonecraft's life reveal her as both an outstanding female leader and human thinker, but also as everywoman. This extraordinary woman, Hays explains, attracted public attention because of her perceptive emotional responses, swift judgments, and powerful intellect. Wollstonecraft's youthful insights into relations between women and men, Hays urges, rendered her incapable of obedience to contemporary mores. Her childhood observations of the tortuous dynamic between her abusive father and passive mother made independence essential to Wollstonecraft. Her wide-ranging curiosity led her to explore new ways of living and knowing that had radical political, personal, and social implications for herself and others. Hays elevates Wollstonecraft to the pantheon of enlightened philosophers, like Robert Robinson, who in innovative ways exercise the right to attempt to live "the idea of being free." Hays adds Wollstonecraft as the first woman to the imaginative lineage of freethinkers.

Hays's memoir complemented and corrected Godwin's and the chorus of critics of his Wollstonecraft. She devised responses to his existing text, as she had in *The Victim of Prejudice*. In contrast to Godwin's portrayal of Wollstonecraft as an heroic political figure, Hays envisions her life from their shared perspectives as women and emphasizes the role resistance to gender prejudice played in Wollstonecraft's development. Godwin had accentuated Wollstonecraft's intuitive ability to apprehend the meaning of an experience, using Wollstonecraft's own term, "intellectual beauty."[11] Hays emphasizes Wollstonecraft's denial of "the existence of a sexual character," that is, her belief that the mind is neither female nor male, and that gender is socially constructed, as are its consequences.[12] Hays adumbrates Wollstonecraft's character in the egalitarian terms Wollstonecraft advocated, her "wild wish to see the distinction of sex confounded."[13] Hays's Wollstonecraft embodies the best of universal *human* qualities that transcend specific cultural assumptions about male and female.

Godwin had described Wollstonecraft as a religious skeptic like himself.[14] By contrast, Hays explains Wollstonecraft's spirituality as compounded of feeling, intellection, and intuition, which Hays understood as that category of human knowledge between emotion and thought. For Hays, Wollstonecraft experienced her God as the only power that might fully release those female talents and impulses that have no scope for expression in the earthly sphere. Hays explains that Wollstonecraft's faith was rather intuitive than rational, meaning that she took little interest in theological disputation about the nature of God, or at least of the sectarian kind that Hays encountered both within and outside the Rational Dissenting community.[15] Wollstonecraft's personal independence extended to her credo, an important model for Hays who continued to suffer from the absence of close community with other Unitarian and Rational Dissenting thinkers. Hays argues that even in relation to her God, Wollstonecraft stood on her own as she had urged Hays to do nearly a decade earlier.

Godwin had attempted to speak from his authorial point of view as an impartial chronicler for posterity.[16] He wrote of Wollstonecraft's isolation and unhappiness during her first years in London. He explained her depression as a consequence of performing perfunctory editorial tasks for Joseph Johnson. Hays, writing of the same period, conjectures about psychological causes: it was not so much the kind of work Wollstonecraft undertook that caused her despair, but that such duties engaged only her rational mental faculties, and not her passions or sympathies towards others. Hays underscores the corrosive effects of one-dimensional endeavors that impeded fulfillment of such a woman's complex desires. In discussing Wollstonecraft's support of her family from her professional earnings, Hays points to the obstacles that any woman has to overcome to be self-supporting, thus highlighting Wollstonecraft's exertions in providing financial support for her many relatives, including her dissolute father.

The momentous effects of *A Vindication of the Rights of Woman*, Hays proposes, emerged out of and had the effect of creating an organic connection among the writer, the subject, and the reader. For Hays Wollstonecraft wrote powerfully as a woman to women about female existence. Hays's prose achieves a new sonorousness as she meditates on the universal conditions of women's lives that inevitably led Wollstonecraft to champion her own sex. Hays extrapolates from Wollstonecraft's experience and her own as thinking women to convey in historical and political terms the terrible, apparently unshakable, feudal bondage of gender that still obtained. "There are few situations," Hays writes, "in which a woman of cultivated understanding has not occasion to observe and deplore, the systematic vassalage, the peculiar disadvantages, civil and social, to which she is subjected, even in the most polished societies, on account of her sex."[17] A woman like Wollstonecraft, Hays explains, who early recognized her intellectual superiority to the majority of men she knew and read, must be skeptical of the historical claim that there exist natural, innate barriers to women's intellectual achievement simply because of their sex.

Hays represents Wollstonecraft as heroine and everywoman, her idiosyncratic history resonant with the life stories of all women. In Hays's memoir, the intrepid Wollstonecraft is nearly crushed by her lack of academic training and economic opportunity, the consequence of gender prejudice, and ostracized as a result of the double standard applied to the sexual activity of men and woman. If Wollstonecraft suffered for attempting to live freely, then all women who dare to express their wants, needs, ambitions, or passions do so at their peril.

Godwin had presented Wollstonecraft's polemic as unique with no known precedent. Hays disagrees and reports that the *Vindication* rested on the feminist principles of an earlier controversial work, historian Catharine Macaulay's *Letters on Education* (1790). Hays implies that the unheralded connection between the ideas of the two distinguished women thinkers provides yet another example of the invisibility of women's intellectual history. Women read each other's works, reflect on, and respond to them. Men read women's texts, but reflexively dismiss women's ideas and their responses to each other's formulations with the effect that women continue to be excluded from the continuum of male responses that is the canon of Western culture. The absence of women is then explained as the result, rather than the cause, of their lack of achievements. Without a parallel history linking female endeavors to each other, each female thinker and her texts are perceived as idiosyncratic, without context, and unconnected to any other. In the absence of a recognized lineage of women's thought, every woman believes that she is alone and must begin anew.

Meditating out loud about Wollstonecraft's eccentric intellectual genealogy, Hays was moved to articulate the enduring conviction of her own life: advances in women's education to prepare them to assume social responsibilities and privileges equal to men's mark human progress from barbarity to civilization.[18] Hays's Wollstonecraft illuminates how the *Vindication* and Wollstonecraft's other experimental texts conjoin lived female suffering and trenchant political analysis. Self-educated, impetuous, and strong-willed, Hays's Wollstonecraft is a thinker for the ages. Still, Hays tempers her own idealized representation of Wollstonecraft. She responds to Godwin's criticisms of Wollstonecraft's sometimes too aggressive postures and her lack of formal training that in his account produced flaws in her thinking and writing. Hays also attends to the more virulent accounts of Wollstonecraft's immorality and impropriety as thinker, writer, and woman. Acknowledging Wollstonecraft's deficiencies signals not a lessening of Hays's revolutionary feminism as some have claimed, but rather a deepening and an advance.[19] Hays knew firsthand the difficulties of being a female acting in opposition to the larger social world. Hays may have felt constrained to demonstrate her impartiality by responding to, not ignoring, Godwin's own attempts at objectivity about his wife and the public conflation of private woman and public advocate. Hays argues that even Wollstonecraft's alleged inconstancy in moving from one lover to another and her intense sexual responses to individual men reveal the depth of her capacity for human engagement. Deprived of free expression for her talents, Wollstonecraft sought fulfillment in the culturally sanctioned female vocation of romantic love.

In her love affairs, too, Hays writes, Wollstonecraft was singularly self-determining: Wollstonecraft embarked on her experiment with Imlay fully cognizant of the consequences of illicit sex. But the ability to live without social approval was another aspect of Wollstonecraft's courage. Exploiting the literary technique she learned from Robert Robinson and deployed in *Emma Courtney*, Hays lets Wollstonecraft's sexual rapture speak for itself in pages of excerpts from the letters to Imlay that chart Wollstonecraft's intensifying anguish at his betrayal. Hays again follows Godwin's lead and comments on Wollstonecraft's failure to accurately read Imlay's character and her denial that he tired of her. Godwin had explained that it was the nature of love to perpetuate itself. Hays, by contrast, points to the psychological dynamics of Wollstonecraft's obsession with Imlay in which fantasy rather than reality was the engine of romance. Reality, she conjectures, sometimes barely intrudes on the idealized dream of the person one desires. This is a subversive hypothesis that denies mutual recognition of a kindred soul as the basis of romantic love. Speaking from her own experiences, as well as Wollstonecraft's, and attempting to justify their respective mistakes, Hays insists that the feelings aroused by one's own fantasies are neither less genuine nor natural because they are self-initiated and self-perpetuating.[20] She refines on her earlier explanation to Godwin about Emma Courtney's dogged yearning for the unavailable Augustus Harley. Hays now claims that imagination alone can fuel great enthusiasms: love of another person, personal ambition, political resistance, or religious martyrdom. This is Hays's most naked defense of female autonomy, even in erotic love. She also anticipates the Romantic belief in the power of the imagination. For Hays, the force of fantasy emerges from her understanding of Lockean psychoperceptual mechanics refined by Erasmus Darwin's hypothesis of embodied or *"innate* desires" and behavior that reveal *"unconscious* mental processes guided by habit."[21] Extending Darwin's ideas, Hays implies that there is an unexplored realm of human activity that is still waiting to be revealed.

Godwin had written about Wollstonecraft's attempts to kill herself as part of his more general philosophical discourse on suicide.[22] Hays particularizes Wollstonecraft's actions as an individual woman's response to the universal situation of disappointed love. She inserts a significant particular to answer Wollstonecraft's bitterest detractors who, following publication of Godwin's *Memoirs*, publicly charged that Wollstonecraft denied her maternity and sacrificed her sacred responsibilities to her daughter by willing herself to die because of a man's rejection. Hays reports that Wollstonecraft thought of her daughter as she contemplated her own death. Perhaps Wollstonecraft confided this to Hays as she convalesced. In any case, Hays had witnessed Wollstonecraft's devotion to her daughter, Fanny Imlay:[23] Hays's Wollstonecraft is at once a loving mother torn between attachment to her child and a desperate woman betrayed by her lover.

Hays expounds on the disastrous effects on the minds of ambitious and passionate women if they stray from conventional behavior, and the high personal price of genius: "Those strong passions, that, ravaging the mind, afflict and deform society, have their origin in opposition and constraint; if in this way talent is sometimes generated, it seems to be purchased too dear."[24] Hays implicitly speaks of herself as much as her subject. Uncommon women, she writes, if they overstep the "bounds prescribed to them, by a single error, they become involved in a labyrinth of perplexity and distress," referring to her own and Wollstonecraft's ignominy. Society condemned Wollstonecraft and Hays and their fictional counterparts to be victims of gender prejudice because there continued to be only one narrow path for women to public approval: they must be chaste, lovely, cautious, and compliant.[25] Hays proposes that women may choose to act on their sexual desire as an expression of autonomy, or they may decide not to marry in an alternative act of self-determination.

In retrospect, Hays prophesies that Wollstonecraft's pioneering life has not been lived in vain. "The spirit of reform is silently pursuing its course," she urges, "Who can mark its limits?"[26] This was the rhetoric of progressive Rational Dissent; it was also Hays's prayer for imagined community in her isolation. Hays's Wollstonecraft evolved to reflect Hays's understanding of the great reformist ideas that had earlier stimulated both women now that these were submerged in the din of conservative reaction in the new century. Hays envisioned Wollstonecraft as the emblem of both female suffering and transcendence over gender prejudice that was at the root of the historical intolerance towards women. Wollstonecraft's ideas would live on, Hays predicted, as had the discoveries of other original thinkers, because she saw beyond the petty squabbles of her day and augured future human possibilities.

Writing Lives: Female Biography

Hays advanced from writing Wollstonecraft's life to the more ambitious enterprise of constructing a history of multiple women. She likely approached this project in the spirit that Priestley advocated in his *History and Present State of Electricity,* as an inquiring student who learned as she worked.[27] After three years of extensive research and writing, Hays offered an alternative to the history of Great Men in *Female Biography; or, Memoirs of Illustrious and Celebrated Women, of All Ages and Countries,* in six volumes, a compendium of the lives of 288 vibrant women who gave hope that, in more advanced stages of society, women's intellectual freedom and political participation would be valued as markers of human progress.[28] In the individual memoirs, Hays argued for the expanded understanding of tolerance she had inherited from Robinson, one modeled on Bayle's concept of religious pluralism.[29] Hays's interest was to provide a counterbalance to the view of history represented by male Dissenters, one that elucidated mostly men's lives in the ongoing battle for the right to freedom of opinion and action. In her account, she chronicled a rich, variegated history of women in which they struggled against male intolerance in a variety of forms.

The memoir of Wollstonecraft was probably intended as the first installment of *Female Biography*, Hays's major life-writing project.[30] Most general biographical dictionaries before and after *Female Biography* dealt almost exclusively with men or with conventionally pious women.[31] Those compilations that included only women were traditionally designed to provide women with principles of exemplary moral behavior rather than models of learning or achievement. The first major work of specifically English female biography was George Ballard's celebratory *Memoirs of Several Ladies of Great Britain, who have been Celebrated for their Writings or Skill in the Learned Languages Arts and Sciences* (1752). More specialized collections of female biography according to idiosyncratic criteria gradually appeared through the century.[32] Dissenters also produced their own anti-establishment personal history in which few women were included.[33] Hays would have read many of these.[34] And despite the repressive political atmosphere at the end of the century, the publication records show that there was continuing interest in women. When Phillips finally published Hays's *Female Biography* in December 1802, several other similar works appeared and at least one other woman writer, Matilda Betham, a poet whom Coleridge promoted, was thinking of undertaking a similar project, but decided not to go forward when she learned that Phillips was publishing Hays's compendium.[35]

The feminist history of women which Mary Hays undertook to compile was an important enterprise for her: a source of income, a medium of and vehicle for scholarship by and about women,[36] and a woman's contribution to the sub-species of history writing which had previously been mainly the province of men.[37] Hays cited her sources at the end of each of the 288 biographies. Though the details about her sources are sketchy or incomplete, they are adequate to indicate the wide variety of information she used.[38] Following Ballard's example, Hays frequently used personal memoirs and autobiographies to supplement more general, standard works.[39] She also referred to primary material.[40] Hays took advantage of her friends' erudition, their private libraries, their publications, and their generosity. William Tooke the Elder (1744–1820), was a learned and adventurous Unitarian who spent time as a minister in St Petersburg. On his return to England he translated a French life of Catherine II of Russia in 1798.[41] Hays used it for her entry on Catherine.[42] Tooke may also have provided Hays access to existing information about other women; he collaborated with William Beloe and others to produce and revise successive editions of *A New and General Biographical Dictionary*, a work that included some women.[43] From her correspondence with the elder Tooke's son, it is clear that Hays borrowed and returned books from their library with some frequency.[44]

Hays incorporated published and unpublished works to construct some of the memoirs, an innovative blending of personal and public texts. In the memoirs of Lady Mary Chudleigh, Mademoiselle de Montpensier, and Isabella of Aragon, among others, she furthered her ideas about gender, education, faith, revolution, rebellion, theological and political schism, heroism, and was explicit about her own role as intermediary between the reader and the reputation of each of her subjects. In the memoir of Anne Askew, a sixteenth-century Protestant martyr, Hays described the interplay of gender, prejudice, and history. Though she used material from Ballard's detailed account of Askew, as well as Foxe's *The Book of Martyrs* (1563), the emphasis on gender prejudice was Hays's own. Hays details how Askew's determination to dispute with chapter and verse the allegations of her male interrogators that she was impious incited them to use extremes of torture against her.[45] But history was also progressive. Following Bayle and Robert Robinson, Hays applauded Marguerite of Navarre, heroine of the early French

Reformation, for supporting Huguenot exiles despite the personal danger to her.[46]
The right to intellectual freedom and personal choice of religious faith remained a
guiding principle of Hays's intellectual life.

Hays has been criticized for succumbing to conservative pressure by omitting
Wollstonecraft from *Female Biography*. This seems an unlikely reason for the
omission since Hays had resisted the oppressive climate of opinion to be the first to
include Manon Roland in a compilation about women, and had also dared to insert
large portions of the text of Manon Roland's revelatory *Appeal to Impartial
Posterity* (1795) in her work.[47] Hays promoted Roland as heroine and martyr of the
French Revolution in an unusually long memoir of 208 pages, explaining that
whatever her readers' political views, they would benefit from the fierce womanly
honesty and courage displayed in Roland's story, an argument she had also used in
the memoirs of Wollstonecraft.

Hays let Roland, like Wollstonecraft, speak for herself, drawing again on
Phillips's working relationship with Johnson, Roland's publisher, to reuse existing
text. Hays chose excerpts in which Roland described her love of learning and her
autodidactism, including the study of Latin. Hays's memoir highlighted Roland's
early resistance to arbitrary authority that sowed the seeds of her radicalism, and
her passionate response to Rousseau's *The New Eloisa* that, like Hays and
Wollstonecraft, suggested new female freedoms to her. At age 21 Roland married
an older man, and Hays related their rise and fatal fall from political power, and
Roland's later, unabashed passion for a younger man. Roland made a point in her
Appeal about the public perils that female authorship invariably aroused. Roland's
last act as a revolutionary was to represent the growth of her mind, no matter the
public and personal consequences because she knew she was already condemned
to die at the guillotine.[48]

Hays added a footnote to Roland's remark, commenting on the inclination of
readers of works by female writers to slander the author with sensational gossip,
obviously drawing on her own experiences as well as Wollstonecraft's.[49] Like
Wollstonecraft, Roland represented herself as an active political feminist,
determined to make structural changes to a corrupt culture that would ensure a new
social order in which the law applied equally to women and men. Hays used
female biography in her account of Roland as she had in the memoir of
Wollstonecraft. She sought to arouse enthusiasm for women's achievements,
irrespective of conventional prejudices toward a political party or religious
persuasion, endorsing figures that did not conform to traditional moral codes.[50]

Hays included women renowned for their erudition, their adventures, their
political influence, their infamy, and their piety. Among the women she included,
90 were English, 50 were French, 32 Roman, and 20 Greek, as well as an
assortment of Italian and Spanish women, and "Matoaks" or Pocahontas. Hays's
relish for research about the existence of other female scholars and enthusiasm for
many of the historical figures she represented sometimes led her to prolixity,
especially in the biographies of better known figures about whom more

information was available. In all but the most cursory entries, the reader can sense Hays's excitement at learning, appropriating, and organizing knowledge for her female readership, as she had done more tentatively in *Letters and Essays*. She frequently juxtaposes conventional gendered assumptions about female competence with male commentary about specific women's achievements. Of Anne Lefèvre Dacier's scholarly translations and adaptations of the texts of early Greek and Latin authors, Hays includes Bayle's comment that Dacier's work was superior to that of her male contemporaries: "Thus," Bayle wrote in the *News from the Republic of Letters,* "we behold our arrogant sex vanquished by this illustrious learned female."[51]

Hays documents her view that women are called to the life of the mind despite the traditional assertion that they are not mentally capable of that pursuit. The exceptional women whose stories she tells refute the misogynist rule by their very existence. Hays offers a welter of specifics about the range of women's interests and variety of talents: for example, Anna Maria von Schurman could draw, paint, and embroider at an early age; she was prodigious in calligraphy, and knew Greek, Hebrew, Syriac, Arabic, Ethiopic, Chaldee, French, Italian, and English. Study of geography, astronomy, and physics led her to theology and fame; she refused marriage and renounced the world, becoming a follower of the quietist, Labadie.[52] Learned women are confronted with the same female dilemmas as less educated women. But the discipline necessary to acquire knowledge and the stories of others' lives that constitute some of their learning can inspire educated women to unusual courage and fortitude: Hays reports that erudite Mary Astell, women's champion, applied the same rigor to being a mastectomy patient that she had applied as a fearless scholar in her critique of Locke, political analyses of misogyny, and proposal for improved, secular female education. "She refused," Hays writes, "on this trying occasion, either to be held or to have her hands confined, and submitted herself to the operator without shrinking." Hays likely retrieved the information from Ballard, but gives the incident additional significance in her account.[53]

Hays learned as she read and wrote, copying and compiling as she had before, but with a difference. Earlier in her career Wollstonecraft and Godwin had accused Hays of an almost slavish dependence on other people's ideas and words as she produced her own. Now she followed her own interests to test out her hypotheses about the existence of a hitherto submerged stratum of learned women. Her omnivorous curiosity served her well, for it is likely that she moved from one text to another as necessary to gather facts about and then to tell the tale of specific women's odysseys. Hays exuberantly enumerates the titles of women's writings in several languages, identifies and adroitly summarizes polemical and political controversies women engendered and/or participated in, all in the interests of demonstrating that women have been inextricably connected to the grand ideas, figures, and conflicts of their times. Information about actual women responds to Wollstonecraft's gloss on the absence of a history of women that refutes the claim that women have not been active in the advance of reason.[54] Hays begins the work of making that new history for future women who might hunger for such knowledge and advance reason even farther.[55] In Hays's work the past teems with significant and competent women. Hays's contribution was to show that their achievements and advances had been made despite the educational, civil, and legal disadvantages they have endured as a class.

Hays composed her preface after nearly three years of intense work in which she reflected on her purpose and method. She explained her intentions in undertaking *Female Biography* as both political and educational, meant to instruct and inspire her readers to surmount gender prejudices by revealing the many kinds of activity, private and public, possible for women. "My pen has been taken up in the cause," she declares, "and for the benefit, of my own sex." Hays says at the end of 1802 what she has said before: women without formal training read primarily for pleasure, secondarily for instruction, a slightly different version of her advice to young Elizabeth's mother in *Letters and Essays*. Hays reiterates her sentiments in *Cursory Remarks* and *Letters and Essays*, now directed exclusively to women, about the Hartleyian chain of causality in which sympathies can be aroused that lead the reader to desire to acquire knowledge. Women's "understandings," she advises, "are principally accessible through their affections," and female sensibilities can be appropriated for rational purposes. Hays speaks knowingly of the female audience she has been participating in, observing, addressing, and reading about for years. The majority of women want personal history, human interest, and minute details, as well as information, in the books they read. Wollstonecraft had complained about this propensity in her criticism of novel reading. Hays, confronting the publishing market of the new century, tacitly accepts that fiction like her own is dismissed as fantasy no matter how rooted in actual female experience. She explicitly acknowledges that few women have been trained to be intellectuals and therefore have not been encouraged to be curious about matters beyond their own lives. Recognizing this fact, Hays sought to catch women's attention with stories of other female lives, providing enough about the substance of their ideas to point interested readers to further study. Hays is as much a teacher as she was in *Letters and Essays,* although less didactic; she is again a lone experimenter, trying out hybrid narrative forms as she had earlier in composing *Emma Courtney*. In *Female Biography*, this experiment combines life-writing, proto-journalist reportage, romance, and historical investigation.

Hays's intent in *Female Biography* was prospective, as well as retrospective, and pedagogical. "I have at heart the happiness of my sex," Hays writes in her preface, rewording her declaration from the memoir of Wollstonecraft, "and their advancement in the grand scale of rational and social existence." She expresses her concern and indignation, echoing Wollstonecraft's in the *Vindication*, at women's complicity in perpetuating their own ignorance. Hays was now nearly alone in wishing to extend their understanding through exposure to Enlightenment ideas to women; she acknowledges that times have changed since the heady days of the early 1790s. If the more explicit struggle for "intellectual equality" has necessarily been suspended, that is no reason for her countrywomen to submit willingly to relinquishing the power to control their own lives because they lack the knowledge to resist.[56] "A woman," she writes, "who, to the graces and gentleness of her own sex, adds the knowledge and fortitude of the other, exhibits the most perfect combination of human excellence," reworking her description of Wollstonecraft as that rare creature, a complete *human* being who transcended arbitrary categories of gender.[57]

Hays addresses with concern the specter of aging in women's lives when women suffer if they have not matured intellectually. Hays promotes cognitive development; she does not advocate pious passivity as the only alternative to youthful activity. She implicitly refutes the notion that once they cease to be ornamental, women must withdraw into seclusion and silence to await death. Instead, the female biographies she has collected illustrate possible alternatives to women's common fashionable pursuits or their search for eternal youth. Her female biographies allow women to look to a past in which their predecessors lived the life of the mind long after they had ceased to be young. Hays speaks especially to her younger readers, not yet fixed in their future selves, "who have not grown old in folly, whose hearts have not been seared by fashion, and whose minds prejudice has not yet warped."

Prejudice reminds Hays of the scars she bears because of others' bigotry against her as Unitarian, unmarried woman, and self-educated scholar. She declares herself independent of political party or sectarian bias, interested only, as she explained in *Cursory Remarks*, in truth and virtue. In her memoirs of individual women she has attempted to represent them in historical contexts; her commentary has no subversive ideological agenda. Underlying her work is the potentially explosive belief that women belong to a great substratum—what the *Monthly* termed "the female world" in its notice about Hays's work-in-progress—that might someday coalesce its incipient power to demand changes in the educational, political, legal, and economic status of all women.[58]

With deliberate irony Hays apologizes to the erudite critic who may claim that she has produced little new information in her volumes, self-deprecation being still a reflexive posture that she shares with other female writers. But Hays no longer speaks with either the youthful breathlessness of Eusebia in *Cursory Remarks* or the heated protestations of *Letters and Essays*. The narrative voice is now older, wiser, more sober, and steadier. Hays reaffirms that her book is for informally trained women, not scholars educated in the classical tradition. She suggests the breadth of her own knowledge by invoking the sentiment of the great Enlightenment biographer, Pierre Bayle, that to abridge a life appropriately is a difficult task.[59] Hays concludes by self-confidently assuring her readers that she has not merely compiled information, but has worked to achieve a comprehensive narrative style and balanced commentary,[60] that she has accomplished this entirely on her own, and that she welcomes the corrections of the frank and experienced critic. Gilbert Wakefield was now dead, but Hays had learned to anticipate complaints about her work from more erudite men.

   Female Biography was a daring experiment in history writing, and Hays knew it. Despite her apologies, disclaimers, and assurances to the reader, in six volumes Hays constructed a parallel story of the past to existing ones like Enfield's adaptation of Brucker's history of philosophy. "Look back through the history of the world," she had directed her readers in *Letters and Essays*, "from its golden days of infancy and innocence, to the maturity of the present times, and you will discern various truths, first dawning like the sun."[61] The emerging truth she had her readers discover was the lineage of women she had constructed. Hays displayed her inventiveness in researching the life of Catharine Macaulay Graham, herself a pioneering female historian. Hays located and corresponded with the sister of Macaulay's second husband, William Graham, 26 years his wife's junior.[62] "Mrs. Macaulay" (the name by which she was known in her time)[63] was severely criticized for the imprudent match; her reputation as an historian and gentlewoman never recovered from the public outcry. Hays's memoir of Macaulay was therefore both provocative and newsworthy. She reported that Macaulay's sister-in-law, Mrs. Arnold, had traveled to France and lived closely with Mrs. Macaulay, and was with her at her death in 1791. Hays detailed the evolution of Macaulay's intellectual passions from her girlhood in terms similar to those she had used for her heroine, Emma Courtney. Like Hays and her heroine, the young Macaulay had recoiled from the vanity of society "to a more improving world of her own" in books.

   As a self-taught woman writing women's history, Hays addressed the fraught question of Macaulay's public career: "A female historian, by its singularity," Hays writes, "could not fail to excite attention: she seemed to have stepped out of the province of her sex; curiosity was sharpened, and malevolence provoked."[64] Macaulay's brilliance was undeniable, so her critics' turned their attention to her appearance. This was a gambit Hays knew well. She spoke for Macaulay and for herself in describing the slurs the female historian incurred: "She is deformed (said her adversaries, wholly unacquainted with her person), she is unfortunately ugly, she despairs of distinction and admiration as a woman, she seeks, therefore, to encroach on the province of man." Fortunately, Mrs. Arnold could offer a firsthand corrective to such caricatures. Hays concluded the entry on Macaulay with a list of her publications to emphasize her intellectual achievements.

   Few modern commentators have noticed *Female Biography* either as life-writing[65] or feminist historiography. Mary Spongberg argues that Hays, rather than Lytton Strachey, should be credited with revolutionizing biography as a genre.[66] Contemporary reviewers, whatever their political convictions, mostly treated *Female Biography* as a serious, but morally flawed, work because it exposed female readers to evidence of licentious and impious women.[67]

   Hays's equivocal reputation among Rational Dissenters continued to dog her. Soon after publication of *Female Biography*, Lucy Aikin, Anna Barbauld's niece, asked her correspondent to give her opinion of Hays's "singular work." Aikin identified Hays as "a great disciple of Mrs. Godwin, you know, and a zealous stickler for the equal rights and equal talents of our sex with the other." Aikin expressed her view that Hays had undercut her own positions in *Female Biography* by selecting role models that readers might find singularly unattractive: "At the same time as [Hays] attempts to make us despise 'the frivolous rivalry of beauty and fashion,'" Aikin advised her correspondent, "she holds forth such tremendous examples of the excesses of more energetic characters, that one is much inclined to imitate those quiet, good folks who bless God they are no geniuses." Aikin was concerned that in the current reactionary climate of opinion, Hays's efforts might also confirm male readers' aversion to learned women. "Alas, alas!," Aikin continued,

> though Miss Hayes has wisely addressed herself to the ladies alone, I am afraid the gentlemen will get a peep at her book and repeat with tenfold energy that women have no business with anything but nursing children and mending stockings. I do not think her book is written quite in an edifying manner neither — the morals are too French for my taste.[68]

Anthony Page reports that when Ann Jebb died in 1812, her biographer "sought to portray [her] as a woman who 'seconded' her husband effectively in print and reformist association, but who did not engage in the 'masculine boldness' displayed by some intellectual females." He omitted Hays's name from the list of people who visited the widow, likely because of Hays's continuing disrepute.[69]

Solitary Wanderer

By 1804, Hays had earned enough money from *Female Biography* to buy a small "cabin" of her own in Camberwell where she lived with a servant whom she considered a friend.[70] She was now, and continued to be until the end of her life, a "solitary wanderer," Wollstonecraft's phrase[71] taken from Rousseau's last, unfinished work, *Rêveries du Promeneur Solitaire*.[72] Hays was restless, discontented, still self-absorbed, and ambivalent about herself. Although she continued to be engaged with her family and read widely, Hays presented herself in her correspondence as haunted by the unresolved desires and disappointments of the past. Hays believed she was all but forgotten by the reading public, or, if not, remembered only as a figure of ridicule and loathing. Unbeknownst to her, the eminent reformer Capel Lofft (1751–1824) had read her two novels and had written to Godwin to express his dismay that so talented a woman had been consigned to ignominy. Lofft, an early admirer of Macaulay, wrote of Hays's "transcendentally powerful Mind," and wondered that the author of the novels and "her greatly to be respected female Biography ... has remained in comparative obscurity or has been insulted by ... malicious cavillings under the name of

Criticism." Lofft was a veteran of Dissenting struggles for reform and had worked with Robert Robinson at grassroots political activities.[73] Lofft knew how the history of a bad reputation could stand in the way of a fair assessment of an individual's later, actual work.[74]

Hays made use of her social isolation to create some emotional distance from the painful events of the past. Her introspection became the subject of her intermittent correspondence with Henry Crabb Robinson, as it had earlier with Godwin. She resumed the narrative of her life to Crabb Robinson as if she had left off speaking to him in mid sentence, although it had been two years since she had last written. Writing in 1806 to Crabb Robinson who was now traveling in Europe, she reported that her older sister had died suddenly, described her loneliness, and complained about his lack of attention to her. She had recently moved yet again, she told him. After her sister's death in 1805, Hays took her three nieces to live with her and opened a school in Islington, which they attended. Once more she represents herself as she had Emma Courtney, as the creature of an over sensitive nature, prone to fervid fantasies, and seduced by "the poison of romance & chivalry." She portrays her consciousness in terms of illness as the "distempered" prism through which she perceives reality. She compares her own susceptibility for wishful thinking with Crabb Robinson's tamer, more rational character. He, she concludes, has secured for himself "a manly independence of action, & a self-possession beyond all price." Despite the repetitiveness of her comments, for once she does not express her accustomed ambivalence. Her tendency to respond intensely to experience, she recognizes, although it produced anguish and alienation, has also fostered ambition and achievement. Away from the bustle of London, she tells him, she walks frequently and feels healthier. Watching the idiosyncratic development of her nieces and students allows comparisons with her own earlier life, and solitude provides her greater perspective. Meditatively, she writes, "I sought & made to myself an extraordinary destiny."[75] The sense of earlier distinction sustained her, as did her involvement in the practical lives of friends and family. She continued to be a staunch friend to Eliza Fenwick, providing loans and her relatives' hand-me-downs, as well as regular visits with Fenwick's schoolboy son, Orlando, while Fenwick attempted to make a living.[76] The two women remained connected by the tragedy of Wollstonecraft's death and by their memories of their participation in an earlier, promising time.[77] Fenwick was more adventurous, if feckless, than Hays. When Godwin began publishing children's literature, Fenwick turned to the genre to make money, as Hays did somewhat later.[78]

Hays continued to represent writing as the means to independence, though she now disavowed it as either passion or vocation.[79] The business of writing, however, turned sour when Phillips asked Hays to complete the third volume of ailing novelist Charlotte Smith's *History of England* (1806).[80] Hays complied; her volume ran well over the length allotted. Phillips refused to pay Hays for her part of the work, and John Aikin mediated between them, judging that Phillips was not responsible for the excess pages Hays had produced, but that Hays had done her work in comparable style to Smith's.[81] Hays sustained her thirst for intellectual stimulation and attempted to make the transition from female biographer to general historian. She sought advice from Southey about writing projects, and then a home with him and his wife in the Lake District, but according to Crabb Robinson he refused to invite her.[82] She wrote the younger Tooke for counsel about a new publisher, having broken with both Johnson and Phillips, and finding Longman unreceptive.[83] When Tooke referred her to another publisher, Hays wrote him that she had already completed 1,700 pages of a new project, a history of recent events from her own perspective.[84] The manuscript was never published and no trace of it survives.

Associates and family moved on with their lives. Both Elizabeth Hays and William Frend married in 1808: Elizabeth to a widower with children; Frend to a younger woman from Francis Blackburne's distinguished clerical family who was related to the wives of John Disney and Theophilus Lindsey.[85] In 1814, Hays moved to Bristol, to live as boarder in the home of Mrs. Penelope Pennington,[86] after a year of deceptively frank correspondence between them of which only Mrs. Pennington's letters survive.[87] The two women detested each other on sight, and for the three years she continued there, Hays wrote Crabb Robinson descriptions of life at the Penningtons' table that are miniature portraits of failed genteel life.[88]

Hays confronted distortions of her former associates and herself again with the publication of *The Sexagenarian; or the Reflections of a Literary Life* (1817) by William Beloe (1756–1817). In the early 1790s Beloe had been a member of the Jacobin circle around Joseph Johnson. In the following years he became a staunch member of the establishment. His book attacked his former friends. Beloe's targets among the Jacobin women included the usual suspects: Wollstonecraft, Hays, Helen Maria Williams, the Plumptre sisters, Elizabeth Inchbald, Amelia Alderson, now married to the painter John Opie, and, surprisingly Hester Lynch Piozzi because she had made a scandalous second marriage to a younger Italian musician. Beloe satirized Godwin's memoirs of Wollstonecraft and "M— H— (a disciple of Wollstonecraft's) fantastic school." His ridicule was especially cutting because he had known Hays earlier than most of her other vocal detractors and could with apparent authority situate the deterioration of her morals and behavior to her involvement with Wollstonecraft and Godwin. He tore *Emma Courtney* to critical shreds; the lapse of many years since its publication in 1796 in no way mitigated his fury. Beloe's final thrust was to refer to Hays as a has-been who was no longer active in polluting the public sphere with her presence or her books: Beloe wrote, "[Mary Hays] had the prudence to stay at home. She might have written other still more mischievous and still more foolish things. It pleased providence to remove her, and, as we earnestly hope, to forgive her."[89]

Despite the ignominy that clung to her, Hays pushed ahead with writing women's lives. The growing scandal about King George IV and his wife, Caroline of Brunswick, offered Hays a newsworthy subject and a new publisher for her next

book, *Memoirs of Queens* (1821).[90] In her last published life-writing, Hays
assembled individual women's stories to document her hypothesis that historically
queenship offered the only relatively unobstructed sphere in which female
competence could be tested and displayed. In her memoirs of Elizabeth, Catherine
II, Catherine de Medici (Queen of France), and other powerful monarchs, Hays
argued that female succession and rule demonstrated unequivocally that queens
could rule as well or better than their male counterparts. *Memoirs of Queens*
presented the lives in brief of 75 female monarchs and included material on two
modern queens, Marie Antoinette and Queen Caroline, estranged wife of George
IV.

It is likely that T. and J. Allman, Hays's new publisher, agreed to publish the
work because of the recent, sensational trial in which the king tried to divorce
Caroline on grounds of adultery. The Queen's cause raised and conflated
disturbing issues of gender, class, and politics. Anna Clark notes that it
"symbolized a myriad of political and social issues" involving multiple layers of
British society and riveted public attention because it joined the issues of public
responsibility for private, unsanctioned sexuality, working class resentment of
governmental oppression, and the as yet unrecognized power of public opinion and
the press.[91] As the Prince of Wales, George had squandered vast sums on horses,
prostitutes and occasionally the arts. Marriage to a foreign princess eventually
became his only way out of enormous debt, although he had previously secretly
married his Catholic mistress, Maria Fitzherbert, a widow.[92] After the wedding of
the Prince and Caroline in 1795, the drunken husband could barely consummate
the marriage. When the couple's daughter was born nine months later, they
effectively separated, and the young princess was brought up at the palace, away
from her mother. In 1806–1807, the prince began a propaganda campaign accusing
Caroline of adultery. His ministers initiated a "Delicate Investigation" conducted
into Caroline's activities. Caroline set about lobbying on her own behalf against
the prince. The situation continued to deteriorate in public view. When George III
finally died in 1820, the stage was set for a regal brawl.

For radicals and former reformers, like Hays, this was a clear case of gender
prejudice in which the woman in question refused to submit to royal pressure to
acknowledge her guilt, whether innocent or not. It was, as well, a subject of
interest to an emerging cross-section of female readers.[93] Hays matched the
feverish temper of the times in her narrative, writing as Caroline's advocate rather
than as the tolerant and even-handed appraiser of "impartial posterity" that she had
claimed to be in *Female Biography*. She adopted a proto-journalist style, and
identified unique facets of the situation, like the attempts by the king to smear
Caroline with planted evidence, attempts that have been corroborated by modern
scholars.[94] "The Caroline Affair of 1820" galvanized public opinion in a new way,
uniting the social classes in defending the honor of the queen, highlighting
gendered hypocrisies about sexual morality in which the king, notoriously
licentious, accused his wife of acts not different from his own, slandered her as an

unfit mother, and demanded that Parliament grant him a divorce. Caroline appealed successfully to the people in defending herself against the unpopular king. Clark reports that "soldiers threatened to mutiny, working-class people demonstrated, and middle-class petitions sent addresses of support."[95] Caroline "became a woman's cause," the first issue of the nineteenth century in which "women acted as defenders of familial values and communal morality."[96]

Hays took the opportunity in her reportage of Caroline to connect past and present. She refuted Edmund Burke's denunciation of the French Revolution for changing gender relations that, Burke lamented, ended the practices of chivalry. She compared the English people's generous, reasoned support of Caroline with Burke's view of the French mob's mistreatment of Marie Antoinette. She pointed out that genuine manners had replaced artificial, courtly ones. Burke, Hays writes, "had he now lived, would have retracted his assertion, that the age of chivalry had passed away; it revived, in all its impassioned fervour, amidst the soberest and gravest people in the civilized world." Hays describes men's earnest reactions to Caroline's vulnerable circumstances: "every manly mind shrank from the idea of driving, by protracted and endless persecutions, a desolate unprotected female from her family, her rank, from society and from the world." Caroline's female subjects understood her dilemma in realistic, gendered terms: "*Woman* considered it as a common cause against the despotism and tyranny of man." Hays extrapolates from the Queen's case the inevitability of human progress because natural law is universal and equitable: "Morals are of no sex, duties are reciprocal between being and being, or they are abrogated by nature and reason. Brute force may subjugate, but in knowledge only is real strength, and to truth and justice is the last and only legitimate appeal." She reiterates her understanding of gender equality as the mark of civilization's advance, commenting that "with the feudal institutions fell the childish privileges and degrading homage paid to the [female] sex; and to *equity* not gallantry do they now prefer their claim."[97] Hays's words reflect her effort to adjust the quest for enlightenment towards what Marshall Brown describes as "a reconciliatory recollection," with the goal of "knowing the light through knowing the dark and the present by means of the past."[98]

Hays cannot and will not forget the past as she thinks about the meaning of Queen Caroline's life, or the personal and public suffering and struggle that have led to the present. She takes a long look back over the historical record and candidly admits that, "Oppression and proscription, it is true, still linger." In 1821 superstition and intolerance still endure, but there is potential for the greater diffusion of knowledge in the future because of the struggles of the past. Hays is oracular for a moment: she discerns the possibility of apocalyptic, if only dimly visible, changes: "Old things appear to be passing away," she writes, "and, in another century probably, should the progress of knowledge bear any proportion to its accelerated march during the latter half of the past, all things will become new." Finally, she acknowledges the necessity of accepting and welcoming inevitable change. "We live in eventful times, and at a critical era of the world," she advises, "happy those who understand the signs of the times; who seek not to oppose to a flood feeble mounds and inadequate barriers; but who suffer its waters gently to flow and expand through prepared appropriate reservoirs and channels, carrying fertility as they glide." Even disgrace and outrage, the mature Hays perceives, may be turned to productive uses.

The Buried Life

In the decades that followed, the exterior of Hays's busy life with family and Unitarian friends concealed what her younger contemporary Matthew Arnold later described as the "buried life"—the memories of unresolved conflicts that arose from the discrepancies between Hays's aspirations for herself and the actual direction her life had taken.[99] Memory and imagination were Hays's constant companions now. Texts sustained their inviolate power for her to embody the writer, a belief she had experimented with in writing *Memoirs of Emma Courtney*. The collection of letters she accumulated as she grew older, her own and others, bore witness that she had lived the life of the mind as passionately as she had once envisioned; that her previous existence had for a brief time been rich with intellectual and social exchanges that she relished as "the feast of reason and the flow of souls." Her cache of manuscripts held tantalizing clues to long-ago mysteries of love and loss and misrepresentation. Like her younger contemporaries, Hays now knew herself in Romantic terms "by remembering what [she] had experienced."[100]

The ambiguities of the past presented themselves again when Hays learned that Godwin had died in April 1836. She took the opportunity to write condolences to his widow and his daughter, and both replied. Mary Jane Godwin answered appreciatively to Hays's attentions, expressed her high regard for what she knew of Hays's character and intellect, and sympathized with her sufferings. The second Mrs. Godwin suggested that in the warmer weather they should meet for the first time.[101] Mary Shelley, Godwin and Wollstonecraft's daughter, now the widow of Percy Shelley, responded to Hays with the compliment that she knew her by reputation as the friend of her parents and as a distinguished woman in her own right.[102] Although 39 years had passed since her original request, in her letter of condolence Hays had asked that her letters and other papers to Godwin, the ones he had withheld after Wollstonecraft's death, be returned to her. As her father's executrix, Mary Shelley promised that she would look through his papers when her health permitted and return whatever manuscripts of Hays's she found.[103] As promised, she returned 26 letters from Hays to Godwin, presumably putting a close to a chapter of Hays's life that had begun nearly four decades earlier.[104]

But not all of the letters had been returned. And Hays had endured the limbo of loss too long not to press further. Godwin's refusal to return her letters after Wollstonecraft's death had continued to cause Hays discomfort, the memory of her texts that she no longer possessed twitching like a phantom limb. Hays's deep conviction that texts embodied their writer made the absence of these letters especially painful. The letters testified that before she composed the lives of other women, she had written her own life as she was living it. Without the letters there was no evidence of the intense life she had lived; they documented the experiences that she counted as among the most formative and significant of her life. The loss of the letters and papers was the loss of a part of herself that she valued highly, albeit with ambivalence. Most importantly, a crucial signifier of Hays's past was missing from the materials Mary Shelley had returned, a brief, confidential memoir that she had written expressly for Godwin.[105] He had esteemed her enough to be curious about her intellectual development; like her letters to him, this life-writing was crucial testimony that she had lived a meaningful existence which he, skeptic and critic that he was, had endorsed.

In a second letter, Hays assured Mary Shelley that she felt gratified that Godwin had preserved her letters, and, after more than 30 years, was not surprised that some might be missing. She seized the opportunity the exchanges with Mary Shelley presented to give her own account of her relations with Mary Shelley's father. Hays wrote that when unidentified circumstances separated her from Godwin, she "never claimed the papers, lest, by the delicate mind to which they were confided, such a claim might be construed into distrust"—using Godwin's criticism of her demand for the letters as an imagined reason for not having made the request, the opposite, in fact, of what she had actually done. Hays wondered aloud in her letter to Mary Shelley if Godwin might have destroyed the autobiographical piece she sought; perhaps, she hoped, it might yet turn up. In this letter Hays represented her relations with Godwin in a carefully edited version of the past. Godwin had supported her work, she wrote, even though he was a reputable author, "and *I* a merely self-taught, obscure young woman"—in fact, she was 35. Their arrangement, she told his daughter, was, "that I was to write to him as to 'my genius in the moon', & he was to reply to me in person. Hence I was favoured but by few of his letters & some brief notes."[106]

Hays presented herself as an appreciative acolyte in the hope that this would interest his daughter. Hays had her own reasons for tempting Mary Shelley with her remembrances of the past. Hays probably knew from Henry Crabb Robinson, with whom both women were in contact,[107] that Godwin's will had named his daughter as his literary executor and biographer.[108] At 77, Hays hoped to be remembered for posterity as the writer whom Godwin had encouraged and whose novel had emerged out of the intense interactions she had shared with him and Wollstonecraft. Hays was compelled by still unfulfilled ambitions to ensure that she would be remembered as a collaborator with her larger-than-life friends in their revolutionary experiments. With the awkward solicitude she had practiced on Robert Robinson so many years before, Hays proposed that Mary Shelley might include her in the memorial Hays knew her father had instructed her in his will to write, and that she was already composing from his manuscripts and correspondence.[109] Hays's letters had been part of the materials Mary Shelley inherited that Godwin directed were to be consulted for this purpose. Hays suggested that her manuscripts, too, might be useful in the daughter's attempt to portray her father's attempts at radical engagement between women and men.[110] Hays had played a vital part in that history by reintroducing Godwin and Wollstonecraft, and in engaging in the "collision of mind with mind" with Godwin.[111] Her unspoken wish was that Mary Shelley, a professional writer, would memorialize Hays as well as her father and mother.

Hays had been preparing for just such a possibility for years: she offered Mary Shelley the mass of papers she still kept from that time, and asked for an interview to discuss the project she hoped Mary Shelley would undertake. Appealing to the future on behalf of the past, Hays expressed her sense of continuity with the next generation in her wish that Mary Shelley would meet with her niece to whom she planned to leave the papers. She was careful to explain that her niece was "not intellectual," signaling her sense that she and Mary Shelley were connected in the present as women intellectuals, as she had been connected so long before with Wollstonecraft.[112] Once again, Hays was contemplating moving, suggesting that her restlessness had not abated, but also that she felt an urgency to be remembered lest she disappear into the oblivion of a succession of unremarkable addresses. She requested that Mary Shelley use the honorific "Mrs." rather than "Miss," that signified Hays's recognition that she was part of an older generation appropriately being supplanted by the next one: "Address to me *Mrs. M. Hays*, a title I have long adopted. My brother's daughter is now Miss Hays."

Hays also sought to stay in contact with the new generation of Unitarian public women to whom she entrusted some of the relics of her former life. Following Godwin's death, but before Mary Shelley had returned her own correspondence with him to Hays, she gave a letter of Wollstonecraft's (likely part of the materials that Godwin did send back in 1797) to Elizabeth Gaskell.[113] The two women may have known each other through the existing networks of Unitarians that were sustained from 1760–1860.[114] Perhaps Hays hoped that Gaskell, a successful writer and public woman, might prove to be an effective inheritor of her unrecorded, uncertain legacy.

Hays knew Harriet Martineau, whose Huguenot and Unitarian lineage afforded her a unique education, even as it kept her, too, at the margins of English culture. Shortly before her death in 1848, Hays wrote to Crabb Robinson about some of the terms of her will. She told him that Mrs. Martineau had taken a mutual friend to visit Mrs. Godwin, now dead. On that occasion, Mrs. Godwin had presented Mrs. Martineau with an engraving of Godwin, and inquired whether Hays would like one. Of course, Hays would. She then went on to say that should Crabb Robinson outlive the friend to whom Hays had promised the engraving on her death, she was making a provision in her will for the image to go to him. In addition, she hoped to see him soon when she would make him a gift of Robert Robinson's controversial *Plan of Lectures on Nonconformity*, a gift from Robinson. Hays remembered that

Robinson's text "was taken to the House of Commons, and read by a member there, as a proof of the disaffected spirit of the Dissenters." Hays confused the Robinson piece read in Parliament: It was his *Political Catechism.*[115] But she evoked Robinson as he had inspired her 50 years before, reminding Crabb Robinson that "this Great and good man was the awakener of my mind, and the Preserver of my life by rousing me by the energy of his genius from the morbid effects of a deep rooted Grief."[116]

In her will, written shortly before she died, Hays composed her own appeal to impartial posterity, against the likelihood that after her death no one would do so for her. She singled out her intellectual works as her most significant achievement. She expressed satisfaction at having risen above the mundane existence she had rejected in her earliest writings, and intimated that her lonely, idiosyncratic struggles over the last 50 years to gain recognition for women's cognitive potential might make a difference to subsequent generations. Despite her persistent sense of female disabilities, she had carried on the legacy of freethinking bequeathed to her by Robert Robinson and other Rational Dissenters, as well as the pioneering Unitarians. Like Wollstonecraft and the other heroes she revered, she too had imagined new human possibilities.[117] She reaffirmed her abiding religious faith and her renewed optimism. "To the Being who gave them, I bequeath my life and my mind," she wrote, "in the humble hope that I may not have lived wholly in vain, or 'folded in a napkin' the talent entrusted to me." Hays consigned to her favorite niece and to the chances of an indeterminate future her collection of texts, her own and those of others. Thus might the evidence of her life make possible the later reconstruction, evaluation, and perhaps affirmation of her own place among learned women who dare to live the life of the mind.

Notes

1   Later, although he was knighted in 1808, Phillips felt called upon to justify himself. In *The Golden Rules of social philosophy, or, A new system of practical ethics*, London: Printed for the author and to be had of all booksellers, 1826, he addresses the ethics of journalism and editing, and claims that he was the exemplar of the upstanding editor: "The writer of this article himself conducted for thirty years the *Monthly Magazine*; and, in the same period, published at least one thousand works on all branches of knowledge and subjects of contemporary interest. Yet, in printing on as many sheets of paper as ever were used by any other individual in England, he never once was questioned by any person whatever, or in any respect called upon to apologize or explain; and his only rule was, to adhere to the truth, to forbear when he could not praise, and to confine the press to its proper business—the public conduct of public men, and the exhibition of subjects of public interest and utility. A thousand times has he himself been the object of slanderous attacks, but he suffered the knaves to smother themselves in their own poison; nevertheless, his connexion with the press enabled

him to baffle malignity, by means which are not within the power of one in a million," p. 287.

2   John Issit, "Introducing Sir Richard Phillips," *Paradigm*, 26 (October 1998).

3   See Laura Marcus, *Auto/biographical Discourses: Criticism, Theory, Practice* (Manchester, 1994), pp. 11–12. For Godwin's experiments with life-writing and history, see "Introduction," *MAV*, pp. 12–14.

4   Charles Lamb advised William Hazlitt that Phillips was the man to publish biographies. "He is perpetually bringing out Biographies," Lamb wrote "without number: little trim things in two easy volumes price 12*s*." Thomas Manning, *Letters of Thomas Manning to Charles Lamb*, ed. G.A. Anderson (London, 1925), vol. I, pp. 273–4, quoted in Helen Braithwaite, *Romanticism, Publishing and Dissent: Joseph Johnson and the Cause of Liberty* (Houndmills, 2003), p. 175. Anthony Trollope portrays the rock bottom of biographical writing in his character, Lady Matilda Carbury, in *The Way We Live Now* (1875). She is the author of "Criminal Queens." Trollope's narrator advises that Lady Carbury "could write after a glib, commonplace, sprightly fashion, and had already acquired the knack of spreading all she knew very thin, so that it might cover a vast surface. She had no ambition to write a good book, but was painfully anxious to write a book that the critics should say was good," *Project Gutenberg*, <http://www.gutenberg.org/etext/5231>.

5   The publication was originally designed to come out annually, but no subsequent issues were published. A second edition was issued in 1805.

6   Peter H. Marshall, *William Godwin* (New Haven, 1984), pp. 255–7.

7   George Eliot creates a similar, sympathetic heroine, Dorothea Brooke in *Middlemarch* who, like Wollstonecraft and Hays, quests for an intellectual life.

8   The *Monthly Review*, 27 (November 1798): 321, *MAV*, p. 179.

9   For a sampling of contemporary responses, see "Appendix D. Critical Reaction," *MAV*, pp. 169–94.

10   William St. Clair, personal correspondence, 12–13 April 2005. See also St. Clair, *The Reading Nation in the Romantic Period* (Cambridge, 2004).

11   *RW*, "Chapter III," p. 160. See also Godwin's comment in *MAV*, p. 121.

12   [Hays,] "Memoirs of Wollstonecraft," *Annual Necrology for 1797–8* (London, 1800), p. 422.

13   *RW*, p. 172; see Barbara Taylor's comprehensive discussion of "Feminists Versus Gallants: Manners and Morals in Enlightenment Britain" that explores Wollstonecraft's denunciation of "'modern philosophers' for purveying prejudicial images of women masked in a rhetoric of sexual compliment," *Representations*, 87 (Summer 2004): 125–48.

14   The poet Anna Seward found Godwin's *Memoirs* valuable, but judged their one great fault Godwin's inaccurate characterization of Wollstonecraft as a religious skeptic like himself. *MAV*, pp. 184–5. See Barbara Taylor's illuminating discussion of Wollstonecraft's theology in "For the love of God," *Mary Wollstonecraft and the Feminist Imagination* (Cambridge, 2003), pp. 96–142.

15   Barbara Taylor notes that Hays wrote that Wollstonecraft's "faith rested not upon critical evidence or laborious investigation." Taylor continues, "Both Godwin and Hays rightly stressed the central role of passion and fantasy in Wollstonecraft's theology. Both also — much less plausibly — represented her as indifferent to theological controversy," *Mary Wollstonecraft and the Feminist Imagination*, p. 96.

Taylor argues that Godwin's "refusal to take Wollstonecraft seriously as a religious intellectual was symptomatic of the anxieties aroused in Godwin by his wife's *savante* status." Ibid., pp. 96–7.

16　Godwin explains that his purpose in his *Memoirs* is to demonstrate "the fairest source of animation and encouragement to those who would follow … in the same career." See "Introduction," *MAV*, p. 20.

17　[Hays,] "Memoirs of Wollstonecraft," pp. 422–3.

18　Hays's understanding of history was shared by her liberal contemporaries. Silvia Sebastiani explains, In "the progressive Enlightenment view … the condition of women was considered the first form of slavery in the history of humankind … The history of women was … a fundamental but ambiguous chapter in the history of civilization," "'Race', Women and Progress in the Scottish Enlightenment," eds Barbara Taylor and Sarah Knott, *Women, Gender and Enlightenment* (Houndmills, 2005), p. 76.

19　Gary Kelly, *Women, Writing and Revolution* (Oxford, 1993), p. 235.

20　Hays to Godwin, 28 July 1795, *Pforz.*, MH6.

21　See Alan Richardson, *British Romanticism and the Science of the Mind* (Cambridge, 2001). See also Barbara Taylor's discussion of the imagination and its sexual dimensions in Wollstonecraft's thought. In *Maria,* Taylor writes, "The problem with Maria's erotic imagination is … not its eroticism … but the fantasmic substitution of the ideal for the real which in her case (that is, in Everywoman's) turns out to be a doomed attempt to make psychological gold out of mere dross," "For the Love of God," *Mary Wollstonecraft and the Feminist Imagination*, p. 137.

22　See William Godwin, "Of Suicide," "Appendix B," *MAV*, vol. I, pp. 135–6.

23　See Wollstonecraft to Hays [15 September 1796], *Pforz.*, MW 2; see also Lyndall Gordon's comments on Wollstonecraft's mothering, *Mary Wollstonecraft: A New Genus* (London, 2005), pp. 353–6.

24　*MAV*, p. 454.

25　Hays represented Wollstonecraft as an exceptional woman, although Wollstonecraft disliked the category, "Chapter IV," *VRW*, p. 197. See also Barbara Taylor: "When Wollstonecraft denounced heroines in 1792 it was on the grounds that praise for Great Women was no substitute for respect for women in general. What was the exceptional woman an exception to, after all, but the frustrated, degraded condition of the majority? As long as most women were second-class citizens, the high-achieving woman would inevitably remain an oddity, a freak, and thus extremely vulnerable," "Mother-Haters and Other Rebels," in *London Review of Books*, 24/1 (3 January 2002).

26　*MAV*, p. 459.

27　Devoney Looser writes, "In the late eighteenth century and early nineteenth centuries, history writing was an occupation not only for ambitious literary workers and statesmen but for dilettantes and hacks. Little education and few special skills were required. The budding historiographer no longer need public experience," "Introduction," *British Women Writers and the Writing of History, 1670–1820* (Baltimore, 2000), p. 15. Looser includes Hays in the list of women who "deserve attention as historiographers."

28　Hays builds on the observations of Alexander Jardine in his *Letters from Barbery, France, Spain, Portugal, &c. By an English Office* (1788) that "The nation that shall first introduce women to their councils, their senates, and seminaries of learning, will probably accelerate most the advances of human nature in wisdom and happiness,". pp. 309–11.

29 Bayle argued for the right to private conscience and intellectual freedom. John Christian Laursen discusses Bayle's complex understanding of "toleration" in "Baylean Liberalism: Tolerance Requires Nontolerance," saying that tolerance has its necessary limits, lest it be extended to complicity with persecution. John Christian Laursen and Cary J. Nederman (eds), *Beyond the Persecuting Society: Religious Toleration Before the Enlightenment* (Philadelphia, 1998), pp. 197–8. Bayle's concept of toleration is also discussed in Sally L. Jenkinson, "The Public Context of Heresy," in John Christian Laursen (ed.) *Histories of Heresy in Early Modern Europe: For, Against, and Beyond Persecution and Toleration* (New York, 2002), pp. 133–5.

30 Kenneth Neill Cameron notes that Hays only included her older contemporaries, Catharine Macaulay and Mrs. Hester Chapone. He judges that Hays has been wrongly criticized for excluding Anna Barbauld, Elizabeth Inchbald, Maria Edgeworth, Amelia Opie, Ann Radcliffe, and Hannah More, as well as Wollstonecraft. *Shelley and his Circle* (Cambridge, 1961), vol. I, p. 161.

31 Brita Rang points out that seventeenth and eighteenth centuries compendia demonstrate the reality of living learned women, including those competent in science and mathematics. "Towards the end of the eighteenth century, the resplendent image of the savante was slowly supplanted by the image of the neurotic, frustrated learned woman," "A 'learned wave': Women of letters and science from the Renaissance to the Enlightenment," in Tjitske Akkerman and Siep Stuurman (eds), *Perspectives on feminist thought in European history: from the Middle Ages to the present* (London, 1998), p. 53.

32 George James published *The lives and amours of the Empresses, consorts to the first twelve Caesars of Rome* (1723), a translation from the French work by Monsieur De Serviez, a study of the interaction of character and power; a misogynist, Jacobite History *Female Revels* (1747); Thomas Amory's *Memoirs: Containing the Lives of Several Ladies of Great Britain* (1755), that was intended to feature 20 women but only included a few; *Biographium Femineum. The Female Worthies: of, Memoirs of the Most Illustrious Ladies of all Ages Nations* (1766); an anonymous *History of Female Favourites* (1772), that included Mary of de Padilla; Livia; Agnes Soreau; Mantilda; Thomas Gibbon's *Memoirs of eminently pious women, who were ornaments to their sex, blessings to their families, and edifying examples to the Church and world* (1777); Ann Thicknesse's *Sketches of the lives and writings of the ladies of France. Addressed to Mrs. Elizabeth Carter* (1778); and William Alexander's *The History of Women, from the Earliest Antiquity, to the Present Time* (1779, 1782).

33 Dissenting minister Andrew Kippis includes ten women in his voluminous *Biographia Britannica* (1778–93).

34 Hays incorporated material from the ten-volume dissenting *Biographia Britannica*, modeled after Bayle; William Enfield's *Biographical sermons: or, a series of discourses on the principal characters in Scripture* (1777); John Aikin's *General Biography; or, lives, critical and historical, of the most eminent persons of all ages, countries, conditions, and professions, arranged according to alphabetical order* (1799).

35   Matilda Betham (1776–1852), "Preface," *A biographical dictionary of the celebrated women of every age and country* (London, 1804), p. 1. See Coleridge's poem to Betham, "That this sweet Hope, by judgment unreproved,/ May boast one Maid, a poetess *indeed*,/ Great as th' impassioned Lesbian, in sweet song,/ And O! of holier mind, and happier fate." "To Matilda Betham, from a Stranger," dated "Keswick, Sept. 9, 1802, S. T. C." *The Poetess Tradition*, <http://www.orgs.muohio.edu/womenpoets/poetess/works/coleridge1802.html>.

36   Although she views Hays as torn between revolutionary feminism and "conservative domestic feminism," Mary Spongberg describes *Female Biography* as "the first and perhaps the most important collection of women's lives," "'Heroines of Domestic Life': Women's History and Female Biography," *Writing Women's History since the Renaissance* (Houndmills, 2002), pp. 115–18.

37   Jane Rendall notes that at about the same time Elizabeth Hamilton was writing her historical work, *The Memoirs of Agrippina, the Wife of Germanicus* (1804). According to Rendall Hamilton used her only historical work to consider the difficulties in imagining and effecting "new roles for British women." Hamilton's work was also reflective about the gendered constraints on women writing in the masculine genre of history. "Writing History for British Women: Elizabeth Hamilton and the *Memoirs of Agrippina*," in Clarissa Campbell Orr (ed.), *Wollstonecraft's Daughters: Womanhood in England and France 1780–1920* (Manchester, 1996), p. 79.

38   Most frequently mentioned are the *Biographia Britannica*, Mrs. Ann Thicknesse's *Ladies of France*, Ballard, the *Female Worthies*, Gibbon's *Pious Women*, the *General Biographical Dictionary*, Granger's *Biographical History of England* (1769), David Baker's *Biographia Dramatica ... of British and Irish dramatic writers* (1782), and *Biographia Gallica: or, the lives of the most eminent French writers of both sexes, in divinity, philosophy, mathematics, history, poetry &c. from the restoration of learning under Francis I. to the present time* (1752).

39   These included a translation of Anglivial de la Beaumelle's *Life of Madame de Maintenon* (1760), the autobiography of Mme Roland, the revolutionary heroine, and Mrs. Elizabeth Rowe's *Friendship in death: in twenty letters from the dead to the living*, with an "account of the life of the author," extracted from *Cibber's Lives of the Poets* (1762). When appropriate, Hays often consulted works in French and/or French works in English translation: Brantome's popular *Vies des dames illustres* and *Vies des dames galantes* (1665–66), the *Nouveau dictionnaire historique portatif, ou Histoire abregee de tous les hommes qui se sont fait un nom par des talents, des vertus, &c &c* (1770), the *Vie de Voltaire*, Bayle's *Dictionary* and his *Lettres ... a sa famille*.

40   For example, in her lengthy account of Elizabeth, Queen of England, Hays refers to a manuscript of Elizabeth's early writings in the royal library at Westminster.

41   *The Life of Catharine II. Empress of Russia. An enlarged translation [by W. Tooke] from the French ... With seven portraits ... and a correct map of the Russian empire* (London, 1798).

42   Cynthia Richards notes that Catherine died seven years before *Female Biography* was published, and that Hays's compilation was the first to include Catherine's scandal-filled "story in an exclusively female context," "Revising History, 'Dumbing Down,' and Imposing Silence: The Female Biography of Mary Hays," *Eighteenth–Century Women, Studies in their Lives, Works, and Culture*, 3 (November 2003): 276.

43 *A new and general biographical dictionary: containing an historical, critical, and impartial account of the lives and writings of the most eminent persons in every nation in the world ... A new edition, etc. / [by] DICTIONARY* ; Alexander Chalmers, F.S.A.; William Tooke the Elder, 1795.

44 Hays to William Tooke the Younger, May 1803, *Pforz.*, MH 29.

45 Hays wrote, "In these perilous times, Anne became a victim to the vengeance of her husband, and to the bigotry of the priests, who accused her to Henry of dogmatizing on the subject of the *real presence*; a notion respecting which, in proportion as it was untenable, he was particularly tenacious. The sex and age of the heretic aggravated, rather than softened, the malice of her adversaries, who could not pardon in a woman the presumption of opposing arguments and reason to their assertions and dogmas," Hays, "Anne Askew," *Female Biography* (1802), vol. I, p. 202.

46 Hays, "Margaret de Valois," *Female Biography*, vol. V, pp. 472–3. Sally Jenkinson notes that in his article that "pays homage" to Navarre, can be "observed in microcosm the range of Bayle's public concerns," from "Navarre," in Jenkinson (ed.), *Bayle: Political Writings*, (Cambridge, 2000), p. 192.

47 See Richards's intriguing discussion of Hays's unwillingness to abridge her memoir of Roland: "What Hays learns ... is to hide her message within the already concluded stories of others and to let her silences, these now compelling abridgements, speak for themselves," "Revising History, 'Dumbing Down,' and Imposing Silence: The Female Biography of Mary Hays," p. 282.

48 Roland's comment reflected Hays's bitter experience as a female writer: "Never," Roland wrote, "did I feel the slightest temptation to become an author. I perceived, at a very early period, that a woman who acquires this title, loses more than she gains. The men do not like, and her own sex criticise [sic], her. If her works are bad, she is ridiculed; if good, she is bereaved of the reputation annexed to them. If the public are forced to acknowledge that she has talents, they sift her character, her morals, her conduct, and balance the reputation of her genius by the publicity which they give to her errors," Hays, "Madame Roland," *Female Biography*, vol. VI, pp. 177–8.

49 Ibid.

50 Ibid., pp. 198–9. Richards notes, "the general arc of Roland's more personal reflections mirrors that found within Hays's own 'autobiographical' work *Emma Courtney*," "Revising History, 'Dumbing Down,' Ibid.

51 Hays, "Madame Dacier," *Female Biography*, vol. IV, p. 6.

52 Hays, "Anna Maria Schurman," *Female Biography*, vol. IV, pp. 384–8.

53 Hays, "Mary Astell," *Female Biography*, vol. I, p. 221.

54 Richards quotes Wollstonecraft's comment in *VWR*, "I shall not go back to the remote annals of history; it is sufficient to allow that [woman] has always been a slave, or a despot, and to remake, that each of these situations equally retards the progress of reason," ibid.

55 Hays's concerns in *Female Biography* are reflected in *Middlemarch* where George Eliot describes Dorothea Brooke's dissatisfaction with "that toy-box history of the world adapted to young ladies which had made the chief part of her education." Dorothea's desire for the life of the mind is sympathetically represented by Eliot; the elderly Mr. Causaban, with his "promises of masculine knowledge," is Dorothea's only resource for that higher learning she aspires to.

56   Hays refers to the Jacobin women's claim that, as the mind is not innately gendered, it is not inevitable that character traits should be. Rather, women should aspire to the best human qualities.

57   See Katherine Binhammer's trenchant discussion of 1790s feminism in "Thinking Gender with Sexuality in 1790s' Feminist Thought," *Feminist Studies*, 28/3 (Fall 2002): 671–80.

58   Hays may have found a call for the kinds of changes in women's status she suggested in Marie Madeleine Jodin's *Legislative Views* (1790), although there was no English translation available. Hays did know Mary Robinson's polemical *A Letter to the Women of England, on the Injustice of Mental Subordination* (1799) that demanded women's greater social and political participation.

59   Richards comments, "What may seem humble in *Female Biography's* preface, that this work comes close to being mere transcription, or in other words, that she is only *copying* these scandalous memoirs, starts to take on a more charged tone ... And through what she chooses to reveal (and what she does not), she will control the tale," "Revising History, 'Dumbing Down,' and Imposing Silence: The Female Biography of Mary Hays," p. 275.

60   Hays is likely also signaling that she has not merely incorporated existing text from others' works as she had in the long excerpts from the letters to Imlay in her memoirs of Wollstonecraft.

61   *L&E*, p. 13.

62   Bridget Hill, *The Republican Virago: The Life and Times of Catharine Macaulay, Historian* (Oxford, 1992), p. 83.

63   Sarah Hutton, "Catherine Macaulay," *Women, Gender and Enlightenment*, p. 738.

64   Hays, "Catherine Macaulay Graham," *Female Biography*, vol. V, p. 292.

65   Alison Booth notices *Female Biography* as an example of women's participation in constructing women's history. *How to Make it as a Woman: Collective Biographical History from Victoria to the Present* (Chicago, 2004), pp. 32, 68. Spongberg sees Hays as "an important transitional figure in women's historiography." Spongberg notes that Hays's techniques in *Female Biography* preceded Lytton Strachey's modern, more personal, approach to life-writing by more than a century." *Writing Women's History since the Renaissance*," pp. 115–18.

66   Ibid.

67   The reviews of *Female Biography* credited Hays for her hard work, noted her interest in combating the prejudice about women's inferior mental competence, but criticized her inclusion of particular women who failed to provide models of moral or chaste behavior. Among the examples cited were Heloise, Aspasia, Ninon l'Enclos, Charlotte Corday, Leontium, an Athenian courtesan, and Aphra Behn. Phillips's *Monthly Magazine* judged Hays successful in her advocacy of women's contributions to the historical record. The *Annual Review* chided the author for selection criteria that privileged talent over virtue, and applauded strong passions as indicative of such talents. They lauded the author's evenhandedness, but called attention to the errors in Latin quotations, and advised that she seek help from a more learned friend for future revisions. The conservative *European Magazine* linked *Female Biography* positively to the recent amelioration of female education, citing learned women and governesses as the prime movers behind this initiative—Hester Chapone, Hannah More, Anna Barbauld, and Sarah Trimmer, but excluding Wollstonecraft and Hays. The critic

devoted space in three separate issues to criticize several aspects of *Female Biography*: the sinfulness of some of the women, particularly actresses and mistresses; its too great length; the inappropriateness of the entry on Catharine Macaulay in which Hays succumbed to Mrs. Arnold's partiality to Macaulay because Arnold was the sister of Macaulay's second, younger husband. The critic advised Phillips to produce a "chaste edition" of the work, more appropriate for young ladies. The critic also noted the absence of Lady Mary Wortley Montagu, but attributed this to the fact that Phillips would soon produce an edition of her letters. *Female Biography* was widely reviewed: in the *Annual Review*, (September 1803): 142; *European Magazine*, (43 June 1803): 431–2; *European Magazine*, (August 1803): 118–19; *Critical Review*, 37/2 (April 1803): 415–20; *The London Review* (June, July, August 1803); *Monthly Review*, 43/2 (January 1804): 92–3; *Monthly Magazine*, 15/103 (28 July 1803): 622, which is a one-paragraph review, with a gallant and somewhat condescending tone, yet it encourages the reader to read the book.

68   Lucy Aikin to Mrs. Taylor, Stoke Newington, 27 January 1803, *Memoirs, Miscellanies and Letters of the Late Lucy Aikin*, ed. Philip Hemery Le Breton (London, 1864), p. 124. I appreciate Felicia Gordon's retrieval and transcription of this excerpt.

69   Anthony Page, "'A great politicianess,'" forthcoming.

70   Hays to Henry Crabb Robinson, 10 September 1804, *DWL*, HCR, 1804, 55.

71   Wollstonecraft to Godwin, [17 August 1796], Janet Todd, *The Collected Letters of Mary Wollstonecraft* (New York, 2003), #230, p. 349. Clemit and Walker characterize Wollstonecraft's use of the phrase as "a persona of social isolation," "Introduction," *MAV*, p. 26.

72   Published posthumously, *Les Rêveries du Promeneur Solitaire* was available in English translation by 1783.

73   Lofft collaborated with Robert Robinson to establish a Dissenting college in Cambridge with George Dyer as a tutor. When Robinson died in 1790, the plan was aborted. Lofft eventually became so disaffected by the failure of reformist efforts that he left England permanently in 1818 and settled on the Continent.

74   Oxford, Bodleian Library, [Abinger] Dep. c. 527. I appreciate Pamela Clemit's calling this quote to my attention. Lofft had much earlier written in praise of his friend Catharine Macaulay, *Observations on Mrs. Macaulay's History of England, (lately published) from the Revolution to the Resignation of Sir Robert Walpole. In a Letter Addressed to that Lady* (London, 1778).

75   Hays compared herself to Petrarch, as she had in her debates with Godwin: "With Petrarch, I sometimes feel inclined to say — 'My short pleasures have been like the light breezes of summer, that refresh the air but for a moment.' Yet my satisfactions, like my pains, are of a vivid nature, & exquisitely felt." Marilyn Brooks notes that Hays incorrectly attributes the remark. It is rather St. Augustine's advice to Petrarch, *CMH*, p. 570, ftnte 93. Hays to Crabb Robinson, 14 February 1806, *DWL*, HCR, 1806, 37.

76   The Fenwicks' son, Eliza wrote, "does not forget Mama Hays," 24 April 1812, A.F. Wedd, *The Fate of the Fenwicks 1798–1822* (London, 1927).

77   Eliza Fenwick also shifted from pillar to post as far away as Barbados, the United States, and Canada; she worked for Godwin and his second wife in their children's bookshop, the Juvenile Library; and published children's books with Tabart Juvenile

Libraries and the Godwins. For an account of Eliza Fenwick's life after Wollstonecraft's death, see Isobel Grundy, "Introduction," *Secresy; or, The Ruin on the Rock* (Peterborough, 1994), pp. 10–20. See also A.F. Wedd's *The Fate of the Fenwicks* for an edited selection of Eliza Fenwick's letters to Hays.

78   Hays published several books for young people: *Harry Clinton; or, a Tale of Youth* (London, 1804); *Historical Dialogues for Young Persons* (London, 1806–1808); *The Brothers; or, Consequences: A Story of What Happens Every Day; Addressed to that Most Useful Part of the Community, the Labouring Poor* (London, 1815), published by Button and Son, who also printed and sold Baptist works; *Family Annals; or, The Sisters*, published by Simpkin & Marshall (London, 1817), publishers of Anna Barbauld's children's books, as well as William Enfield's, and others of Hays's associates.

79   Hays wrote William Tooke, "I wish to be employed, but I do not wish so severely to task my poor brain. I should be content with dull, plodding, inglorious occupation, so as, in these hard times, it promised to bring me a little [help?]. The wings of my ambition are clipped; I want not to be farther known, flattered or abused, but merely to live independent and free. I would engage either in compilation, abridgement or translation, & promise sober drudgery and punctual performance. But as a *woman,* I feel myself under peculiar disadvantage in seeking or procuring connections," May 1803, *Pforz.,* MH 29.

80   The full title is *History of England, from the Earliest Records, to the Peace of Amiens: in a series of Letters to a Young Lady at School* (3 vols, London, 1806). While at work on *Female Biography*, Hays received a letter from Charlotte Smith, on the advice of Eliza Fenwick, asking her to complete the manuscript of Smith's life for Phillips's *Public Characters.* Hays did, and the article was published in 1807 after Smith's death in 1806.

81   See five letters from John Aikin to Hays about this matter between 27 September and 15 January 1805; see *CMH*, pp. 337–41 for transcriptions that include a "Statement" of Aikin's decision, *Pforz.,* 2147–51.

82   See Crabb Robinson's account of Southey's curt refusal and Hays's chagrin at the rebuff: Robinson wrote that he "tried to weaken the impression of a disrespectful letter, but I dare say her letter was thought *too* sentimental." He reported Hays's view of the situation: "Miss Hays is now thrown upon the world. She seeks a residence in some picturesque country. I fear she will not easily find one to her taste," Henry Crabb Robinson, *On Books and their Writers*, ed. Edith J. Morley (London, 1938), pp. 124–5.

83   Hays to Tooke, 24 January 1807, *Pforz.,* MH 31.

84   "I thought it better to … weave my reflections into the subject. I do not pretend to enter learnedly and profoundly into my subject but to *write* (not compile) a popular history, which may entertain & inform common readers," Hays to Tooke, 24 January 1807, *Pforz.,* MH 31.

85   Coleridge reported that Frend wrote Hays to announce his marriage "in a very dry letter." Hays had prophesized to Godwin that she would be deprived of the chance to share a benevolent future with William Frend when he refused to be her lover or father children with her. She was right.

86   Hays's sister Elizabeth described Pennington to Crabb Robinson as "an ecstatic lady who had been the friend of Mrs. Siddons, Helen Maria Williams, Hannah More, and

other well-known women of the time, and whose tastes and temperament must have been closely allied to Mary's own," 14 November 1816, *DWL*.

87   Hays's reputation preceded her. Hays referred to her publications in an early letter. Pennington asked for the titles. On receiving them from Hays, Pennington commented that she had "read 'Emma Courtney' long ago — I will ingenuously say with more admiration of its Ingenuity, than approbation of its *Tendency, which I probably mistook, so apt are we, in those sort of lighter Productions, to confound* 'Warning' *and* 'Example,'" Penelope Pennington to Hays, 11 March 1814, *Pforz.*, 2182.

88   Crabb Robinson noted earlier in his diary that Hays had shown him her correspondence with Pennington. Crabb Robinson feared that Hays's "overstrained sensibility joined to precise manners will make her offensive and ridiculous to the many, infinitely below herself in all essential qualities," *On Books and their Writers*, pp. 130–31. See *CMH*, pp. 506–31, 573–9.

89   "[M—H—] had, really, when first known, appeared lively, ingenuous, innocent and interesting. It is not pretended to say who or what perverted her principles, but she was a friend of Wolstonecraft [sic], a follower of Helvetius, and a great admirer of Rousseau. As ill luck would have it, she must needs write a novel, and as her evil genius prompted, was induced to publish it. What thinkest thou, gentle Reader, was the outline of the story? Why this:—The heroine, Emma Courtney Hight, falls in love, desparately [sic] in love, with a youth whom she had never seen. At length, she counters him—worse and worse! Passion now boils over, and she exercises every female artifice to captivate his affections in return. But it will not do. All her efforts prove ineffectual. What's next to be done? Why take him by storm; or, which is much the same thing, she voluntarily offers herself to live with him as his mistress. [...] But this will not do: his heart proves made of impenetrable stuff; at length, the heroine compelled by dire necessity marries, contrary to her inclination, a man she dislikes exceedingly. But still she retains her first passion; and what is more, disregarding the obligations of duty imposed by her new character, she attends on his dying bed, the man for whom she first suffered love … But after all, things might have been yet worse, with respect to this same M.H. She might, like her friends Mesdames W. and H.M.W. have emigrated to France, and disgraced herself and her country." William Beloe, *The Sexagenarian; or the Reflections of a Literary Life* (London, 1817), pp. 353–62.

90   In 1821, T. and J. Allman, identified as "Booksellers to her Majesty," published *Memoirs of Queens Illustrious and Celebrated*, an alphabetical presentation of the lives in brief of 75 female monarchs from ancient to contemporary times. The entries are mainly derived from *Female Biography*, but Hays includes 27 new entries, many of them non-Western. Hays did not identify many of her sources, as she had in *Female Biography*. For the account of Queen Caroline she appears to have relied primarily on the numerous newspaper accounts of the "Queen's Trial," as it was called, including William Cobbett's reporting of events in *Cobbett's Weekly Political Register*.

91   Anna Clark, "Queen Caroline and the Sexual Politics of the British Constitution," *Scandal: The Sexual Politics of the British Constitution* (Princeton, 2004), p. 177.

92   Clark points out that the Prince had violated the Royal Marriage Act and so the marriage was considered invalid, "Queen Caroline and the Sexual Politics of the British Constitution," p. 178.

93   For transcriptions of Pennington's letters to Hays see *CMH*, pp. 506–31.

94 See Clarissa Campbell Orr's account in "Introduction: Court Studies, Gender and Women's History," *Queenship in Britain, 1660–1837: royal patronage, court culture, and dynastic politics*, ed. Clarissa Campbell Orr (Manchester, 2002), pp. 1–52.
95 Clark, "Queen Caroline and the Sexual Politics of the British Constitution," pp. 177–207.
96 See Clark, "Queen Caroline and the Sexual Politics of Popular Culture in London, 1820," *Representations*, "Special Issue: The Margins of Identity in Nineteenth-Century England," (Summer 1990): 47–68; Dror Wahrman, "'Middle Class' Domesticity Goes Public: Gender, Class, and Politics from Queen Caroline to Queen Victoria," *The Journal of British Studies*, 32/4, Making the England Middle Class, ca. 1700–1850, (October, 1993): 396–432; T.W. Laqueur, "The Queen Caroline Affair: Politics as Art in the Reign of George IV," *Journal of Modern History*, 54 (1982): 417–66.
97 Wollstonecraft expressed this as, "It is justice, not charity, that is wanting in the world!," "Chap. IV.," "Observations on the State of Degradation to Which Woman Is Reduced by Various Causes," *VRW*, p. 190.
98 Marshall Brown, "Romanticism and Enlightenment," *The Cambridge Companion to British Romanticism* (Cambridge, 1993), pp. 42–3.
99 Matthew Arnold, "There rises an unspeakable desire/ After the knowledge of our buried life;/ A thirst to spend our fire and restless force/ In tracking out our true, original course;/ A longing to inquire into this heart that beats/ so wild, so deep within us—to know/ Whence our lives come and where they go," "The Buried Life" (1852), ll. 47–54, ed. H. Kerpneck, *Representative Poetry Online*, University of Toronto, <http://rpo.library.utoronto.ca/poem/86.html>.
101 Mary Jane Godwin to Hays, 30 November 1837, *Pforz.*, MJG 6.
102 Mary Shelley acknowledged Hays's importance in her parents' private lives by describing her father's funeral and his request to be buried with Wollstonecraft. She wrote, "My dear father left it in his will to be placed as near my Mother as possible. Her tomb in St. Pancras Church Yd was accordingly opened — at a depth of twelve feet her coffin was found uninjured — the cloth still over it — and the plate tarnished but legible. The funeral was plain and followed only by a few friends. There might have been many more, but being private, we restricted the number. My son, now sixteen, was among the mourners," 20 April 1836. *Pforz.*, MWS 361.
103 Mary Shelley read Hays's request from her own perspective. In her letter to Hays she commented, "There is nothing more detestable or cruel than publication of letters meant for one eye only," ibid. It is likely that she had not read *Memoirs of Emma Courtney*.
104 Hays added her letters to Godwin to the archive she collected over six decades, beginning with her "book" of love letters. She bequeathed the collection to her favorite niece, Mrs. George Wedd, who passed them down to other female members of the Hays-Wedd family. Eventually, Anne F. Wedd, who published an edited selection in 1925 as *The Love-Letters of Mary Hays*, inherited the archive. Wedd left the collection of manuscripts to her younger friend Jill Organ, later Hansen, who sold them to the Pforzheimer Library in 1971.
105 The autobiography Hays refers to is one of several she seems to have written over the years for particular men. The first was for John Eccles who writes to Hays, "You gave me a little history of yourself yesterday," "Love Letters," 28 October 1779; the second

for Robert Robinson, "Short as the narrative you give of yourself is," Robinson writes Hays, "it is a miniature portrait of a lady in danger and distress, the work of an exquisite artist calculated to touch the heart," Robinson to Hays, 11 January 1783, *Pforz.*, 2154; and the third for Godwin. A.F. Wedd also refers in her introduction to Volume II of "Love Letters" that she described as containing "autobiographical fragments" by Hays, but Volume II has also disappeared.

106 Hays to Mary Shelley, 30 November 1836. Oxford, Bodleian Library [Abinger], Dep. B. 227/8.

107 "Editor's Introduction," "Life of William Godwin," *Mary Shelley's Literary Lives and Other Writings*, ed. Pamela Clemit (with the assistance of A.A. Markley) (London, 2002), vol. 4, p. xiii.

108 Pamela Clemit advises that Godwin "effectively appointed [Mary Shelley] as his authorised biographer and as the creator of his posthumous image," ibid.

109 Ibid. Mary Shelley never completed the life of her father.

110 Pamela Clemit writes that Mary Shelley "sought to defend Godwin's early, much-criticised views on marriage, providing a nuanced account of his egalitarian relationships with women, notably Wollstonecraft," ibid., p. xvi.

111 In the unfinished manuscript, Mary Shelley wrote that Godwin recorded meeting Wollstonecraft for the second time in his diary for 8 January 1796, "Tea Miss Hayes's with Holcroft & Wollstonecraft," ibid., p. 103.

112 Hays and Mary Shelley had in common their works that promoted "feminist historiography." Nora Crook notes that Mary Shelley's choice of subjects in her *Literary Lives* "rather than the inclusion of a few already canonized celebrated females, enable Mary Shelley's *Literary Lives* to take its place, as Greg Kucich has argued, alongside other examples of nineteenth-century feminist historiography such as Mary Hays's *Female Biography* (1803), and Anna Jameson's *Memoirs of Female Sovereigns (1831)*," "General Editor's Introduction," *Mary Shelley's Literary Lives and Other Writings*, ed. Tilar J. Mazzeo (London, 2002), vol. 1, p. xxviii. Crook cites Greg Kucich, "Mary Shelley's *Lives* and the Reengendering of History" in *Mary Shelley in Her Times*, pp. 198–213. Mary Shelley published *Lives of the Most Eminent Literary and Scientific Men of Italy, Spain, and Portugal*, volumes 86–8 of *The Cabinet of Biography*, in *Lardner's Cabinet Cyclopedia*, conducted by Reverend Dionysius Lardner (London, 1835–37); republished in part as *Lives of the Most Eminent Literary and Scientific Men of Italy* (2 vols, Philadelphia, 1841); *Lives of the Most Eminent Literary and Scientific Men of France*, volumes 102 and 103 of *The Cabinet of Biography* (London, 1838, 1839); republished in part as *Lives of the Most Eminent French Writers* (2 vols, Philadelphia, 1840).

113 There is a note in Mrs. Gaskell's hand on a page of a letter from Wollstonecraft to Hays that she gave Mrs. Gaskell, now in the Pforzheimer Collection. The note reads, "This letter written by Mrs. Wolstonecraft [sic] authoress of the Rights of Woman and addressed to Miss Hays authoress of The Lives of Illustrious Women was given me by Miss Hays 1st May 1836. It may have been written 1792–96 and certainly before her marriage with Godwin."

114 Elizabeth Gaskell (1810–65) was a Unitarian as well as a famous novelist. See Ruth Watts, "Unitarian networks," *Gender, Power and the Unitarians in England 1760–1860* (London, 1998), pp. 207–13.

115 *The Parliamentary Register; or History of the Proceedings and Debates of the House of Commons* (London, 1790), vol. XXVII, pp.180, 139, 179–88.

116 Mary Hays to Crabb Robinson, April 1842. *DWL*, HCR 154 (a).

117 At the end of *The Prelude*, Wordsworth describes the experience of

"the animating faith
That Poets, even as Prophets, each with each
Connected in a mighty scheme of truth,
Have each his own peculiar faculty,
Heaven's gift, a sense that fits him to perceive
Objects unseen before, thou wilt not blame
The humblest of this band who dares to hope
That unto him hath also been vouchsafed
An insight that in some sort he possesses,
A privilege whereby a work of his,
Proceeding from a source of untaught things
Creative and enduring, may become
A power like one of Nature's,"

THE PRELUDE, "BOOK THIRTEENTH," "IMAGINATION AND TASTE, HOW IMPAIRED AND RESTORED (concluded)," ll. 300–12, William Wordsworth, *The Complete Poetical Works* (London, 1888) from *Bartleby.com, Inc.*, 1999, <http://www.bartleby.com/145/>.

Bibliography

Manuscript Sources

Alderson, Amelia, Letter to William Godwin, 1 November 1796. Oxford, Bodleian Library, [Abinger] Dep. b. 210/6.

———, Letter to William Godwin, 22 December 1796. Oxford, Bodleian Library, [Abinger] Dep. b. 210/6.

———, Letter to Mary Wollstonecraft (Mrs. Imlay), 28 August [undated]. Oxford, Bodleian Library, [Abinger] Dep. b. 210/6.

———, Letter to Mary Wollstonecraft (Mrs. Imlay), 15 December 1796. Oxford, Bodleian Library, [Abinger] Dep. b. 210/6.

Cambridge University, Letters to and from William Frend. Cambridge, England.

Dr. Williams's Library, Letters to and from John Disney, Eliza Fenwick, William Frend, Mary Hays, Theophilus Lindsey, Henry Crabb Robinson, and Gilbert Wakefield.

Eliza Fenwick's Letters to Hays (1789–1828), Fenwick Family Papers, New-York Historical Society.

Godwin, William, Capel Lofft to William Godwin [undated]. Oxford, Bodleian Library, [Abinger] Dep. c. 527.

———, Letter to Anthony Carlisle, unsigned, 15 September 1797. Oxford, Bodleian [Abinger], Dep. b. 215/2.

———, Diary. Oxford, Bodleian Library, [Abinger] Dep. e. 196–227.

———, Letter to [Mary Hays], 5 October 1797: Oxford, Bodleian Library, [Abinger] Godwin Letter-Press Copies, fols. 58–9.

———, Letter to [Mary Hays], 10 October 1797: Oxford, Bodleian Library, [Abinger] Godwin Letter-Press Copies, fols. 60–61.

———, Letter to [Mary Hays], 22 October 1797: Oxford, Bodleian Library, [Abinger] Dep. b. 277/7, fols. "153–6."

———, Letter to [Mary Hays], 27 October 1797: Oxford, Bodleian Library, [Abinger] Godwin Letter-Press Copies, fols. 78–9.

Hays, Mary. Correspondence and Manuscripts. The Carl H. and Lily Pforzheimer Collection of Shelley and His Circle, The New York Public Library, Astor, Lenox, and Tilden Foundations.

———, Letter to Mary Shelley, 30 November 1836. Abinger MSS, Dep. b. 227/8.

———, Letter to Hugh Worthington, 3 July 1792, MS, in private hands.

Parish Records, Richmond, Yorkshire (North Yorkshire County Records Office, Northallerton), PR/RM 1–5.

Primary Sources

Aikin, J., *General Biography; or, lives, critical and historical, of the most eminent persons of all ages, countries, conditions, and professions, arranged according to alphabetical order* (London: G.G. and J. Robinson, 1799).

Aikin, L., *Memoir of John Aikin* (London: Baldwin, Cradock, and Joy, 1823).

Analytical Review, 1793, 1797, 1798.

A new and general biographical dictionary: containing an historical, critical, and impartial account of the lives and writings of the most eminent persons in every nation in the world ... A new edition, etc. / [by] DICTIONARY, ed. A. Chalmers, F.S.A. and W. Tooke the Elder (London: Proprietors, 1795).

Annual Review, 1803.

The Anti-Jacobin Review and Magazine, 1799.

Arnold, M., "The Buried Life" (1852), ed. H. Kerpneck, *Representative Poetry Online*, University of Toronto, http://rpo.library.utoronto.ca/poem/86.html.

Austen, J., *Persuasion* (1818) (New York: Bantam, 1984).

Bacon, F., "The Advancement of Learning: Book Two (1605)," *Renascence: An Online Repository of Works Printed in English Between the Years 1477 and 1799*, The University of Oregon, <http://darkwing.uoregon.edu/~rbear/adv2.htm>.

Ballard, G., *Memoirs of several ladies of Great Britain: who have been celebrated for their writings or skill in the learned languages, arts, and sciences*, ed. R. Perry. (Detroit: Wayne State University Press, 1985).

Barbauld, A., "Remarks on Mr. Wakefield's Enquiry...." (London: J. Johnson, 1792).

Bayle: Political Writings, ed. S.L. Jenkinson (Cambridge: Cambridge University Press, 2000).

Beloe, W., *The Sexagenarian; or the Reflections of a Literary Life* (London: F.C. and J. Rivington, 1817).

Belsham, T., "The Christian Character Exemplified in A Discourse occasioned by the death of Mrs. Hannah Lindsey, and delivered at Essex Street Chapel, January 26th, 1812; by Thomas Belsham" (London: J. Johnson & Co., 1812).

Benger, E., *Memoirs of the Late Mrs. Elizabeth Hamilton, with a Selection from Her Correspondence, and Other Unpublished Writings*, 2nd edn (London: Longman, Hurst, Rees, Orme, & Brown, 1819).

Betham, M., *A biographical dictionary of the celebrated women of every age and country* (London: B. Crosby and Co.; Tegg and Castleman; and E. Lloyd, 1804).

Blake, W., *Visions of the Daughters of Albion*, ed. R.N. Essick (Huntington: University of California Press, 2002).

The British Critic, A New Review, 1797.

Brooke, F., *Emily Montague* (London: J. Dodsley, 1769).

Brooks, M.L., ed., *The Correspondence (1779–1843) of Mary Hays, British Novelist* (Lewiston: Edwin Mellen Press, 2004).

Brown, I.V., ed., *Joseph Priestley: Selections from His Writings* (University Park, Pennsylvania State University Press, 1962).

Burke, E., *A Philosophical Enquiry into the Origin of Our Ideas of the Sublime and Beautiful* (1757).

Burney, F., *Cecilia, or Memoirs of an Heiress, By the Author of Evelina*, 5 vols (London: T. Payne and Son and T. Cadell, 1782).

The Cabinet, 1795.

Cappe, C., *Memoirs of the Life of the Late Mrs. Catherine Cappe* (London: Longman, 1822).

Claude, J., *Cruel Persecutions of the PROTESTANTS in the Kingdom of France*, first American reprint of the English translation…["Les plaintes des protestans, cruellement opprimez dans le royaume de France," 1686] (Boston: Narcisse Cyr, 1893).

Coleridge, S.T., *The Collected Works of Samuel Taylor Coleridge: Poetical Works I, Poems (Reading Text): Part 1*, ed. J.C.C. Mays (Princeton: Princeton University Press, 2001).

———, "To Matilda Betham, from a Stranger," dated "Keswick, Sept. 9, 1802, S. T. C." *The Poetess Tradition*, <http://www.orgs.muohio.edu/womenpoets/poetess/works/coleridge1802.html>.

Conduct Literature for Women 1770–1803, ed. P. Morris, vols 1 and 3 (London: Pickering & Chatto, 2005).

Crabb Robinson, H., *On Books and Their Writers*, ed. E.J. Morley (London: J.M. Dent & Sons Ltd., 1938).

Cristall, A.B., *Poetical Sketches* (Johnson, 1795) *Electronic Text Center*, University of Virginia Library, <http://etext.lib.virginia.edu/subjects/Women-Writers.html>.

Critical Review, 1793, 1799, 1803.

Darwin, E., *Zoönomia; or, The Laws of Organic Life* (London: 1794–96), vol. I.

Dear Miss Heber: An 18th Century Correspondence, ed. F. Bamford with introductions by G. and S. Sitwell (London: Constable, 1936).

de la Barre, F.P., *Three Cartesian Feminist Treatises*, ed. M.M. Welch, trans. V. Bosley (Chicago: University of Chicago Press, 2002).

Disney, John, "An ARRANGED CATALOGUE of the Several Publications which have appeared relation to the enlargement of the Toleration of PROTESTANT-DISSENTING-MINISTERS; and the Repeal of the Corporation and Test acts: with reference to the Agitation of those Questions in Parliament, from the Year

M.DCC.LXXII, to M.DCC.XC, Inclusive," (St. Paul's Church Yard: Joseph Johnson, 1790).

————, *The Works Theological, Medical, Political, and Miscellaneous of John Jebb, with Memoirs of the Life of the Author by John Disney* (London: T. Cadell, J. Johnson, J. Stockdale, 1787).

Dyer, G., *Complaint of the Poor People of England* 2nd edn (London: J. Ridgway and H.D. Symonds, 1793).

————, *Memoirs of the Life and Writings of Robert Robinson* ... (London: G.G. and J. Robinson, 1796).

————, *Poems* (London: J. Johnson, 1792).

Enfield, W., *Biographical sermons: or, a series of discourses on the principal characters in Scripture* (1777).

————, *The History of Philosophy: from the earliest times to the beginning of the present century: drawn up from Brucker's Historia Critica Philosophiae*, 2 vols (London: J. Johnson, 1791).

The English Review, 1793.

European Magazine, 1803.

Frend, W., *Peace and Union recommended to the associated bodies of republican and anti-republicans* (St. Ives: printed for the author, by P.C. Croft, 1793).

Godwin & Mary: Letters of William Godwin and Mary Wollstonecraft, ed. R.M. Wardle, (Lincoln and London: University of Nebraska Press, 1967).

Godwin, W., *An Enquiry concerning Political Justice, and its Influence on General Virtue and Happiness*, ed. M. Philp. *Political and Philosophical Writings of William Godwin*, vol. 3 (London: Pickering and Chatto, 1993).

————, *Collected Novels and Memoirs of William Godwin*, ed. M. Philp (London: William Pickering, 1992).

————, *Fleetwood: Or, the New Man of Feeling*, ed. G. Handwerk and A.A. Markley (Peterborough, ON: Broadview Press, 2001).

[————], "The Law of Parliament in the Present Situation of Great Britain Considered," *Enlightenment and Dissent*, 20 (2001):194–225.

————, *Memoirs of the Author of A Vindication of the Rights of Woman*, ed. P. Clemit and G.L. Walker (Peterborough, ON: Broadview Press, 2001).

[————], "Reflexions on the Late Consequences of His Majesty's Recovery from His Late Indisposition," *Enlightenment and Dissent*, 20 (2001): 228–48.

————, *Things as they are; or, the Adventures of Caleb Williams*, 1794, ed. M. Hindle (London: Penguin Books, 1987).

Hackney New College Sermons and Reports (London, 1786–91).

Hall, R., *An Apology for the Freedom of the Press, and for General Liberty*...(London: G.G. and J. Robinson, 1793).

Hamilton, E., *Letters on Education* (Bath: R. Crutwell for G.G. & J. Robinson, 1801).

————, *Memoirs of Modern Philosophers*, ed. C. Grogan (Peterborough, ON: Broadview Press, 2000).

————, *Translations of the Letters of a Hindoo Rajah*, ed. Perkins, P. and Russell, S. (Peterborough, ON: Broadview Press, 1999).

Hartley, D., *Observation on man, his frame, his duty, and his expectations. In two parts...; to which are now added notes and additions to the second part; translated from the German of the Rev. Andrew Herman Pistorius*, (London: Johnson, 1791).

[Hays, M.], "Advertisement to the Reader," *Appeal to the Men of Great Britain in Behalf of Women* (London, 1798).

————, *Analytical Review*, 25 (January 1797): 25–6.

————, "Are Mental Talents Productive of Happiness?" as "M.H." *Monthly Magazine*, 3 (1797): 358–60.

[————], "Art. XL. Translation of the Letters of a Hindoo Rajah; written previous to, and during the Period of his Residence in England," *Analytical Review*, (October 1796): 429.

————, *The Brothers; or, Consequences: A Story of What Happens Every Day; Addressed to that Most Useful Part of the Community, the Labouring Poor* (London: Button and Son, 1815).

[————], "Cursory Remarks on *An Enquiry into the Expediency and Propriety of Public or Social Worship*: Inscribed to Gilbert Wakefield, B.A., Late Fellow of Jesus-College, Cambridge. By EUSEBIA," 2nd edn (London: J. Deighton, 1792).

————, "Defence of Helvetius," as "M.H." *Monthly Magazine*, 3 (1797): 26–8.

————, *Female Biography; or, Memoirs of Illustrious and Celebrated Women of All Ages and Countries* (London: R. Phillips, 1803).

————, *Harry Clinton; or, a Tale of Youth* (London: Johnson, 1804).

————, *Historical Dialogues for Young Persons* (London: Johnson, 1806–1808).

[————], *History of England, from the Earliest Records, to the Peace of Amiens: in a series of Letters to a Young Lady at School*, 3 vols (London: Phillips, 1806).

————, "Improvements Suggested in Female Education," as "M.H." *Monthly Magazine*, (March 1797): 94.

[————], "Letter from 'A Woman' on the Talents of Women," *Monthly Magazine*, 2 (November 1796): 784–7.

[————], "Letter from M.H.," *Monthly Magazine*, 1 (June 1796): 385–6.

————, *Letters and Essays, Moral, and Miscellaneous*, 1793, ed. G. Luria (New York: Garland, 1974).

————, *Memoirs of Emma Courtney*, 1796, 2 vols, ed. G. Luria (New York: Garland, 1974).

————, *Memoirs of Emma Courtney*, ed. M.L. Brooks (Peterborough, ON: Broadview Literary Texts, 2000).

[————], "Memoirs of Wollstonecraft," *Annual Necrology for 1797–98* (London: Phillips, 1800).

[————], as "M.H." *Monthly Magazine,* 3 (May 1797): 358–60.

[————], "Obituary of Mary Wollstonecraft," *The Monthly Magazine*, 4 (September 1797), 231–33.

————, "On Novel-Writing," *Monthly Magazine*, 4 (September 1797): 180.

[————], "M.H." "Remarks on Dr. Reid on Insanity," *Monthly Magazine*, 9 (1800): 523–4.

[————], "Reply to J.T. on Helvetius," as "M.H." *Monthly Magazine*, 1 (June 1796): 385–7.

————, *The Victim of Prejudice*, ed. E. Ty (Peterborough, ON: Broadview Press, 1996).

Jardine, A., *Letters from Barbary, France, Spain, Portugal by a Soldier* (London: G. Cadwell, 1788).

Johnson, S., *The Rambler*, in W.J. Bate and A.B. Strauss (eds), *Yale Edition of the Works of Samuel Johnson* (New Haven: Yale University Press, 1969), vol. 3.

Jump, H., *Lives of the Great Romantics III: Godwin, Wollstonecraft & Mary Shelley by their Contemporaries*, vol. 2, ed. H. Jump (London: Pickering & Chatto, 1999).

Kant, I., *Observations on the Feeling of the Beautiful and Sublime* (1764).

Kell, E., "Memoir of Mary Hays: with some unpublished letters addressed to her by Robert Robinson, of Cambridge, and others," *The Christian Reformer*, CXXIX/XI (1844): 943–4.

Law, W., *A Serious Call to a Devout and Holy Life* (1728), in D.A. Johnson, *Women in English Religion, 1700–1925, Studies in Women and Religion* (New York: The Edwin Mellen Press, 1983), vol. 10, pp. 22–40.

Le Faye, D., ed., *Jane Austen's Letters* (New York: Oxford University Press, 1995).

Lloyd, C., *Edmund Oliver* (Bristol: J. Cottle, 1798).

Lofft, C., *Observations on Mrs. Macaulay's History of England, (lately published) from the Revolution to the Resignation of Sir Robert Walpole. In a Letter Addressed to that Lady* (London: Edward and Charles Dilly, 1778).

The London Review, 1803.

The Letters of Charles and Mary Lamb, ed. E.W. Marrs, Jr. (Ithaca: Cornell University Press, 1975).

Lindsey, T., *A Farewell Address to the Parishioners of Catterick* (London: J. Johnson, 1774).

————, "*A SERMON* preached at the Opening of the Chapel in Essex House, Essex-Street ... April 17, 1774," *Conversations on Christian Idolatry* (London: J. Johnson, 1791).

Manning, T., *Letters of Thomas Manning to Charles Lamb*, ed. G.A. Anderson (London: Secker, 1925).

Meadley, G.W., *Memoirs of Mrs. Jebb* (London: T. Davison, [1812]).

Memoirs, Miscellanies and Letters of the Late Lucy Aikin, ed. P.H. Le Breton (London: Longman, Green, Longman, Roberts and Green, 1864).

Monthly Magazine, 1796, 1797, 1798, 1803.

Monthly Review, 1797, 1804.

More, H., *Strictures on the Modern System of Female Education*, 1799, ed. G. Luria (New York: Garland Publishing, 1974).

New Annual Register, 1793.

New Letters of Robert Southey, 2 vols, ed. K. Curry (New York: Columbia University Press, 1965).

The Parliamentary Register; or History of the Proceedings and Debates of the House of Commons (London: J. Debrett, 1790), vol. XXVII.

Polwhele, R., *The Unsex'd Females: A Poem, Addressed to the Author of the Pursuits of Literature*, 1798, ed. G. Luria (New York: Garland Publishing, 1974).

Priestley, J. *The History and Present State of Electricity: with original experiments* (London: J. Dodsley, J. Johnson and B. Davenport, and T. Cadell, 1767).

———, *Letters to a Young Man, occasioned by Mr. Wakefield's Essay on Public Worship* (London: J. Johnson, 1792).

———, *Life and Correspondence of Joseph Priestley, LL.D., F.R.S., & C.*, ed. J.T. Rutt (London: R. Hunter, 1831).

Robinson, M., *A Letter to the Women of England and The Natural Daughter*, ed. S.M. Setzer (Peterborough, ON: Broadview Press, 2003).

Robinson, R., *A Political Catechism* (London: printed for J. Buckland; C. Dilly; J. Mathews; J. Debrett; and W. Lepard, 1782).

———, *Arcana, or the Principles of the Late Petitioners to Parliament* (Cambridge: Fletcher & Hodson, 1774).

———, *History of Baptism*, (London: T. Knott, 1790).

———, "Memoirs of the Reformation in France, and of the Life of the Rev. James Saurin, The Preface to the First Volume of a Translation of Saurin's Sermons," *Miscellaneous Works of Robert Robinson*, ed. B. Flower (Harlow: B. Flower, 1807), vol. I, pp. 1–63.

———, *Select Works of the Rev. Robert Robinson, of Cambridge, Edited, with Memoir, by the Rev. William Robinson*, 1772 (London: J. Heaton, 1861).

———, *Slavery Inconsistent with the Spirit of Christianity*, 1786. (Baltimore: Abner Neal, 1819).

Roland, Madame Manon, *An Appeal to Impartial Posterity, by Citizenness Roland, Wife of the Minister of the Home Department; or, A Collection of Pieces Written by her during her Confinement in the Prisons of the Abbey, and St. Pélagie. Translated from the French*, 2 vols (London: J. Johnson, 1795).

Rousseau, J-J., *Emile*, ed. P.D. Jimack, trans. B. Foxley (London: J.M. Dent, 1993).

———, *La Nouvelle Heloise: Julie, or the New Eloise. Letters of two lovers, inhabitants of a small town at the foot of the alps*, trans. and abridged J.H. McDowell (University Park: The Pennsylvania State University Press, 1968).

Search, E., [Tucker, Abraham], *The Light of Nature Pursued* (1768–78).

Seward, T., *A Collection of Poems in Six Volumes. By Several Hands. With notes*, ed. R. Dodsley (London: J. Dodsley, 1782), vol. II, with a new Introduction, Notes, and Indices by M.F. Suarez, S.J. (London: Routledge/Thoemmes Press, 1997).

Smith, C., *Desmond*, ed. A. Blank and J. Todd (Peterborough, ON: Broadview Press, 2001).

Southey, R., *Life and Correspondence of Robert Southey*, ed. Rev. C.C. Southey (New York: Harper and Bros, 1851).

Thomas, D.O., ed., "John Disney's Diary. I January 1783–17 May 1784," *Enlightenment and Dissent*, 21 (2002): 42–127.

Thompson, W., and Wheeler, A.D., *Appeal of One Half of the Human Race, Women, against the pretensions of the other half, Men, to retain them in political and thence in civil and domestic slavery, in reply to a paragraph of Mr. Mill's celebrated article on Government*, 1825 (New York: Source Book Press, 1970).

Thomson, J., "Spring," *The Seasons* (Yorkshire: Scolar Press, 1970), p. 52.

Trollope, A., *The Way We Live Now* (1875) *Project Gutenberg*, <http://www.gutenberg.org/etext/5231>.

Vives, J.L., *On the Education of a Christian Woman: A Sixteenth-Century Manual*, ed. and trans. C. Fantazzi (Chicago: University of Chicago Press, 2000).

Wakefield, G., "A General Reply to the Arguments Against the Enquiry into Public Worship," 1792.

———, *Memoirs of the Life of Gilbert Wakefield, B.A. … in two volumes. Vol. I. Written by Himself, A new edition, with his latest corrections and notes by the editors, To which is subjoined, An Appendix of Original Letters* (London: J. Johnson, 1804).

Walker, G., F.R.S., *The Dissenter's Plea: or the Appeal of the Dissenters to the justice, the honour, and the religion of the Kingdom, against the Test Laws* (Birmingham: Printed by J. Thompson and sold by J. Johnson, 1790).

Wedd, A.F., ed., *The Fate of the Fenwicks* (London: Methuen & Co., 1927).

———, "The Story of Mary Hays," *The Love-Letters of Mary Hays (1779–1780)* (London: Methuen & Co., Ltd., 1925).

Wollstonecraft, M., *A Vindication of the Rights of Woman, The Vindications*, ed. E.L. Macdonald and K. Scherf (Peterborough, ON: Broadview Press, 1997).

———, *The Collected Letters of Mary Wollstonecraft*, ed. J. Todd (New York: Columbia University Press, 2003).

———, *Mary, a Fiction*, 1788, ed. G. Luria (New York: Garland Publishing, 1974).

———, "Review of Hester Lynch Piozzi's *Observations and Reflection, made in the Course of a Journey through France, Italy and Germany* (1789)," *Analytical Review*, IV (1789): 127.

———, *The Works of Mary Wollstonecraft*, 7 vols, ed. J. Todd and M.L. Butler (London: Pickering and Chatto, 1989).

Wordsworth, W., *THE PRELUDE,* "BOOK THIRTEENTH," "IMAGINATION AND TASTE, HOW IMPAIRED AND RESTORED (concluded)," *The Complete Poetical Works* (London, 1888) *Bartleby.com, Inc.,* <http://www.bartleby.com/145/>.

Worthington, H., "Wednesday the 6th of May, 1789, At the Meeting-house in the Old Jewry, London, to the supporters of a New Academical Institution among Protestant Dissenters," (London: printed by H. Goldney, for T. Cadell; and J. Johnson, 1789).

Secondary Sources

Addicott, Len, "Introduction," *Church Book: St Andrew's Street Baptist Church, Cambridge 1720–1832* (London: Baptist Historical Society, 1991), pp. i–xxxii.

Akkerman, Tjitske and Stuurman, S., eds, *Perspectives on Feminist Thought in European History: from the Middle Ages to the Present* (London: Routledge, 1998).

Barber, Elizabeth Wayland, *Woman's Work: The First 20,000 Years* (New York: W.W. Norton, 1994).

Barker-Benfield, G.J., *The Culture of Sensibility: Sex and Society in Eighteenth-Century Britain* (Chicago: University of Chicago Press, 1992).

Barker, Hannah, and Chalus, E., eds, *Gender in Eighteenth-Century England: Roles, Representations and Responsibilities* (London: Longman, 1997).

Binhammer, Katherine, "Thinking Gender with Sexuality in 1790's Feminist Thought," *Feminist Studies,* 28/3 (Fall 2002): 667–90.

———, "The Persistence of Reading: Governing Female Novel-Reading in *Memoirs of Emma Courtney* and *Memoirs of Modern Philosophers*," *Eighteenth-Century Life,* 27/2 (Spring 2003): 1–22.

Bodenheimer, Rosemarie, *The Real Life of Mary Ann Evans: George Eliot, Her Letters and Fiction* (Ithaca: Cornell University Press, 1994).

Booth, Alison, *How to Make it as a Woman: Collective Biographical History from Victoria to the Present* (Chicago: University of Chicago Press, 2004).

Bour, Isabelle, "Sensibilité et Répétition dans les Romans Revolutionnaires de Mary Hays," *Études Anglaises,* 51/2 (1998): 143–55.

Bradley, James E., "Religion and Reform at the Polls: Nonconformity in Cambridge Politics, 1774–1784," *Journal of British Studies* 23 (Spring 1984): 55–78.

———, *Religion, Revolution, and English Radicalism: Nonconformity in Eighteenth-Century Politics and Society* (Cambridge: Cambridge University Press, 1990).

Braithwaite, Helen, *Romanticism, Publishing and Dissent: Joseph Johnson and the Cause of Liberty* (Houndmills: Palgrave Macmillan, 2003).

Brekke, Tone, "Authoring 'The Illustrious Dead': Godwin's Memoirs as Paratext," Centre for Romantic Studies, University of Bristol, Panel Discussion, 24 July 2004.

Brewer, John, *Pleasures of the Imagination: English Culture in the Eighteenth Century* (New York: HarperCollins, 1997).

Brooks, Marilyn, "Priestley's Plan for a 'Continually Improving' Translation of the Bible," *Enlightenment and Dissent*, 15 (1996): 89–106.

Brown, Marshall, "Romanticism and Enlightenment," in Stuart Curran (ed.), *The Cambridge Companion to British Romanticism* (Cambridge: Cambridge University Press, 1993), p. 38.

Butler, Marilyn L., *Jane Austen and the War of Ideas* (Oxford: Clarendon Press, 1987), 2nd edn.

———, *Romantics, Rebels and Reactionaries: English Literature and its Background 1760–1830* (Oxford: Oxford Paperbacks, 1982).

Byrne, Paula, *Perdita: the Life of Mary Robinson* (London: HarperCollins, 2005).

Cameron, Kenneth N., ed., *Shelley and his Circle, 1773–1882* (Harvard: Harvard University Press, 1970), vol. I.

Cassirer, Ernst, *The Philosophy of the Enlightenment*, trans. Fritz C.A. Koelln and James P. Pettegrove (Boston: Beacon Press, 1964).

Chernock, Arianne, "Champions of the Fair Sex: Men and the Creation of Modern British Feminism, 1788–1800," Ph.D. Diss. (UC Berkeley, 2004).

Clark, Anna, *Scandal: The Sexual Politics of the British Constitution* (Princeton: Princeton University Press, 2004).

———, "Queen Caroline and the Sexual Politics of Popular Culture in London, 1820," *Representations* (Summer 1990): 47–68.

Clarke, Norma, *The Rise and Fall of the Woman of Letters* (London: Pimlico, 2004).

Clemit, P., "Editor's Introduction," in P. Clemit (ed.), (with the assistance of A.A. Markley) *Mary Shelley's Literary Lives and Other Writings*, 4 vols (London: Pickering & Chatto, 2002).

———, "Godwin, Women, and 'The Collision of Mind with Mind,'" *The Wordsworth Circle*, XXV/2 (Spring 2004): 72–6.

———, *The Godwinian Novel: The Rational Fictions of Godwin, Brockden Brown, Mary Shelley* (Oxford: Oxford University Press, 1993).

———, "Introduction," *Lives of the Great Romantics: Godwin, Wollstonecraft & Mary Shelley by their Contemporaries* (London: Pickering & Chatto, 1999), vol. I.

———, "Philosophical Anarchism in the Schoolroom: William Godwin's Juvenile Library, 1805–1825," *Biblion: The Bulletin of The New York Public Library*, 9/1–2 (Fall 2000/Spring 2001): 44–70.

———, "Two Pamphlets on the Regency Crisis by William Godwin," *Enlightenment and Dissent*, 20 (2001): 185–93.

————, "William Godwin and James Watt's Copying Machine: Wet-Transfer Copies in the Abinger Papers," *Bodleian Library Record*, 18:5 (April 2005).

Clery, E.J., "Bluestocking 'Feminism' and the Fame Game," *British Journal for Eighteenth-Century Studies*, 28/2 (Autumn 2005): 277–8.

Cole, G.A., "Doctrine, Dissent and the Decline of Paley's Reputation 1805–1825," *Enlightenment and Dissent*, 6 (1987): 19–30.

Corfield, Penelope J. and Evans C., eds, *Youth and Revolution in the 1790s: Letters of William Pattisson, Thomas Amyot and Henry Crabb Robinson* (Phoenix Mill: Alan Sutton Publishing, Ltd., 1996).

Craciun, Adriana, and Lokke K.E., eds, *Rebellious Hearts: British Women Writers and the French Revolution*, (Albany State: University of New York Press, 2001).

Dart, Gregory, *Rousseau, Robespierre and English Romanticism* (Cambridge: Cambridge University Press, 1999).

De Montluzin, Emily Lorraine, *The Anti-Jacobins, 1798–1800: The Early Contributors to the* Anti-Jacobin Review (New York: St Martin's Press, 1988).

De Palacio, Jean, "La 'Fortune' de Godwin en France: Le Cas d'Elizabeth Hamilton,"*Revue de Littérature Comparée*, 41 (1967): 326–9.

Deutscher, Penelope, "'Imperfect Discretion': Intervention into the history of philosophy by twentieth-century French women philosophers," *Hypatia*, 15/2 (Spring 2000): 160–80.

Ditchfield, G.M., "*A History of the University of Cambridge* — Review," *English Historical Review* (April 1999).

————, "Friends of Dr. Williams's Library 51st Lecture: Theophilus Lindsey: From Anglican to Unitarian," (1998).

————, *George III: An Essay in Monarchy* (Houndmills: Palgrave Macmillan, 2002).

————, "'How Narrow will the limits of this Toleration appear?' Dissenting petitions to Parliament, 1772–1773," in S. Taylor and D. Wykes (eds) "Parliament and Dissent," (Parliamentary History Trust, Edinburgh University Press, 2005), pp. 91–106.

————, "Theophilus Lindsey and the Cause of Protestantism in eighteenth-century Britain," (London: Dr Williams's Trust and Library, forthcoming, 2006).

Dixon, Thomas, *From Passions to Emotions: The Creation of a Secular Psychological Category* (Cambridge: Cambridge University Press, 2003).

Donoghue, Frank, *The Fame Machine: Book Reviewing and Eighteenth-Century Literary Careers* (Stanford: Stanford University Press, 1996).

Doody, Margaret Anne, *La femme en Angleterre et dans les colonies américaines aux XVIIe et XVIIIe siècles* (Paris: Actes du Colloque tenir à Paris, Université de Lille III, 1975).

————, *The True Story of the Novel* (New Brunswick: Rutgers University Press, 1996).

Earle, Rebecca, *Epistolary Selves: Letters and Letter Writers, 1600–1945* (Aldershot: Ashgate, 1999).

Fara, Patricia, *An Entertainment for Angels: Electricity in the Enlightenment* (Cambridge: Icon Books, 2002).

———, *Pandora's Breeches: Women, Science and Power in the Enlightenment* (London: Pimlico, 2004).

———, *Sympathetic Attractions: Magnetic Practices, Beliefs, and Symbolism in Eighteenth-Century England* (Princeton: Princeton University Press, 1996).

Favret, Mary A., *Romantic Correspondence: Women, Politics and the Fiction of Letters* (Cambridge: Cambridge University Press, 1992).

Gilbert, Sandra M., and Gubar, S., *The Madwoman in the Attic: The Woman Writer and the Nineteenth-Century Literary Imagination* (Yale: Yale University Press, 1979).

Gleadle, Kathryn, "British Women and Radical Politics in the Late Nonconformist Enlightenment, c. 1780–1830," in Amanda Vickery (ed.), *Women, Privilege, and Power: British Politics, 1750 to the Present* (Stanford: Stanford University Press, 2001), p. 139.

———, *The Early Feminists: Radical Unitarians and the Emergence of the Women's Rights Movement, 1831–51* (New York: St Martin's Press, 1995).

Goodwin, Albert, *The Friends of Liberty: The English Democratic Movement in the Age of the French Revolution* (Cambridge, MA: Harvard University Press, 1979).

Gordon, Lyndall, *Mary Wollstonecraft: A New Genus* (London: Little Brown, 2005).

Graham, Jenny, *Revolutionary in Exile: The Emigration of Joseph Priestley to America 1794–1804* (Philadelphia: The American Philosophical Society, 1995).

Gray, Arthur and Brittain, F., *A History of Jesus College Cambridge* (London: Heinemann, 1960).

Grenby, M.O., *The Anti-Jacobin Novel: British Conservatism and the French Revolution* (Cambridge: Cambridge University Press, 2001).

Grogan, Claire, "The Politics of Seduction in British Fiction of the 1790s: The Female Reader and Julie, ou La nouvelle Héloïse," *Eighteenth-Century Fiction*, 11/4 (July 1999): 459–76.

Grundy, Isobel, ed., "Introduction," *Secresy; or, The Ruin on the Rock* (Peterborough, ON: Broadview Press, 1994), pp. 10–20.

Gunther-Canada, Wendy, *Rebel Writer: Mary Wollstonecraft and Enlightenment Politics* (DeKalb: Northern Illinois University Press, 2001).

Haakonssen, Knud, ed., *Enlightenment and Religion: Rational Dissent in Eighteenth-Century Britain.* (Cambridge: Cambridge University Press, 1996).

Hill, Bridget, *The Republican Virago: The Life and Times of Catharine Macaulay, Historian* (Oxford: Clarendon Press, 1992).

Hoagwood, Terence Allan, *Introduction to Victim of Prejudice by Mary Hays* (Delmar, NY Scholars, 1990).

How, James, *Epistolary Spaces: English Letter Writing from the Foundation of the Post Office to Richardson's Clarissa* (Aldershot: Ashgate, 2003).

Israel, Jonathan I., *Radical Enlightenment: Philosophy and the Making of Modernity, 1650–1750* (New York: Oxford University Press, 2001).

Issitt, John, "Introducing Sir Richard Phillips," *Paradigm*, 26 (October, 1998).

Jacobus, Mary, *Psychoanalysis and the Scene of Reading* (Oxford: Oxford University Press, 1999).

Jenkinson, Sally L., ed., *Bayle: Political Writings.* (Cambridge: Cambridge University Press, 2000).

———, "The Public Context of Heresy," in John Christian Laursen (ed.), *Histories of Heresy in Early Modern Europe: For, Against, and Beyond Persecution and Toleration* (New York: Palgrave, 2002), pp. 119–38.

Jewson, C.B., *The Jacobin City: a Portrait of Norwich in its Reaction to the French Revolution 1788–1802* (Glasgow: Blackie & Son, 1975).

Johnson, Claudia L., *Equivocal Beings: Politics, Gender, and Sentimentality in the 1790s: Wollstonecraft, Radcliffe, Burney, Austen* (Chicago: The University of Chicago Press, 1995).

———, *Jane Austen: Women, Politics, and the Novel* (Chicago: University of Chicago Press, 1988).

Johnson, Dale A., *Studies in Women and Religion* (New York: The Edwin Mellen Press, 1983).

Johnson, Patricia J., "Constructions of Venus in Ovid's Metamorphoses V," *Arethusa*, 29/1 (1996): 125–49.

Jones, Vivien, "The Death of Mary Wollstonecraft," *British Journal for Eighteenth-Century Studies*, 20/2 (Autumn 1997): 187–205.

———, "Placing Jemima: Women Writers of the 1790s and the Eighteenth-Century Prostitution Narrative," *Women's Writing*, 4/2 (1997): 201–20.

———, "'The Tyranny of the Passions': Feminism and Heterosexuality in the Fiction of Wollstonecraft and Hays," in Sally Ledger, Josephine McDonagh, and Jane Spencer (eds), *Political Gender: Texts and Contexts* (London: Harvester Wheatsheaf, 1994), pp. 173–88.

Jump, Harriet, "Introduction" in Mullan, John, ed., *Lives of the Great Romantics II* (London: Pickering & Chatto, 1999), p. x.

———, ed., *Wollstonecraft. Lives of the Great Romantics III*, vol. 2 (London: Pickering and Chatto, 1999).

Laqueur, T.W., "The Queen Caroline Affair: Politics as Art in the Reign of George IV," *Journal of Modern History*, 54 (1982): 417–66.

Keane, Angela, *Women Writers and the English Nation in the 1790s: Romantic Belongings* (Cambridge: Cambridge University Press, 2000).

Keeble, N.H., *The Literary Culture of Nonconformity in Later Seventeenth-Century England* (Athens: The University of Georgia Press, 1987).

Keen, Paul, "A Revolution in Female Manners," in Paul Keen (ed), *Revolutions in Romantic Literature: An Anthology of Print Culture, 1780–1832,* (Peterborough, ON: Broadview Press, 2004), p. 235.

———, *The Crisis of Literature in the 1790s: Print Culture and the Public Sphere* (Cambridge: Cambridge University Press, 1999).

Kelly, Gary, *English Fiction of the Romantic Period, 1789–1830* (London: Longman Literature in English Series, 1989).

———, "Mary Hays," in Gary Kelly and Edd Applegate (eds), *Dictionary of Literary Biography 158: British Reform Writers, 1789–1832* (Detroit: Bruccoli Clark Layman, 1996), pp. 124–30.

———, *Women, Writing, and Revolution 1790–1827* (Oxford: Clarendon Press, 1993).

Klancher, Jon, *The Making of English Reading Audiences, 1790–1832* (Madison: University of Wisconsin Press, 1987).

Knight, Frida, *University Rebel: The Life of William Frend (1757–1841)* (London: Victor Gollancz, Ltd., 1971).

Knox, Kevin C., "'The Revolting Propositions of Newtonian Mechanicks': Natural Philosophy and the Trial of William Frend," *Enlightenment and Dissent,* 17 (1998): 126–53.

Kramnick, Isaac, *Bourgeois Radicalism and English Dissent: Political Ideology in Late Eighteenth-Century England and America* (Ithaca: Cornell University Press, 1990).

Kucich, Greg, "Mary Shelley's *Lives* and the Reengendering of History" in Betty T. Bennett and Stuart Curran (eds), *Mary Shelley in Her Times* (Baltimore and London: The Johns Hopkins University Press, 2000).

Laursen, John Christian, "The Beneficial Lies Controversy in the Huguenot Netherlands, 1705–31: an unpublished manuscript at the root of the *cas Saurin,*" *Studies On Voltaire & The Eighteenth Century,* 319 (1994): 96.

———, "Brucker in English and the Uses of the History of Philosophy in the Revolutionary Era," Paper presented at "Construction of the Past in Modern Political Philosophy, The Conference for the Study of Political Thought," Colorado Springs, 9–11 November 2001.

———, and Nederman, C.J., eds, *Beyond the Persecuting Society: Religious Toleration Before the Enlightenment* (Philadelphia: University of Pennsylvania Press, 1998).

Le Doeuff, Michèle, *The Sex of Knowing,* trans. Kathryn Hamer and Lorraine Code (New York: Routledge, 2003).

Lincoln, Anthony, *Some Political and Social Ideas of English Dissent 1763–1800* (Cambridge: Cambridge University Press, 1938).

Logan, Peter Melville, *Nerves and Narratives: A Cultural History of Hysteria in Nineteenth-Century British Prose* (Berkeley: University of California Press, 1997).

Looser, Devoney, *British Women Writers and the Writing of History, 1670–1820* (Baltimore: The Johns Hopkins University Press, 2000).

Luria, Gina, "Mary Hays: A Critical Biography," Unpublished Ph.D. Diss. (New York University, 1972).

———, "Mary Hays's Letters & Manuscripts," *Signs: Journal of Women in Culture and Society*, 3/2 (Winter 1977): 524–30.

Marcus, Laura, *Auto/biographical Discourses: Criticism, Theory, Practice* (Manchester: Manchester University Press, 1994).

Marshall, Peter H., *William Godwin* (New Haven: Yale University Press, 1984).

Mazzeo, Tilar J., "General Editor's Introduction," in Nora Crook (ed.), *Mary Shelley's Literary Lives and Other Writings*, 4 vols (London: Pickering & Chatto, 2002).

McCarthy, William, and Kraft, E., *Anna Laetitia Barbauld: Selected Poetry and Prose* (Peterborough, ON: Broadview Press, 2002).

McEvoy, J.G., "Perspectives on Priestley's Science," *Enlightenment & Dissent*, 19 (2000): 63–4.

McFarland, Thomas, *Originality & Imagination* (Baltimore: The Johns Hopkins University Press, 1985).

McLachlan, H. John, "Mary Priestley: A Woman of Character," in A. Truman Schwartz and John G. McEvoy (eds), *Motion Towards Perfection: The Achievement of Joseph Priestley* (Boston: Skinner House Books, 1990), p. 251.

Mellor, Anne K., *Romanticism & Gender* (New York: Routledge, 1993).

Mercer, Matthew, "Dissenting Academies and The Education of the Laity, 1750–1850," *History of Education*, 30/1 (2001): 35–58.

Miller, Jim, *Rousseau: Dreamer of Democracy* (New Haven: Yale University Press, 1984).

Moskal, Jeanne, and Wooden, S.R., eds, *Teaching British Women Writers 1750–1900* (New York: Peter Lang Publishing, 2005).

Newlyn, Lucy, *Reading, Writing, and Romanticism: The Anxiety of Reception* (Oxford: Oxford University Press, 2000).

Newman, Gerald, *The Rise of English Nationalism: A Cultural History 1740–1830* (New York: St Martin's Press, 1997).

Nye, Andrea, "A Woman's Thought or a Man's Discipline? The Letters of Abelard and Heloise," *Hypatia*, 7/3 (Summer 1992): 6.

Orr, Clarissa Campbell, *Queenship in Britain 1660–1837: Royal Patronage, Court Culture and Dynastic Politics* (Manchester: Manchester University Press, 2002).

———, *Wollstonecraft's Daughters: Womanhood in England and France 1780–1920* (Manchester: Manchester University Press, 1996).

Oxford English Dictionary Online, Oxford University Press, <http://dictionary. oed.com/cgi/display/50215528>.

Page, Anthony, "'A great politicianess': Ann Jebb, Rational Dissent and politics in late eighteenth-century Britain," forthcoming.

————, *John Jebb and the Enlightenment Origins of British Radicalism* (Westport: Praeger, 2003).

————, "Review of Richard C. Allen's *Hartley on Human Nature*," *Enlightenment and Dissent*, 20 (2001): 126–38.

Paul, Charles Kegan, *William Godwin: His Friends and Contemporaries* (London: H.S. King, 1876).

Pearson, Jacqueline, "Women Reading, Reading Women," in Helen Wilcox (ed.), *Women and Literature in Britain 1500–1700* (Cambridge: Cambridge University Press, 1996), pp. 80–99.

Perkins, Pamela and Russell, S., "Introduction," in Elizabeth Hamilton, *Translations of the Letters of a Hindoo Rajah* (Peterborough, ON: Broadview Press, 1999), p. 15.

Phillips, M., and Tompkinson, W.S., *English Women in Life and Letters* (Oxford: H.P. Milford, 1926).

Philp, Mark, *Godwin's Political Justice* (Ithaca: Cornell University Press, 1986).

Plant, Helen, *Unitarianism, philanthropy and feminism in York, 1782–1821: the career of Catherine Cappe*, Borthwick Paper No. 103 (Borthwick: Borthwick Institute of Historical Research, 2003).

Pointon, Marcia, *Strategies for Showing: Women, Possession, and Representation in English Visual Culture 1665–1800* (New York: Oxford University Press, 1997).

Pollin, Burton R., "Mary Hays on Women's Rights in the Monthly Magazine," *Etudes Anglaises*, 24/3 (1971): 271–82.

Porter, Roy, *Enlightenment: Britain and the Creation of the Modern World* (London: The Penguin Press, 2000).

————, *Flesh in the Age of Reason* (London: Allen Lane, 2003).

Rajan, Tillotama, "Autonarration and Genotext in Mary Hays' Memoirs of Emma Courtney," *Studies in Romanticism*, 32/2 (Summer 1993): 149–76.

Reeves, Marjorie, *Pursuing the Muses: Female Education and Nonconformist Culture, 1700–1900* (London: Leicester University Press, 1997).

Reiman, Donald H., "Introduction," in Charles Lloyd, *Charles Lloyd, Poems on Various Subjects…* (New York: Garland Publishing, 1978).

Rendall, Jane, "Writing History for British Women: Elizabeth Hamilton and the *Memoirs of Agrippina*," in Clarissa Campbell Orr (ed.), *Wollstonecraft's Daughters: Womanhood in England and France 1780–1920* (Manchester: Manchester University Press, 1996), pp. 79–93.

Reynolds, Myra, *The Learned Lady in England 1650–1760*, 1920 (Gloucester, MA: Peter Magnolia, 1964).

Richards, Cynthia, "Revising History, 'Dumbing Down,' and Imposing Silence: The Female Biography of Mary Hays," *Eighteenth–Century Women, Studies in their Lives, Works, and Culture*, 3 (November 2003): 276.

Richardson, Alan, *British Romanticism and the Science of the Mind* (Cambridge: Cambridge University Press, 2001).

Riskin, Jessica, *Science in the Age of Sensibility: The Sentimental Empiricists of the French Enlightenment* (Chicago: University of Chicago Press, 2002).

Rivers, Isabel, *Reason, Grace, and Sentiment: The Study of the Language of Religion and Ethics in England, 1660–1780* (Cambridge: Cambridge University Press, 1990), vol. II.

Roe, Nicholas, ed., *Samuel Taylor Coleridge and the Sciences of Life* (Oxford: Oxford University Press, 2001).

———, *Wordsworth and Coleridge: The Radical Years* (Oxford: Clarendon Press, 1988).

Rogers, Katharine M., "The Contribution of Mary Hays," *Prose Studies*, 10/2 (September 1987): 131–42.

Rosenblatt, Helena, "The Christian Enlightenment," in Timothy Tackett and Stewart Brown (eds), *The Cambridge History of Christianity, vol VII: Enlightenment, Revolution and Reawakening (1660–1815)* (Cambridge: Cambridge University Press, 2006).

Ruether, Rosemary Radford, *Women-Church: Theology and Practice of Feminist Liturgical Communities* (San Francisco: Harper & Row, 1985).

Russell, Gillian, and Tuite, C., eds, *Romantic Sociability: Social Networks and Literary Culture in Britain 1770–1840* (Cambridge: Cambridge University Press, 2002).

Schiebinger, Londa, *The Mind Has No Sex? Women in the Origins of Modern Science* (Cambridge, MA: Harvard University Press, 1989).

Schneider, Ben Ross, *Wordsworth's Cambridge Education* (Cambridge: Cambridge University Press, 1957).

Searby, Peter, *A History of the University of Cambridge: Volume III, 1750–1870* (Cambridge: Cambridge University Press, 1998).

Seed, John, "Gentlemen Dissenters: The Social and Political Meanings of Rational Dissent in the 1770s and 1780s," *The Historical Journal*, 28/2 (June 1985): 324–5.

Sherman, Sandra, "The Law, Confinement, and Disruptive Excess in Hays' *The Victim of Prejudice*," *1650–1850: Ideas, Aesthetics, and Inquiries in the Early Modern Era* (New York: AMS Press, 1998), vol. 5.

Skedd, S.J., "More, Hannah (1745–1833)," *Oxford Dictionary of National Biography* (Oxford: Oxford University Press, 2004), p. 7.

Simonutti, Luisa, "Between Political Loyalty and Religious Liberty: Political Theory and Toleration in Huguenot Thought in the Epoch of Bayle," *History of Political Thought*, XVII/4 (Winter 1996): 535.

Smith, J.W. Ashley, *The Birth of Modern Education: The Contribution of the Dissenting Academies 1660–1800* (London: Independent Press, Ltd., 1954).

Smith, Tania, "The Rhetorical Education of Eighteenth-Century British Women Writers," Unpublished Ph.D. Diss. (The Ohio State University, 2002), pp. 267–85.

Spencer, Jane, *The Rise of the Woman Novelist: From Aphra Behn to Jane Austen* (Oxford: Blackwell, 1986).

Spender, Dale, *Mothers of the Novel: 100 Good Women Writers Before Jane Austen* (New York: Pandora, 1986).

Spongberg, Mary, *Writing Women's History Since the Renaissance* (Houndmills: Palgrave Macmillan, 2002).

St. Clair, William, *The Reading Nation in the Romantic Period* (Cambridge: Cambridge University Press, 2004).

Stott, Anne, *Hannah More: The First Victorian* (Oxford: Oxford University Press, 2003).

Tayler, Irene, and Luria, G., "Gender and Genre: Women in British Romantic Literature," in Marlene Springer (ed.), *What Manner of Women – Essays in English and American Life and Literature* (New York: New York University Press, 1977), pp. 98–123.

Taylor, Barbara, *Eve and the New Jerusalem: Socialism and Feminism in the Nineteenth Century* (New York: Pantheon Books, 1983).

————, "Feminists Versus Gallants: Manner and Morals in Enlightenment Britain," *Representations*, 87 (Summer 2004): 127.

————, *Mary Wollstonecraft and the Feminist Imagination* (Cambridge: Cambridge University Press, 2003).

————, "Mother-Haters and Other Rebels" *London Review of Books*, 24/1 (3 January 2002).

Taylor, Barbara, and Knott, S., eds, *Women, Gender and Enlightenment* (Houndmills: Palgrave Macmillan, 2005).

Tenger, Zeynep and Trolander, P., "The Politics of Literary Production: The Reaction to the French Revolution and the Transformation of the English Literary Periodical," *Studies in Eighteenth-Century Culture*, 24 (1995): 285.

Terry, Richard, "'In Pleasing Memory of All He Stole': Plagiarism and Literary Detraction, 1747–1785," in Paulina Kewes (ed.), *Plagiarism in Early Modern England* (Houndmills: Palgrave Macmillan, 2003), pp.181–200.

Thomas, D.O., "Preface and introduction to John Disney's Diary," *Enlightenment and Dissent*, 21 (2002): 1–41.

Todd, Janet, ed., *A Dictionary of British and American Women Writers 1660–1800* (Totowa, NJ: Rowman & Littlefield, 1987).

————, *Sensibility: An Introduction* (London: Methuen, 1986).

————, *Mary Wollstonecraft: A Revolutionary Life* (London: Weidenfeld & Nicolson, 2000).

————, *The Sign of Angellica: Women, Writing and Fiction, 1660–1800* (London: Virago, 1989).

Tompkins, J.M.S., *The Popular Novel in England 1770–1800* (London: Constable, 1932).

Thomas, D.O., "Preface and introduction to John Disney's Diary," *Enlightenment and Dissent*, 21(2002): 1–41.

Ty, Eleanor, "Female Philosophy Refunctioned: Elizabeth Hamilton's Parodic Novel," *Ariel: A Review of International English Literature*, 22/4 (October 1991): 111–29.

———, "The Imprisoned Female Body in Mary Hays' *The Victim of Prejudice*," in Linda Lang-Peralta (ed.), *Women, Revolution and the Novels of the 1790s* (East Lansing: Michigan State University Press, 1999), pp. 133–54.

———, "Mary Hays," in S. Serafin (ed.), *Dictionary of Literary Biography 142: Eighteenth-Century British Literary Biographers* (Detroit: Bruccoli Clark Layman, 1994), pp. 152–60.

———, *Unsex'd Revolutionaries: Five Women Novelists of the 1790s* (Toronto: University of Toronto Press, 1993).

Wahrman, Dror, "'Middle Class' Domesticity Goes Public: Gender, Class, and Politics from Queen Caroline to Queen Victoria," *The Journal of British Studies*, 32/4 (October 1993): 396–432.

Walker, Gina Luria, "'The Emancipated Mind': Robinson's *History of the Reformation in France* and Mary Hays's View of Censorship and Persecution," *Understandings of Censorship and Persecution in the Eighteenth-Century*, International Society for Eighteenth Century Studies Congress, The Clark Library, UCLA, 7 August 2003.

———, "Mary Hays (1759-1843): An Enlightened Quest," in Sarah Knott and Barbara Taylor (eds), *Women, Gender and Enlightenment* (Houndmills: Palgrave Macmillan, 2005), pp. 493–518.

———, "Mary Hays's 'Love Letters'" *Keats-Shelley Journal*, LI (2002): 94–115.

———, "'Sewing in the Next World': Mary Hays as Dissenting Autodidact in the 1780s," *Romanticism on the Net* 25 (February 2002): 45 pars, <http://users.ox.ac.uk/~scat0385/25walker.html>.

———, "The Two Marys: Hays Writes Wollstonecraft," *Romantic Circles* University of Maryland, 2002, <http://www.rc.umd.edu/features/features/ chambermusic>.

Wallace, Miriam L., "Mary Hays's 'Female Philosopher,'" *Rebellious Hearts: British Women Writers and the French Revolution* (Albany: State University of New York Press, 2001).

Waters, Mary A., *British Women Writers and the Profession of Literary Criticism, 1789–1832* (Houndmills: Palgrave Macmillan, 2004).

Watts, Ruth, *Gender, Power and the Unitarians in England 1760–1860* (London: Longman, 1998).

Watson, J.R., *The English Hymn: A Critical and Historical Study* (Oxford: Clarendon Press, 1997).

Watson, Nicola J., *Revolution and the Form of the British Novel, 1790–1825: Intercepted Letters, Interrupted Seductions* (Oxford: Clarendon Press, 1994).

Webb, R.K., "Religion," in Iain McCalman (ed.), *An Oxford Companion to the Romantic Age: British Culture, 1776–1832* (Oxford: Oxford University Press, 1999), pp. 93–101.

Wedd, Imogen, "Annie Frances Wedd," (unpublished MS, 2004).

Whelan, Ruth, "'Liberating the Bible from Patriarchy': Pouillain de la Barre's Feminist Hermeneutics," in Allison P. Coudert, Sarah Hutton, Richard H. Popkin, and Gordon M. Weinter (eds), *Judaeo-Christian Intellectual Culture in the Seventeenth Century* (Dordrecht: Kluwer Academic Publishers, 1999), pp. 119–43.

Whitehead, Barbara J., *Women's Education in Early Modern Europe: A History 1500–1800* (New York: Garland Press, 1999).

Winstanley, D.A., *Unreformed Cambridge: A Study of Certain Aspects of the University in the Eighteenth Century* (Cambridge: Cambridge University Press, 1935).

Wood, Marcus, "William Cobbett, John Thelwall, Radicalism, Racism and Slavery: A Study in Burkean Parodics," *Romanticism On the Net* 15 (August 1999), <http://users.ox.ac.uk/~scat0385/thelwall.html>.

Woolf, D.R., "A Feminine Past? Gender, Genre, and Historical Knowledge in England, 1500–1800," *American Historical Review* (June 1997): 667–77.

Wooten, David, "Helvétius: From Radical Enlightenment to Revolution," *Political Theory*, 28/3 (June 2000): 307–36.

Wykes, David L., "The Contribution of the Dissenting Academy to the Emergence of Rational Dissent," in Knud Haakonssen (ed.), *Enlightenment and Religion: Rational Dissent in eighteenth-century Britain* (Cambridge: Cambridge University Press, 1996), pp. 99–139.

Index

Abelard, 12, 13, 53
abolitionism, 36, 42, 97, 98, 165
Adams, Abigail, 107n48
Adams, John, 109n69
Addison, Joseph, 71, 79n31
aging, 227
Aikn, Anna, 90, 98; *see also* Barbauld,
    Anna
Aikn, John, 44, 57n37, 118, 164, 171,
    179n25, 181n40, 230–31,
    240n34, 245n8
Aikin, Lucy, 44–5, 57n37, 228–9
Akenside, Mark, 67, 181n40
Alderson, Amelia, 130n37, 149n4, 162,
    163, 164, 165, 167, 172,
    178n12, 178n13, 179n20,
    180n33, 181n48, 199, 205n3,
    212n94, 231, 240n30
Alexander, William, 240n32
"Amasia", 71, 72, 81n63–64, 81–2n63
America, 89
American Revolution, 22–3, 36, 98,
    109n69
Amory, Thomas, 240n32
Analytical Review, The, 74, 118,
    153n59, 188, 210n67
Hays's reviews for, 161, 165, 171, 173,
    182n60
    reviews of Hays's works, 74, 148,
    194–5, 197
    Wollstonecraft and, 74, 115
Annual Necrology for 1797–1978, 216
Annual Review, The, 243–4n67
anti-Catholicism, 29n27, 68
Anti-Jacobin Review, The, 148, 195,
    199, 200–201, 202, 203, 211n84
*Appeal to the Men of Great Britain in
    Behalf of Women*, 187, 195–7,
    197, 205–6n4, 208–9n43

Arabian Nights, The, 150, 153n64
Arianism, 37n1
Arnold, Matthew, 234
Arnold, Mrs., 228, 243–4n67
Askew, Anne, 41, 223, 242n45
Astell, Mary, 225
Augustine, Saint, 134, 244n75
Austen, Jane, 149, 156n98
    Mansfield Park, 57n39
    Northanger Abbey, 81n55
    Persuasion, 29n36, 102
    Sense and Sensibility, 102
autodidactism, 96, 101
    of Hays, 4, 35–6, 67
    of Robinson, 37
    women and, 5–6, 145
autonomy, female, 121; *see also*
    freedom
    chastity as a vehicle for, 33
    Hays on, 12, 27, 193–4, 222
    Hortensia as representation of, 100
    sexuality as a vehicle for, 14
    Wollstonecraft as an example of,
    222

Bacon, Francis, 55n25
Ballard, George, 222, 223, 225
Barbauld, Anna, 34, 44, 45, 46, 50, 51–
    2, 57n37, 74, 88, 89, 90, 96–7,
    98, 104n4, 130n37, 162, 164,
    168, 172, 178–9n17, 178n14,
    199, 228, 240n30, 243–4n67,
    245n78
Barbauld, Rochemont, 43, 98, 162,
    178n14
Barker-Benfield, G.J., 31n73
Barry, James, 130n37, 212n94
Baxter, Richard, 37
Bayle, 222, 223–4, 225, 240n29

in *Letters and Essays*, 74, 99, 102
*Letters Written During a Short
    Residence in Sweden, Norway,
    and Denmark*, 136, 150n18,
    150n21, 151n39
Mary, A Fiction, 81n56, 143, 194
More and, 94
as a mother, 221
Newington Green school and, 91
omission from *Female Biography*,
    224, 240n30
political activity of, 111, 114–15
Posthumous Works, 217–8
as a professional writer, 76–7n4
refutation of Rousseau's depiction
    of women, 100
reputation of, 115, 170, 209n45
response to Burke, 115
romantic life of, 120, 123–4, 142,
    146, 220–21
sexual life of, 120, 121, 123–4, 135
spirituality of, 218–19
suicide attempts of, 115, 123, 125,
    221
The Victim of Prejudice and, 192,
    193
A Vindication of the Rights of Men,
    80n39, 115

*A Vindication of the Rights of
    Woman*, 61–4, 66, 76n1, 77n14,
    78n26, 78n29, 79n35, 80n39,
    81n55, 99, 115, 165, 167–8,
    181n45, 195, 197, 201, 217,
    219–20, 226, 242n54
on women writers, 77–8n19
on women's education, 66–7
Wrongs of Woman, 41, 193, 194

women; *see also* sexuality, female
    autodidactism of, 5–6
    education of, 3, 4, 5–6, 8n18, 11,
        12, 20, 29n35, 29n39, 34, 44,
        64–7, 70–73, 75–6, 82n73, 90,
        95–6, 99, 118, 145, 161, 168–9,
        170, 182n54, 184n85, 193–4,
        196, 200–3, 208n34, 210–
        11n78, 243–4n67
    enlightenment of, 67, 73
    freedom of, 193–4
    intellectual history of, 4, 5–6, 7n5,
        90, 169, 220
    life-writing about, 2, 4, 169, 214,
        222–9, 240n32, 243n65
    Rational Dissenters on, 23–4
    rights of, 64, 67, 74, 76; *see also*
        feminism
    slavery and, 42
    solidarity between, 24–5
    "women's work", 73, 76
    as writers, 61, 64, 74, 77–8n19, 145,
        159–60, 172–3
women's rights, 197
"women's work", 96
Wooten, David, 150n15
Wordsworth, William, 3, 4, 212n94,
    249n117
Worthington, Hugh, 12, 35, 44, 46, 62–
    3, 62–3, 64, 65, 70, 71, 73, 74,
    77n10, 80n45, 81n55, 87, 91,
    92, 117, 127, 138, 217
Worthington, Susanna, 62, 88, 92
writing, 12, 230

Yearsley, Ann, 199